Y0-ADY-310

S$1.95 A

The Basic Writings of
TROTSKY

The Basic Writings of
TROTSKY

Edited
and Introduced by
IRVING HOWE

SCHOCKEN BOOKS · NEW YORK

First published by SCHOCKEN BOOKS 1976

© Copyright 1963, by Random House, Inc.

Library of Congress Cataloging in Publication Data

Trotskii, Lev, 1879-1940.
 The basic writings of Trotsky.

  Reprint of the ed. published by Random House, New York under title: Basic writings.
  1. Russia—Politics and government—1917- —Collected works. 2. Communism—Collected works. 3. Trotskii, Lev, 1879-1940. I. Howe, Irving. II. Title.

DK254.T6A263 1976   947.084′092′4   75-44439

Manufactured in the United States of America

The Editor acknowledges with gratitude the permission of the following publishers to reprint in this book materials by Leon Trotsky:

Stein and Day, Publishers, for "Three Concepts of the Russian Revolution" from *Stalin,* copyright © 1941 by Harper & Brothers. Copyright renewed © 1969 by Stein and Day, Inc. Reprinted with permission of Stein and Day, Publishers.

Harvard University Press, for "Diary in Exile—1935." Reprinted by permission of the publishers from *Trotsky's Diary In Exile, 1935,* Cambridge, Mass.: Harvard University Press, © 1958 by the President and Fellows of Harvard College.

The University of Michigan Press, for "Five Days (February 23-27, 1917)," and "Dual Power" from *History of the Russian Revolution,* copyright 1933 by The University of Michigan Press; for "The Red Terror and the Freedom of the Press" and "The Metaphysics of Democracy" from *Terrorism and Communism,* © 1961 by The University of Michigan Press.

The Trotsky Estate and Pathfinder Press, for "My First Exile" and "The Train" from *My Life,* copyright 1930 by The Trotsky Estate; for " 'War Communism,' The New Economic Policy (NEP), and The Course Toward the Kulak," " 'Five Year Plan in Four Years' and 'Complete Collectivization,' " "The Degeneration of the Bolshevik Party," "Is the Bureaucracy a Ruling Class?" from *The Revolution Betrayed,* copyright 1972 by Pathfinder Press; for "The Revolution in Spain," "Democracy and Fascism," "For a Workers' United Front Against Fascism," "The Popular Front," "I Stake My Life!" "The USSR in War," and "Stalinism and Bolshevism;" for "The Moscow Trials and Terrorism," and "Why and Wherefore These Trials?" from *The Case of Leon Trotsky;* and for "Céline: Novelist and Politician," copyright 1935 by The Trotsky Estate, first published by Atlantic Monthly Co.

Holt, Rinehart and Winston, Inc., for "The Events in St. Petersburg" from *Our Revolution* by Leon Trotsky. Translated by Moissaye J. Olgin. All rights reserved. Reprinted by permission of Holt, Rinehart and Winston, Publishers.

A Prefatory Note

In compiling this anthology I have kept in mind primarily those readers who did not live through the experiences touched upon by Trotsky in his writings or by myself in the Introduction. I have therefore tried, in the Introduction, to devote myself to a general survey of his political-intellectual career, rather than to detailed consideration of the problems it raises. In behalf of this larger view, I have deliberately risked an excess of compression and perhaps simplification: the reader will have to judge. But if this book stimulates him to further study, he will find no lack of other materials.

The principle of organization is simple. In Part I there is a sequence of selections roughly following the chronology and main events of Trotsky's career; in Part II, a sampling of miscellaneous writings. Before each selection I have appended the source and, unless otherwise noted, the date of publication in English translation.

For some of the quotations from Trotsky's speeches and writings, I am indebted to the multi-volume biography now being published by Mr. Isaac Deutscher.

I wish, finally, to express my gratitude to two old friends. One is Emanuel Geltman, steadfast collaborator for a quarter of a century, who helped with the problem of selection. The other is Max Shachtman, the literary executor of Trotsky's estate, who extended his co-operation with characteristic generosity.

Contents

INTRODUCTION 3

PART ONE: *Outline of a Career*

1. *The Motive Forces of the Russian Revolution* 43
2. *The Events in Petersburg* 62
3. *My First Exile* 67
4. *Five Days (February 23-27, 1917)* 77
5. *Dual Power* 101
6. *The Train* 111
7. *Two Military Declarations* 120
8. *Three Concepts of the Russian Revolution* 123
9. *The Red Terror and the Freedom of the Press* 142
10. *The Metaphysics of Democracy* 154
11. *"War Communism," The New Economic Policy (NEP), and The Course Toward the Kulak* 160
12. *Bureaucratism and the Revolution* 170

13 *"Five Year Plan in Four Years" and "Complete Collectivization"* 178
14 *The Degeneration of the Bolshevik Party* 188
15 *Thermidor and Anti-Semitism* 206
16 *Is the Bureaucracy a Ruling Class?* 216
17 *The Revolution in Spain* 223
18 *Democracy and Fascism* 234
19 *For a Workers' United Front Against Fascism* 245
20 *The German Catastrophe* 257
21 *The Popular Front in France* 267
22 *I Stake My Life!* 278
23 *The Moscow Trials and Terrorism* 290
24 *Why and Wherefore These Trials?* 299
25 *The USSR in War* 305

PART TWO: *Samples of Opinion*

26 *Gogol: An Anniversary Tribute* 317
27 *The Young Lenin* 325
28 *The Family and Ceremony* 338
29 *Céline: Novelist and Politician* 343
30 *Stalinism and Bolshevism* 356
31 *Their Morals and Ours* 370
32 *Diary in Exile—1935* 400

GLOSSARY OF NAMES 415

INDEX 423

The Basic Writings of
TROTSKY

Introduction

Has any major figure of the twentieth century left so complete a record of his thought and experience as Leon Trotsky? Perhaps Churchill, perhaps De Gaulle; but neither of these men combined so fully or remarkably as did Trotsky the roles of historical actor and historian, political leader and theorist, charismatic orator and isolated critic. Trotsky made history, and kept an eye on history. He was a man of heroic mold, entirely committed to the life of action, but he was also an intellectual who believed in the power and purity of the word. At no point in his career, whether as a revolutionary émigré or commander of revolutionary armies, did Trotsky allow his public activities or personal condition to keep him long from his desk. "In my eyes," he once wrote, "authors, journalists and artists always stood for a world that was more attractive than any other, a world open only to the elect."

An exile in Siberia, he wrote about the 1905 Russian Revolution, the great Russian novelists of the nineteenth century, the rise of the Freemasons. An exile in Europe, he wrote about the controversies of European Marxism, the special problems of Russian society, and his own theory of "permanent revolution." A leader of the Bolshevik regime, he wrote about military affairs, literary disputes, the economics of statification, manners and morals in a proletarian state, the rise of the Stalinist bureaucracy. An exile in Turkey, France, Norway and finally Mexico, he wrote his monumental history of the Russian Revolution, his political autobiography, studies of Lenin and Stalin, and a stream of books, pamphlets, articles on the Chinese revolution of the late twenties, the tactics of the German Left confronting Hitler, the anatomy of the new despotism in Russia, the failure of the Popular Front in Europe, problems of political morality, the need for Marxist reconstruction. And in 1939, when an agent of the Russian GPU drove an ax into Trotsky's skull, the murderer gained access to his victim's study on the pretext of discussing an article.

With full, almost naïve conviction Trotsky believed in the creative possibilities of the word. But he believed not as most Western intellectuals have: not in some ironic or contemplative or symbolic way. The common distinction between word and deed Trotsky scorned as a sign of philistinism, worthy—he might have added—of liberal professors and literary dilettantes. He regarded his outpouring of brilliant composition as the natural privilege of a thinking man, but more urgently, as the necessary work of a Marxist leader who had pledged his life to socialism. The heritage of the Russian writers of the nineteenth century is stamped upon his books, for he took from them the assumption that to write is to engage in a serious political act, a gesture toward the redemption or re-creation of man.

Trotsky's life is so interwoven with the complexities and tragedies of twentieth-century experience that it would be absurd to suppose any selection from his writings could give a full historical or intellectual portrait of the man. He is too complex for that. The Marxist theoretician and scathing polemicist; the great historian; the organizer of the Bolshevik seizure of power and leader of the Red Army; the literary man devoted to the Russian classics while alert to the novelties of French prose; the defeated but unyielding critic of the Stalin dictatorship, resisting with his pen a worldwide apparatus of terror and lies; the founder of the Fourth International trying vainly, at the end of his life, to rebuild a revolutionary movement—these are but some of his public roles.

A few of them can be glimpsed in the pages that follow. But whole sides of Trotsky's life and thought do not appear at all in this book: his analyses of revolutionary strategy in China are too recondite for inclusion; the detailed criticisms of the Stalinist theory of "socialism in one country" would require more space than is available and may, in any case, be somewhat dated; and the numerous intra-Marxist polemics, torn from their contexts, are not likely to interest the audience for whom this collection is meant.

Trotsky appears in this book mainly as a public writer, so that no intimate knowledge of radical ideology or history is needed to grasp the significance of his work. The selections have been made to provide examples of his analytic sweep and brilliance, his authority as spokesman for the Marxist worldview, and his distinction as a writer. They are likely to inspire admiration even from those who do not agree with Trotsky's politics, as well as elicit disapproval from all but his most devoted followers. Trotsky the polemical in-fighter barely appears in this book; Trotsky the historian does, though he can be fully appreciated only by those who have read from beginning to end *The History of the Russian Revolution.* Yet if this anthology cannot display Trotsky's thought in its depth and detail, it may have the virtue of tracing his intellectual career in its essential rhythm of development. A good part of the material has been rescued from obscure journals and yellowed pamphlets, and some of it appears in English for the first time.

Lev Davidovich Bronstein—only as a young revolutionist did he adopt the name of Trotsky—was born in 1879, the son of Jewish farmers living near the Black Sea. The life of the Bronsteins was somewhat unusual for Russian Jews: they worked a large farm instead of trading in cramped ghetto villages, they became well-to-do *kulaks* who could mistreat peasants as readily as gentile landowners did, and they showed little feeling for the religious pieties that still gripped most Jews in eastern Europe.

Growing up in the Bronstein household, young Lev Davidovich could observe something of that endless misery which had been the traditional lot of the Russian peasant; it disturbed the boy, and by the time he was sent off to school in Odessa he was already a rebel of sorts. He participated in a demonstration against an unpopular teacher and was suspended from the school for a year: the kind of incident which in a free society need not have serious repercussions but which in Czarist Russia would contribute heavily to the formation of character. For in a closed authoritarian society all behavior has political implications, and even the most innocent gesture can take on a rebellious cast. Whatever the case, young Bronstein returned to school with a heightened sense of his powers. Years later, in his autobiography, he would write:

> Such was my first political test, as it were. The class was henceforth divided into two distinct groups: the talebearers and envious on one side, the frank and courageous boys on the other, and the neutral and vacillating mass in the middle. These three groups never quite disappeared even in later years.

The passage is typical of the mature Trotsky. In his conscious thought he insisted, as a Marxist, that moral criteria were determined by social relations, or at least were crucially dependent upon them; but in part of himself he held fast to traditional valuations of character and reponded strongly to such "supra-class" sentiments as honor, courage and frankness.

A gifted student, especially in mathematics, young Bronstein was sent in 1896 to the town of Nikolayev to complete his education. It was here, in a provincial city first acquiring both modern industry and a proletariat, that he encountered the socialist ideas which had begun to filter into Czarist Russia. In the hut of a poor gardener, a group of students and workers met to discuss radical theories, and soon Bronstein's was a leading voice among them, first as a sentimental partisan of Russian populism who declared himself an enemy of "Marxist dryness," and then as a spokesman for the more rigorous concepts of Marxism, to which he was converted by a lively young woman who would soon become his first wife and always remain a political colleague. At the age of eighteen, in the tradition of sacrifice that had been established by the Russian radicals of the nineteenth century, Lev Davidovich Bronstein chose the life of a professional revolutionary. What such a life could mean has been eloquently described by Edmund Wilson in his book *To the Finland Station:*

> Whoever has known the Russian revolutionaries of these pre-war generations at their best has been impressed by the effectiveness of the Czarist regime as a training school for intellect and character in those who were engaged in opposing it. Forced to pledge for their conviction their careers and their lives, brought by the movement into contact with all classes of people, driven to settle in foreign countries whose languages they readily mastered . . . —these men and women combine an unusual range of culture with an unusual range of social experience and, stripped of so many of the trimmings with which human beings have swathed themselves, have, in surviving, kept the sense of those things that are vital to the honor of human life.

In the spring of 1897 Bronstein and his friends organized a clandestine group, the South Russian Workers' Union, which held political discussions and issued leaflets about conditions in local factories; the writing and hectographing, at the rate of two hours a page, was done by Bronstein himself. Inevitably the police closed in, and early the next year most of the members of this embryonic radical movement were arrested; some were subjected to flogging and Bronstein was kept for several months in lice-ridden solitary confinement. Next he was transferred to an Odessa prison, where he remained a year and a half, and then sentenced to four years in Siberia. The young revolutionist now found himself settled along the Lena River, above the Arctic Circle, where, as he later wrote, life was "dark and repressed, utterly remote from the world." But meanwhile he had been studying the Marxist classics, and in Siberia he saw copies of the Social Democratic paper *Iskra* and Lenin's pamphlet *What Is to Be Done?* in which the future leader of Bolshevism argued that only by creating a highly disciplined party staffed by full-time revolutionists could the Russian Social Democracy survive the persecution of the Czarist police.

In exile Bronstein felt himself sufficiently self-assured as a publicist to write essays on a range of literary figures—Ibsen, Zola, Gogol among them—and to enter the discussion as to future politics and organizational structure that was occupying the Russian Social Democrats. Most of the important Russian Marxists were then living as exiles in western Europe, debating their political course in relation to the seemingly invincible monolith of Czarism and preparing to establish an organization that might ensure tighter relations between themselves and the scattered illegal groups in Russia. Eager to meet and learn from such Marxist leaders as Plekhanov, Martov and Lenin, young Bronstein escaped from Siberia in the fall of 1902, made his way secretly across Russia and, taking the pseudonym by which the world would come to know him, managed to smuggle himself across the frontier.

Once in Europe, Trotsky immediately threw himself into the political life of the Russian émigrés. In London he met Lenin for the first time, and the two men took long walks through the streets of the alien city, exchanging political ideas and impressions as to the underground in Russia. Trotsky began to write articles for *Iskra* distinguished by revolutionary enthusiasm, but florid and immature in style; the hard aphoristic brilliance of his later prose would come only from an accumulation of experience and a conscious self-discipline.

By all accounts the young man made a powerful impression on the leaders of Russian Marxism. Marvelously young, alive with eagerness and zeal, bristling with unformed talents, intellectually quick and receptive, somewhat imperious in manner and abrupt in personal relations but still reverent toward the men and women he regarded as the great names of the Russian revolutionary movement, Trotsky seemed to his new friends an incarnation of that political élan they hoped would spark and revive their movement. Vera Zasulich, veteran of the underground, felt him to be "undoubtedly a genius." Julius Martov, future leader of Menshevism and himself a gifted man, wrote that Trotsky's literary works "reveal indubitable talent . . . and already he wields great influence here thanks to his uncommon oratorical gifts. He speaks magnificently. Of this both I and Vladimir Ilyich [Lenin] have had sufficient proof. He possesses knowledge and works hard to increase it."

By the time the Russian Social Democratic Party held its Second Congress in 1903, Trotsky, though still in his early twenties, was a figure of some importance. He refused to align himself completely with either of the factions that were hardening into shape, the Bolsheviks led by Lenin and the Mensheviks led by Martov. This division can now be seen as a partial anticipation of the great split that would come during the First World War between revolutionists and reformists within the socialist movement, but at the time the issues were still murky, and Trotsky, disinclined in his earlier years to tie himself to a party apparatus, sided now with one group and now with the other. At stake, apparently, was a bit of phrasing as to who could be considered a member of the party: someone who "personally participates in one of its organizations" (Lenin), or someone prepared to "co-operate personally and regularly under the guidance of one of the organizations" (Martov). Scholastic as this difference might seem—two years later the Mensheviks virtually took over Lenin's phrasing—it was nevertheless a sign of divergences in political outlook that went deeper than the participants could yet grasp.

Immediately after the Congress, Trotsky sided with the Mensheviks, composing vitriolic attacks on what he regarded as Lenin's dictatorial and "Jacobin" views concerning party organization. In a pamphlet he wrote denouncing Lenin there appeared a sentence that has since been quoted many times as a prophetic anticipation, ignored by the later Trotsky himself, of the decline of the Russian Revolution:

> Lenin's methods lead to this: the party organization at first substitutes itself for the party as a whole; then the Central Committee substitutes itself for the organization;

and finally a single "dictator" substitutes himself for the Central Committee.

The remark is a striking one, of course, in its anticipation of the ways in which the highly centralized structure of the Bolshevik party would encourage an authoritarian psychology among the leaders and intellectual dependence among the followers. As a sociological insight, it remains valuable for the study of modern politics and political organization. Yet it is hardly as prescient as some historians have supposed, and it certainly is not sufficient evidence for the claim that in his youth Trotsky grasped the causes of the degeneration of the Russian Revolution in a way that the older Trotsky, even after his downfall, refused to acknowledge. Though anticipating the debacle of the Bolshevik party in the era of Stalinist totalitarianism, Trotsky's remark does not—nor could it—touch upon the complex of causes behind that degeneration. Any effort to explain a major historical phenomenon (like the rise of Stalinism) by the workings of an exclusive cause (like Bolshevik centralization) is doomed to be superficial, and the later Trotsky was right in rejecting such a mode of explanation.

Though siding with the Mensheviks on party organization, Trotsky began, in the early years of the century, to express views on another fundamental problem—the relationship in the coming Russian Revolution between the socialists and the liberal bourgeois parties—which brought him closer to Lenin. Since, as all Russian Marxists agreed, the first task was to overthrow the Czar and establish democratic rights, the Mensheviks argued that the liberal bourgeoisie would have to take the lead and the working class serve as a loyal opposition. Trotsky, by contrast, insisted that the socialists should keep a clear distance from the bourgeois parties and not compromise with liberalism.

These discussions, apparently so academic, soon involved the destinies of millions. For the moment, however, they were happily put aside when the Russian people, long voiceless and dormant, began in 1905 to stir against the Czarist regime. In Petersburg a demonstration led by an Orthodox priest called for democratic rights; the Czar ordered his troops to fire into the crowd. From Geneva, Trotsky wrote in a state of high excitement:

> One day of revolution was enough, one magnificent contact between the Czar and the people was enough for the idea of constitutional monarchy to become fantastic, doctrinaire, and disgusting. The priest Gapon rose with his idea of the monarch against the real monarch. But, as behind him there stood not monarchist liberals but revolutionary proletarians, this limited "insurrection" immediately manifested its rebellious content in barricade fighting and in the outcry: Down with the Czar. The real monarch has destroyed the idea of the monarch. . . . The revolution has come and she has put an end to our political childhood.

Throughout the year 1905 Russia was in a turmoil of rebellion. Strikes closed the factories, street demonstrations broke out in the cities, the crew of the warship *Potemkin* revolted. One of the first exiles to return to Petersburg, Trotsky for a time lived a political life that was half-public, half-clandestine. Belonging to neither the Menshevik nor Bolshevik faction, but contributing frequently to the press of both and acting with a boldness neither could match, Trotsky became the popular tribune of the revolutionary left. In October there met in the capital the Soviet of Workers' Delegates, a kind of rump parliament of representatives from the unions, left parties and popular organizations, in which Trotsky soon rose to the post of chairman. Unlike the Bolsheviks, who until Lenin's arrival in November were skeptical about the Soviet because of fear it would threaten their political identity, Trotsky grasped the enormous revolutionary potential of this new and spontaneous organ of political action. His personal fearlessness, his combination of firm political ends with tactical ingenuity, and his incomparable gifts as an orator helped transform him, at twenty-six, into a leader of the first rank: he had entered upon the stage of modern history and only the ax of a murderer would remove him. Here is a passage from one of his speeches before the Soviet, a characteristic flare of virtuosity, in which he tells about a conversation with a liberal who had urged him to moderation:

> I recalled to him an incident from the French Revolution, when the Convention voted that "the French people will not parley with the enemy on their own territory." One of the members of the Convention interrupted: "Have you signed a pact with victory?" They answered him: "No, we have signed a pact with death." Comrades, when the liberal bourgeoisie, as if boasting of its treachery, tells us: "You are alone. Do you think you can go on fighting without us? Have you signed a pact with victory?" we throw our answer in their face: "No, we have signed a pact with death."

In the fifty days of its existence the Soviet experienced the dilemma so frequently faced by revolutionary institutions: it was strong enough to frighten the government but not strong enough to overthrow it. Finally, Czarism regained the initiative, for it was not yet as fully discredited as it would be in 1917 and the revolutionary movements were still unripe and inexperienced. In the repressions that followed, thousands were killed and imprisoned; reaction once again held Russia. Together with the other leaders of the Soviet, Trotsky faced public trial, at the climax of which—for now he stood firm in the sense of his powers, secure in the knowledge that he had established himself in the line of the great European rebels, convinced that he had found the key to history—he made a brilliant, openly defiant speech:

> A rising of the masses is not made, gentlemen the judges. It makes itself of its own accord. It is the result of social relations and conditions and not of a scheme drawn up on paper. A popular insurrection cannot be staged. It can only be foreseen. For reasons that were as little dependent on us as on Czardom, an open conflict has become inevitable. . . .
>
> . . . no matter how important weapons may be, it is not in them, gentlemen the judges, that great power resides.

No! Not the ability of the masses to kill others, but their great readiness themselves to die, this secures in the last instance the victory of the popular uprising. . . .

Again Siberia: this time deportation "for life." But it was a saving feature of pre-totalitarian despotisms that they were often inefficient, so that even before reaching his Arctic destination Trotsky could make a superbly bold escape, being driven by a vodka-besotted peasant for a whole week across the frozen tundra and through ferocious blizzards.

For the young Marxist who only a few months earlier had been sentenced to Siberia "for life," the escape was a personal triumph: in retrospect one might say, a personal triumph with historic portents. But now that he was safe again in Europe, Trotsky turned back to his pen, composing his first major work, *1905*, an historical study that in scope and vigor anticipates the *History of the Russian Revolution*. (The opening chapter of *1905* appears on p. 43 of this collection.)

These were hard times for the Russian revolutionists. The Czar took a merciless revenge as he cut away almost every vestige of popular rights. In Russia the socialist movements came close to collapse from police harassment and inner demoralization, while in exile they kept fragmenting into embittered factions. Trotsky continued vainly to urge that the Bolsheviks and Mensheviks reunite: perhaps he did not fully grasp the extent of their disagreements, perhaps he feared what the consequence of grasping it might be. Wandering from country to country, often after being expelled by the police, and earning a bare living through political journalism, he found himself in New York during the war years, and there he wrote for a radical Russian paper until word of the March 1917 revolution brought him rushing back to his homeland. During the years between the two Russian revolutions Trotsky's main intellectual work was the development—and defense against critics within the movement—of his theory of permanent revolution, a bold set of speculations concerning Marxist strategy in backward countries. Trotsky's own statement of this theory appears in the following pages, but it may be useful here to attempt a schematic and condensed summary:

1) Czarist Russia is a backward country in which the immediate task is the bourgeois-democratic revolution that will confront those problems which, historically, have been solved by the great bourgeois revolutions of the past: such problems as the overthrow of the autocracy, the abolition of semi-feudal relations in the countryside, the right to self-determination for oppressed national minorities, the convocation of a constituent assembly to establish a republic, the proclamation of democratic liberties, etc.

2) These tasks, however, must be faced in Russia long after the bourgeoisie as a class has lost the revolutionary élan of its youth. Because of the special backwardness and isolation of Russian society, the Russian bourgeoisie is characterized by timidity and indecision. It has many social and economic reasons for opposing the Czarist autocracy, yet is bound to it by links of petty interest, prestige and cowardice. Above all, it shares with the autocracy a growing fear of the two main classes at the base of Russian society: the peasantry and the workers. Because of these congenital weaknesses, the Russian bourgeoisie is incapable of a revolutionary initiative even in behalf of its own interests; it cannot make "its own" revolution. Consequently the tasks of the bourgeois revolution in a backward country like Russia must now be fulfilled by the plebeian classes. Or to put forward a seeming paradox, the bourgeois revolution has to be made *against* the bourgeoisie.

3) While it rests with the working class and the peasantry to carry through the bourgeois revolution, these classes are not socially or historically of equal weight. The peasantry—because of its geographical dispersion, centuries-long passivity, tradition of petty ownership, and lack of common outlook—has shown itself incapable of taking the historical lead. Its role has always been to serve as a crucial but subordinate ally of an urban class.

4) The sole urban ally now available to the peasantry—unless it remain the collective serf of Czarism—is the proletariat. For Trotsky, then, the inevitable conclusion is that the bourgeois-democratic revolution could be completed in a backward country only under the leadership of the working class, small and inexperienced though it may be—which means, more particularly, only under the leadership of the revolutionary party speaking for the working class. But the workers, having gained power, will not be able to stop short before the problems of the bourgeois revolution. The very effort to cope with these will inevitably force them to go beyond the limits of bourgeois property, so that, as Trotsky would write later, "the democratic revolution grows over immediately into the socialist, and thereby becomes a *permanent* revolution."

5) The socialist revolution thus begun in a backward country cannot be completed within national limits. For that, there would be neither a sufficiently secure economic base nor a working class sufficiently strong and conscious. Power could be held and steps toward socialism taken only if there speedily followed victorious revolutions in the advanced European countries. Russia's very backwardness would thrust her forward in the revolutionary scale and bring her under the rule of the working class, perhaps before any of those countries which, because of their economic maturity, were commonly regarded as most ripe for socialism. But this same backwardness, after having forced the working class to power, would overtake it and drag it down unless it received aid from abroad. Or as Trotsky later put it: "In a country where the proletariat has power . . . as the result of the democratic revolution, the subsequent fate of the dictatorship and socialism is not only and not so much dependent in the final analysis upon the national productive forces, as it is upon the development of the international socialist revolution."

Unquestionably this was the boldest theory, the most extreme prognosis, advanced by any Russian Marxist in the years before the first world war. The full measure of its audacity can be grasped even today by anyone who troubles to break past the special barriers of the Marxist vocabulary and examine the theory in terms of the tensions between "underdeveloped" and advanced countries in the twentieth century. The vexing problem of the relation between backwardness and industrialization, which today preoccupies all serious political thinkers, was to be solved, as Trotsky saw it, by the historical audacity of the barely-developed proletariat in the colonial countries. For the Mensheviks, who believed that the bourgeoisie would have to lead the forthcoming bourgeois revolution, Trotsky's theory was an absurdity. Lenin, though agreeing with Trotsky as to the historical impotence of the Russian bourgeoisie, felt that the Russian working class was still too weak and inexperienced to play the grandiose role assigned to it by Trotsky and that the revolution would have to be carried through by an alliance between proletariat and peasantry, the exact relationship between whom he refused to specify or predict. Later, after the Russian Revolution, Lenin acknowledged the prescience of Trotsky's theory, and in retrospect it seems no exaggeration to add that of all the Marxists it was Trotsky who best foresaw the course of events in Russia.

But not entirely. There were at least two crucial respects in which history would cross his expectations. Like most Marxists, Trotsky did not foresee the extent to which the working class in western Europe, increasingly absorbed into national life and having won for itself major economic and political benefits, would choose parliamentarism, rather than revolution, as the way to realize its aims. The help from a victorious European proletariat which Trotsky hoped would salvage the Russian Revolution was not to be forthcoming. Secondly, he failed to anticipate certain consequences of an isolated revolution in a backward country. He knew it might collapse or be overthrown, but he did not imagine that a consolidation of power from within its ranks might undo its original values. That the working class in a backward country, or a party acting in its name, could in moments of crisis approach and even take power, but that it would then reveal a fundamental incapacity to reconstruct economic and cultural life on a level high enough for achieving socialism—all this he foresaw brilliantly.

But what he did not count on was that in such a debacle the revolutionary party, or a bonapartist sector of it, would concentrate power in its upper ranks and establish itself as a bureaucratic elite above all classes—above exhausted proletariat, supine peasantry, dispersed bourgeoisie. The result would be a new, collectivist mode of authoritarianism, neither capitalist nor socialist in character. The first of these miscalculations did not necessarily call into question the validity of Marxism, but the second involved historical possibilities with which traditional Marxism was not well prepared to cope.

With the outbreak of the Russian Revolution in 1917, Trotsky moves into the center of modern history. His achievements as revolutionary leader are sufficiently known not to require a full account in these pages, but a few details may help us in tracing the curve of his political career.

Returning to Petersburg after the overthrow of the Czar, Trotsky thrust himself into the excitements of Russian politics, a politics that was chaotic and ultimatistic but, for the first time in history, free. Parties sprang up, debate rang passionately, the long-silent masses began to find their voice. The provisional governments that had replaced the Czar—first under the liberal monarchist Prince Lvov, then the Constitutional Democrat Miliukov and finally the populist Kerensky—were inherently unstable. Their incapacity or unwillingness to permit a division of landed estates among the peasants and their failure to end Russia's participation in a fruitless and exhausting war made them increasingly unpopular. Since Trotsky opposed in principle any political collaboration with these regimes, even when they included some Menshevik ministers under Kerensky, he found himself at odds with both the Mensheviks and the "conciliationist" wing of the Bolsheviks. By the same token he was now closer to Lenin, whose entire political strategy beginning with the spring of 1917, to the astonishment even of many of his own comrades, was directed toward preparing the Bolshevik party for a seizure of power. In July, Trotsky formally joined the Bolsheviks, though for some months he had already been collaborating with them.

Supported by Lenin and for the first time in his political career working closely with a disciplined party organization,

Trotsky became the popular spokesman for Bolshevism. Sukhanov, the gifted Menshevik whose eyewitness chronicle of the revolution is a major historical source, has recalled that Trotsky "spoke everywhere simultaneously. Every worker and soldier at Petrograd knew him and listened to him. His influence on the masses and the leaders alike was overwhelming." His biographer, Isaac Deutscher, offers a vivid picture of Trotsky as a mass orator:

> . . . he established his platform in the Cirque Moderne, where almost every night he addressed enormous crowds. The amphitheatre was so densely packed that Trotsky was usually shuffled towards the platform over the heads of the audience, and from his elevation he would catch the excited eyes of the daughters of his first marriage . . . He spoke on the topics of the day and the aims of the revolution with his usual piercing logic; but he also absorbed the spirit of the crowd, its harsh sense of justice, its desire to see things in sharp and clear outline . . . Later he recollected how at the mere sight of the multitude words and arguments he had prepared well in advance receded and dispersed in his mind and other words and arguments, unexpected by himself but meeting a need in his listeners, rushed up as if from his subconscious. He then listened to his own voice as to that of a stranger, trying to keep pace with the tumultuous rush of his own ideas and phrases and afraid lest like a sleepwalker he might suddenly wake and break down. Here his politics ceased to be the distillation of individual reflection or of debates in small circles of professional politicians. He merged emotionally with the dark warm human mass in front of him . . .

Trotsky was more than a superb orator, more than a remarkably sensitive medium between the aroused masses and the straining Bolshevik leadership. In the Soviets, those improvised institutions of popular sovereignty where the left-wing parties struggled for domination, he became the main political spokesman for the Bolshevik point of view. And as preparations for the October Revolution proceeded, "all the work of practical organization of the insurrection"—even Joseph Stalin had to admit shortly afterwards—"was conducted under the immediate leadership of the President of the Petrograd Soviet, Comrade Trotsky. It is possible to declare with certainty that the swift passing of the garrison to the side of the Soviet, and the bold execution of the work of the Military Revolutionary Committee [the body directing the October insurrection], the party owes principally and first of all to Comrade Trotsky."

In the government now formed under Lenin, Trotsky became foreign minister, intending, as he joked, to issue "a few revolutionary proclamations and then close shop," but in reality having to conduct the difficult Brest-Litovsk negotiations with imperial Germany, which at a heavy price brought peace to Russia. In 1918, when the Civil War broke out across the whole of Russia, Trotsky became minister of war. Without military experience, he applied himself to creating a revolutionary army from almost nothing. He began with a few thousand Bolsheviks, Red Guards who had fought in the revolution; a considerable group of Russian army officers willing to serve the new regime in a nonpolitical capacity; and masses of untrained recruits who lacked discipline and often enough arms. For almost two years Trotsky lived in an armored train which served as the political-military headquarters of the new army. Moving from front to front, working with ferocious energy, exposing himself in crucial battles to rally frightened men, insisting upon the military authority of the old officers while checking their power through a network of political commissars, holding fast to standards of efficiency and discipline among soldiers who had long been demoralized, but above all else, stirring his followers to fight and die through the exaltation of his speeches and manifestoes, Trotsky created an effective army which finally defeated the Whites. He understood that in a revolutionary army it is the will to struggle which is often decisive; victory would come to his troops only as they believed themselves to be crusaders in behalf of a better world, only as they were ready to face death out of a conviction that they were—to quote from one of Trotsky's speeches to his soldiers—"participants in an unprecedented historic attempt . . .

to create a new society, in which all human relations will be based on . . . co-operation and man will be man's brother, not his enemy."

Once the Red Army had ended the threat of counterrevolution, the young Bolshevik regime had for the first time to face the problems of social reconstruction. In these difficult years, when Russian economic life was reduced to chaos and hunger swept across the land, Trotsky argued in behalf of compulsory work and labor armies based on military discipline—draconian measures, he admitted, but necessary for lifting the economy to that minimal level of production where ordinary incentives might begin operating. (It is but fair to add that Trotsky advocated these measures only after his proposal for modifying "War Communism" had been rejected and that he was among the first Bolshevik leaders to urge the economic relaxation that went under the name of NEP.)

In the public debates that followed—for a certain measure of political opposition could still be expressed in Russia—the Menshevik leader Raphael Abramovich opposed such forced labor battalions with the query: "Wherein does your socialism differ from Egyptian slavery? It was just by similar methods that the Pharaohs built the pyramids, forcing the masses to labor." Trotsky replied: "Abramovich sees no difference between the Egyptian regime and our own. He has forgotten the class nature of government. . . . It was not the Egyptian peasants who decided through their Soviets to build the pyramids . . . our compulsion is applied by a workers' and peasants' government. . . ."

It was an unfortunate argument, Trotsky at his weakest. In advancing it he failed to acknowledge that by 1920 the Russian workers were not deciding very much on their own; it was the Bolshevik government that made the decisions. A great deal of the support the Bolsheviks had enjoyed among the workers since the October revolution had by now been lost or badly weakened. The policies of this government could not be justified simply because it was, or called itself, a workers' government; its rights to that title might better be justified by the nature of the policies it put forward. But most unfortunate of all, Trotsky's argument provided the formula that could later be used all too easily for rationalizing the Stalinist plunge into totalitarianism.

In arguing for labor armies and also in justifying the suppression of dissident socialist groups, Trotsky invoked the harsh necessities of fighting a desperate civil war and salvaging a collapsed economy. As he began, upon the completion of the civil war, to work at the revival of industrial production, all his enormous talents came into play; but his political role took on a harsh and authoritarian cast which cannot be justified even to the extent that certain of his measures during the Civil War might be. Driven by the force of intolerable circumstances, but also trapped in the vise of a Bolshevik exclusivism which led to greater concentrations of power at the summit of the ruling party just when an opening of political and economic life might alone have saved the situation, Trotsky now condoned acts of repression which undercut the remnants of "Soviet democracy." A few years earlier the left-Menshevik leader, Julius Martov, had warned against the tendency of the Bolsheviks to equate the power of their party with the interests of the proletariat. Trotsky, flushed with the conquest of power, had replied: "You are bankrupt; your role is played out. Go where you belong from now on—into the rubbish-can of history!" Sad words, from the man who in a few years would himself be harried into exile; sad words, as they reflect a failure to see that it is not always the least intelligent or good or even politically "correct" who are cast into that rubbish-can.

In the years after the revolution, Lenin was more flexible, less doctrinaire than Trotsky. He opposed Trotsky's scheme for labor battalions and argued against a facile identification of the Bolshevik state with the proletariat; he described the regime as a "*deformed* workers' state" in which the workers' organization had to defend not only the state against its enemies but themselves against the state. But while this led him to propose an easing of economic life, he did not urge a parallel easing of political life. On the contrary, the turn toward the NEP in 1921, with its attendant threat to the Communist political monopoly, became for Lenin an argument against the reintroduction of even limited political freedoms.

In a speech before the Third Congress of the Comintern

(1921), Lenin repeated the assumption that had been common to all the Bolshevik leaders:

> It was clear to us that without aid from the international world revolution, a victory of the proletarian revolution [in Russia] is impossible. Even prior to the Bolshevik revolution, as well as after it, we thought that the revolution would also occur either immediately or at least very soon in other backward countries and in the more highly developed capitalist countries. Otherwise we would perish.

Russia, Lenin kept insisting, was a backward peasant land that lacked technology, industry and the accumulated culture required for surpassing the achievements of the Western capitalist countries. Consequently the fate of the Russian Revolution depended on the ability of the Communist movement to achieve power in at least one major advanced country, so that assistance could come for besieged Russia. With the defeat of the 1919-1921 revolutions in western Europe, however, there were already signs that Lenin's prophecy—"otherwise we perish"—would be realized. But realized in ways that neither Lenin nor Trotsky had foreseen.

The Bolshevik party could preserve itself as master of a beleaguered state within the limits of a shrunken Russia, but in doing so it underwent large transformations in political ideology, social character and moral quality. In a country where all the means of production are owned by the state, and the state is totally in the grip of the only legal party, major changes in the nature of the party are equivalent to a social revolution creating new relationships between rulers and ruled.

Both the Russian economy and the Russian people were exhausted. To prevent economic collapse or social explosion, Lenin proposed as part of the NEP major concessions to an already hostile peasantry; but this in turn helped bring into existence a whole new conservative stratum of "rich" and middle peasants. When the mass of soldiers, demobilized after the civil war, came back drained of their revolutionary or patriotic fervor, the conservative tendencies within the villages were further reinforced.

So too in the cities. The workers were sapped of their social energy, some having fallen into demoralization and others turning against the regime. Many of the most devoted Bolsheviks had died during the civil war; others had been worn out; and still others, lacking the iron will of a Lenin or a Trotsky, displayed the characteristics of officials everywhere, with vested interests of their own which set them in increasing opposition to the workers in whose name they ruled. Apart from large amounts of economic help, what the country needed most was the ventilation of ideas, a gust of freedom to bring new life and strength; but after 1921 the Bolsheviks refused to allow any party but their own to function legally and thus contributed heavily to their own degeneration. Ruling as a minority dictatorship, though at times with mass support, the Bolshevik regime had planted the seeds of counterrevolution at the very moment the revolution triumphed. Each repressive measure taken by the dictatorship, even when truly the consequence of an emergency created by civil war or economic collapse, further undermined the ideological claims to which many of its supporters were devoted and helped create within the regime a cancerous social growth flourishing upon deprivation, cynicism and brutality.

A new social stratum—it had sprung up the very morning after the revolution—began to consolidate itself: the party-state bureaucracy which found its roots in the technical intelligentsia, the factory managers, the military officials and above all the Communist functionaries. It was narrow in outlook, provincial and boorish in tone, primitive in culture. It was committed to a nationalist perspective, and instinctively authoritarian in method. It looked upon the workers as material to be shaped, upon intellectuals as propagandists to be employed, upon the international Communist movement as an auxiliary to be exploited, and upon Marxist thought as a crude process for rationalizing its new ambitions.

To speak of a party-state bureaucracy in a country where industry has been nationalized means to speak of a new ruling group or class which parasitically fastened upon every institution of Russian life. That many members of this new party-state bureaucracy were unaware of the significance of this process seems obvious; it was, in many respects, an historical novelty for which little provision had been made in the Marxist scheme of things. Years later, in 1928, the Bolshevik leader Bukharin, who had joined with Stalin to defeat Trotsky and was then himself shattered by Stalin, remarked that the disasters of the post-revolutionary period were all due to a "single mistake": the identification of the party with the state. There were people in the "rubbish-can of history" who had been saying that for some time.

At precisely which point the revolutionary dictatorship of Leninism gave way to the totalitarianism of Stalin is hard and perhaps profitless to say. This transformation—a gradual counterrevolution—began during or shortly after the revolution itself, in the inner structure of the Leninist regime; came to its decisive moment in the mid-twenties; and reached full expression in the thirties, with the mass deportation of peasants, the Moscow trials and the blood purges. Having consolidated its power, the new bureaucratic class proceeded to exploit the opportunities for centralized economic planning that are peculiar to a nationalized economy; it undertook a "primitive accumulation of capital" so cruel and bloody as to make the earlier accumulation of bourgeois society seem a model of humaneness.

Of this whole process Trotsky was a powerful critic, from the publication in 1923 of his brochure *The New Course*, in which he first explored the social physiognomy of bureaucratism, to his final writings in 1940, in which he showed signs of uncertainty as to some of his earlier sociological analyses of Stalinism. But especially in the earlier critiques, Trotsky made the error of supposing that in alliance with the new conservative elements in the countryside (whose interests he saw reflected in the "Right Communist" group led by Bukharin), the bureaucracy might constitute a nucleus for the restoration of private capitalism. Actually, as it slowly gathered into its hands control of the entire state, which meant control over the socio-economic life of the nation, this new ruling stratum had every interest in preventing a return to private capitalism, for it neither owned nor could own property but instead controlled the state in whose legal custody property resided. Private capitalism would have meant the end of its power and privilege. It turned instead against every real or potential source of opposition both within and outside the party, destroying the bulk of the Bolshevik "Old Guard" in the purges of the next decades, reducing the intellectuals to a traumatized obedience, terrorizing the workers into passivity, and establishing itself as the sole center of power.

Until the late twenties, criticism of this bureaucratic trend could still be voiced in Russia, though in the later years not with impunity. Various opposition groups struggled to change the Bolshevik course between 1920 and 1923, that is, before Trotsky became the major critic of Stalinism and indeed, without his badly-needed help. One respected Bolshevik oppositionist, G. Myasnikov, wrote: "The Soviet power must maintain at its own expense a body of detractors as did once the Roman Emperors." These words went unheeded, and their author suffered rebuke from the Central Committee. The questions Trotsky would raise in his struggle against Stalinism—questions concerning revolutionary strategy abroad, economic development at home, democracy within the ruling party—were surely important; but now it seems clear that the main significance of all the opposition groups, both Trotskyist and non-Trotskyist, was as a series of ill-connected efforts to stop or slow the trend toward totalitarianism.

For some years, roughly between 1923 and 1928, Trotsky was both political leader and intellectual guide of the left opposition groups in Russia which attacked the growing despotism of the Stalin regime. Far more skillful as the spokesman of a revolutionary upsurge than as a factional maneuverer, painfully aware that he was caught in a moment of social retreat which must prove inhospitable to his austere demands and standards, Trotsky fought doggedly, with intellectual flair and personal pride. But he fought on the terrain of the enemy, accepting the destructive assumption of a Bolshevik monopoly of power, and there were times when he suddenly withdrew into silence and illness, as if in disgust at having to cope with the hooliganism and intellectual vulgarity of his opponents. The very aspects of post-revolutionary Russia which Trotsky saw as conducive to the rise of Stalinism—social weariness, pervasive poverty, lack of culture, asphyxiation of independent thought, loss of spirit among Bolshevik cadres learning to prefer the comforts of administration to the heroism of revolution, the decline in strength and numbers of a proletariat bled white by civil war and industrial collapse—all this made it almost inevitable that Trotsky, no matter what his tactics, would fail. Years earlier, in 1909, he had provided a vivid description of parallel circumstances:

> When the curve of historical development rises, public thinking becomes more penetrating, braver and more ingenious. . . . But when the political curve indicates a drop, public thinking succumbs to stupidity. The priceless gift of political generalization vanishes somewhere without leaving a trace. Stupidity grows in insolence and, baring its teeth, heaps insulting mockery on every attempt at a serious generalization. Feeling that it is in command of the field, it begins to resort to its own means.

Many centuries earlier Thucydides had put the matter in his own words:

> Those who enjoyed the greatest advantages were the men of limited intelligence. The consciousness of their inability and of the talent of their adversaries made them fear that they would be duped by the fine speeches or the subtlety of spirit of their enemies and therefore they advanced straight toward their aim; while the others, scorning even to foresee the schemes of their adversaries and believing that action was superfluous when talk seemed to suffice, found themselves disarmed and defeated.

In only one way could Trotsky possibly have wrested power, and this was through a military coup taking advantage of his popularity in the army. But such a coup would have contributed to the acceleration of the very authoritarian decline he was now opposing; and in any case, he was too much a man of ideological rigor, too much a man devoted to his own sense of historical place and honor, to succumb to the smallness of a Bonapartist adventure. In a bitterly ironic turn of events, he was suffering from the vindication of his own theory of permanent revolution, by means of which he had predicted that a proletarian revolution in a backward country would, if it continued to suffer isolation, find itself in an historical limbo. Only, as it happened, neither he nor anyone else could predict how terrible that limbo would be.

The programs advanced by Trotsky during these years are far too complex, and far too deeply imbedded in the historical context of the time, to allow for easy summary. In general, however, at least three major themes can be noted. To cope with the economic crisis in which Soviet Russia found itself during the early and middle twenties—what Trotsky described as the problem of "the scissors," the two blades of which, moving farther apart from one another, were the rising prices of industrial goods and the declining prices of agricultural products —the Trotskyist opposition put forward an elaborate plan for the reorganization of the economy. The goals of this plan included strengthening the "socialist" industrial sector, raising the productivity of labor, supporting the poorer peasants against the new *kulaks* who had sprung up in the countryside since the NEP, improving the living standards of the workers and drawing them into a more active role in economic life. What was needed, wrote Trotsky, was "a *socialist* accumulation of capital," an harmonious development of the various departments of industrial production, and toward this end "Soviet democracy has become an *economic* necessity." Together with his economic program, Trotsky concentrated on the problems of democracy within the Bolshevik party and the state-dominated institutions of social life:

> Free discussion within the party has in fact disappeared; the party's social mind has been choked off. In these times the broad masses of the party do not nominate and elect the provincial committees and the Central Committee. . . . On the contrary, the secretarial hierarchy of the party to an ever greater degree selects the membership of conferences and congresses, which to an ever greater degree are becoming executive consultations of the hierarchy.

Trotsky did not propose the restoration of freedom for the outlawed socialist parties, but confined himself to urging democracy within the Bolshevik party so that its intellectual life could be refreshed. And finally, he urged a reassertion of the principles of "socialist internationalism" in the work of the Communist parties abroad, charging that under Stalin's domination the Communist movement was being reduced to an appendage of Russian nationalism. As Trotsky saw it, the struggle between Stalin and himself was not primarily a personal dispute or a competition for power; it involved profound differences of principle between a bureaucracy that had become encrusted on the workers' state and the oppositionist forces that spoke for the socialist tradition.

Some years later, when the triumph of Stalinism had become complete in Russia and a good number of Western liberals had succumbed to an uncritical acceptance of its pretensions, it became fashionable to say that Stalin, having embarked upon a frenzied program of industrialization through his successive Five Year Plans, had "stolen Trotsky's thunder." Such remarks ignored the fact that what mattered for Trotsky was not industrialization as an end in itself, but industrialization in behalf of what he took to be socialist ends. Industrialization might be effected in any backward country prepared to employ centralized power with sufficient ruthlessness in order to sweat capital accumulation out of the people, but that was not what Trotsky believed to be the issue. For him, as he kept insisting, industrialization mattered as a means for "raising the specific gravity of the proletariat in society," and thereby moving toward the harmonious world of socialism. The industrialization of Stalin, by contrast, was achieved through the social exploitation of the working class, the imposition of totalitarian controls upon the entire country, and the destruction of political life and consciousness; it brought with it grave economic imbalances, profound social disruption, and extreme political barbarism, the effects of which will be felt for decades to come. No, this was not the "thunder" that Trotsky or any other Bolshevik leader of the twenties had proposed or even imagined. An observation by one of Trotsky's former collaborators, Max Shachtman, is worth quoting here:

The workers' power in Russia, even in the already attenuated form of a dictatorship of the Bolshevik party, stood as an obstacle in the path of [capital] accumulation precisely because, on the one hand, genuine socialist accumulation was impossible under conditions of an isolated and backward country and, on the other hand, workers' power was incompatible with any other kind of accumulation. This power, then, had to be shattered.

It had, that is, to be shattered by Stalin's totalitarian dictatorship, which did indeed manage to impose a layer of industrialization on Russia's backward economy but in doing so created a socio-political structure profoundly in conflict with socialist values.

A more cogent criticism of Trotsky's course in the twenties concerns his failure to speak out in behalf of a multi-party democracy within the limits of "Soviet legality." In 1917, a few weeks before the October revolution, when Trotsky was elected President of the Petrograd Soviet, he had promised: "we shall conduct the work of the Pegrograd Soviet in a spirit of lawfulness and of full freedom for all parties." Toward the end of his life Trotsky would write that "Only when the Civil War began, when the most decisive elements of the Mensheviks and Social Revolutionaries took part in the Civil War on the other side of the barricades, we prohibited them. It was a military measure, not a permanent step." All recent political experience inclines us to suspect such arguments from necessity, so badly abused have they been; and even if one grants some force to Trotsky's claim, one must also heed the careful documentation in Leonard Schapiro's *The Origin of the Communist Autocracy*, an account of the repeated violations of democratic procedures by the Bolshevik regime in the years between 1917 and 1922, a good many of which could not be attributed to the pressures of the Civil War. In any case, Trotsky's decision to limit himself during the factional struggles of the twenties to a demand for democracy within the Bolshevik party placed him in a severe contradiction. Democracy within a ruling party, especially if it dominates a society in which property has become the possession of the state, is finally impossible unless it is extended beyond the limits of that party. Trotsky was demanding both a monopoly of power and a monopoly of freedom for the Bolsheviks: something just barely possible for a brief interval, but surely not for longer. There is no reason to suppose that if he had raised the demand for multi-party democracy it would have strengthened his cause or re-established his popularity. Such a demand would probably have isolated him still further within the Bolshevik hierarchy, and very likely not have sparked any great enthusiasm among the weary and impoverished masses. But what it would have done was to make his political and moral position more secure in the eyes of that historical posterity upon whose verdict he seemed so heavily to bank.

By 1928 Stalin had consolidated his power. The Left Opposition of Trotsky was crushed and the Right Opposition of Bukharin rendered powerless; the members of both groups were driven into exile, silenced in prison, or broken to recant. Trotsky himself was sent to a distant region of Asian Russia and early in 1929 deported from the country. A pall of obedience fell over Russia, and then: terror.

It was now, in his years as a powerless and harassed exile, that Trotsky achieved his greatest moral stature. No longer were there masses of cheering listeners to inflame with his eloquence; no longer armies to spur into heroism; no longer parties to guide to power. The most brilliant figure of the revolution was cast by the usurping dictatorship as a heretic, then a traitor, and finally, in the macabre frame-ups of the Moscow Trials, an agent of fascism.

Driven from country to country, partly because of the pressures brought to bear by the Stalin regime and partly because the presence of the famous revolutionist, helpless and isolated though he might be, made governments feel uncomfortable, Trotsky found his final exile in Mexico. He lived forever in danger of assassination, and at least one effort involving the Mexican Communist painter David Siqueiros was made upon his life before the actual murder. A number of Trotsky's political associates were killed by agents of the Russian secret police, and his children, including a son who had never shown any interest in politics, were systematically hounded in Russia.

But Trotsky continued to cry out his defiance, unbent and unyielding, caustic and proud, a solitary Promethean figure; he continued to write his trenchant analyses of the totalitarian regime in Russia, its terrorism directed against defenseless millions, its byzantine deification of the dictator, its blundering ventures into European politics. One need not accept in whole or part the ideas of Trotsky in order to recognize that during his last decade he rose to an intellectual eminence and personal strength surpassing anything he had shown during the years of power. His productivity as a writer was amazing. Unburdened by office, he was once again the independent political analyst, historian and literary man; it was the role in life, as he had once said, that he most enjoyed; and he wrote now with an authority of statement, an incisiveness of structure, a cutting sharpness of phrase, a brilliant freedom of metaphor which require that he be placed among the great writers of our time.

Trotsky's writings on Germany in the immediate pre-Hitler years are a model of Marxist polemic and analysis, but also of polemic and analysis that can be valuable to the non-Marxist as well. With blazing sarcasm and urgency—he was never patient toward fools—he attacked the insane policy of the German Communists, which declared the Social Democrats to be "social fascists" representing a greater danger than the Nazis, and thereby prevented the formation of that united front of the left which he kept insisting was the one way to stop Hitler. Had his advice been followed (the Stalinists attacked him for "capitulating" to Social Democracy!), the world might have been spared some of the horrors of our century; at the very least, the German working class would have gone down in battle rather than allowing the Nazi thugs to take power without resistance. Only a little less important are Trotsky's writings on Spain during the thirties, writings in which he analyzed the difficulties of modernizing a stagnant country, the way the Spanish bourgeoisie, out of social greed and cowardice, would block measures toward reform or even a dynamic economy, thereby opening the way to fascism—in short, that complex of problems which in a few years would lead to the Spanish Civil War. Equally incisive though, as it now seems, marred by dogmatic rigidity are the writings Trotsky devoted to the social crisis of France during the late thirties, in which he analyzed the Popular Front as an unstable, inherently pusillanimous amalgam of bourgeois, socialist, and Stalinist parties lacking coherent purpose or will. With an excess of revolutionary hopefulness, he saw the French working class as an historical agent striving toward revolutionary action but restrained by its corrupted leaders.

Trotsky's most important political commentary of the thirties—a commentary which has influenced and been used by even those writers who sharply disagree with him—was devoted to the problem of Stalinism. Step by step he followed the transformation of the Stalin dictatorship into a full-scale totalitarian state, denouncing the economic policies by which the regime aggravated the exploitation of the masses in behalf of its mania for super-industrialization, enriching (though sometimes also confusing) his description of Stalinism with historical analogies drawn from the decline of the French Revolution, and riddling the claims of those Western liberals who had begun to praise the Soviet Union only after it had sunk into totalitarianism. Again and again Trotsky was accused of exaggeration and spite in his attacks on the Stalin regime; the American liberal weeklies printed recondite discussions of the "psychological causes" behind his attacks; but almost everything he wrote would later be confirmed by the revelations that started coming out of the Soviet Union after Stalin's death. In the mid-thirties Trotsky was also forced to devote his time to refuting the lies of the Moscow Trials; he did not live long enough to hear Khrushchev admit they had been frame-ups contrived by the state, though he did live long enough to hear some American liberals accept them as truth and praise them as therapy.

All the while Trotsky kept working to create a new movement of the revolutionary left, the Fourth International, which would be loyal to the original principles of Marxism-Leninism. This effort failed. The masses of radical workers in Europe remained attached, however passively, to the traditional parties of the left and showed no interest in the tiny Trotskyist groups, while those intellectuals who broke away from Stalinism often found themselves reconsidering and then abandoning the whole Leninist outlook. As a political leader in these years Trotsky tended to be fractious and inflexible, perhaps because his imagination was still caught up with the myth of the Russian Revolution and could not easily adapt itself to the reduced scale of political action to which he was now confined. Among the scattered groups of the non-Communist left he won more admiration than adherence.

The most enduring portion of Trotsky's writings during the years of exile was not, however, directly polemical or narrowly political. It was directed to the world at large, rather than the constricted circles of radicalism, and today it is surely the most immediately accessible to readers untrained in radical ideology. Trotsky's autobiography, his unfinished book on Lenin, his severely controlled study of Stalin, that masterful compression of his basic views on Stalinism called *The Revolution Betrayed*, but above all, *The History of the Russian Revolution* —these are among the major works of his eleven years of exile. The *History* is Trotsky's masterpiece, the single greatest work of historical composition in the Marxist vein. It is a work on the grand scale, epic in proportion and tone, brilliant in color, vibrant with the passions of strongly-remembered events. Throughout the book there is a rising tension, so characteristic of modern writing, between the subjective perceptions of a highly self-conscious author and the unfolding of a sequence of history taken to be determined by objective law. The book develops into great complexity—the complexity of revolutionary craft and assurance—from a simple but commanding image: the meeting of Russian worker and Russian peasant, often in his guise as soldier or Cossack, their first hesitant gropings toward each other, the subsequent drama of retreat and reconciliation, and finally, a clasp of unity. Apart from its claim to being a faithful record and true interpretation, the *History* is a major work of twentieth-century literature, deserving to be placed besides the masterpieces of modernism.

During the last years of his life Trotsky not merely wrote with great vigor in reply to the calumnies of the Moscow trials, not merely composed a number of major works, not merely produced a steady barrage of topical pieces on political and literary themes; he also engaged in sharp debates with intellectual opponents ranging from independent Marxists who disagreed with him on the "class nature" of the Russian state to liberals and socialists who challenged his assumption that between Bolshevism and Stalinism there was a fundamental conflict rather than a deep continuity. To support this assumption he wrote an ambitious essay, "Their Morals and Ours," in which he argued for the historical relativity of moral standards, tried to show the social causes of the moral distance between Bolshevism and Stalinism, reiterated his defense of the methods employed by the early Bolshevik regime, and had little difficulty in demonstrating that his liberal critics were necessarily quite as committed to the belief that "the end justifies the means" as they charged he was. In the less polemical sections of this essay Trotsky struggled with the problem of the relation between historically-conditioned moral values, reflecting the interests of social classes and therefore in constant flux, and those moral "absolutes" he was inclined to depreciate as excessively abstract, but which he nevertheless found it impossible to avoid using himself.

In the last year or two of his life Trotsky plunged into a discussion concerning the political role and sociological nature of Stalinist Russia, which had been provoked by some of his American followers who found increasingly unsatisfactory his view that Russia merited "critical support" in the war because it remained a "degenerated workers' state." Trotsky clung hard to this position. When the Russian armies marched into Finland, he denounced the invasion as another instance of Stalinist reaction, yet because he saw the Russo-Finnish war as part of a larger conflict between the bourgeois West and the Soviet Union, he continued in his writings to give the latter "critical support."

This discussion might seem, at first glance, another of those exercises in ideological hair-splitting which occupy radical sects; but it had a genuine value, since the issues that were being discussed would have to be faced by anyone trying to provide a theoretical framework for the study of Stalinism. Trotsky held that Stalinist Russia should still be designated as a "degenerated workers' state" because it preserved the nationalized property forms that were a "conquest" of the Russian Revolution; in his view it was a society without an independent historical perspective, one that would soon have to give way either to capitalist restoration or workers' democracy. His critics insisted that the loss of political power by the Russian working class meant that it no longer ruled in any social sense, for as a propertyless class it could rule only through political means and not in those indirect ways that the bourgeoisie had employed in its youthful phase. Stalinism, they continued, showed no signs of producing from within itself a bourgeois restoration; quite the contrary, for the bureaucracy had become a new ruling class, with interests of its own in opposition to both capitalism and socialism. Trotsky did not live long enough to follow this dispute into the postwar years.

The last years of his life were difficult. Neither poverty nor powerlessness seemed to trouble him as much as the constrictedness of his daily existence; he worked under the constant protection of the guard his friends provided him, and he chafed at being unable to move about freely. For many years he had been living with his second wife, Natalia Sedov, in a marriage that was a model of mutual considerateness and devotion; together they now suffered blow after blow, as the news came of the death or disappearance of sons and friends. In his public conduct Trotsky remained firm and vigorous; privately, he suffered from intervals of depression. Once he apparently contemplated suicide. The indignity of needing to defend himself against the slanders pouring out of Moscow, the frustrations he suffered trying to rebuild a political movement ("I give advice because I have no other way to act," he wrote to a friend in France), the annoyance of having to write certain articles and books for merely financial reasons, the pain he felt at seeing so many people close to him persecuted by the Russian regime, the anxiety that he might not live long enough to fulfill the tasks he had set himself—all these left their mark. Trotsky was a man of enormous self-discipline, with an unshakable conviction as to his place in history and his responsibility to the idea of socialism; but he was also a complex and sensitive human being, impatient with the turn of history which had left him helpless—but only for the moment, he believed—to influence events. In the mid-thirties he kept a diary which reveals sudden flashes of unhappiness and irritation, as if he were rebelling against the disproportion between his intellectual powers and his political opportunities. But the diary also reveals capacities for human warmth and intensity of feeling, above all toward his admirable wife. And there are sentences which open a more intimate view of him: "Old age," he wrote, "is the most unexpected of all the things that happen to a man."

Only sixty when he was murdered, Trotsky was still a vigorous man who might otherwise have lived on for a number of years and continued to write and work. It would have been profoundly interesting to see how he would have responded to the intellectual crises of the postwar years, when as it seemed to many observers, all political systems, including both Marxism and classical liberalism, proved insufficient. Trotsky's mind was a mixture of the rigid and the flexible: he held unquestioningly to the basic tenets of Marxism, but within those limits was capable of innovation and risk. The problems he was forced to grapple with were qualitatively different from those which the greatest minds in his tradition had had to confront; for Trotsky was living in the time of the debacle of socialism and the triumph of totalitarianism, events that none of his intellectual ancestors had foreseen.

In one of his last articles, "The USSR in War," he showed a readiness at least to consider the possibility that the proletariat might not fulfill the revolutionary role that he and other Marxists had so long expected. He knew quite well that in such an event he would have to initiate a fundamental shift in political thought:

> If this war provokes, as we firmly believe, a proletarian revolution, it must inevitably lead to the overthrow of the bureaucracy in the USSR and regeneration of Soviet democracy on a far higher economic and cultural basis than in 1918. . . . If, however, it is conceded that the present war will provoke not revolution but a decline of the proletariat, then there remains another alternative: the further

decay of monopoly capitalism, its further fusion with the state and the replacement of democracy wherever it still remained by a totalitarian regime. The inability of the proletariat to take into its hands the leadership of society could actually lead under these conditions to the growth of a new exploiting class. . . .

There were other problems—already present during the last years of Trotsky's life but visible in their full significance only during the decades since his death—which call into question at least parts of his political outlook. Can, for instance, the modern phenomenon of totalitarianism, with its profound irrationality, its systematized terrorism, and its tendency to suppress traditional class dynamics, be understood adequately in terms of Trotsky's Marxism? Trotsky, it is true, had kept writing that in the absence of socialism, there would be a relapse into a kind of modern barbarism, and the Europe of the thirties and forties certainly sustained this prediction. But to predict a phenomenon is not necessarily to describe it fully or understand it adequately; and for those purposes his intellectual outlook did not, in the era of totalitarianism, suffice. Or again: can the murder of six million Jews in Europe be satisfactorily explained through his theory that nazism represented the last brutal attempt by the German bourgeoisie to retain power? Similarly, with his treatment of the problem of democracy. He was extremely sensitive to the numerous signs of the decay of European democracy during the years between the two world wars, and his writings on Germany, France and Spain often brilliantly register the ways in which the crisis of capitalism endangered the survival of democracy. But the "class analysis" of democracy, to which Trotsky was committed, seems not at all sufficient for an era in which it has become so painfully clear that freedom and liberty—far from being mere guises of class domination—are the most precious values of human life and that without them little remains but servitude.

Staying within the limits of Trotsky's ideology, it would be difficult to account for the considerable stability and the marked rise in living standards that have characterized the life of Western capitalism and that now call into question the whole revolutionary perspective. This does not approximate what he called "the death agony of capitalism," though there does of course remain the possibility that the crises he predicted have merely been delayed. Nor have his prognoses concerning Russia been realized: the post-Stalin society ruled by Khrushchev has achieved a relative stability; it is neither threatened by bourgeois restoration nor within measurable distance of socialist democracy, but maintains itself as an authoritarian dictatorship, keeping terror in reserve but not employing it with the maniacal consistency of Stalin.

These apparent failures in historical prediction are not as disturbing as Trotsky's refusal or inability to reconsider some of his intellectual premises. In his last book, the biography of Stalin, there are perhaps one or two signs that he had begun to feel some uneasiness about the Bolshevik heritage, but for the most part he continued to defend it to the last. His powers of mind operated within the boundaries of a fixed political tradition, but not toward scrutinizing his own assumptions. One could hardly have expected him to repudiate his lifework, and much of the anti-Bolshevism directed against him in the late thirties must be acknowledged to have been crude in method and purpose. Yet for a Marxist theoretician who so fiercely and effectively criticized every move of the Stalinist regime and who so contemptuously swept aside all of its pretexts for the suppression of freedom, there should have been a stronger impetus to turn back to the early years of Bolshevism and submit them to the kind of objective critical study that historical distance alone makes possible.

It is very hard to imagine that Trotsky's influence in the future will be of the kind he anticipated: a renewal of orthodox Marxism in theory and proletarian revolution in practice, along the lines that have come to be known as "Trotskyism." We are living in times that disintegrate all fixed ideologies, and the idea of socialism, if it is to survive as more than an historical memory or a label incongruously attached to authoritarian states, will surely go through a good many transmutations and critical revisions in the coming years. But the writings of this extraordinary man are likely to survive, and the example of his energy and heroism likely to grip the imagination of generations to come. In the eastern European countries heretics turn instinctively to his forbidden books. In the West political thinkers must confront his formidable presence, parrying his sharp polemics and learning from his significant mistakes. Trotsky embodied the modern historical crisis with an intensity of consciousness and a gift for dramatic response which few of his contemporaries could match: he tried, on his own terms, to be equal to his time. In his power and his fall, Leon Trotsky is one of the titans of our century.

PART ONE
Outline of a Career

I

The Motive Forces of the Russian Revolution

TRANSLATED BY I. A. LANGNAS
from the 1922 Russian edition of *1905* (previously untranslated).

In Europe 5.4 million square kilometers, in Asia 17.5 million, and a population of 150 million. In this enormous area, all stages of human development: from the primitive savagery of northern forests, where men eat raw fish and worship trees, to the most modern social relations of the capitalist city, where the Socialist worker regards himself as an active participant in world politics and eagerly follows the course of events in the Balkans or the debates of the German Reichstag. The most concentrated industry in Europe, based on the most backward agriculture of Europe. The most colossal governmental machinery in the world, using all the achievements of technical progress to arrest the historical progress of its own country. This is the soil on which social classes grow, live and fight. The revolution will show us these classes engaged in the most severe of struggles. But direct action in political life is confined to consciously formed groups: parties, unions, army, bureaucracy, press, and—above them—ministers, leaders, demagogues and executioners. The classes cannot be seen at first; they usually remain behind the scenes. Nonetheless, the political parties, with their leaders, ministers and executioners, are only the organs of classes. They may be clever or stupid organs, and this is by no means unimportant in determining the course and outcome of events. If the ministers are merely the servants of "the objective reason of state," this by no means frees them from the obligation of having some brains in their skulls, even if they quite often fail to live up to this condition. Just as, on the other side, the logic of class struggle does not free us from the obligation of using our own subjective logic. Anyone who does not find room, within the framework of economic necessity, for initiative, energy, talent, and heroism has not mastered the philosophical secret of Marxism. On the other hand, if we want to grasp the total meaning of a political process—in this case, a revolution—we must be able to uncover, beneath the motley wardrobe of parties and programs, the cunning and cruelty of some and the courage and idealism of others, the actual outlines of the social classes which are rooted in the deep strata of the processes of production and unfold their flowers in the high spheres of ideology.

THE MODERN CITY

The character of the capitalist classes is closely linked with the historical development of industry and of the city. True, the industrial population of Russia does not quite coincide with its urban population. In addition to industrial suburbs, not formally included within city boundaries, there are dozens of important industrial centers to be found in villages. Generally speaking, 57 per cent of all enterprises and 58 per cent of all workers are in cities. Nonetheless, the capitalist city remains the most complete expression of the new society.

Modern urban Russia is a product of the last few decades. In the first quarter of the eighteenth century, Russia's urban population was 328 thousand, 3 per cent of the total. In 1812, 1.6 million people lived in cities, still only 4.4 per cent of the total. In the middle of the nineteenth century, the urban population numbered 3.5 million, or 7.8 per cent of the total. Finally, the 1897 census gave an urban population of as much as 16.3 million, about 13 per cent of the total. From 1885 to 1897, Russia's urban population grew by 33.8 per cent; her rural population only by 12.7 per cent. Individual cities grew faster still. The population of Moscow increased in the last 35 years from 604,000 to 1,359,000, i.e., by 123 per cent. Other cities, like Odessa, Rostov, Yekaterinoslav, and Baku, have had an even faster rate of growth.

This increase in the number and size of cities in the second half of the nineteenth century was accompanied by a complete transformation of their economic role and their internal class structure.

Contrary to the trade guild cities of Europe, which fought energetically—and often successfully—to concentrate all manufacturing industry within their walls, the cities of old Russia, like those of the Oriental despotisms, had almost no productive function. They were military and administrative strongholds, field fortresses, and, in some cases, trading centers. Their population comprised officials maintained by the Treasury, merchants, and, finally, peasants seeking a refuge within city walls. Even Moscow, the largest city of Old Russia, was nothing but a big village adjoining the Czar's residence.

The crafts had an insignificant place in the city, since the manufacturing industry of the day was scattered in the villages and practiced at home. The four million artisans of the home industry enumerated in the 1897 census performed the productive functions of the guild artisans of European cities, but, unlike the latter, they generally took no part in the creation of manufacturing industries and factories. When modern industry finally appeared in Russia, it proletarianized the greater part of the home-working artisans and directly or indirectly subordinated the rest to its interests.

Just as Russian industry did not pass through the stage of medieval handicraft, so the Russian cities did not know the gradual growth of the third estate through guilds, corporations, communes and municipalities. European capital created Russian industry in a few decades, and Russian industry in turn created the modern cities, in which the basic productive functions are performed by the proletariat.

THE BIG BOURGEOISIE

Big capital thus obtained its economic rule without a struggle. But the enormous role that foreign capital played in this process had a deadly effect on the political influence of the Russian bourgeoisie. Because of government indebtedness, a considerable share of the national income went abroad every year to enrich and strengthen the financial bourgeoisie of Europe. The aristocracy of the stock exchange, which dominates European countries and which, without making any special effort, turned the Czarist government into its vassal, did not want to join the bourgeois opposition in Russia—if only because no other government secured for it such usurious profits. This is true not only of financial capital. European industrial capital as well, which exploits Russia's natural resources and labor power, exercises its political power in the parliaments of France, England and Belgium.

Nor could native capital take the lead in the national struggle against Czarism, because it was, from the very start, the enemy of the national masses: of the proletariat, which it exploited directly, and of the peasants, which it fleeced through the intermediary of the state. This applies especially to heavy industry, which today everywhere depends on government, and especially military, decisions. True, it is interested in a "strict and legal public order"; but it needs even more a centralized government, that great giver of the good things of life. And in their own factories, the entrepreneurs of the metal industry face the most active and advanced part of the working class, which uses every weakening of Czarism to assault capital.

The textile industry is less dependent on the state. It is, moreover, directly interested in raising the purchasing power of the masses, which is unthinkable without a broad land reform. This is why, in 1905, the opposition of textile Moscow to Czarist bureaucracy was so much sharper and more energetic than that of metallurgic Petersburg. The Moscow city council viewed the rising storm with undoubted benevolence. But when the revolution revealed its social content and made the textile workers follow the course of the metal workers, the Moscow council returned all the more decisively and "ideologically" to the side of strong government. And counterrevolutionary capital, after allying itself with counterrevolutionary landlordism, found its leader in the Moscow merchant Guchkov, majority leader in the Third Duma.

BOURGEOIS DEMOCRACY

When European capital nipped in the bud the development of Russian handicrafts, it also tore bourgeois democracy from the social soil that would make it grow. Can the Moscow or Petersburg of today really be equated with the Berlin or Vienna of 1848 or, *a fortiori*, with the Paris of 1789, where the railroad and the telegraph were not even dreams and where a factory with three hundred workers was considered a major industry? We don't even have a memory of that four-square burgess class, schooled for centuries in self-government and political action, and then allying itself with an as yet undifferentiated proletariat to take the feudal Bastille by assault. What do we have instead? A "new middle class" of professional intelligentsia—lawyers, journalists, doctors, engineers, professors, teachers. This social stratum lacks a significance of its own in the general production, is small in number and economically dependent. Judging itself—and correctly—to be powerless, it invariably looks for a massive social class to lean upon. A remarkable task! Such support is found, primarily, not among the capitalists, but among the landlords.

The Constitutional Democratic Party (*Kadets*), which took the lead in the first two Dumas, was formed in 1905 by the union of the *zemstvo* [provincial assembly] constitutionalists and the Liberation League [*Soyuz Osvobozhdeniya*]. The liberal front of the *zemstvo* men expressed two things: the envious discontent felt by the agrarians with the monstrous industrial protectionism practiced by the government, and an opposition of the more progressive landlords who were unable, because of the barbarism of Russian agrarian relations, to put their properties on a capitalist footing. The Liberation League comprised the elements of the intelligentsia which were too "decent"—and too satiated—to take the revolutionary path. The opposition of the *zemstvos* was marked by timidity and weakness, so that the august youth [the young Czar Nicholas II] only told them the bitter truth when, in 1894, he called their political ambitions "senseless fancies." On the other hand, the privileged part of the intelligentsia, being materially dependent either directly or indirectly on the government, the protection of big capital, and the more liberal landlords, was unable to develop an inspiring opposition.

The *Kadet* party was therefore, in its origin, a union of the powerless *zemstvo* men with the general weakness of intellectuals holding professional diplomas. The superficial character of *zemstvo* liberalism manifested itself clearly at the end of 1905, when the landlords, under the influence of agrarian disorders, quickly made their peace with the old order. And the liberal intelligentsia had to make a tearful departure from the manor house, where it had been—strictly speaking—only an adopted child, and look for recognition toward its historical family home, the city. But what company did it find there? A conservative big capital, a revolutionary proletariat, and an unbridgeable antagonism between them.

This antagonism also split small-scale production to its very foundations, in all the branches of industry where it managed to remain significant. The proletariat of craftsmen has developed in an atmosphere of big industry, and differs little from the proletariat of factory workers. Squeezed between big industry and the workers' movement, the Russian artisans are an ignorant, half-starved and exasperated class ready to join the *Lumpenproletariat* in providing fighting personnel for political manifestations of the reactionary "Black Hundreds" and for pogroms.

And so a hopelessly belated bourgeois intelligentsia, born to the sound of socialist curses, is hanging over the abyss of class contradictions, burdened by the traditions of landlordism, and wrapped in professional prejudices, without initiative, without influence over the masses, and without faith in tomorrow.

THE PROLETARIAT

The same world-wide historical causes which have made bourgeois democracy in Russia a head without a body—and a completely confused head at that—have bred the conditions for the outstanding role of the young Russian proletariat. First of all, what are its numbers? The very incomplete figure of the 1897 census give us the following reply:

NUMBER OF WORKERS

A	Mining and manufacturing industry, transport, construction and trade	3,322,000
B	Agriculture, forestry, fishing and hunting	2,723,000
C	Day-laborers and artisans	1,195,000
D	Servants, doormen, house-porters	2,132,000
	Total (men and women)	9,372,000

Together with its dependents, the proletariat formed 27.6% of the entire population in 1897, or little more than a fourth. The degree of political activity differs considerably among the various strata of this human mass, and leadership in the revolution is almost exclusively confined to the workers of group A. However, to judge the actual and potential importance of the Russian revolutionary proletariat by its relative numbers would be to fall into the gross error of failing to perceive the social relations behind the bare figures.

The importance of the proletariat is determined by its role in modern economy. The most powerful means of production depend directly and immediately on the workers. The 3.3 million workers of group A produce no less than half of each year's national income. The railroads, those most important means of communication which—as shown by the course of events—are primary in turning the enormous country into an economic whole, represent in the hands of the proletariat an economic and political asset of immeasurable importance. To them we must add the mails and the telegraph, which depend on the proletariat less directly but very effectively.

Whereas the peasantry is scattered all over the country, the proletariat is strategically concentrated in great masses in factories and industrial centers. It forms the core of the population of every city of any economic or political importance. The advantages which the city enjoys in a capitalist country—concentration of the means and forces of production, presence of the most active elements of the population, availability of the best cultural values—naturally become class advantages of the proletariat. Its self-determination as a class grew here at a speed unparalleled in history. Barely out of its cradle, the Russian proletariat found itself facing the most concentrated power of the government and an equally concentrated power of capitalism. The traditions of guilds and the prejudices of craftsmen had no hold whatever on its outlook. With its very first steps, it took the path of an implacable class struggle.

The insignificance of handicrafts and of small-scale production generally, and the very high development of Russia's big industry, led to the political displacement of bourgeois democracy by proletarian democracy. The working class took over from the petty bourgeoisie not only its productive functions but also its former political role, its historical responsibility to lead the peasant masses in the age of their emancipation from serfdom to the landlords and the Treasury.

The land question is the political test to which history put the political parties of the city.

NOBILITY AND AGRICULTURE

The *Kadet*—or, rather, the former *Kadet*—program of compulsory expropriation of large and medium properties according to a "just" assessment, represents, in the opinion of the *Kadets*, the maximum achievement that can be attained through "creative legislation." What actually happened was that the liberal attempt to expropriate large estates by legislation produced the expropriation of the right to vote by the government and the coup d'etat of June 3, 1907. The *Kadets* viewed the liquidation of the landowning nobility as a purely financial operation and scrupulously tried to make their "just assessment" more palatable to the landlords. But the nobility looked at things with very different eyes. Guided by an infallible instinct, it immediately understood that what was at stake was not a simple sale of 50 million *desyatinas* of land, even at a high price, but a liquidation of its entire social position as a ruling class. And so it refused point-blank to surrender its power. As Count Saltykov cried to the landlords at the time of the first Duma: "Let your slogan and your motto be: Not an inch of our soil; not one grain of sand from our fields; not one blade of grass of our meadows; not one knot in the wood of our forests!" And this was not a voice crying in the desert. No, the years of the revolution were for the Russian nobility a period of class concentration and political invigoration. In the darkest years of reaction under Alexander III, the nobility was but one social class, albeit the first. The autocracy, vigilant in the defense of its independence, did not leave the nobility free even for one minute from the rigors of police supervision. But today the nobility is the class that gives the orders, in the full meaning of that phrase: It makes the provincial governors dance to its tune, threatens ministers and openly dismisses them, issues ultimatums to the government and gets them carried out. And its slogan is: "Not an inch of our soil; not a jot of our privileges!"

Sixty thousand private landowners, each with an annual income of over 1,000 rubles, own about 75 million *desyatinas* of land. At current market values, this land is worth 56 billion rubles and earns its owners an annual net profit of more than 450 million rubles. The share of the nobility is no less than two-thirds of this sum.

The bureaucracy is closely linked with agriculture. Almost 200 million rubles are spent every year for the maintenance of 30,000 government officials with an annual income of over 1,000 rubles. And nobility, once again, notably predominates in the middle and upper ranks of the bureaucracy. Finally, the nobility has an exclusive hold on the organs of self-government of the *zemstvos* and the revenues which pertain to them.

Before the revolution, a good half of the *zemstvos* were headed by "liberal" landlords, who become prominent through "cultural" activities in the assemblies. The revolution brought a complete change here, and the most implacable representatives of reactionary landlordism are now in the front ranks. The all-powerful Soviet of the united nobility nips in the bud any attempts of the government to foster the interests of the capitalist industry, to democratize the *zemstvos,* or to loosen the class shackles of the peasantry.

In view of these facts, the *Kadet* land program, as a foundation of a *legislative consent,* is a hopeless utopia and it is not surprising that the *Kadets* themselves tacitly reject it.

The Social Democrats concentrated their criticism of the *Kadet* land program on the "just assessment," and rightly so. Even from the financial point of view, the purchases of all estates with an annual income of over 1,000 rubles would add some 5 to 6 billion rubles to our national debt of 9 billion. The interest alone would then cost us 750 million rubles per annum. However, it is not the financial aspect of the transaction that is decisive, but the political.

The 1861 "Liberation of the Peasants," accomplished by raising the prices which the peasants had to pay for their land, actually compensated the landlords for the serfs they lost to the extent of a quarter of a billion rubles, i.e., 25 per cent of the entire redemption price. On that occasion, great historical rights and privileges of the nobility were liquidated with the aid of a "just assessment." The nobility managed to adapt itself to this "half-liberation" and reconcile itself to it. Its instinct was correct then, just as it is correct now when it resolutely refuses to commit class suicide, even through a "just assessment." Under the slogan of "Not an inch of our soil, not a jot of our privileges!" the nobility finally captured the machinery of government, which had been shaken by the revolution, and showed that it would fight as ferociously as any ruling class engaged in a life-and-death struggle.

The land question cannot be solved by a parliamentary agreement with the nobility, but only by the revolutionary pressure of the masses.

THE PEASANTS AND THE CITY

The knot of Russian social and political barbarism is tied in the village; but this does not mean that the village has brought forth a class capable of cutting it. The peasantry, scattered among 500,000 settlements over the 5 million square *versts* of European Russia, has not acquired from its past any traditions of united struggle. Until the agrarian disorders of 1905-6, the task of the rebellious peasants was limited to expelling the landlords from their village, their *volost* or their *uyezd* [smaller or larger rural districts]. The landowning nobility could mobilize the centralized machinery of government against a peasant revolution. The peasantry could overcome it only by a simultaneous and resolute country-wide rising. But the living conditions of the peasants made them incapable of such a rising. A cretinous localism has been the historical curse of peasant risings, from which they can free themselves only insofar as they cease being purely peasant risings and merge with the revolutionary movements of new social classes.

Already in the German Peasant Rebellion of the first quarter of the sixteenth century, the peasants accepted as a matter of course the leadership of urban parties, even though the German cities were politically insignificant at the time. The German peasantry, though predisposed to a social revolution by its objective interests, was, politically speaking, scattered and powerless. Unable to produce a political party of its own, it favored one of the two urban parties—that of bourgeois opposition or that of plebeian revolution, according to local conditions. The latter party was the only power that could have secured victory for the peasant revolution. But though it represented the most radical social class of the day, the embryo of the modern proletariat, it had no national organization nor any clear awareness of revolutionary aims. It lacked these two things because Germany was then economically undeveloped, her means of communication were primitive, and her political structure split. Therefore, the problem of revolutionary collaboration between the rebellious peasantry and the urban plebs was not and could not be solved, and the peasant rebellion was suppressed. . . .

The same kind of thing occurred some three centuries later in the Revolution of 1848. Not only was the liberal bourgeoisie unwilling to call for a peasant revolt and to unite the peasantry under its leadership; more than that, the bourgeoisie feared a peasant rising above all else, because such a rising would strengthen and consolidate the radical and plebeian elements which opposed bourgeois rule in the cities. On the other hand, these plebeian radicals had not yet overcome their social and political shapelessness and atomization, and were therefore unable to cast aside the liberal bourgeoisie and assume the leadership of the peasant masses. The Revolution of 1848 was defeated. . . .

Yet, six decades earlier, we had witnessed a victorious realization of revolutionary tasks in France, precisely through the co-operation of the peasants and the urban plebs, i.e., the proletarians, semi-proletarians and *lumpen*-proletarians of the day. This took the form of a dictatorship of the National Convention, i.e., a dictatorship of the city over the village, Paris over the provinces, and the *sans-culottes* over Paris.

In Russia, under present conditions, the social advantage of the industrial population over the agricultural is very much greater than it was in the days of the old European revolutions. Moreover, in the Russian cities of today we no longer have chaotic plebeians, but a clearly defined industrial proletariat. One thing, however, has not changed: in a revolution, the only party that can win the support of the peasantry is the party that leads the most revolutionary masses of the city and that does not hesitate to assault feudal property because it is afraid of the property-owning bourgeoisie. Only the Social Democracy is such a party today.

THE CHARACTER OF THE RUSSIAN REVOLUTION

The Russian Revolution, if defined in terms of its direct and immediate tasks, is a "bourgeois" revolution. It attempts to free bourgeois society from the shackles and fetters of absolutism and feudal property. But the chief motive force of that revolution is the proletariat, and the Russian Revolution is therefore a "proletarian" one, if defined in terms of its methods. The pedants who determine the historical role of the proletariat by displays of statistical figures or by formal historical analogies find this contradiction impossible to swallow. For these pedants, bourgeois democracy is the providential leader of the Russian Revolution and, faced with the fact that the proletariat has actually led the revolution in all its stages, they try to wrap it in the swaddling clothes of their own theoretical immaturity. They believe that the history of one capitalist nation must repeat itself in the history of any other capitalist nation, with larger or smaller deviations. What these pedants fail to see is that the world is now undergoing a unified process of capitalist development which absorbs all the countries it meets on its way and creates in them a social amalgam combining local conditions with the general conditions of capitalism. The actual nature of this amalgam cannot be determined by mouthing historical clichés, but only by applying a materialistic analysis.

There is no historical analogy, though there is a deep internal connection, between, for example, England and the modern colonies. England was pioneer of the capitalist development which produced, in the course of centuries, new social forms and a powerful bourgeoisie acting as their carrier, whereas in the colonies European capital had ready-made armor-clad ships to import ready-made rails, sleepers, nails and drawing-room cars for colonial administrators, as well as rifles and bayonets to expel the natives from their ancestral land and force it into capitalist civilization. There is no historical development here analogous to that of Europe, though there is a deep inner resemblance.

The new Russia thus acquired its completely peculiar character by the circumstance of having received its capitalist baptism in the second half of the nineteenth century at the hands of a European capital which had already reached its most concentrated and abstract form, that is, finance capital. Its own previous history is in no way linked with the previous history of Russia. Before it could climb, in its own countries, the pinnacles of modern high finance, it had to do a number of things. First, it had to fight its way out of the narrow streets and alleys of the handicraft towns in which it learned to crawl and walk. Then it had to develop science and technology while waging a ceaseless struggle against the church; unite the whole nation around it; conquer power by revolting against dynastic and feudal privileges; clear an open stage for itself; and finish off the independent small industry from which it had once arisen. It was only after it severed its national umbilical cord and cut itself off from the dust of its ancestors, from political prejudices, racial sympathies, and geographical latitude and longitude, that it was able to cast its carnivorous shadow over the entire earth. And so today it sends opium to the Chinese artisan it has ruined; tomorrow it enriches the Russian seas with yet another warship; and the day after it conquers the diamond-bearing sands of South Africa.

But when English or French capital, the historical precipitation of several centuries, makes its appearance on the steppes of the Donets Basin, it is quite unable to bring forth the forces, relations and passions which it had once successively absorbed. It does not repeat in the new territory the development which it underwent in the old, but starts from the level it attained in its native land. It carries its machines across the seas and through the customs houses; and then, immediately and without intermediate stages, it concentrates around them the masses of the proletariat. And into this class it pours the revolutionary energy of the old generations of the bourgeoisie that is no longer active in its old home.

During the heroic period of French history we see the bourgeoisie, which has not yet become aware of the contradictions inherent in its position, being charged by history with the leadership of the struggle for a new order of things, not only against the obsolete institutions of France but also against the reactionary forces of Europe as a whole. And so the bourgeoisie, in all its different strata, considers itself and actually is the leader of the nation. It draws the masses into the struggle, gives them their political slogans and dictates to them what tactics they should adopt. Democracy unites the nation by a political ideology. The people—petty bourgeois, peasants

The Motive Forces of the Russian Revolution

and workers—send bourgeois deputies to the national parliament, and the orders they receive from their authorities are couched in the language of a bourgeoisie that has become conscious of its messianic role. During the revolution itself, class antagonisms are indeed uncovered; but the inherent logic of the revolutionary struggle successively removes from the political path the most inert strata of the bourgeoisie. However, before each stratum is removed, it transmits its energy to the strata that succeed it. And while all this goes on, the nation as a whole continues to fight for its objectives, using ever sharper and more decisive means. When, after the national core begins to move, the top strata of the well-to-do bourgeoisie separate themselves from it and ally themselves with Louis XVI, the democratic necessities of the nation turn against this part of the bourgeoisie, and produce universal suffrage and the republic as inescapably logical forms of democracy.

The Great French Revolution is a genuine national revolution. But it is also more than that. Within its national framework the world-wide struggle of the bourgeoisie for rule, power, and undivided triumph finds its classical expression.

In 1848 the bourgeoisie can no longer play a similar role. It could not and dared not take upon itself the responsibility for a revolutionary liquidation of the existing social order that impeded its rule. Its task was—and it knew this—to introduce into the old order some indispensable guarantees, not of its exclusive rule, but of its rule in partnership with the forces of the past. And so the bourgeoisie did not lead the masses in an assault on the old order; it leaned on that order and resisted the pressure of the masses attempting to push it forward. Its consciousness rebelled against the objective conditions of its rule. It viewed the democratic institutions not as the aim of its struggles but as a threat to its happiness. The revolution could not be carried out by it; only against it. This is why, in 1848, a successful revolution required the existence of a class able to take leadership in spite of the bourgeoisie and against the bourgeoisie, a class ready not only to push forward the revolution by the force of its own momentum but also to remove the political corpse of the bourgeoisie from its own path when the decisive moment came.

But neither the petty bourgeoisie nor the peasantry could satisfy these conditions.

The petty bourgeoisie viewed with hostility not only the past but also the future. It was still tied to medieval conceptions, but was already unable to resist "free" industry; it still marked the city with its stamp, but it was already yielding its influence to the medium and big bourgeoisie. It was immersed in its prejudices, deafened by the explosive events. Exploiting and exploited, greedy and impotent in its greed, the isolated petty bourgeoisie was unable to direct events on a world-wide scale.

The peasantry still largely lacked any initiative of its own. Scattered, separated from the cities that were political and cultural nerve centers, backward, incapable of looking beyond its own locality, indifferent to everything concerning the city, the peasantry could not supply a significant leadership. As soon as the burden of feudal rights was taken from its shoulders, it was appeased. It repaid with a black ingratitude the cities that had fought for its rights: once liberated, the peasants became the fanatical adherents of "order."

The democratic intelligentsia lacked class strength of its own. And so it alternately followed the lead of its older sister, the liberal bourgeoisie, acting as its appendage and parting company with it at critical moments to reveal its own impotence. It tied itself into knots of invisible contradictions and carried these wherever it went.

The proletariat was too weak, and lacked organization, experience and knowledge. The development of capitalism had reached the stage at which liquidation of the old feudal structures became necessary; but it had not yet reached the stage at which the working class, the product of new processes of production, became a decisive political force. The antagonism between the proletariat and the bourgeoisie had gone too far to permit the bourgeoisie to assume dauntlessly the role of national leader; it had not gone far enough to permit the proletariat to assume this role.

Austria offers an especially sharp and tragic picture of these uncompleted political relations in a revolutionary period.

The Viennese proletariat exhibited in 1848 a wild heroism

and a great revolutionary energy. Time and again it faced the fire, driven only by an obscure class instinct, lacking any general concept of the aims of its struggle and groping its way from slogan to slogan. The leadership of the proletariat passed, strangely, to the students, who were the only democratic group, and who because of their activities exercised a great influence on the masses. But though the students could fight heroically on the barricades and honestly fraternize with the workers, they were quite unable to determine the general course of the revolution which had handed them a "dictatorship" over the street. On May 26, all working-class Vienna rose up to answer the call of the students for a fight against the disarmament of the "academic legion." But when the population actually had the city in its hands, when the monarchy was in flight and had lost its significance, when the last troops left Vienna under the pressure of the people, when the government of Austria thus showed itself to be the relic of a dead past, there was no political force left in the capital to take the helm. The liberal bourgeoisie deliberately refused to exercise a power acquired in such a bandit fashion. It longed only for the return of the emperor, who had gone to the Tyrol and left Vienna orphaned. The workers were brave enough to defeat the reaction but insufficiently organized and self-conscious to pick up its inheritance. Unable to grasp the helm itself, the proletariat could not persuade bourgeois democracy to dare this historic deed: in its usual fashion, it went into hiding at the last moment. The general situation has been well described by a contemporary: "In Vienna a republic was established in fact but, unfortunately, nobody seemed to have noticed it." And here is Lassalle's incontrovertible judgment on the lesson of the events of 1848-49: "No struggle can be won in Europe unless it is proclaimed from the very start to be a purely socialist struggle; and no struggle can be won here any longer if social problems form only a vague element of it and remain in the background, while it is outwardly fought under the banner of national renaissance or bourgeois republicanism. . . ."

In the revolution which history will say started in 1905, the proletariat for the first time fought under its own flag and for its own aims. And yet it is certain that none of the old revolutions consumed such a great mass of national energy and won such insignificant positive gains as the Russian Revolution has done up to now. We have no wish to prophesy the immediate course of events. But we are sure about one thing: victory is possible only if the revolution takes the path defined in 1849 by Lassalle. There is no road back from the class struggle to the unity of the bourgeois nation. The "lack of results" of the Russian Revolution is nothing but a temporary reflection of its deep social character. In this "bourgeois" revolution without a revolutionary bourgeoisie, the proletariat naturally drives toward hegemony over the peasant and struggle for political power. The first wave of the Russian Revolution was broken by the political stupidity of the peasant who first fought the landlord of his village to take over his land, and then put on the soldier's uniform and shot at workers. We may view the events of this revolution as a series of pitiless object lessons by which history knocks into the head of the peasant the awareness of the links which exist between his local need for land and the central problem of political power. The foundations of the future victory of the revolution are being hammered out in the historical school of severe clashes and cruel defeats.

As Marx wrote in 1852 in his *Eighteenth Brumaire of Louis Bonaparte:*

> Bourgeois revolutions rapidly advance from success to success, their dramatic effects are striking, men and events are illuminated by a kind of Bengal fire, and ecstasy is the dominant mood of every day. But their course is rapid, they quickly reach their apogee and then society falls prey to an apathetic hangover in which it soberly tries to absorb the results of the period of storm and stress. Proletarian revolutions, on the contrary, constantly criticize themselves, their course is often broken, they turn back and start all over again what has been clearly finished. They ridicule, with a pitiless severity, the half-heartedness, weakness, and defects of their first attempts, and defeat their opponents only to permit them to rise again with re-

newed strength. They retreat again and again, scared by the colossal size and the undefined character of their task until, at last, conditions arise which make further retreat impossible, when Life itself proclaims majestically: *Hic Rhodus, hic salta!*

2

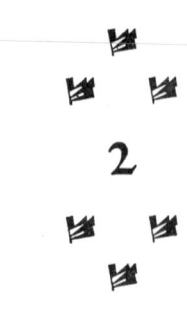

The Events in Petersburg

TRANSLATED BY M. J. OLGIN
from *Our Revolution* (1918).

How invincibly eloquent are facts! How utterly powerless are words!

The masses have made themselves heard! They have kindled revolutionary flames on Caucasian hilltops; they have clashed, breast against breast, with the guards' regiments and the cossacks on that unforgettable day of January Ninth; they have filled the streets and squares of industrial cities with the noise and clatter of their fights. . . .

The revolutionary masses are no more a theory, they are a fact. For the Social Democratic Party there is nothing new in this fact. We had predicted it long ago. We had seen its com-

[This essay, here slightly condensed, was written on January 20, 1905, eleven days after the "Bloody Sunday" on which thousands of workers marched to the Czar's Winter Palace, and were shot at and killed by the police.—Ed.]

//
ing at a time when the noisy liberal banquets seemed to form a striking contrast with the political silence of the people. *The revolutionary masses are a fact,* was our assertion. The clever liberals shrugged their shoulders in contempt. Those gentlemen think themselves sober realists solely because they are unable to grasp the consequences of great causes, because they make it their business to be humble servants of each ephemeral political fact. They think themselves sober statesmen in spite of the fact that history mocks at their wisdom, tearing to pieces their school books, making to naught their designs, and magnificently laughing at their pompous predictions.

There are no revolutionary people in Russia as yet. . . . The Russian workingman is backward in culture, in self-respect, and (we refer primarily to the workingmen of Petersburg and Moscow) he is not yet prepared for organized social and political struggle.

Thus Mr. Struve wrote in his *Osvoboshdenie.* He wrote it on January 7, 1905. Two days later the proletariat of Petersburg arose.

"*There are no revolutionary people in Russia as yet.*" These words ought to have been engraved on the forehead of Mr. Struve were it not that Mr. Struve's forehead already resembles a tombstone under which so many plans, slogans, and ideas have been buried—socialist, liberal, "patriotic," revolutionary, monarchic, democratic, and other ideas, all of them calculated not to run too far ahead, and all of them hopelessly dragging behind.

"*There are no revolutionary people in Russia as yet.*" So it was declared through the mouth of *Osvoboshdenie* by Russian liberalism, which in the course of three months had succeeded in convincing itself that liberalism was the main figure on the political stage and that its program and tactics would determine the future of Russia. Before this declaration had reached its readers, the wires carried into the remotest corners of the world the great message of the beginning of a National Revolution in Russia.

Yes, the Revolution has begun. We had hoped for it, we had

had no doubt about it. For long years, however, it had been to us a mere deduction from our "doctrine," which all nonentities of all political denominations had mocked at. They never believed in the revolutionary role of the proletariat, yet they believed in the power of *zemstvo* petitions, in Witte, in "blocs" combining naughts with naughts, in Svyatopolk-Mirski, in a stick of dynamite.... There was no political superstition they did not believe in. Only the belief in the proletariat to them was a superstition.

History, however, does not question political oracles, and the revolutionary people do not need a passport from political eunuchs.

The Revolution has come. One move of hers has lifted the people over scores of steps, up which in times of peace we would have had to drag ourselves with hardship and fatigue. The Revolution has come and destroyed the plans of so many politicians who had dared to make their little political calculations with no regard for the master, the revolutionary people. The Revolution has come and destroyed scores of superstitions, and has manifested the power of the program which is founded on the revolutionary logic of the development of the masses.

The Revolution has come, and the period of our political infancy has passed. Down to the archives went our traditional liberalism, whose only resource was the belief in a lucky change of administrative figures. Its period of bloom was the stupid reign of Svyatopolk-Mirski. Its ripest fruit was the Ukase of December 12. But now, January Ninth has come and effaced the "Spring," and has put military dictatorship in its place, and has promoted to the rank of Governor-General of Petersburg the same Trepov, who just before had been pulled down from the post of Moscow Chief of Police by the same liberal opposition.

That liberalism which did not care to know about the revolution, which hatched plots behind the scenes, which ignored the masses, which counted only on its diplomatic genius, has been swept away. *We are done with it for the entire period of the revolution.*

The liberals of the left wing will now follow the people. They will soon attempt to take the people into their own hands. The people are a power. One must *master* them. But they are, too, a *revolutionary* power. One, therefore, must *tame* them. This is, evidently, the future tactics of the *Osvoboshdenie* group. Our fight for a revolution, our preparatory work for the revolution must also be our merciless fight against liberalism for influence over the masses, for a leading rôle in the revolution. In this fight we shall be supported by a great power, the very logic of the revolution!

The Revolution has come.

The *forms* taken by the uprising of January Ninth could not have been foreseen. A revolutionary priest, in perplexing manner placed by history at the head of the working masses for several days, lent the events the stamp of his personality, his conceptions, his rank. This form may mislead many an observer as to the real substance of the events. The actual meaning of the events, however, is just that which social democracy foresaw. The central figure is the proletariat. The workingmen start a strike, they unite, they formulate political demands, they walk out into the streets, they win the enthusiastic sympathy of the entire population, they engage in battles with the army. . . . The hero, Gapon, has not created the revolutionary energy of the Petersburg workingmen, he only unloosed it. He found thousands of thinking workingmen and tens of thousands of others in a state of political agitation. He formed a plan which united all those masses—for the period of one day. The masses went to speak to the Czar. They were faced by Ulans, cossacks, guards. Gapon's plan had not prepared the workingmen for that. What was the result? They seized arms wherever they could, they built barricades. . . . They fought, though apparently they went to beg for mercy. This shows that they went *not to beg, but to demand.*

The proletariat of Petersburg manifested a degree of political alertness and revolutionary energy far exceeding the limits of the plan laid out by a casual leader. Gapon's plan contained many elements of revolutionary romanticism. On January Ninth, the plan collapsed. Yet the revolutionary proletariat of Petersburg is no romance; it is a living reality. So is the proletariat of other cities. An enormous wave is rolling over Russia. It has not yet quieted down. One shock, and the proletarian crater will begin to erupt torrents of revolutionary lava.

The proletariat has arisen. It has chosen an incidental pretext and a casual leader—a self-sacrificing priest. That seemed enough to *start* with. It was not enough to *win*.

Victory demands not a romantic method based on an illusory plan, but revolutionary tactics. *A simultaneous action of the proletariat of all Russia must be prepared.* This is the first condition. No local demonstration has a serious political significance any longer. After the Petersburg uprising, only an all-Russian uprising should take place. Scattered outbursts would only consume the precious revolutionary energy with no results. Wherever spontaneous outbursts occur, as a late echo of the Petersburg uprising, *they must be made use of to revolutionize and to solidify the masses, to popularize among them the idea of an all-Russian uprising* as a task of the approaching months, perhaps only weeks. . . .

The Russian Revolution has approached its climax—a national uprising. The organization of this uprising, which would determine the fate of the entire revolution, becomes the day's task for our party.

No one can accomplish it but we. Priest Gapon could appear only once. He cherished extraordinary illusions: that is why he could do what he has done. Yet he could remain at the head of the masses for a brief period only. The memory of George Gapon will always be dear to the revolutionary proletariat. Yet his memory will be that of a hero who opened the sluices of the revolutionary torrent. Should a new figure step to the front now, equal to Gapon in energy, revolutionary enthusiasm and power of political illusions, his arrival would be too late. What was great in George Gapon may now look ridiculous. There is no room for a second George Gapon, as the thing now needed is not an illusion, but clear revolutionary thinking, a decisive plan of action, a flexible revolutionary organization which would be able to give the masses a slogan, to lead them into the field of battle, to launch an attack all along the line and bring the revolution to a victorious conclusion.

3

My First Exile

From *My Life* (1930).

We were going down the river Lena, a few barges of convicts with a convoy of soldiers, drifting slowly along with the current. It was cold at night, and the heavy coats with which we covered ourselves were thick with frost in the morning. All along the way, at villages decided on beforehand, one or two convicts were put ashore. As well as I can remember, it took about three weeks before we came to the village of Ust-Kut. There I was put ashore with one of the woman prisoners, a close associate of mine from Nikolayev. Alexandra Lvovna had one of the most important positions in the South Russian Workers' Union. Her utter loyalty to socialism and her complete lack of any personal ambition gave her an unquestioned moral authority. The work that we were doing bound us closely together, and so, to avoid being separated, we had been married in the transfer prison in Moscow.

The village comprised about a hundred peasant huts. We settled down in one of them, on the very edge of the village. About us were the woods; below us, the river. Farther north, down the Lena, there were gold mines. The reflection of the gold seemed to hover about the river. Ust-Kut had known lusher times, days of wild debauches, robberies, and murders. When we were there the village was very quiet, but there was still plenty of drunkenness. The couple who owned the hut that we took were inveterate tipplers. Life was dark and repressed, utterly remote from the rest of the world. At night, the cockroaches filled the house with their rustlings as they crawled over table and bed, and even over our faces. From time to time we had to move out of the hut for a day or so and keep the door wide open, at a temperature of 35 degrees (Fahrenheit) below zero.

In the summer our lives were made wretched by midges. They even bit to death a cow that had lost its way in the woods. The peasants wore nets of tarred horsehair over their heads. In the spring and autumn the village was buried in mud. To be sure, the country was beautiful, but during those years it left me cold. I hated to waste interest and time on it. I lived between the woods and the river, and I almost never noticed them—I was so busy with my books and personal relations. I was studying Marx, brushing the cockroaches off the page.

The Lena was the great water route of the exiled. Those who had completed their terms returned to the south by way of the river. But communication was continuous between these various nests of the banished which kept growing with the rise of the revolutionary tide. The exiles exchanged letters with each other, some of them so long that they were really theoretical treatises. It was comparatively easy to get a transfer from one place to another from the governor of Irkutsk. Alexandra Lvovna and I moved to a place 250 versts east on the river Ilim, where we had friends. I found a job there, for a while, as clerk to a millionaire merchant. His fur depots, stores and saloons were scattered over a territory as big as Belgium and Holland put together. He was a powerful merchant-lord. He referred to the thousands of Tunguses under him as "my little Tunguses." He couldn't even write his name; he had to mark it with a cross. He lived in niggardly fashion the whole year round, and then would squander tens of thousands of rubles at the annual fair at Nijni-Novgorod. I worked under him for a month and a half. Then one day I entered on a bill a pound of red lead as "one pood" (forty pounds), and sent this huge bill to a distant store. This completely ruined my reputation with my employer, and I was discharged.

So we went back to Ust-Kut. The cold was terrific; the temperature dropped as low as 55 degrees (Fahrenheit) below zero. The coachman had to break the icicles off the horses' muzzles as we drove along. I held a ten-months-old baby girl on my knees. We had made a fur funnel to put over her head, arranged so that she could breathe through it and at every stop we removed her fearfully from her coverings, to see if she was still alive. Nothing untoward happened on that trip, however. We didn't stay long at Ust-Kut. After a few months, the governor gave us permission to move a little farther south, to a place called Verkholensk, where we had friends.

The aristocracy among the exiles was made up of the old Populists who had more or less succeeded in establishing themselves during the long years they had been away. The young Marxists formed a distinct section by themselves. It was not until my time that the striking workers, often illiterates who by some freak of fate had been separated from the great mass, began to drift to the north. For them, exile proved an invaluable school for politics and general culture. Intellectual disagreements were made the more bitter by squabbles over personal matters, as is natural where a great many people are forcibly confined. Private, and especially romantic, conflicts frequently took on the proportions of drama. There were even suicides on this account. At Verkholensk, we took turns at guarding a student from Kiev. I noticed a pile of shining metal shavings on his table. We found out later that he had made lead bullets for his shotgun. Our guarding him was in vain. With the barrel of the gun against his breast, he pulled the trigger with his foot. We buried him in silence on the hill. At that time, we were still shy about making speeches, as if there were something artificial about them. In all the big exile colonies, there were graves of suicides. Some of the exiles became absorbed into the local populations, especially in the towns; others took to drink. In exile, as in prison, only hard intellectual work could save one. The Marxists, I must admit, were the only ones who did any of it under these conditions.

It was on the great Lena route, at that time, that I met Dzerzhinsky, Uritzky, and other young revolutionaries who were destined to play such important rôles in the future. We awaited each arriving party eagerly. On a dark spring night, as we sat around a bonfire on the banks of the Lena, Dzerzhinsky read one of his poems, in Polish. His face and voice were beautiful, but the poem was a slight thing. The life of the man was to prove to be one of the sternest of poems.

Soon after our arrival at Ust-Kut, I began to contribute articles to an Irkutsk newspaper, the *Vostochnoye Obozreniye* (*The Eastern Review*). It was a provincial organ within the law, started by the old Populist exiles, but occasionally it fell into the hands of Marxists. I began as a village correspondent, and I waited anxiously for my first article to appear. The editor encouraged my contributions, and I soon began to write about literature, as well as about public questions. One day when I was trying to think of a pen name, I opened the Italian dictionary and "antidoto" was the first word that met my eye. So for several years I signed myself "Antid Oto," and jestingly explained to my friends that I wanted to inject the Marxist antidote into the legitimate newspapers. After a while, my pay jumped suddenly from two kopecks a line to four. It was the best proof of success. I wrote about the peasantry; about the Russian classic authors; about Ibsen, Hauptmann and Nietzsche; de Maupassant, Andreyev and Gorky. I sat up night after night scratching up my manuscripts, as I tried to find the exact idea or the right word to express it. I was becoming a writer.

Since 1896, when I had tried to ward off revolutionary ideas, and the following year, when I had done the same to Marxist doctrines even though I was already carrying on revolutionary work, I had traveled far. At the time of my exile, Marxism had definitely become the basis of my philosophy. During the exile, I tried to consider, from the new point of view I had acquired, the so-called "eternal" problems of life: love, death, friendship, optimism, pessimism, and so forth. In different epochs, and in varying social surroundings, man loves and hates and hopes differently. Just as the tree feeds its leaves, flowers, and fruits with the extracts absorbed from the soil by its roots, so does the individual find food for his sentiment and ideas, even the most "sublime" ones, in the economic roots of society. In my literary articles written in this period, I developed virtually one theme only: the relations between the individual and society. Not very long ago, these articles were published in a single volume, and when I saw them collected I realized that although I might have written them differently today, I should not have had to change the substance of them.

At that time, official or so-called "legal" Russian Marxism was in the throes of a crisis. I could see then from actual experience how brazenly new social requirements create for themselves intellectual garments from the cloth of a theory that was intended for something quite different. Until the nineties, the greater part of the Russian intelligentsia was stagnating in Populist theories, with their rejection of capitalist development and idealization of peasant communal ownership of the land. And capitalism in the meantime was holding out to the intelligentsia the promise of all sorts of material blessings and political influence. The sharp knife of Marxism was the instrument by which the bourgeois intelligentsia cut the Populist umbilical cord, and severed itself from a hated past. It was this that accounted for the swift and victorious spread of Marxism during the latter years of the last century.

As soon as Marxism had accomplished this, however, it began to irk this same intelligentsia. Its dialectics were convenient for demonstrating the progress of capitalist methods of development, but finding that it led to a revolutionary rejection of the whole capitalist system, they adjudged it an impediment and declared it out of date. At the turn of the century, at the time when I was in prison and exile, the Russian intelligentsia was going through a phase of widespread criticism of Marxism. They accepted its historical justification of capitalism, but discarded its rejection of capitalism by revolutionary means. In this roundabout way the old Populist intelligentsia, with its archaic sympathies, was slowly being transformed into a liberal bourgeois intelligentsia.

European criticisms of Marxism now found a ready hearing in Russia, irrespective of their quality. It is enough to say that Eduard Bernstein became one of the most popular guides from socialism to liberalism. The normative philosophy, shouting victory with more and more assurance, was ousting the materialist dialectics. Bourgeois public opinion, in its formative stages, needed inflexible norms, not only to protect it against the tyrannies of the autocratic bureaucracy, but against the wild revolutionism of the masses. Kant, although he overthrew Hegel, did not in turn hold his position very long. Russian liberalism came very late, and lived from the first on volcanic soil. The categorical imperative, it found, gave it too abstract and unreliable a security. Much stronger measures were needed to resist the revolutionary masses. The transcendental idealists became orthodox Christians. Bulgakov, a professor of political economy, began with a revision of Marxism on the agrarian question, went on to idealism, and ended by becoming a priest. But this last stage was not reached until some years later.

In the early years of this century, Russia was a vast laboratory of social thinking. My work on the history of Freemasonry had fortified me in a realization of the subordinate place of ideas in the historical process. "Ideas do not drop from the sky," I repeated after old Labriola. Now it was no longer a question of pure scientific study, but of the choice of a political path. The revision of Marxism that was going on in all directions helped me as it did many another young Marxist—it helped us to make up our minds and sharpen our weapons. We needed Marxism, not only to rid ourselves of Populism, which touched us but slightly, but actually to begin a stout war against capitalism in its own territory. The struggles against the Revisionists toughened us politically, as well as in the field of theory. We were becoming proletarian revolutionaries.

During this same period, we met with a great deal of criticism from our left. In one of the northern colonies—I think it was Viluysk—lived an exile called Makhaisky, whose name soon became generally known. Makhaisky began as a critic of social democratic opportunism. His first hectographed essay, devoted to an exposure of the opportunism of the German social democracy, had a great vogue among the exiles. His second essay criticized the economic system of Marx and ended with the amazing conclusion that socialism is a social order based on the exploitation of the workers by a professional intelligentsia. The third essay advocated the rejection of political struggle, in the spirit of anarchist syndicalism. For several months, the work of Makhaisky held first place in the interest of the Lena exiles. It gave me a powerful inoculation against anarchism, a theory very sweeping in its verbal negations, but lifeless and cowardly in its practical conclusions.

The first time I ever met a living anarchist was in the Moscow transfer prison. He was a village schoolteacher, Luzin, a man reserved and uncommunicative, even cruel. In prison he always preferred to be with the criminals and would listen intently to their tales of robbery and murder. He avoided discussions of theory. But once when I pressed him to tell me how railways would be managed by autonomous communities, he answered: "Why the hell should I want to travel on railways under anarchism?" That answer was enough for me. Luzin tried to win the workers over, and we carried on a concealed warfare which was not devoid of hostility.

We made the journey to Siberia together. During the high floods on the river, Luzin decided to cross the Lena in a boat. He was not quite sober and challenged me to go with him. I agreed. Loose timber and dead animals were floating on the surface of the swollen river; there were many whirlpools. We made the crossing safely, though not without exciting moments. Luzin gave me a sort of verbal testimonial: a "good comrade," or something to that effect, and we became friendlier. Soon after, however, he was transferred to a place farther north. A few months later he stabbed the local police chief with a knife. The policeman was not a bad sort of fellow and the wound did not prove dangerous. At the trial Luzin declared that he had nothing against the man personally, but that he wanted, through him, to strike at the tyranny of the state. He was sentenced to hard labor.

While hot discussions were seething in the far-flung, snow-covered Siberian exile colonies—discussions of such things as the differentiation of the Russian peasantry, the English trades unions, the relationship between the categorical imperative and the class interests, and between Marxism and Darwinism—a struggle of a special sort was taking place in government spheres. In February, 1901, the Holy Synod excommunicated Leo Tolstoy.

The edict was published in all the papers. Tolstoy was accused of six crimes: 1. "He rejects the personal, living God, glorified in the Holy Trinity." 2. "He denies Christ as the God-man risen from the dead." 3. "He denies the Immaculate Conception and the virginity, before and after the birth, of the God-mother." 4. "He does not recognize life after death and retribution for sins." 5. "He rejects the benefaction of the Holy Ghost." 6. "He mocks at the sacrament of the Eucharist." The gray-bearded metropolitans, Pobedonostzev, who was inspiring them, and all the other pillars of the state who looked upon us revolutionaries as half-mad fanatics, not to say criminals—whereas they, in their own eyes, were the representatives of sober thought based on the historical experience of man—it was these people who demanded that the great artist-realist subscribe to the faith in the Immaculate Conception, and in the transubstantiation of the Holy Ghost through wafers. We read the list of Tolstoy's heresies over and over again, each time with fresh astonishment, and said to ourselves: No, it is we who rest on the experience of man, it is we who represent the future, while those men at the top are not merely criminals but maniacs as well. We were absolutely sure that we would get the better of that lunatic asylum.

The old structure of the state was cracking all through its foundations. The students were still the ringleaders in the struggle, and in their impatience began to employ the methods of terrorism. After the shots fired by Karpovich and Balmashov,[1] all the exiles were as much aroused as if they had heard the bugle-call of alarm. Arguments about the use of terrorist methods began. After individual vacillations, the Marx-

[1] [Karpovich shot Bogolyepov, Minister of Education, in 1901. Balmashov shot Sipyagin, Minister of the Interior, in 1902.—Tr.]

ist section of the exiled went on record against terrorism. The chemistry of high explosives cannot take the place of mass action, we said. Individuals may be destroyed in a heroic struggle, but that will not rouse the working class to action. Our task is not the assassination of the Czar's ministers, but the revolutionary overthrow of Czarism. This is where the line was drawn between the social democrats and the Social Revolutionaries. While my theoretical views were formed in prison, my political self-determination was achieved in exile.

Two years had passed in this way, and much water had flowed under the bridges of St. Petersburg, Moscow, and Warsaw. A movement begun underground was now walking the streets of the cities. In some districts, the peasantry was beginning to stir. Social democratic organizations sprang up even in Siberia, along the line of the Trans-Siberian railway. They got in touch with me, and I wrote proclamations and leaflets for them. After a three years' interval, I was rejoining the ranks for active struggle.

The exiles were no longer willing to stay in their places of confinement, and there was an epidemic of escapes. We had to arrange a system of rotation. In almost every village there were individual peasants who as youths had come under the influence of the older generation of revolutionaries. They would carry the "politicals" away secretly in boats, in carts, or on sledges, and pass them along from one to another. The police in Siberia were as helpless as we were. The vastness of the country was an ally, but an enemy as well. It was very hard to catch a runaway, but the chances were that he would be drowned in the river or frozen to death in the primeval forests.

The revolutionary movement had spread far and wide, but it still lacked unity. Every district and every town were carrying on their individual struggles. Czarism had the invaluable advantage of concerted action. The necessity for creating a centralized party was engaging the minds of many revolutionaries. I devoted an essay to this, and copies of it were circulated throughout the colonies; it was discussed with avidity. It seemed to us that our fellow social democrats in Russia and abroad were not giving this question enough thought. But they did think and act. In the summer of 1902, I received, by way of Irkutsk, a number of books in the binding of which were concealed the latest publications from abroad, printed on extremely fine paper. We learned from them that there was a Marxian newspaper published abroad, the *Iskra,* which had as its object the creation of a centralized organization of professional revolutionaries who would be bound together by the iron discipline of action. A book by Lenin also reached us, a book published in Geneva, entitled *What Is to Be Done?* which dealt exclusively with the same problem. My handwritten essays, newspaper articles, and proclamations for the Siberian Union immediately looked small and provincial to me in the face of the new and tremendous task which confronted us. I had to look for another field of activity. I had to escape from exile.

At that time we already had two daughters. The younger was four months old. Life under conditions in Siberia was not easy, and my escape would place a double burden on the shoulders of Alexandra Lvovna. But she met this objection with the two words: "You must." Duty to the revolution overshadowed everything else for her, personal considerations especially. She was the first to broach the idea of my escape when we realized the great new tasks. She brushed away all my doubts.

For several days after I had escaped, she concealed my absence from the police. From abroad, I could hardly keep up a correspondence with her. Then she was exiled for a second time; after this we met only occasionally. Life separated us, but nothing could destroy our friendship and our intellectual kinship.

4

Five Days

(FEBRUARY 23-27, 1917)

TRANSLATED BY MAX EASTMAN
from *The History of the Russian Revolution* (1932).

The twenty-third of February was International Woman's Day. The Social Democratic circles had intended to mark this day in a general manner: by meetings, speeches, leaflets. It had not occurred to anyone that it might become the first day of the revolution. Not a single organization called for strikes on that day. What is more, even a Bolshevik organization, and a most militant one—the Vyborg borough committee, all workers—was opposing strikes. The temper of the masses, according to Kayurov, one of the leaders in the workers' district, was very tense; any strike would threaten to turn into an open fight. But since the committee thought the time unripe for militant action—the party not strong enough and the workers having too few contacts with the soldiers—they decided not to call for strikes but to prepare for revolutionary action at some indefinite time in the future. Such was the course followed by the committee on the eve of the twenty-third of February, and everyone seemed to accept it. On the following morning, however, in spite of all directives, the women textile workers in several factories went on strike, and sent delegates to the metal workers with an appeal for support. "With reluctance," writes Kayurov, "the Bolsheviks agreed to this, and they were followed by the workers—Mensheviks and Social Revolutionaries. But once there is a mass strike, one must call everybody into the streets and take the lead." Such was Kayurov's decision, and the Vyborg committee had to agree to it. "The idea of going into the streets had long been ripening among the workers; only at that moment nobody imagined where it would lead." Let us keep in mind this testimony of a participant, important for understanding the mechanics of the events.

It was taken for granted that in case of a demonstration the soldiers would be brought out into the streets against the workers. What would that lead to? This was wartime; the authorities were in no mood for joking. On the other hand, a reserve soldier in wartime is nothing like an old soldier of the regular army. Is he really so formidable? In revolutionary circles they had discussed this much, but rather abstractly. For no one, positively no one—we can assert this categorically upon the basis of all the data—then thought that February 23 was to mark the beginning of a decisive drive against absolutism. The talk was of a demonstration which had indefinite, but in any case limited, perspectives.

Thus the fact is that the February revolution was begun from below, overcoming the resistance of its own revolutionary organizations, the initiative being taken of their own accord by the most oppressed and downtrodden part of the proletariat—the women textile workers, among them no doubt many soldiers' wives. The overgrown bread lines had provided the last stimulus. About 90,000 workers, men and women, were on strike that day. The fighting mood expressed itself in demonstrations, meetings, encounters with the police. The movement began in the Vyborg district with its large industrial establishments; from there it crossed over to the Petersburg side. There were no strikes or demonstrations elsewhere, according to the testimony of the secret police. On that day detachments of troops were called in to assist the police —evidently not many of them—but there were no encounters with them. A mass of women, not all of them workers, flocked to the Municipal Duma demanding bread. It was like demanding milk from a he-goat. Red banners appeared in different parts of the city, and inscriptions on them showed that the workers wanted bread, but neither autocracy nor war. Woman's Day passed successfully, with enthusiasm and without victims. But what it concealed in itself, no one had guessed even by nightfall.

On the following day the movement not only fails to diminish, but doubles. About one-half of the industrial workers of Petrograd are on strike on the twenty-fourth of February. The workers come to the factories in the morning; instead of going to work they hold meetings, then begin processions toward the center. New districts and new groups of the population are drawn into the movement. The slogan "Bread!" is crowded out or obscured by louder slogans: "Down with autocracy!" "Down with the war!" Continuous demonstrations on the Nevsky[1]—first compact masses of workmen singing revolutionary songs, later a motley crowd of city folk interspersed with the blue caps of students. "The promenading crowd was sympathetically disposed toward us, and soldiers in some of the war hospitals greeted us by waving whatever was at hand." How many clearly realized what was being ushered in by this sympathetic waving from sick soldiers to demonstrating workers? But the Cossacks constantly, though without ferocity, kept charging the crowd. Their horses were covered with foam. The mass of demonstrators would part to let them through, and close up again. There was no fear in the crowd. "The Cossacks promise not to shoot," passed from mouth to mouth. Apparently some of the workers had talks with individual Cossacks. Later, however, cursing, half-drunken dragoons appeared on the scene. They plunged into the crowd,

[1] [Nevsky Prospect, the main avenue of the city.—Tr.]

began to strike at heads with their lances. The demonstrators summoned all their strength and stood fast: "They won't shoot." And in fact they didn't.

A liberal senator was looking at the dead streetcars—or was that on the following day and his memory failed him?—some of them with broken windows, some tipped over on the tracks, and was recalling the July days of 1914 on the eve of the war. "It seemed that the old attempt was being renewed." The senator's eyes did not deceive him; the continuity is clear. History was picking up the ends of the revolutionary threads broken by the war, and tying them in a knot.

Throughout the entire day, crowds of people poured from one part of the city to another. They were persistently dispelled by the police, stopped and crowded back by cavalry detachments and occasionally by infantry. Along with shouts of "Down with the police!" was heard oftener and oftener a "Hurrah!" addressed to the Cossacks. That was significant. Toward the police the crowd showed ferocious hatred. They routed the mounted police with whistles, stones, and pieces of ice. In a totally different way the workers approached the soldiers. Around the barracks, sentinels, patrols and lines of soldiers, stood groups of working men and women exchanging friendly words with the army men. This was a new stage, due to the growth of the strike and the personal meeting of the worker with the army. Such a stage is inevitable in every revolution. But it always seems new, and does in fact occur differently every time: those who have read and written about it do not recognize the thing when they see it.

In the State Duma that day they were telling how an enormous mass of people had flooded Znamensky Square and all Nevsky Prospect and the adjoining streets, and that a totally unprecedented phenomenon was observed: the Cossacks and the regiments with bands were being greeted by revolutionary and not patriotic crowds with shouts of "Hurrah!" To the question, "What does it all mean?" the first person accosted in the crowd answered the deputy: "A policeman struck a woman with a knout; the Cossacks stepped in and drove away the police." Whether it happened in this way or another will never be verified. But the crowd believed that it was so, that this was possible. The belief had not fallen out of the sky; it arose from previous experience, and was therefore to become an earnest of victory.

The workers at the Erikson, one of the foremost mills in the Vyborg district, after a morning meeting came out on the Sampsonievsky Prospect—a whole mass, 2,500 of them—and in a narrow place ran into the Cossacks. Cutting their way with the breasts of their horses, the officers first charged through the crowd. Behind them, filling the whole width of the Prospect, galloped the Cossacks. Decisive moment! But the horsemen, cautiously, in a long ribbon, rode through the corridor just made by the officers. "Some of them smiled," Kayurov recalls, "and one of them gave the workers a good wink." This wink was not without meaning. The workers were emboldened with a friendly, not hostile, kind of assurance, and slightly infected the Cossacks with it. The one who winked found imitators. In spite of renewed efforts from the officers, the Cossacks, without openly breaking discipline, failed to force the crowd to disperse, but flowed through it in streams. This was repeated three or four times and brought the two sides even closer together. Individual Cossacks began to reply to the workers' questions and even to enter into momentary conversations with them. Of discipline there remained but a thin transparent shell that threatened to break through any second. The officers hastened to separate their patrol from the workers, and, abandoning the idea of dispersing them, lined the Cossacks out across the street as a barrier to prevent the demonstrators from getting to the center. But even this did not help: standing stock-still in perfect discipline, the Cossacks did not hinder the workers from "diving" under their horses. The revolution does not choose its paths: it made its first steps toward victory under the belly of a Cossack's horse. A remarkable incident! And remarkable the eye of its narrator—an eye which took an impression of every bend in the process. No wonder, for the narrator was a leader; he was at the head of over two thousand men. The eye of a commander watching for enemy whips and bullets looks sharp.

It seems that the break in the army first appeared among the Cossacks, those age-old subduers and punishers. This does not mean, however, that the Cossacks were more revolutionary than others. On the contrary, these solid property owners, riding their own horses, highly valuing their Cossack peculiarities, scorning the plain peasants, mistrustful of the workers, had many elements of conservatism. But just for this reason the changes caused by the war were more sharply noticeable in them. Besides, they were always being pulled around, sent everywhere, driven against the people, kept in suspense—and they were the first to be put to the test. They were sick of it, and wanted to go home. Therefore they winked: "Do it boys, if you know how—we won't bother you!" All these things, however, were merely very significant symptoms. The army was still the army, it was bound with discipline, and the threads were in the hands of the monarchy. The worker mass was unarmed. The leaders had not yet thought of the decisive crisis.

On the calendar of the Council of Ministers that day there stood, among other questions, the question of disorders in the capital. Strikes? Demonstrations? This isn't the first time. Everything is provided for. Directions have been issued. Return to the order of business.

And what were the directions? In spite of the fact that on the twenty-third and twenty-fourth twenty-eight policemen were beaten up—persuasive exactness about the number!—the military commander of the district, General Khabalov, almost a dictator, did not resort to shooting. Not from kind-heartedness: everything was provided for and marked down in advance, even the time for the shooting.

The revolution caught them unawares only with regard to the exact moment. Generally speaking, both sides, the revolutionary and the governmental, were carefully preparing for it, had been preparing for years, had always been preparing. As for the Bolsheviks, all their activity since 1905 was nothing but preparation for a second revolution. And the activities of the government, an enormous share of them, were preparations to put down the new revolution. In the fall of 1916 this part of the government's work had assumed an aspect of particularly careful planning. A commission under Khabalov's chairmanship had completed by the middle of January, 1917,

Five Days (February 23-27, 1917)

a very exact plan for crushing a new insurrection. The city was divided into six police districts, which in turn were subdivided into rayons. The commander of the reserve guard units, General Chebykin, was placed at the head of all the armed forces. Regiments were assigned to different rayons. In each of the six police districts, the police, the gendarmes and the troops were united under the command of special staff officers. The Cossack cavalry was at the disposal of Chebykin himself for larger-scale operations. The order of action was planned as follows: first the police act alone, then the Cossacks appear on the scene with whips, and only in case of real necessity do the troops go into action with rifles and machine guns. It was this very plan, developed out of the experience of 1905, that was put into operation in the February days. The difficulty lay not in lack of foresight, nor defects of the plan itself, but in the human material. Here the whole thing threatened to hang fire.

Formerly the plan was based on the entire garrison, which comprised one hundred and fifty thousand soldiers, but in reality only some ten thousand came into the count. Besides the policemen, numbering three and a half thousand, a firm hope was placed in the military training schools. This is explained by the makeup of the Petrograd garrison, which at that time consisted almost exclusively of reserve units, primarily of the fourteen reserve battalions attached to the regiments of the Guard which were then at the front. In addition to that, the garrison comprised one reserve infantry regiment, reserve bicycle battalion, a reserve armored car division, small units of sappers and artillerymen and two regiments of Don Cossacks. That was a great many—it was too many. The swollen reserve units were made up of a human mass which had either escaped training almost entirely, or succeeded in getting free of it. But for that matter, substantially the same thing was true of the entire army.

Khabalov meticulously adhered to the plan he had worked out. On the first day, the twenty-third, the police operated alone. On the twenty-fourth, for the most part, the cavalry was led into the streets, but only to work with whip and lance. The use of infantry and firearms was to depend on the further development of events. But events came thick and fast.

On the twenty-fifth, the strike spread wider. According to the government's figures, 240,000 workers participated that day. The most backward layers are following up the vanguard. Already a good number of small establishments are on strike. The streetcars are at a standstill. Business concerns are closed. In the course of the day students of the higher schools join the strike. By noon tens of thousands of people pour to the Kazan cathedral and the surrounding streets. Attempts are made to organize street meetings; a series of armed encounters with the police occurs. Orators address the crowds around the Alexander III monument. The mounted police open fire. A speaker falls wounded. Shots from the crowd kill a police inspector, wound the chief of police and several other policemen. Bottles, petards and hand grenades are thrown at the gendarmes. The war has taught this art. The soldiers show indifference, at times hostility, to the police. It spreads excitedly through the crowd that when the police opened fire by the Alexander III monument, the Cossacks let go a volley at the horse "Pharaohs" (such was the nickname of the police) and the latter had to gallop off. This apparently was not a legend circulated for self-encouragement, since the incident, although in different versions, is confirmed from several sources.

A worker-Bolshevik, Kayurov, one of the authentic leaders in those days, relates how at one place, within sight of a detachment of Cossacks, the demonstrators scattered under the whips of the mounted police, and how he, Kayurov, and several workers with him, instead of following the fugitives, took off their caps and approached the Cossacks with the words: "Brothers —Cossacks, help the workers in a struggle for their peaceable demands; you see how the Pharaohs treat us, hungry workers. Help us!" This consciously humble manner, those caps in their hands—what an accurate psychological calculation! Inimitable gesture! The whole history of street fights and revolutionary victories swarms with such improvisations. But they are drowned without a trace in the abyss of great events—the shell remains to the historian, the generalization. "The Cossacks glanced at each other in some special way," Kayurov continues, "and we were hardly out of the way before they rushed into the fight." And a few minutes later, near the station gate, the crowd were tossing in their arms a Cossack who before their eyes had slaughtered a police inspector with his saber.

Soon the police disappear altogether—that is, begin to act secretly. Then the soldiers appear—bayonets lowered. Anxiously the workers ask them: "Comrades, you haven't come to help the police?" A rude "Move along!" for answer. Another attempt ends the same way. The soldiers are sullen. A worm is gnawing them, and they cannot stand it when a question hits the very center of the pain.

Meanwhile disarmament of the Pharaohs becomes a universal slogan. The police are fierce, implacable, hated and hating foes. To win them over is out of the question. Beat them up and kill them. It is different with the soldiers: the crowd makes every effort to avoid hostile encounters with them; on the contrary, seeks ways to dispose them in its favor, convince, attract, fraternize, merge them in itself. In spite of the auspicious rumors about the Cossacks, perhaps slightly exaggerated, the crowd's attitude toward the mounted men remains cautious. A horseman sits high above the crowd; his soul is separated from the soul of the demonstrator by the four legs of his beast. A figure at which one must gaze from below always seems more significant, more threatening. The infantry are beside one on the pavement—closer, more accessible. The masses try to get near them, look into their eyes, surround them with their hot breath. A great role is played by women workers in the relation between workers and soldiers. They go up to the cordons more boldly than men, take hold of the rifles, beseech, almost command: "Put down your bayonets—join us." The soldiers are excited, ashamed, exchange anxious glances, waver; someone makes up his mind first, and the bayonets rise guiltily above the shoulders of the advancing crowd. The barrier is opened, a joyous and grateful "Hurrah!" shakes the air. The soldiers are surrounded. Everywhere arguments, reproaches, appeals—the revolution makes another forward step.

Nicholas from headquarters sent Khabalov a telegraphic command to put an end to the disorders "tomorrow." The Czar's will fell in with the next step in Khabalov's "plan," and the telegram served merely as an extra stimulus. Tomorrow the troops will say their say. Isn't it too late? You can't tell yet. The question is posed, but far from answered. The indulgence of the Cossacks, the wavering of certain infantry lines—these are but much-promising episodes repeated by the thousand-voiced echo of the sensitive street. Enough to inspire the revolutionary crowd, but too little for victory. Especially since there are episodes of an opposite kind. In the afternoon a detachment of dragoons, supposedly in response to revolver shots from the crowd, first opened fire on the demonstrators near Gostinny Dvor. According to Khabalov's report to headquarters three were killed and ten wounded. A serious warning! At the same time Khabalov issued a threat that all workers registered in the draft would be sent to the front if they did not go to work before the twenty-eighth. The general issued a three-day ultimatum—that is, he gave the revolution more time than it needed to overthrow Khabalov and the monarchy into the bargain. But that will become known only after the victory. On the evening of the twenty-fifth nobody guessed what the next day had in its womb.

Let us try to get a clearer idea of the inner logic of the movement. On February 23, under the flag of Woman's Day, began the long-ripe and long-withheld uprising of the Petrograd working masses. The first step of the insurrection was the strike. In the course of three days it broadened and became practically general. This alone gave assurance to the masses and carried them forward. Becoming more and more aggressive, the strike merged with the demonstrations, which were bringing the revolutionary mass face to face with the troops. This raised the problem as a whole to the higher level where things are solved by force of arms. The first days brought a number of individual successes, but these were more symptomatic than substantial.

A revolutionary uprising that spreads over a number of days can develop victoriously only if it ascends step by step, and scores one success after another. A pause in its growth is dangerous; a prolonged marking of time, fatal. But even successes by themselves are not enough; the masses must know about them in time, and have time to understand their value. It is possible to let slip a victory at the very moment when it is within arm's reach. This has happened in history.

The first three days were days of uninterrupted increase in the extent and acuteness of the strife. But for this very reason the movement had arrived at a level where mere symptomatic successes were not enough. The entire active mass of the people had come out on the streets. It was settling accounts with the police successfully and easily. In the last two days the troops had been drawn into the events—on the second day the cavalry, on the third the infantry too. They barred the way, pushed and crowded back the masses, sometimes connived with them, but almost never resorted to firearms. Those in command were slow to change their plan, partly because they underestimated what was happening—the faulty vision of the reaction supplemented that of the leaders of the revolution—partly because they lacked confidence in the troops. But exactly on the third day, the force of the developing struggle, as well as the Czar's command, made it necessary for the government to send the troops into action in dead earnest. The workers understood this, especially their advance ranks; the dragoons had already done some shooting the day before. Both sides now faced the issue unequivocally.

On the night of the twenty-sixth about a hundred people were arrested in different parts of the city—people belonging to various revolutionary organizations, and among them five members of the Petrograd Committee of the Bolsheviks. This, also, meant that the government was taking the offensive. What will happen today? In what mood will the workers wake up after yesterday's shooting? And most important: what will the troops say? The sun of February 26 came up in a fog of uncertainty and acute anxiety.

In view of the arrest of the Petrograd Committee, the guidance of the entire work in the city fell into the hands of the Vyborg rayon. Perhaps this was just as well. The upper leadership in the party was hopelessly slow. Only on the morning of the twenty-fifth, the Bureau of the Bolshevik Central Committee at last decided to issue a handbill calling for an all-Russian general strike. At the moment of issue, if indeed it ever did issue, the general strike in Petrograd was facing an armed uprising. The leaders were watching the movement from above; they hesitated, they lagged—in other words, they did not lead. They dragged after the movement.

The nearer one comes to the factories, the greater the decisiveness. Today, however, the twenty-sixth, there is anxiety even in the rayons. Hungry, tired, chilled, with a mighty historic responsibility upon their shoulders, the Vyborg leaders gather outside the city limits, amid vegetable gardens, to exchange impressions of the day and plan the course . . . of what? Of a new demonstration? But where will an unarmed demonstration lead, now the government has decided to go the limit? This question bores into their minds. "One thing seems evident: the insurrection is dissolving." Here we recognize the voice of Kayurov, already familiar to us, and at first it seems hardly his voice. The barometer falls so low before the storm.

In the hours when hesitation seized even those revolutionists closest to the mass, the movement itself had gone much further than its participants realized. Even the day before, toward evening of the twenty-fifth, the Vyborg side was wholly in the hands of the insurrection. The police stations were wrecked, individual officers had been killed, and the majority had fled. The city headquarters had completely lost contact with the greater part of the capital. On the morning of the twenty-sixth it became evident that not only the Vyborg side, but also Peski almost up to Liteiny Prospect, was in control of the insurrection. At least so the police reports defined the situation. And it was true in a sense, although the revolutionists could hardly realize it: the police in so many cases abandoned their lairs before there was any threat from the workers. But even aside from that, ridding the factory districts of the police could not have decisive significance in the eyes of the workers: the troops had not yet said their final word. The uprising is "dissolving," thought the boldest of the bold. Meanwhile it was only beginning to develop.

The twenty-sixth of February fell on a Sunday; the factories were closed, and this prevented measuring the strength of the mass pressure in terms of the extent of the strike. Moreover the

Five Days (February 23-27, 1917)

workers could not assemble in the factories, as they had done on the preceding days, and that hindered the demonstrations. In the morning the Nevsky was quiet. In those hours the Czarina telegraphed the Czar: "The city is calm."

But this calmness does not last long. The workers gradually concentrate, and move from all suburbs to the center. They are stopped at the bridges. They flock across the ice: it is only February and the Neva is one solid bridge of ice. The firing at their crowds on the ice is not enough to stop them. They find the city transformed. Posses, cordons, horse-patrols everywhere. The approaches to the Nevsky are especially well guarded. Every now and then shots ring out from ambush. The number of killed and wounded grows. Ambulances dart here and there. You cannot always tell who is shooting and where the shots come from. One thing is certain: after their cruel lesson, the police have decided not to expose themselves again. They shoot from windows, through balcony doors, from behind columns, from attics. Hypotheses are formed that easily become legends. They say that in order to intimidate the demonstrators, many soldiers are disguised in police uniforms. They say that Protopopov has placed numerous machine gun nests in the garrets of houses. A commission created after the revolution did not discover such nests, but this does not mean that there were none. However, the police on this day occupy a subordinate place. The troops come decisively into action. They are given strict orders to shoot, and the soldiers, mostly training squads—that is, noncommissioned officers' regimental schools—do shoot. According to the official figures, on this day about forty are killed and as many wounded, not counting those led or carried away by the crowd. The struggle arrives at a decisive stage. Will the mass ebb before the lead and flow back to its suburbs? No, it does not ebb. It is bound to have its own.

Bureaucratic, bourgeois, liberal Petersburg was in a fright. On that day Rodzianko, the President of the State Duma, demanded that reliable troops be sent from the front; later he "reconsidered" and recommended to the War Minister Belyaev that the crowds be dispersed, not with lead, but with cold water out of fire hose. Belyaev, having consulted General Khabalov, answered that a douse of water would produce precisely the opposite effect "because it excites." Thus in the liberal and bureaucratic upper circles they discussed the relative advantages of hot and cold douches for the people in revolt. Police reports for that day testify that the fire hose was inadequate:

> In the course of the disorders it was observed as a general phenomenon that the rioting mobs showed extreme defiance towards the military patrols, at whom, when asked to disperse, they threw stones and lumps of ice dug up from the street. When preliminary shots were fired into the air, the crowd not only did not disperse but answered these volleys with laughter. Only when loaded cartridges were fired into the very midst of the crowd, was it found possible to disperse the mob, the participants in which, however, would most of them hide in the yards of nearby houses, and as soon as the shooting stopped come out again into the street.

This police report shows that the temperature of the masses had risen very high. To be sure, it is hardly probable that the crowd would have begun of itself to bombard the troops—even the training squads—with stones and ice: that would too much contradict the psychology of the insurrectionary masses, and the wise strategy they had shown with regard to the army. For the sake of supplementary justification for mass murders, the colors in the report are not exactly what they were, and are not laid on the way they were, in actual fact. But the essentials are reported truly and with remarkable vividness: the masses will no longer retreat, they resist with optimistic brilliance, they stay on the street even after murderous volleys, they cling, not to their lives, but to the pavement, to stones, to pieces of ice. The crowd is not only bitter, but audacious. This is because, in spite of the shooting, it keeps its faith in the army. It counts on victory and intends to have it at any cost.

The pressure of the workers upon the army is increasing—countering the pressure from the side of the authorities. The Petrograd garrison comes into the focus of events. The expectant period, which has lasted almost three days, during which

Five Days (February 23-27, 1917)

it was possible for the main mass of the garrison to keep up friendly neutrality toward the insurrection, has come to an end. "Shoot the enemy!" the monarchy commands. "Don't shoot your brothers and sisters!" cry the workers. And not only that: "Come with us!" Thus in the streets and squares, by the bridges, at the barrack-gates, is waged a ceaseless struggle—now dramatic, now unnoticeable—but always a desperate struggle, for the heart of the soldier. In this struggle, in these sharp contacts between working men and women and the soldiers, under the steady crackling of rifles and machine guns, the fate of the government, of the war, of the country, is being decided.

The shooting of demonstrators increased the uncertainty among the leaders. The very scale of the movement began to seem dangerous. Even at the meeting of the Vyborg committee the evening of the twenty-sixth—that is, twelve hours before the victory—arose discussions as to whether it was not time to end the strike. This may seem astonishing. But remember, it is far easier to recognize victory the day after than the day before. Besides, moods change frequently under the impact of events and the news of them. Discouragement quickly gives way to a flow of enthusiasm. Kayurovs and Chugurins have plenty of personal courage, but at moments a feeling of responsibility for the masses clutches them. Among the rank-and-file workers there were fewer oscillations. Reports about their moods were made to the authorities by a well-informed agent in the Bolshevik organization, Shurkanov.

> Since the army units have not opposed the crowd, [wrote this *provocateur*] and in individual cases have even taken measures paralyzing the initiative of the police officers, the masses have got a sense of impunity, and now, after two days of unobstructed walking the streets, when the revolutionary circles have advanced the slogans "Down with war" and "Down with the autocracy!", the people have become convinced that the revolution has begun, that success is with the masses, that the authorities are powerless to suppress the movement because the troops are with it, that a decisive victory is near, since the troops

will soon openly join the side of the revolutionary forces, that the movement begun will not subside, but will ceaselessly grow to a complete victory and a state revolution.

A characterization remarkable for compactness and clarity! The report is a most valuable historic document. This did not, of course, prevent the victorious workers from executing its author.

These *provocateurs*, whose number was enormous, especially in Petrograd, feared, more than anyone else did, the victory of the revolution. They followed a policy of their own: in the Bolshevik conferences Shurkanov defended the most extreme actions; in his reports to the secret police he suggested the necessity of a decisive resort to firearms. It is possible that with this aim, Shurkanov tried even to exaggerate the aggressive confidence of the workers. But in the main he was right: events would soon confirm his judgment.

The leaders in both camps guessed and vacillated, for not one of them could estimate *a priori* the relation of forces. External indications ceased absolutely to serve as a measure. Indeed one of the chief features of a revolutionary crisis consists in this sharp contradiction between the present consciousness and the old forms of social relationship. A new relation of forces was mysteriously implanting itself in the consciousness of the workers and soldiers. It was precisely the government's offensive, called forth by the previous offensive of the revolutionary masses, which transformed the new relation of forces from a potential to an active state. The worker looked thirstily and commandingly into the eyes of the soldier, and the soldier anxiously and diffidently looked away. This meant that, in a way, the soldier could no longer answer for himself. The worker approached the soldier more boldly. The soldier sullenly, but without hostility—guiltily rather—refused to answer. Or sometimes—now more and more often—he answered with pretended severity in order to conceal how anxiously his heart was beating in his breast. Thus the change was accomplished. The soldier was clearly shaking off his soldiery. In doing so he could not immediately recognize himself. The authorities said that the revolution intoxicated the soldier. To the soldier it seemed, on the contrary, that he was sobering up from the opium of the barracks. Thus the decisive day was prepared—the twenty-seventh of February.

However, on the eve of that day an incident occurred which in spite of its episodic nature paints with a new color all the events of the twenty-sixth. Towards evening the fourth company of the Pavlovsky regiment of the Imperial Guard mutinied. In the written report of a police inspector the cause of the mutiny is categorically stated: "Indignation against the training squad of the same regiment which, while on duty in the Nevsky, fired on the crowd." Who informed the fourth company of this? A record has been accidentally preserved. About two o'clock in the afternoon, a handful of workers ran up to the barracks of the Pavlovsky regiment. Interrupting each other, they told about a shooting on the Nevsky. "Tell your comrades that the Pavlovtsi, too, are shooting at us—we saw soldiers in your uniform on the Nevsky." That was a burning reproach, a flaming appeal. "All looked distressed and pale." The seed fell not upon the rock. By six o'clock the fourth company had left the barracks without permission under the command of a noncommissioned officer—who was he? His name is drowned forever among hundreds and thousands of equally heroic names—and marched to the Nevsky to recall its training squad. This was not a mere soldiers' mutiny over wormy meat; it was an act of high revolutionary initiative. On their way down, the company had an encounter with a detachment of mounted police. The soldiers opened fire. One policeman and one horse were killed; another policeman and another horse were wounded. The further path of the mutineers in the hurricane of the streets is unknown. The company returned to the barracks and aroused the entire regiment. But their arms had been hidden. According to some sources, they nevertheless got hold of thirty rifles. They were soon surrounded by the Preobrazhentsi. Nineteen Pavlovtsi were arrested and imprisoned in the fortress; the rest surrendered. According to other information, the officers on that evening found twenty-one soldiers with rifles missing. A dangerous leak! These twenty-one soldiers would be seeking allies and defenders all night long. Only the victory of the revolution could save them. The workers would surely learn from them what had happened. This was not a bad omen for tomorrow's battles.

Nabokov, one of the most prominent liberal leaders, whose truthful memoirs seem at times to be the very diary of his party and of his class, was returning home from a visit at one o'clock in the morning along the dark and watchful streets. He was "perturbed and filled with dark forebodings." It is possible that at one of the crossings he met a fugitive Pavlovetz. Both hurried past: they had nothing to say to each other. In the workers' quarters and the barracks some kept watch or conferred, others slept the half-sleep of the bivouac, or dreamed feverishly about tomorrow. Here the fugitive Pavlovetz found shelter.

How scant are the records of the mass fighting in the February days—scant even in comparison with the slim records of the October fights. In October the party directed the insurrection from day to day; in its articles, proclamations, and reports, at least the external continuity of the struggle is recorded. Not so in February. The masses had almost no leadership from above. The newspapers were silenced by the strike. Without a look back, the masses made their own history. To reconstruct a living picture of the things that happened in the streets is almost unthinkable. It would be well if we could re-create at least the general continuity and inner order of events.

The government, which had not yet lost hold of the machinery of power, observed the events on the whole even less ably than the Left parties, which, as we know, were far from brilliant in this direction. After the "successful" shootings of the twenty-sixth, the ministers took heart for an instant. At dawn of the twenty-seventh Protopopov reassuringly reported that, according to information received, "part of the workers intend to return to work." But the workers never thought of going back to the shops. Yesterday's shootings and failures had not discouraged the masses. How to explain this? Apparently the losses were outbalanced by certain gains. Pouring through the streets, colliding with the enemy, pulling at the arms of soldiers, crawling under horses' bellies, attacking, scattering, leaving their corpses on the crossings, grabbing a few firearms,

Five Days (February 23-27, 1917)

spreading the news, catching at rumors, the insurrectionary mass becomes a collective entity with numberless eyes, ears, and antennae. At night, returning home from the arena of struggle to the workers' quarter, it goes over the impressions of the day, and sifting away what is petty and accidental, casts its own thoughtful balance. On the night of the twenty-seventh, this balance was practically identical with the report made to the authorities by the *provocateur*, Shurkanov.

In the morning the workers streamed again to the factories, and in open meetings resolved to continue the struggle. Especially resolute, as always, were the Vyborgtsi. But in other districts too these morning meetings were enthusiastic. To continue the struggle! But what would that mean today? The general strike had issued in revolutionary demonstrations by immense crowds, and the demonstrations had led to a collision with the troops. To continue the struggle today would mean to summon an armed insurrection. But nobody had formulated this summons. It had grown irresistibly out of the events, but it was never placed on the order of the day by a revolutionary party.

The art of revolutionary leadership in its most critical moments consists nine-tenths in knowing how to sense the mood of the masses—just as Kayurov detected the movement of the Cossack's eyebrow, though on a larger scale. An unexcelled ability to detect the mood of the masses was Lenin's great power. But Lenin was not in Petrograd. The legal and semi-legal "socialistic" staffs, Kerensky, Cheidze, Skobelev, and all those who circled around them, pronounced warnings and opposed the movement. But even the central Bolshevik staff, composed of Shliapnikov, Zalutsky and Molotov, was amazing in its helplessness and lack of initiative. In fact, the districts and barracks were left to themselves. The first proclamation to the army was released only on the twenty-sixth by one of the Social Democratic organizations close to the Bolsheviks. This proclamation, rather hesitant in character—not even containing an appeal to come over to the people—was distributed throughout all the city districts on the morning of the twenty-seventh. "However," testifies Yurenev, the leader of this organization, "the tempo of the revolutionary events was such

that our slogans were already lagging behind it. By the time
the leaflets had penetrated into the thick of the troops, the
latter had already come over." As for the Bolshevik center—
Shliapnikov, at the demand of Chugurin, one of the best
worker-leaders of the February days, finally wrote an appeal
to the soldiers on the morning of the twenty-seventh. Was it
ever published? At best it might have come in at the finish. It
could not possibly have influenced the events of February 27.
We must lay it down as a general rule for those days that the
higher the leaders, the further they lagged behind.

But the insurrection, not yet so named by anyone, took its
own place on the order of the day. All the thoughts of the
workers were concentrated on the army. "Don't you think we
can get them started?" Today haphazard agitation would no
longer do. The Vyborg section staged a meeting near the barracks of the Moscow regiment. The enterprise proved a failure.
Is it difficult for some officer or sergeant-major to work the
handle of a machine gun? The workers were scattered by a
cruel fire. A similar attempt was made at the barracks of a
reserve regiment. And there too: officers with machine guns
interfered between the workers and soldiers. The leaders of
the workers fumed, looked for firearms, demanded them from
the party. And the answer was: "The soldiers have the firearms,
go get them." That they knew themselves. But how to get
them? Isn't everything going to collapse all at once today?
Thus came on the critical point of the struggle. Either the machine gun will wipe out the insurrection, or the insurrection
will capture the machine gun.

In his recollections, Shliapnikov, the chief figure in the Petrograd center of the Bolsheviks, tells how he refused the demands of the workers for firearms—or even revolvers—sending
them to the barracks to get them. He wished in this way to
avoid bloody clashes between workers and soldiers, staking
everything on agitation—that is, on the conquest of the soldiers
by work and example. We know of no other testimony which
confirms or refutes this statement of a prominent leader of
those days—a statement which testifies to sidestepping rather
than foresight. It would be simpler to confess that the leaders
had no firearms.

Five Days (February 23-27, 1917)

There is no doubt that the fate of every revolution at a certain point is decided by a break in the disposition of the army. Against a numerous, disciplined, well-armed and ably led military force, unarmed or almost unarmed masses of the people cannot possibly gain a victory. But no deep national crisis can fail to affect the army to some extent. Thus along with the conditions of a truly popular revolution there develops a possibility—not, of course, a guarantee—of its victory. However, the going over of the army to the insurrection does not happen of itself, nor as a result of mere agitation. The army is heterogeneous, and its antagonistic elements are held together by the terror of discipline. On the very eve of the decisive hour, the revolutionary soldiers do not know how much power they have, or what influence they can exert. The working masses, of course, are also heterogeneous. But they have immeasurably more opportunity for testing their ranks in the process of preparation for the decisive encounter. Strikes, meetings, demonstrations are not only acts in the struggle, but also measures of its force. The whole mass does not participate in the strike. Not all the strikers are ready to fight. In the sharpest moments the most daring appear in the streets. The hesitant, the tired, the conservative sit at home. Here a revolutionary selection takes place of itself; people are sifted through the sieve of events. It is otherwise with the army. The revolutionary soldiers—sympathetic, wavering or antagonistic—are all tied together by a compulsory discipline whose threads are held, up to the last moment, in the officer's fist. The soldiers are told off daily into first and second files, but how are they to be divided into rebellious and obedient?

The psychological moment when the soldiers go over to the revolution is prepared by a long molecular process, which, like other processes of nature, has its point of climax. But how to determine this point? A military unit may be wholly prepared to join the people, but may not receive the needed stimulus. The revolutionary leadership does not yet believe in the possibility of having the army on its side, and lets slip the victory. After this ripened but unrealized mutiny, a reaction may seize the army. The soldiers lose the hope which flared in their breasts; they bend their necks again to the yoke of discipline, and in a new encounter with the workers, especially at a distance, will stand opposed to the insurrection. In this process there are many elements imponderable or difficult to weigh, many cross-currents, collective suggestions and autosuggestions. But out of this complicated web of material and psychic forces one conclusion emerges with irrefutable clarity: the more the soldiers in their mass are convinced that the rebels are really rebelling—that this is not a demonstration after which they will have to go back to the barracks and report, that this is a struggle to the death, that the people may win if they join them, and that this winning will not only guarantee impunity, but alleviate the lot of all—the more they realize this, the more willing they are to turn aside their bayonets, or go over with them to the people. In other words, the revolutionists can create a break in the soldiers' mood only if they themselves are actually ready to seize the victory at any price whatever, even the price of blood. And this highest determination never can, or will, remain unarmed.

The critical hour of contact between the pushing crowd and the soldiers who bar their way has its critical minute. That is when the gray barrier has not yet given way, still holds together shoulder to shoulder, but already wavers, and the officer, gathering his last strength of will, gives the command: "Fire!" The cry of the crowd, the yell of terror and threat, drowns the command, but not wholly. The rifles waver. The crowd pushes. Then the officer points the barrel of his revolver at the most suspicious soldier. From the decisive minute now stands out the decisive second. The death of the boldest soldier, to whom the others have involuntarily looked for guidance, a shot into the crowd by a corporal from the dead man's rifle, and the barrier closes, the guns go off of themselves, scattering the crowd into the alleys and backyards. But how many times since 1905 it has happened otherwise! At the critical moment, when the officer is ready to pull the trigger, a shot from the crowd—which has its Kayurovs and Chugurins—forestalls him. This decides not only the fate of the street skirmish, but perhaps the whole day, or the whole insurrection.

The task which Shliapnikov set himself of protecting the workers from hostile clashes with the troops by not giving fire-

Five Days (February 23-27, 1917)

arms to the insurrectionists could not in any case be carried out. Before it came to these clashes with the troops, innumerable clashes had occurred with the police. The street fighting began with the disarming of the hated Pharaohs, their revolvers passing into the hands of the rebels. The revolver by itself is a weak, almost toy-like weapon against the muskets, rifles, machine guns and cannon of the enemy. But are these weapons genuinely in the hands of the enemy? To settle this question the workers demanded arms. It was a psychological question. But even in an insurrection psychic processes are inseparable from material ones. The way to the soldier's rifle leads through the revolver taken from the Pharaoh.

The feelings of the soldiers in those hours were less active than those of the workers, but not less deep. Let us recall again that the garrison consisted mainly of reserve battalions many thousand strong, destined to fill up the ranks of those at the front. These men, most of them fathers of families, had the prospect of going to the trenches when the war was lost and the country ruined. They did not want war; they wanted to go home to their farms. They knew well enough what was going on at court, and had not the slightest feeling of attachment to the monarchy. They did not want to fight with the Germans, and still less with the Petrograd workers. They hated the ruling class of the capital, who had been having a good time during the war. Among them were workers with a revolutionary past, who knew how to give a generalized expression to all these moods.

To bring the soldiers from a deep but as yet hidden revolutionary discontent to overt mutinous action—or, at least, first to a mutinous refusal to act—that was the task. On the third day of the struggle the soldiers totally ceased to be able to maintain a benevolent neutrality toward the insurrection. Only accidental fragments of what happened in those hours along the line of contact between workers and soldiers have come down to us. We heard how yesterday the workers complained passionately to the Pavlovsky regiment about the behavior of its training squad. Such scenes, conversations, reproaches, appeals, were occurring in every corner of the city. The soldiers had no more time for hesitation. They were compelled to shoot yesterday, and they would be again today. The workers will not surrender or retreat; under fire they are still holding their own. And with them their women—wives, mothers, sisters, sweethearts. Yes, and this is the very hour they had so often whispered about: "If only we could all get together. . . ." And in the moment of supreme agony, in the unbearable fear of the coming day, the choking hatred of those who are imposing upon them the executioner's role, there ring out in the barrack room the first voices of open indignation, and in those voices—to be forever nameless—the whole army with relief and rapture recognizes itself. Thus dawned upon the earth the day of destruction of the Romanov monarchy.

Dual Power

TRANSLATED BY MAX EASTMAN
from *The History of the Russian Revolution* (1932).

What constitutes the essence of a dual power?[1] We must pause upon this question, for an illumination of it has never appeared in historic literature. And yet this dual power is a distinct condition of social crisis, by no means peculiar to the Russian Revolution of 1917, although there most clearly marked out.

Antagonistic classes exist in society everywhere, and a class deprived of power inevitably strives to some extent to swerve the governmental course in its favor. This does not as yet

[1] [*Dual power* is the phrase settled upon in Communist literature as an English rendering of *dvoevlastie*. The term is untranslatable both because of its form—twin-powerdom—and because the stem, *vlast*, means *sovereignty* as well as *power*. *Vlast* is also used as an equivalent of *government*, and in the plural corresponds to our phrase *the authorities*. In view of this, I have employed some other terms besides *dual power: double sovereignty, two-power regime,* etc.—Tr.]

101

mean, however, that two or more powers are ruling in society. The character of a political structure is directly determined by the relation of the oppressed classes to the ruling class. A single government, the necessary condition of stability in any regime, is preserved so long as the ruling class succeeds in putting over its economic and political forms upon the whole of society as the only forms possible.

The simultaneous dominion of the German Junkers and the bourgeoisie—whether in the Hohenzollern form or the republic—is not a double government, no matter how sharp at times may be the conflict between the two participating powers. They have a common social basis, therefore their clash does not threaten to split the state apparatus. The two-power regime arises only out of irreconcilable class conflict—is possible, therefore, only in a revolutionary epoch, and constitutes one of its fundamental elements.

The political mechanism of revolution consists of the transfer of power from one class to another. The forcible overturn is usually accomplished in a brief time. But no historic class lifts itself from a subject position to a position of rulership suddenly in one night, even though a night of revolution. It must already on the eve of the revolution have assumed a very independent attitude towards the official ruling class; moreover, it must have focused upon itself the hopes of intermediate classes and layers, dissatisfied with the existing state of affairs, but not capable of playing an independent role. The historic preparation of a revolution brings about, in the pre-revolutionary period, a situation in which the class which is called to realize the new social system, although not yet master of the country, has actually concentrated in its hands a significant share of the state power, while the official apparatus of the government is still in the hands of the old lords. That is the initial dual power in every revolution.

But that is not its only form. If the new class, placed in power by a revolution which it did not want, is in essence an already old, historically belated, class; if it was already worn out before it was officially crowned; if on coming to power it encounters an antagonist already sufficiently mature and reaching out its hand toward the helm of state; then instead of one unstable two-power equilibrium, the political revolution produces another, still less stable. To overcome the "anarchy" of this twofold sovereignty becomes at every new step the task of the revolution—or the counterrevolution.

This double sovereignty does not presuppose—generally speaking, indeed, it excludes—the possibility of a division of the power into two equal halves, or indeed any formal equilibrium of forces whatever. It is not a constitutional, but a revolutionary fact. It implies that a destruction of the social equilibrium has already split the state superstructure. It arises where the hostile classes are already each relying upon essentially incompatible governmental organizations—the one outlived, the other in process of formation—which jostle against each other at every step in the sphere of government. The amount of power which falls to each of these struggling classes in such a situation is determined by the correlation of forces in the course of the struggle.

By its very nature such a state of affairs cannot be stable. Society needs a concentration of power, and in the person of the ruling class—or, in the situation we are discussing, the two half-ruling classes—irresistibly strives to get it. The splitting of sovereignty foretells nothing less than a civil war. But before the competing classes and parties will go to that extreme—especially in case they dread the interference of a third force—they may feel compelled for quite a long time to endure, and even to sanction, a two-power system. This system will nevertheless inevitably explode. Civil war gives to this double sovereignty its most visible, because territorial, expression. Each of the powers, having created its own fortified drill ground, fights for possession of the rest of the territory, which often has to endure the double sovereignty in the form of successive invasions by the two fighting powers, until one of them decisively installs itself.

The English revolution of the seventeenth century, exactly because it was a great revolution shattering the nation to the bottom, affords a clear example of this alternating dual power, with sharp transitions in the form of civil war.

At first the royal power, resting upon the privileged classes or the upper circles of these classes—the aristocrats and bishops—is opposed by the bourgeoisie and the circles of the squirarchy that are close to it. The government of the bourgeoisie is the Presbyterian Parliament supported by the City of London. The protracted conflict between these two regimes is finally settled in open civil war. The two governmental centers—London and Oxford—create their own armies. Here the dual power takes a territorial form, although, as always in civil war, the boundaries are very shifting. Parliament conquers. The king is captured and awaits his fate.

It would seem that the conditions are now created for the single rule of the Presbyterian bourgeoisie. But before the royal power can be broken, the parliamentary army has converted itself into an independent political force. It has concentrated in its ranks the Independents, the pious and resolute petty bourgeoisie, the craftsmen and farmers. This army powerfully interferes in the social life, not merely as an armed force, but as a Praetorian Guard, and as the political representative of a new class opposing the prosperous and rich bourgeoisie. Correspondingly the army creates a new state organ rising above the military command: a council of soldiers' and officers' deputies ("agitators"). A new period of double sovereignty has thus arrived: that of the Presbyterian Parliament and the Independents' army. This leads to open conflicts. The bourgeoisie proves powerless to oppose with its own army the "model army" of Cromwell—that is, the armed plebeians. The conflict ends with a purgation of the Presbyterian Parliament by the sword of the Independents. There remains but the rump of a parliament; the dictatorship of Cromwell is established. The lower ranks of the army, under the leadership of the Levellers—the extreme left wing of the revolution—try to oppose to the rule of the upper military levels, the patricians of the army, their own veritably plebeian regime. But this new two-power system does not succeed in developing: the Levellers, the lowest depths of the petty bourgeoisie, have not yet, nor can have, their own historic path. Cromwell soon settles accounts with his enemies. A new political equilibrium, and still by no means a stable one, is established for a period of years.

In the great French Revolution, the Constituent Assembly,

the backbone of which was the upper levels of the Third Estate, concentrated the power in its hands—without however fully annulling the prerogatives of the king. The period of the Constituent Assembly is a clearly-marked period of dual power, which ends with the flight of the king to Varennes, and is formally liquidated with the founding of the Republic.

The first French constitution (1791), based upon the fiction of a complete independence of the legislative and executive powers, in reality concealed from the people, or tried to conceal, a double sovereignty: that of the bourgeoisie, firmly entrenched in the National Assembly after the people's capture of the Bastille, and that of the old monarchy, still relying upon the upper circles of the priesthood, the clergy, the bureaucracy, and the military, to say nothing of their hopes of foreign intervention. In this self-contradictory regime lay the germs of its inevitable destruction. A way out could be found only in the abolition of bourgeois representation by the powers of European reaction, or in the guillotine for the king and the monarchy. Paris and Coblenz must measure their forces.

But before it comes to war and the guillotine, the Paris Commune enters the scene—supported by the lowest city layers of the Third Estate—and with increasing boldness contests the power with the official representatives of the national bourgeoisie. A new double sovereignty is thus inaugurated, the first manifestation of which we observe as early as 1790, when the big and medium bourgeoisie are still firmly seated in the administration and in the municipalities. How striking is the picture—and how vilely it has been slandered!—of the efforts of the plebeian levels to raise themselves up out of the social cellars and catacombs, and stand forth in that forbidden arena where people in wigs and silk breeches are settling the fate of the nation. It seemed as though the very foundation of society, tramped underfoot by the cultured bourgeoisie, was stirring and coming to life. Human heads lifted themselves above the solid mass, horny hands stretched aloft, hoarse but courageous voices shouted! The districts of Paris, bastards of the revolution, began to live a life of their own. They were recognized —it was impossible not to recognize them!—and transformed into sections. But they kept continually breaking the boundaries of legality and receiving a current of fresh blood from below, opening their ranks in spite of the law to those with no rights, the destitute *sans-culottes*. At the same time the rural municipalities were becoming a screen for a peasant uprising against that bourgeois legality which was defending the feudal property system. Thus from under the second nation arises a third.

The Parisian sections at first stood opposed to the Commune, which was still dominated by the respectable bourgeoisie. In the bold outbreak of August 10, 1792, the sections gained control of the Commune. From then on the revolutionary Commune opposed the Legislative Assembly, and subsequently the Convention, which failed to keep up with the problems and progress of the revolution—registering its events, but not performing them—because it did not possess the energy, audacity and unanimity of that new class which had raised itself up from the depths of the Parisian districts and found support in the most backward villages. As the sections gained control of the Commune, so the Commune, by way of a new insurrection, gained control of the Convention. Each of the stages was characterized by a sharply marked double sovereignty, each wing of which was trying to establish a single and strong government—the right by a defensive struggle, the left by an offensive. Thus, characteristically—for both revolutions and counterrevolutions—the demand for a dictatorship results from the intolerable contradictions of the double sovereignty. The transition from one of its forms to the other is accomplished through civil war. The great stages of a revolution—that is, the passing of power to new classes or layers—do not at all coincide in this process with the succession of representative institutions, which march along after the dynamic of the revolution like a belated shadow. In the long run, to be sure, the revolutionary dictatorship of the *sans-culottes* unites with the dictatorship of the Convention. But with what Convention? A Convention purged of the Girondists, who yesterday ruled it with the hand of the Terror—a Convention abridged and adapted to the dominion of new social forces. Thus by the steps of the dual power the French Revolution rises in the course of four years to its culmination. After the ninth of Thermidor it begins—again by the steps of the dual power—to descend. And again civil war precedes every downward step, just as before it had accompanied every rise. In this way the new society seeks a new equilibrium of forces.

The Russian bourgeoisie, fighting with and co-operating with the Rasputin bureaucracy, had enormously strengthened its political position during the war. Exploiting the defeat of Czarism, it had concentrated in its hands, by means of the Country and Town unions and the Military-Industrial Committees, a great power. It had at its independent disposition enormous state resources, and was in the essence of the matter a parallel government. During the war the Czar's ministers complained that Prince Lvov was furnishing supplies to the army, feeding it, medicating it, even establishing barber shops for the soldiers. "We must either put an end to this, or give the whole power into his hands," said Minister Krivoshein in 1915. He never imagined that a year and a half later Lvov would receive "the whole power"—only not from the Czar, but from the hands of Kerensky, Cheidze and Sukhanov. But on the second day after he received it, there began a new double sovereignty: alongside of yesterday's liberal half-government—today formally legalized—there arose an unofficial, but so much the more actual government of the toiling masses in the form of the Soviets. From that moment the Russian Revolution began to grow up into an event of world-historic significance.

What, then, is the peculiarity of this dual power as it appeared in the February Revolution? In the events of the seventeenth and eighteenth centuries, the dual power was in each case a natural stage in a struggle imposed upon its participants by a temporary correlation of forces, and each side strove to replace the dual power with its own single power. In the Revolution of 1917, we see the official democracy consciously and intentionally creating a two-power system, dodging with all its might the transfer of power into its own hands. The double sovereignty is created, or so it seems at a glance, not as a result of a struggle of classes for power, but as the result of a voluntary "yielding" of power by one class to another. In so far as the Russian "democracy" sought for an escape from the two-power regime, it could find one only in its own removal from power. It is just this that we have called the paradox of the February Revolution.

A certain analogy can be found in 1848, in the conduct of the German bourgeoisie with relation to the monarchy. But the analogy is not complete. The German bourgeoisie did try earnestly to divide the power with the monarchy on the basis of an agreement. But the bourgeoisie neither had the full power in its hands, nor by any means gave it over wholly to the monarchy. "The Prussian bourgeoisie nominally possessed the power, it did not for a moment doubt that the forces of the old government would place themselves unreservedly at its disposition and convert themselves into loyal adherents of its own omnipotence" (Marx and Engels).

The Russian democracy of 1917, having captured the power from the very moment of insurrection, tried not only to divide it with the bourgeoisie, but to give the state over to the bourgeoisie absolutely. This means, if you please, that in the first quarter of the twentieth century the official Russian democracy had succeeded in decaying politically more completely than the German liberal bourgeoisie of the nineteenth century. And that is entirely according to the laws of history, for it is merely the reverse aspect of the upgrowth in those same decades of the proletariat, which now occupied the place of the craftsmen of Cromwell and the *sans-culottes* of Robespierre.

If you look deeper, the twofold rule of the Provisional Government and the Executive Committee had the character of a mere reflection. Only the proletariat could advance a claim to the new power. Relying distrustfully upon the workers and soldiers, the Compromisers were compelled to continue the double bookkeeping—of the kings and the prophets. The twofold government of the liberals and the democrats only reflected the still concealed double sovereignty of the bourgeoisie and the proletariat. When the Bolsheviks displace the Compromisers at the head of the Soviet—and this will happen within a few months—then that concealed double sovereignty will come to the surface, and this will be the eve of the October Revolution. Until that moment the revolution will live in a world of political reflections. Refracted through the rationalizations of the socialist intelligentsia, the double sovereignty, from being a stage in the class struggle, became a regulative principle. It was just for this reason that it occupied the center of all theoretical discussions. Every thing has its uses: the mirror-like character of the February double government has enabled us better to understand those epochs in history when the same thing appears as a full-blooded episode in a struggle between two regimes. The feeble and reflected light of the moon makes possible important conclusions about the sunlight.

In the immeasurably greater maturity of the Russian proletariat in comparison with the town masses of the older revolutions, lies the basic peculiarity of the Russian Revolution. This first led to the paradox of a half-spectral double government, and afterwards prevented the real one from being resolved in favor of the bourgeoisie. For the question stood thus: Either the bourgeoisie will actually dominate the old state apparatus, altering it a little for its purposes, in which case the Soviets will come to nothing: or the Soviets will form the foundation of a new state, liquidating not only the old governmental apparatus but also the dominion of those classes which it served. The Mensheviks and the Social Revolutionaries were steering toward the first solution, the Bolsheviks toward the second. The oppressed classes, who, as Marat observed, did not possess in the past the knowledge, or skill, or leadership to carry through what they had begun, were armed in the Russian Revolution of the twentieth century with all three. The Bolsheviks were victorious.

A year after their victory the same situation was repeated in Germany, with a different correlation of forces. The social democracy was steering for the establishment of a democratic government of the bourgeoisie and the liquidation of the Soviets. Luxemburg and Liebknecht steered toward the dictatorship of the Soviets. The Social Democrats won. Hilferding and Kautsky in Germany, Max Adler in Austria, proposed that they should "combine" democracy with the Soviet system, including the workers' Soviets in the constitution. That would have meant making potential or open civil war a constituent part of the state regime. It would be impossible to imagine a more curious utopia. Its sole justification on German soil is perhaps an old tradition: the Württemberg democrats of '48 wanted a republic with a duke at the head.

Does this phenomenon of the dual power—heretofore not sufficiently appreciated—contradict the Marxian theory of the state, which regards government as an executive committee of the ruling class? This is just the same as asking: Does the fluctuation of prices under the influence of supply and demand contradict the labor theory of value? Does the self-sacrifice of a female protecting her offspring refute the theory of a struggle for existence? No, in these phenomena we have a more complicated combination of the same laws. If the state is an organization of class rule, and a revolution is the overthrow of the ruling class, then the transfer of power from the one class to the other must necessarily create self-contradictory state conditions, and first of all in the form of the dual power. The relation of class forces is not a mathematical quantity permitting a priori computations. When the old regime is thrown out of equilibrium, a new correlation of forces can be established only as the result of a trial by battle. That is revolution.

It may seem as though this theoretical inquiry has led us away from the events of 1917. In reality it leads right into the heart of them. It was precisely around this problem of twofold power that the dramatic struggle of parties and classes turned. Only from a theoretical height is it possible to observe it fully and correctly understand it.

6

The Train

From *My Life* (1930).

What was the train of the Chairman of the Revolutionary Military Council seeking on the civil-war fronts? The general answer is obvious: it was seeking victory. But what did it give the fronts? What methods did it follow? What were the immediate objects of its endless runs from one end of the country to the other? They were not mere trips of inspection. No, the work of the train was all bound up with the building-up of the army, with its education, its administration, and its supply. We were constructing an army all over again, and under fire at that. This was true not only at Sviyazhsk, where the train recorded its first month, but on all the fronts. Out of bands of irregulars, of refugees escaping from the Whites, of peasants mobilized in the neighboring districts, of detachments of workers sent by the industrial centers, of groups of communists and trade-unionists—out of these we formed at the front companies, battalions, new regiments, and sometimes even entire divisions. Even after defeats and retreats, the flabby, panicky mob would be transformed in two or three weeks into an efficient fighting force. What was needed for this? At once much and little. It needed good commanders, a few dozen experienced fighters, a dozen or so communists ready to make any sacrifice, boots for the barefooted, a bath-house, an energetic propaganda campaign, food, underwear, tobacco and matches. The train took care of all this. We always had in reserve a few zealous communists to fill in the breaches, a hundred or so of good fighting men, a small stock of boots, leather jackets, medicaments, machine guns, field glasses, maps, watches and all sorts of gifts. Of course, the actual material resources of the train were slight in comparison with the needs of the army, but they were constantly being replenished.

But—what is even more important—tens and hundreds of times they played the part of the shovelful of coal that is necessary at a particular moment to keep the fire from going out. A telegraph station was in operation on the train. We made our connections with Moscow by direct wire, and my deputy there, Sklyansky, took down my demands for supplies urgently needed for the army, sometimes for a single division or even for a regiment. They were delivered with a dispatch that would have been absolutely impossible without my intervention. Of course, this is not exactly a proper way of doing things—a pedant would tell us that in the supply service, as in military departments in general, the most important thing is system. That is absolutely true. I am myself rather inclined to err on the side of pedantry. But the point is that we did not want to perish before we could build up a smoothly running system. That is why, especially in that early period, we had to substitute improvisations for a system—so that later on we might develop a system on their foundations.

On all of my trips, I was accompanied by the chief workers in all the principal departments of the army, especially in those connected with the supply service. We had inherited from the old army supply service officers who tried to work in the old way or in even worse fashion, for the conditions became infinitely more difficult. On these trips, many of the old specialists had to learn new ways, and new ones received their training in live experience. After making the round of a division and ascertaining its needs on the spot, I would hold a conference in the staff-car or the dining-car, inviting as many representatives as possible, including those from the lower commanding force and from the ranks, as well as from the local party organizations, the Soviet administration, and the trade-unions. In this way I got a picture of the situation that was neither false nor highly colored. These conferences always had immediate practical results. No matter how poor the organs of the local administration might be, they always managed to squeeze a little tighter and cut down some of their own needs to contribute something to the army.

The most important sacrifices came from institutions. A new group of communists would be drawn from the institutions and put immediately into an unreliable regiment. Stuff would be found for shirts and for wrappings for the feet, leather for new soles, and an extra hundredweight of fat. But of course the local sources were not enough. After the conference, I would send orders to Moscow by direct wire, estimating our needs according to the resources of the center, and, as a result, the division would get what it desperately needed, and that in good time. The commanders and commissaries of the front learned from their experience on the train to approach their own work—whether they were commanding, educating, supplying or administering justice—not from above, from the standpoint of the pinnacle of the staff, but from below, from the standpoint of the company or platoon, of the young and inexperienced new recruit.

Gradually, more or less efficient machinery for a centralized supply service for the front and the armies was established. But, alone, it did not and could not satisfy all needs. Even the most ideal organization will occasionally misfire during a war, and especially during a war of maneuvers based entirely on movement—sometimes, alas! in quite unforeseen directions. And one must not forget that we fought without supplies. As early as 1919, there was nothing left in the central depots. Shirts were sent to the front direct from the workshop. But the supply of rifles and cartridges was most difficult of all. The

Tula munition factories worked for the needs of the current day. Not a carload of cartridges could be sold anywhere without the special authorization of the Commander-in-chief. The supply of munitions was always as taut as a string. Sometimes the string would break, and then we lost men and territory.

Without constant changes and improvisations, the war would have been utterly impossible for us. The train initiated these, and at the same time regulated them. If we gave an impulse of initiative to the front and its immediate rear, we took care to direct it into the channels of the general system. I do not want to say that we always succeeded in this. But, as the civil war has demonstrated, we did achieve the principal thing —victory.

The trips to the sections of the front where often the treason of the commanding officers had created catastrophes were especially important. On August 23, 1918, during the most critical period before Kazan, I received a coded telegram from Lenin and Sverdlov: "Sviyazhsk Trotsky. Treason on the Saratov front, though discovered in time, has yet produced very dangerous wavering. We consider your going there at once absolutely necessary, for your appearance at the front has an effect on soldiers and the entire army. Let us together arrange for your visits to other fronts. Reply stating date of your departure, all by code, August 22, 1918. Lenin. Sverdlov."

I thought it quite impossible to leave Sviyazhsk, as the departure of the train would have shaken the Kazan front, which was having a difficult enough time as it was. Kazan was in all respects more important than Saratov. Lenin and Sverdlov themselves soon agreed with me on this. I went to Saratov only after the recapture of Kazan. But telegrams like this reached the train at all stages of its travels. Kiev and Vyatka, Siberia and the Crimea would complain of their difficult positions and would demand, in turn or at the same time, that the train hasten to their rescue.

The war unrolled on the periphery of the country, often in the most remote parts of a front that stretched for eight thousand kilometers. Regiments and divisions were cut off from the rest of the world for months at a time. Very often they had not enough telephone equipment even for their own intercommunication, and would then succumb to hopelessness. The train, for them, was a messenger from other worlds. We always had a stock of telephone apparatus and wires. A wireless aerial had been arranged over a particular car in our train, so that we could receive radio messages from the Eiffel Tower, from Nauen, and from other stations, thirteen in all, with Moscow, of course, foremost. The train was always informed of what was going on in the rest of the world. The more important telegraphic reports were published in the train newspaper, and given passing comment, in articles, leaflets and orders. Kapp's raid, conspiracies at home, the English elections, the progress of grain collections, and feats of the Italian Fascismo were interpreted while the footprints of events were still warm, and were linked up with the fates of the Astrakhan or Archangel fronts.

These articles were simultaneously transmitted to Moscow by direct wire, and radioed from there to the press of the entire country. The arrival of the train put the most isolated unit in touch with the whole army, and brought it into the life not only of the country, but of the entire world. Alarmist rumors and doubts were dispelled, and the spirit of the men grew firm. This change of morale would last for several weeks, sometimes until the next visit of the train. In the intervals, members of the Revolutionary Military Council of the front or the army would make trips similar in character, but on a smaller scale.

All my work in the train, literary and otherwise, would have been impossible without my assisting stenographers, Glazman and Syermuks, and the younger assistant, Nechayev. They worked all day and all night in the moving train, which, disregarding all rules of safety in the fever of war, would rush over shaken ties at a speed of seventy or more kilometers an hour, so that the map that hung from the ceiling of the car would rock like a swing. I would watch in wondering gratitude the movements of the hand that, despite the incessant jerking and shaking, could inscribe the finely shaped symbols so clearly. When I was handed the typed script half an hour later, no corrections were necessary. This was not ordinary work; it took on a character of heroic sacrifice. Afterward, Glazman and Syermuks paid dearly for their sacrifices in the service of the revolution. Glazman was driven to suicide by the Stalinites, and Syermuks has been shut away in the wilds of Siberia.

Part of the train was a huge garage holding several automobiles and a gasoline tank. This made it possible for us to travel away from the railway line for several hundred *versts*. A squad of picked sharpshooters and machine-gunners, amounting to from twenty to thirty men, occupied the trucks and light cars. A couple of hand machine guns had also been placed in my car. A war of movement is full of surprises. On the steppes, we always ran the risk of running into some Cossack band. Automobiles with machine guns insured one against this, at least when the steppe had not been transformed into a sea of mud. Once during the autumn of 1919, in the province of Voronezh, we could move at a speed of only three kilometers an hour. The automobiles sank deep into the black, rain-soaked earth. Thirty men had to keep jumping off their cars to push them along. And once, when we were fording a river, we got stuck in midstream. In a rage, I blamed everything on the low-built machine which my excellent chauffeur, an Estonian named Puvi, considered the very best machine in the world. He turned round to me, and raising his hand to his cap, said in broken Russian:

"I beg to state that the engineers never foresaw that we should have to sail on water."

In spite of the difficulty of the moment, I felt like embracing him for the cold aptness of his irony.

The train was not only a military-administrative and political institution, but a fighting institution as well. In many of its features it was more like an armored train than a staff headquarters on wheels. In fact, it was armored, or at least its engines and machine-gun cars were. All the crew could handle arms. They all wore leather uniforms, which always make men look heavily imposing. On the left arm, just below the shoulder, each wore a large metal badge, carefully cast at the mint, which had acquired great popularity in the army. The cars were connected by telephone and by a system of signals. To keep the men on the alert while we were traveling, there were frequent alarms, both by day and by night. Armed detachments would be put off the train as "landing parties." The appearance of a leather-coated detachment in a dangerous place invariably had an overwhelming effect. When they were aware of the presence of the train just a few kilometers behind the firing-line, even the most nervous units, their commanding officers especially, would summon up all their strength. In the unstable poise of a scale, only a small weight is enough to decide. The role of that weight was played by the train and its detachments a great many times during its two and a half years of travel. When we took the returned "landing party" aboard, we usually found some one missing. Altogether, the train lost about fifteen men in killed and wounded, not counting the ones who joined the units in the field and disappeared from our view. For instance, a squad was made up from our train crew for the model armored train named for Lenin; another joined the troops in the field before Petrograd. For its share in the battles against Yudenich, the train as a whole was decorated with the order of the Red Flag.

Sometimes the train was cut off and shelled or bombed from the air. No wonder it was surrounded by a legend woven of victories both real and imagined. Time and again the commander of a division, of a brigade, or even of a regiment would ask me to stay at his staff headquarters for an extra half hour, just whiling away the time, or to drive with him by automobile or on horseback to some distant sector, or even to send a few men from the train there with supplies and gifts, so that the news of the train's arrival might be spread far and wide. "This will be as good as a division in reserve," commanders would say. The news of the arrival of the train would reach the enemy lines as well. There people imagined a mysterious train infinitely more awful than it really was. But that only served to increase its influence on morale.

The train earned the hatred of its enemies and was proud of it. More than once, the Social Revolutionaries made plans to wreck it. At the trial of the Social Revolutionaries, the story was told in detail by Semyonov, who organized the assassination of Volodarsky and the attempt on Lenin's life, and who also took part in the preparations to wreck the train. As a matter of fact, such an enterprise presented no great difficulty, except that by that time the Social Revolutionaries, weakened politically, had lost faith in themselves and no longer had much influence with the younger generation.

On one of our trips south, the train was wrecked at the station of Gorki. In the middle of the night, I was suddenly jerked out of bed, and was seized by that creepy feeling one has during an earthquake, of the ground slipping away under one's feet, with no firm support anywhere. Still half-asleep, I clutched the sides of the bed. The familiar rumbling had stopped at once; the car had turned on its edge, and stood stock-still. In the silence of the night, a single, pitiful voice was the only thing to be heard. The heavy car doors were so bent that they could not even be opened, and I could not get out. No one appeared, which alarmed me. Was it the enemy? With a revolver in my hand, I jumped out of the window and ran into a man with a lantern. It was the commander of the train, unable to get to me.

The car was standing on a slope, with three wheels buried deep in the embankment, and the other three rising high above the rails. The rear and front of the car had crumpled. The front grating had pinned down a sentry, and it was his pitiful little voice, like the crying of a child, that I had heard in the darkness. It was no easy matter to release him from the grating covering him so tightly. To everyone's surprise, he got off with nothing but bruises and a scare. In all, eight cars were destroyed. The restaurant car, which was used as the club for the train, was a heap of polished splinters. A number of men had been reading or playing chess while they waited for their turn to go on duty, but they had all left the club at midnight, ten minutes before the accident. The trucks with books, equipment and gifts for the front were all badly damaged as well. None of the men was seriously hurt. The accident was due to faulty switching, whether because of negligence or deliberate action we never found out. Fortunately for us, the train was passing a station at the time, running at a speed of only thirty kilometers.

The train crew performed many other tasks beside their special duties. They lent their help in time of famine, during epidemics of disease, in propaganda campaigns, and at international congresses. The train was the honorary head of a rural district and of several children's homes. Its communist local published its own paper, *On Guard*. Many an incident of adventure and battle is recorded in its pages, but unfortunately this, like many other records, is not in my present traveling archives.

When I was leaving to prepare an offensive against Wrangel, who had intrenched himself in the Crimea, I wrote in the train newspaper *En Route*, on October 27, 1920:

> Our train is again bound for the front.
>
> The fighting men of our train were before the walls of Kazan in the grave weeks of 1918, when we were fighting for the control of the Volga. That fight ended long ago. Today the Soviet power is approaching the Pacific Ocean.
>
> The fighting men of our train fought gallantly before the walls of Petrograd. Petrograd has been saved and has since been visited by many representatives of the world proletariat.
>
> Our train visited the western front more than once. Today, a preliminary peace has been signed with Poland.
>
> The fighting men of our train were on the steppes of the Don when Krasnov and, later, Denikin advanced against Soviet Russia from the south. The days of Krasnov and Denikin are long since past.
>
> There now is left only the Crimea, which the French government has made its fortress. The White Guard garrison of this French fortress is under the command of a hired German-Russian general, Baron Wrangel.
>
> The friendly family of our train is starting on a new campaign. Let this campaign be the last.

The Crimean campaign was actually the last campaign of the civil war. A few months later, the train was disbanded. From these pages, I send fraternal greetings to all my former comrades-in-arms.

7

Two Military Declarations

TRANSLATED BY I. A. LANGNAS.

TO THE REBELLIOUS TROOPS OF KAZAN FIGHTING AGAINST THE WORKERS' AND PEASANTS' RED ARMY, TO THE DELUDED CZECHOSLOVAKS, THE DELUDED PEASANTS AND THE DELUDED WORKERS.

What on earth are you fighting for?

The landlords, the capitalists and the old officers want to recover their power and their wealth.

The French and Japanese speculators want profits.

And you, soldiers—Czechoslovaks, workers and peasants?

You have been deceived. You are cannon fodder. You are shedding workingmen's blood for the benefit of the rich.

[These statements, previously untranslated, were issued by Trotsky in the Civil War of 1918-20.—Ed.]

The revolting White Guardists have no chance.

Kazan is surrounded on all sides. Our forces are incomparably bigger than yours—on land, on water and in the air.

Your leaders, having grabbed the government gold, are hurrying to leave Kazan. They know their cause is lost.

Czechoslovak soldiers! Peasants and Workers!

Do you want to perish with them?

I proclaim to all:

The Soviet power wages war only against the rich, the oppressors, and the imperialists.

To working people we extend a brotherly hand. Any one of you who crosses to our side will receive from us a full pardon and a brotherly reception.

Dozens of you have already come over to us. None of them has suffered. They are all free and unharmed.

In the name of the Council of People's Commissars I now give you a last warning.

All of you come over to the side of the Soviet troops!

Sviyazhsk, August 26, 1918.

ON FORMER OFFICERS

A Necessary Declaration

The frequent and often unjustified attacks on military specialists from the former officers' cadres now working for the Red Army have produced, in some units of the command, an uncertain and harrowing atmosphere. On the other hand, former officers who are now on government duty behind the front are wary about moving into the Red Army because of the prevailing distrust towards them, artificially fanned by unbalanced elements in the Soviet ranks. These facts create obvious and serious damage to the armies in the field.

I therefore feel it necessary to issue the following declaration:

A general hostility to former regular officers is alien to both the Soviet Power and to the best units on active duty. Every officer who wants to defend our country against the invasion of foreign imperialists and its Krasnov and Dutov agents is a welcome worker for the cause. Every officer who wants to and can co-operate in forming the internal structure of the army and thus help it to achieve its objectives with a minimum loss of workers' and peasants' blood, is a welcome collaborator with the Soviet power, has a right to be respected, and shall be respected in the ranks of the Red Army.

The Soviet power will continue to bear down hard on rebels and to punish traitors; but its policies are guided by the interests of the working people and the aims of the revolution, and not by a blind urge for vengeance.

The Soviet power knows full well that many thousands and tens of thousands of officers who graduated from the schools of the Old Regime and were brought up in a bourgeois-monarchist spirit cannot accustom themselves at once to the New Regime, understand it or respect it. But during the thirteen months of Soviet power it has become clear to many, many officers that the Soviet regime is not an accident; it is a regularly constituted structure, based on the will of the working millions. It has become clear to many, many officers that there is now no other regime capable of securing the freedom and independence of the Russian people against foreign intervention.

The officers who, guided by this new awareness, honestly join our ranks, will find full oblivion there for the crimes against the people in which they took part because of their old upbringing and their insufficiently developed political and revolutionary consciousness.

In the Ukraine, in Krasnov's army, in Siberia, in the ranks of the Anglo-French imperialists in the North, there are not a few former Russian officers who would be willing to submit to the Soviet Republic if they did not fear a drastic punishment for their previous activities. To them, the repentant apostates, applies what we said above about the general policy of the Workers' and Peasants' Government: it is guided in all its actions by its revolutionary objectives, not by blind vengeance, and it opens its doors to every honest citizen willing to work in the Soviet ranks.

8

Three Concepts of the Russian Revolution

TRANSLATED BY CHARLES MALAMUTH
from *Stalin* (1946).

Russia's development is first of all notable for its backwardness. But historical backwardness does not mean a mere retracing of the course of the advanced countries a hundred or two hundred years late. Rather, it gives rise to an utterly different "combined" social formation, in which the most highly developed achievements of capitalist technique and structure are integrated into the social relations of feudal and pre-feudal barbarism, transforming and dominating them, fashioning a unique relationship of classes. The same is true of ideas. Precisely because of its historical tardiness, Russia proved to be the only European country in which Marxism, as a doctrine, and the Social Democracy, as a party, enjoyed a powerful development even prior to the bourgeois revolution —and naturally so, because the problem of the relation between the struggle for democracy and the struggle for socialism was subjected to the most profound theoretical examination in Russia.

The idealistic democrats—for the most part, the Populists—superstitiously refused to recognize the advancing revolution as a bourgeois revolution. They called it "democratic," attempting to hide under that neutral political label—not only from others, but from themselves as well—its social content. But Plekhanov, the founder of Russian Marxism, in his fight against Populism, showed as far back as the eighties of the past century that Russia had no reason whatsoever to rely on preferential ways of development; that, like the "profane" nations, it would have to go through the purgatory of capitalism; and that on this very path it would wrest political freedom, which was indispensable to the proletariat in its continuing fight for socialism. Plekhanov not only segregated the bourgeois revolution, as the immediate task, from the socialist revolution, which he in turn relegated to the vague future, but he foresaw distinct combinations of forces for each of them. The proletariat would secure political freedom jointly with the liberal bourgeoisie; then, after many decades, on a high level of capitalist development, the proletariat would proceed with the socialist revolution in direct conflict against the bourgeoisie.

To the Russian intellectual . . . , [Lenin wrote toward the end of 1904] it always seems that to recognize our revolution as bourgeois means to make it colorless, to humiliate it, to vulgarize it. . . . The struggle for political freedom and the democratic republic in bourgeois society is to the proletarian merely one of the necessary stages in the struggle for the social revolution.

The Marxists are thoroughly convinced, [he wrote in 1905] of the bourgeois character of the Russian Revolution. What does that mean? It means that those democratic transformations . . . which became indispensable for Russia not only do not signify in themselves the undermining of capitalism, the undermining of the domination of the bourgeoisie, but, on the contrary, they will be the first to really clear the ground for a widespread and rapid, a European rather than an Asiatic, development of capitalism; they will be the first to make possible the rule of the bourgeoisie as a class. "We cannot jump out of the bourgeois-democratic framework of the Russian Revolution," he insisted, "but we can considerably broaden that framework"—that is, create within the bourgeois society more favorable conditions for the further struggle of the proletariat. To that extent Lenin followed in the footsteps of Plekhanov. The bourgeois character of the revolution was the meeting of the crossroads for the two factions of the Russian social democracy.

For Plekhanov, Axelrod, and the leaders of Menshevism generally, the characterization of the revolution as bourgeois had, above all, the political value of avoiding the premature taunting of the bourgeoisie with the red specter of socialism and thus "frightening it away" into the camp of reaction. Said Axelrod, the chief tactician of Menshevism, at the Unification Congress:

> The social relations of Russia have ripened only for a bourgeois revolution. While this general political lawlessness persists, we must not even so much as mention the direct fight of the proletariat against other classes for political power. . . . It is fighting for the conditions of bourgeois development. Objective historical conditions doom our proletariat to an inevitable collaboration with the bourgeoisie in the struggle against our common enemy.

The content of the Russian Revolution was thus confined beforehand to changes that were compatible with the interests and the views of the liberal bourgeoisie.

This was the starting point for the fundamental divergence between the two factions. Bolshevism resolutely refused to acknowledge that the Russian bourgeoisie was capable of consummating its own revolution. With immeasurably greater force and consistency than Plekhanov, Lenin advanced the agrarian question as the central problem of the democratic revolution in Russia:

> The crux of the Russian Revolution is the agrarian [the land] question. We must make up our minds about the

defeat or victory of the revolution . . . on the basis of accounting for the condition of the masses in their struggle for land.

At one with Plekhanov, Lenin regarded the peasantry as a petty-bourgeois class and the peasant land program as the program of bourgeois progressivism.

> Nationalization is a bourgeois measure [he insisted at the Unification Congress]. It will give impetus to the development of capitalism by intensifying the class struggle, by strengthening the mobilization of land and the investment of capital in agriculture, by lowering the prices on grain.

Notwithstanding the admitted bourgeois character of the agrarian revolution, the Russian bourgeoisie was nevertheless hostile to the expropriation of the land owned by the landed gentry, and precisely for that reason strove for a compromise with the monarchy on the basis of a constitution after the Prussian model. To the Plekhanovite idea of union between the proletariat and the liberal bourgeoisie Lenin counterposed the idea of union between the proletariat and the peasantry. He proclaimed the task of the revolutionary collaboration of these two classes to be the establishment of a "democratic dictatorship," as the only means for radically purging Russia of its feudal refuse, creating a free class of farmers and opening the way for the development of capitalism after the American rather than the Prussian model.

The victory of the revolution, he wrote, can be attained

> only through dictatorship, because the realization of the transformations immediately and unconditionally necessary for the proletariat and the peasantry will call forth the desperate resistance of the landlords, of the big bourgeoisie and of Czarism. Without dictatorship it would be impossible to break that resistance, it would be impossible to defeat counterrevolutionary efforts. That would be, needless to say, not a socialist, but a democratic dictatorship. It would not be able to dispose of (without a whole series of intermediary stages in revolutionary develop-

ment) the foundations of capitalism. At best, it would be able to introduce a radical redistribution of land ownership for the benefit of the peasantry, carry out a consistent and complete democratization, including a republic; uproot all the oppressive Asiatic characteristics in the life of the factory as well as the village; lay down the beginnings of important improvements in the condition of the workers; raise their standard of living; and finally, last but not least, carry the revolutionary conflagration into Europe.

Lenin's conception represented a tremendous step forward, proceeding as it did from the agrarian revolution rather than from constitutional reforms as the central task of the revolution, and indicating the only realistic combination of social forces that could fulfill that task. The weak point of Lenin's concept was its inherently contradictory notion, "the democratic dictatorship of the proletariat and the peasantry." Lenin himself emphasized the basic limitations of that "dictatorship" when he openly called it *bourgeois*. He was thus implying that, for the sake of maintaining unity with the peasantry, the proletariat would be obliged to forego posing the socialist task directly during the impending revolution. But that would have meant the repudiation by the proletariat of its *own* dictatorship. The dictatorship was consequently, in essence, of the peasantry, although with the workers participating. On certain occasions that was precisely how Lenin spoke; for example, at the Stockholm Congress, when he replied to Plekhanov, who had rebelled against the "utopia" of seizing power: "What program are we talking about? About an agrarian program. Who in that program is supposed to seize the government? The revolutionary peasantry. Is Lenin confounding the government of the proletariat with that of the peasantry?" No, he said with reference to himself: Lenin sharply differentiated between the socialist government of the proletariat and the bourgeois-democratic government of the peasantry. "And how is a victorious peasant revolution possible," he exclaimed again, "without seizure of power by the revolutionary peasantry?" In that polemical formulation Lenin very clearly exposed the vulnerability of his position.

The peasantry was dispersed over the surface of an immense country, with cities as points of contact. By itself the peasantry was incapable even of formulating its own interests, for in each region they were differently conceived. Economic contact between provinces was established by the market and by the railroads; but both the market and the railroads were in the city's hands. In trying to break through the confines of the village and pool their interests, the peasantry necessarily succumbed to political dependence on the city. Neither was the peasantry homogeneous in its social relations: its *kulak* stratum naturally strove to entice it to unite with the city bourgeoisie, while the lower strata of the village pulled in the direction of the city workers. Under these circumstances, the peasantry as a whole was utterly incapable of assuming the reins of government.

True, in ancient China revolutions brought the peasantry to power, or rather, the military leaders of peasant insurrections. That led each time to a redivision of the land and the establishment of a new "peasant" dynasty, after which history began all over again: new concentration of lands, a new aristocracy, new usury, new uprisings. So long as the revolution maintained its purely peasant character, society did not emerge from these hopeless rotations. Such was the basis of ancient Asiatic, including ancient Russian, history. In Europe, beginning with the emergence of the Middle Ages, each victorious peasant uprising did not place a peasant government in power but a Leftist burgher party. More precisely, a peasant uprising proved victorious only to the extent that it managed to establish the position of the city population's revolutionary sector. Seizure of power by a revolutionary peasantry was out of the question in twentieth-century bourgeois Russia.

The attitude toward the liberal bourgeoisie thus became the touchstone in the divergence between revolutionists and opportunists among Social Democrats. How far the Russian Revolution could venture, what character would be assumed by the future provisional revolutionary government, what tasks would confront it, and in what order it would dispose of them —these questions could be correctly posed in all their importance only in reference to the basic character of the proletariat's politics, and that character was determined, above all, by its relation to the liberal bourgeoisie. Plekhanov demonstratively and stubbornly shut his eyes to the fundamental object-lession of nineteenth-century political history: wherever the proletariat appeared as an independent force, the bourgeoisie shifted to the camp of the counterrevolution. The bolder the struggle of the masses, the quicker the reactionary transformation of liberalism. No one has yet invented a way to paralyze the workings of the law of the class struggle.

"We must prize the support of the non-proletarian parties," Plekhanov was wont to repeat during the years of the First Revolution, "and not drive them away from us by tactless behavior." With such monotonous moralizings the sage of Marxism demonstrated that he was unable to grasp the living dynamics of society. "Tactlessness" might drive away an occasional oversensitive intellectual. But classes and parties are drawn or repelled by their social interests. "It may be safely said," Lenin retorted to Plekhanov, "that the liberals among the landed gentry will forgive you millions of 'tactless' acts, but they will never forgive incitements to take away their land." And not only the landed gentry: the upper crust of the bourgeoisie, bound to the landowners by identity of property interests and even more closely by the banking system, as well as the upper crust of the petty-bourgeoisie and of the intellectuals, materially and morally dependent on the large and middling property owners, dreaded the independent movement of the masses. Yet in order to overthrow Czarism, it was necessary to arouse scores upon scores of millions of the oppressed for a heroic, self-sacrificing, reckless, supreme revolutionary onslaught. The masses could be aroused to this uprising only under the banner of their own interests; hence, in the spirit of unreconcilable hostility toward the exploiting classes, and first of all, the landlords. The "frightening away" of the oppositional bourgeoisie from the revolutionary peasants and workers was therefore the immanent law of the revolution itself and could not be forestalled by "tactfulness" or diplomacy.

Each new month confirmed Lenin's estimate of liberalism. Notwithstanding the fondest hopes of the Mensheviks, the

Kadets not only made no move to lead the "bourgeois" revolution but, on the contrary, more and more found their historic mission in fighting it. After the crushing defeat of the December Insurrection, the liberals, who, thanks to the ephemeral Duma, stepped out before the political footlights, strove with all their might to explain to the monarchy their insufficiently active counterrevolutionary behavior in the autumn of 1905, when the holiest pillars of "culture" were in danger. The leader of the liberals, Miliukov, who carried on sub rosa negotiations with the Winter Palace, argued quite properly in the press that by the end of 1905 the *Kadets* were unable even to appear before the masses.

> Those who now blame the [*Kadet*] party [he wrote] for not protesting then, by convoking meetings, against the revolutionary illusions of Trotskyism . . . simply do not understand or do not remember the moods then prevalent among the democratic public that attended these meetings.

By the "illusions of Trotskyism" the liberal leader meant the independent policy of the proletariat, which attracted to the Soviets the sympathies of the cities' lower classes, soldiers, peasants and of all the oppressed, thus alienating "cultivated" society. The evolution of the Mensheviks developed along parallel lines. Time and again they had to alibi themselves to the liberals for having found themselves in a bloc with Trotsky after October, 1905. The explanations of that talented publicist of the Mensheviks, Martov, came to this—that it was necessary to make concessions to the "revolutionary illusions" of the masses.

Populists regarded all workers and peasants as simply "toilers" and "exploited ones," who were equally interested in socialism, while to Marxists a peasant was a petty bourgeois, capable of becoming a socialist only to the extent that he either materially or spiritually ceased being a peasant. With a sentimentality characteristic of them, Populists saw in that sociological characterization a dire insult to the peasantry. Along that line was fought for two generations the principal battle between the revolutionary tendencies of Russia. In order to understand the subsequent conflict between Stalinism and Trotskyism, it is necessary to emphasize that, in consonance with all Marxist tradition, Lenin never regarded the peasant as a socialist ally of the proletariat; on the contrary, it was the overwhelming preponderance of the peasantry which had led Lenin to conclude that a socialist revolution was impossible in Russia. That idea recurs time and again in all his articles that directly or indirectly touch upon the agrarian question.

"We support the peasant movement," wrote Lenin in September, 1905, "insofar as it is revolutionary and democratic. We are preparing (at once, immediately preparing) to fight against it insofar as it asserts itself as a reactionary anti-proletarian movement. The whole essence of Marxism is in that twofold task. . . ." Lenin saw the Western proletariat and to some extent the semi-proletarians of the Russian village as socialist allies, but never the whole of the peasantry. "At first, we support to the very end, with all means, including confiscation," he repeated with persistence typical of him, "the peasant in general against the landed proprietor, but later (and not even later, but at the very same time) we support the proletariat against the peasant in general."

"The peasantry will win in a bourgeois democratic revolution," he wrote in March, 1906, "and thereby will completely exhaust its revolutionism as a peasantry. The proletariat will win in a bourgeois democratic revolution, and thereby will only begin really to unfold its true socialist revolutionism." "The movement of the peasantry," he repeated in May of the same year, "is the movement of another class; it is a struggle not against the foundations of capitalism but for their purging of all the remnants of serfdom." That view may be traced in Lenin from article to article, from year to year, from volume to volume. Expressions and illustrations vary, but the basic thought is unalterable. Nor could it have been otherwise. Had Lenin seen a *socialist* ally in the peasantry, he would not have had the slightest basis for insisting upon the *bourgeois* character of the revolution and limiting it to "the dictatorship of the proletariat and the peasantry," to purely democratic tasks. On the occasions when Lenin accused me of "underestimating" the peasantry, he did not have in mind my failure to recognize the socialist tendencies of the peasantry but rather my failure to realize sufficiently, from Lenin's point of view, the bourgeois-democratic independence of the peasantry, its capacity to create its *own* power and through it impede the establishment of the socialist dictatorship of the proletariat.

The revaluation of that question commenced only during the years of the Thermidorian reaction, the beginning of which coincided by and large with Lenin's illness and death. From then on the union of Russian workers and peasants was declared to be in itself sufficient guaranty against the dangers of restoration and a firm pledge that socialism would be achieved within the borders of the Soviet Union. Having substituted the theory of socialism in a separate country for the theory of international revolution, Stalin began to call the Marxist evaluation of the peasantry "Trotskyism," and moreover not only with reference to the present but retroactively to the entire past.

It is, of course, possible to ask whether the classical Marxist view of the peasantry had not proved erroneous. That theme would lead us far beyond the limits of this essay. Suffice it to say for the present that Marxism never ascribed an absolute and immutable character to its estimation of the peasantry as a non-socialist class. Marx said long ago that the peasant is capable of judgment as well as prejudgment. The very nature of the peasantry is altered under altered conditions. The regime of the dictatorship of the proletariat discovered very great possibilities for influencing the peasantry and for reeducating it. History has not yet plumbed to the bottom the limits of these possibilities. But it is already clear that the growing role of state compulsion in the USSR has, far from refuting, basically confirmed the very view of the peasantry that distinguished Russian Marxists from Populists. Yet, whatever the situation on that score today, after twenty-odd years of the new regime, the fact remains that prior to the October Revolution, or rather prior to the year 1924, no one in the Marxist camp, and least of all Lenin, had regarded the peasantry as a factor of socialist development. Without the aid of a proletarian revolution in the West, he reiterated time and again, restoration is unavoidable in Russia. He was not mistaken: the Stalinist bureaucracy is nothing else than the first stage of bourgeois restoration.

Such were the divergent positions of the two main factions of the Russian social democracy. But alongside them, as early as the dawn of the First Revolution, a third position was formulated, which met with practically no recognition in those days, but which we must explain—not only because it was confirmed by the events of 1917, but particularly because seven years after the revolution, after being turned upside down, it began to play an utterly unforeseen role in the political evolution of Stalin and of the entire Soviet bureaucracy.

Early in 1905 I published in Geneva a pamphlet which analyzed the political situation as it existed around the winter of 1904. I came to the conclusion that the independent campaign of liberal petitions and banquets had exhausted its possibilities; that the radical intellectuals, who had shifted their hopes to the liberals, had found themselves in a blind alley together with the latter; that the peasant movement was creating conditions favorable for victory yet incapable of assuring it; that the showdown could be brought about only through an armed insurrection of the proletariat; that the very next stage along that way must be the general strike. This pamphlet, called "Until the Ninth of January," had been written prior to the Bloody Sunday in Petersburg. The powerful wave of strikes which began that day, together with the first armed clashes that supplemented it, was an unequivocal confirmation of the pamphlet's strategic prognosis.

The preface to my work was written by Parvus, a Russian émigré, who had already become by then a prominent German writer. Parvus was an extraordinarily creative personality, capable of becoming infected with the ideas of others as well as enriching others with his ideas. He lacked the inward balance and application necessary to contribute anything worthy of his talents as a thinker and writer to the labor movement. There is no doubt that he exerted considerable influence on my personal development, especially with respect to the social-revolutionary understanding of our epoch. A few years before our first meeting Parvus passionately defended the idea of a general strike in Germany; but the country was passing through prolonged industrial prosperity, the Social Democracy was adjusting itself to the Hohenzollern regime, and foreigners' revolutionary propaganda met nothing but ironical indifference. Having read my pamphlet in manuscript, the very next day after the bloody events in Petersburg, Parvus was overwhelmed with the thought of the exceptional role which the proletariat of backward Russia was called upon to play. Several days spent jointly in Munich were filled with conversations that clarified much to both of us and brought us personally close together. The preface Parvus then wrote to the pamphlet entered permanently into the history of the Russian Revolution. In a few pages he shed light on those social peculiarities of backward Russia which, true enough, were already well known, but from which no one before him had drawn all the necessary inferences:

> Political radicalism throughout western Europe [wrote Parvus], as everybody knows, depended primarily on the petty bourgeoisie. These were artisans and generally all of that part of the bourgeoisie which was caught up by the industrial development but which at the same time was superseded by the class of capitalists. . . . In Russia of the pre-capitalist period, cities developed on the Chinese rather than on the European model. These were administrative centers, purely official and bureaucratic in character, devoid of any political significance, while in the economic sense they were trade bazaars for the landlord and peasant milieu of its environs. Their development was still rather inconsiderable, when it was terminated by the capitalist process, which began to establish large cities in its own image, that is, factory towns and centers of world trade. . . . That which had hindered the development of petty bourgeois democracy came to benefit the class consciousness of the proletariat in Russia —the weak development of the artisan form of production. The proletariat was immediately concentrated in the factories. . . .
>
> Greater and greater masses of peasants will be drawn

into the movement. But all they can do is to aggravate the political anarchy rampant in the country and thus weaken the government; they cannot become a compact revolutionary army. Hence, as the revolution develops, an even greater portion of political work will fall to the lot of the proletariat. At the same time its political awareness will be enhanced and its political energy will grow apace. . . .

The Social Democracy will be confronted with this dilemma: to assume responsibility for the provisional government or to stand aloof from the labor movement. The workers will regard that government as their own, no matter what the attitude of the Social Democracy. . . . In Russia only workers can accomplish a revolutionary insurrection. In Russia the revolutionary provisional government will be a government of the *workers' democracy.* That government will be social democratic, should the Social Democracy be at the head of the revolutionary movement of the Russian proletariat. . . .

The Social Democratic provisional government cannot accomplish a socialist insurrection in Russia, but the very process of liquidating the autocracy and establishing a democratic republic will provide it with fertile ground for political activity.

In the heyday of revolutionary events in the autumn of 1905, I met Parvus again, this time in Petersburg. Remaining organizationally independent of both factions, we jointly edited *Russkoye Slovo* (The Russian World), a newspaper for the working class masses, and, in coalition with the Mensheviks, the important political newspaper *Nachalo* (The Beginning). The theory of permanent revolution was usually associated with the names of "Parvus and Trotsky." That was only partially correct. Parvus attained revolutionary maturity at the end of the preceding century, when he marched at the head of the forces that fought so-called Revisionism, i.e., the opportunistic distortions of Marx's theory. But his optimism was undermined by the failure of all his efforts to push the German Social Democracy in the direction of a more resolute policy. Parvus grew increasingly more reserved about the perspectives of a socialist revolution in the West. At the same time he felt that "the Social-Democratic provisional government cannot accomplish a socialist insurrection in Russia." Hence, his prognosis indicated, instead of the transformation of the democratic into the socialist revolution, merely the establishment in Russia of a regime of workers' democracy, more or less as in Australia, where the first labor government, resting on a farmerist foundation, did not venture beyond the limits of the bourgeois regime.

I did not share that conclusion. Australian democracy, maturing organically on the virgin soil of a new continent, immediately assumed a conservative character and dominated the youthul yet rather privileged proletariat. Russian democracy, on the contrary, could come about only in consequence of a large-scale revolutionary insurrection, the dynamics of which would never permit the labor government to maintain itself within the framework of bourgeois democracy. Our differences of opinion, which began soon after the Revolution of 1905, led to a complete break at the beginning of the war, when Parvus, in whom the skeptic had completely killed the revolutionist, proved to be on the side of German imperialism and subsequently became the counselor and inspirer of the first President of the German Republic, Ebert.

After writing my pamphlet, "Until the Ninth of January," I repeatedly returned to the development and the grounding of the theory of permanent revolution. In view of the significance it subsequently acquired in the intellectual evolution of the hero of this biography, it is necessary to present it here in the form of exact quotations from my works of the years 1905 and 1906.

> The nucleus of population in a contemporary city—at least, in a city of economic and political significance—is the sharply differentiated class of hired labor. It is this class, essentially unknown to the Great French Revolution, which is fated to play the decisive role in our revolution. . . . In an economically more backward country the proletariat may come to power sooner than in a country more advanced capitalistically. The conception of a kind

of automatic dependence of the proletarian dictatorship on a country's technical forces and means is a prejudice of extremely simplified "economic" materialism. Such a view has nothing in common with Marxism. . . . Notwithstanding the fact that the productive forces of United States industry are ten times greater than ours, the political role of the Russian proletariat, its influence on the politics of its own country and the possibility that it may soon influence world politics are incomparably greater than the role of significance of the American proletariat. . . .

It seems to me that the Russian Revolution will create such conditions that the power may (in the event of victory, *must*) pass into the hands of the proletariat before the politicians of bourgeois liberalism will find it possible fully to unfold their genius for statecraft. . . . The Russian bourgeoisie will surrender all the revolutionary positions to the proletariat. It will also have to surrender revolutionary hegemony over the peasantry. The proletariat in power will come to the peasantry as the class liberator. . . . The proletariat, leaning on the peasantry, will bring into motion all the forces for raising the cultural level of the village and for developing political consciousness in the peasantry. . . .

But will not perhaps the peasantry itself drive the proletariat away and supersede it? That is impossible. All historic experience repudiates that supposition. It shows that the peasantry is utterly incapable of an *independent* political role . . . From the aforesaid it is clear how I look upon the idea of the "dictatorship of the proletariat and the peasantry." The point is not whether I deem it admissible in principle, whether I "want" or "do not want" such a form of political cooperation. I deem it unrealizable—at least, in the direct and immediate sense.

The foregoing already shows how incorrect is the assertion that the conception here expounded "jumped over the bourgeois revolution," as has been subsequently reiterated without end. "The struggle for the democratic renovation of Russia . . ." I wrote at the same time, "is in its entirety derived from capitalism, is being conducted by forces formed on the basis of capitalism, and *immediately, in the first place*, is directed against the feudal and vassal obstacles that stand in the way of developing a capitalist society." But the substance of the question was with what forces and by which methods these obstacles could be overcome.

The framework of all the questions of the revolution may be limited by the assertion that our revolution is *bourgeois* in its objective goals and consequently, in all its inevitable results, and it is possible at the same time to close one's eyes to the fact that the principal active force of that bourgeois revolution is the proletariat, which is pushing itself toward power with all the impact of the revolution. . . . One may comfort himself with the thought that Russia's social conditions have not yet ripened for a socialist economy—and at the same time overlook the thought that, upon coming to power, the proletariat would inevitably, with all the logic of its situation, push itself toward the management of the economy at the expense of the state. . . . Coming into the government not as helpless hostages but as the leading force, the representatives of the proletariat will by virtue of that alone smash the demarcation between the minimal and maximal program, i.e., *place collectivism on the order of the day*. At what point in that tendency the proletariat would be stopped will depend on the interrelation of forces, but certainly not on the initial intentions of the proletariat's party. . . .

But we may already ask ourselves: must the dictatorship of the proletariat inevitably smash itself against the framework of the bourgeois revolution or can it, on the basis of the existing historical situation of the *world*, look forward to the perspective of victory, after smashing this limiting framework? . . . One thing may be said with certainty: without the direct governmental support of the European proletariat, the working class of Russia will not be able to maintain itself in power and transform its temporary reign into an enduring socialist dictatorship.

But this does not necessarily lead to a pessimistic prognosis:

> The political liberation, led by the working class of Russia, will raise the leader to a height unprecedented in history, transmit to him colossal forces and means, and make him the initiator of the world-wide liquidation of capitalism, for which history has created all the objective prerequisites.

As to the extent to which international Social Democracy will prove capable of fulfilling its revolutionary task, I wrote in 1906:

> The European socialist parties—and in the first place, the mightiest of them, the German party—have developed their conservatism, which grows stronger in proportion to the size of the masses embraced by socialism and the effectiveness of the organization and the discipline of these masses. Because of that, the Social Democracy, as the organization that embodies the political experience of the proletariat, may at a given moment become the immediate obstacle on the path of an open clash between the workers and the bourgeois reaction.

Yet I concluded my analysis by expressing the assurance that

> the Eastern revolution will infect the Western proletariat with revolutionary idealism and arouse in it the desire to start talking "Russian" with its enemy . . .

To sum up. Populism, like Slavophilism, proceeded from illusions that Russia's course of development would be utterly unique, escaping capitalism and the bourgeois republic. Plekhanov's Marxism concentrated on proving the identity in principle of Russia's historical course with that of the West. The program that grew out of that ignored the very real and far from mystical peculiarities of Russia's social structure and revolutionary development. The Menshevik view of the revolution, purged of its episodic stratifications and individual deviations, was tantamount to the following: the victory of the Russian bourgeois revolution was possible only under the leadership of the liberal bourgeoisie and must put the latter in power. Later the democratic regime would let the Russian proletariat, with incomparably greater success than heretofore, catch up with its elder Western brothers on the road of the struggle for socialism.

Lenin's perspective may be briefly expressed in the following words: the backward Russian bourgeoisie is incapable of completing its own revolution! The complete victory of the revolution, through the intermediacy of the "democratic dictatorship of the proletariat and the peasantry," would purge the land of medievalism, invest the development of Russian capitalism with American tempo, strengthen the proletariat in city and village, and make really possible the struggle for socialism. On the other hand, the victory of the Russian Revolution would give tremendous impetus to the socialist revolution in the West, while the latter would not only protect Russia from the dangers of restoration but would also enable the Russian proletariat to come to the conquest of power in a comparatively brief historical period.

The perspective of permanent revolution may be summarized in the following way: the complete victory of the democratic revolution in Russia is conceivable only in the form of the dictatorship of the proletariat, leaning on the peasantry. The dictatorship of the proletariat, which would inevitably place on the order of the day not only democratic but socialistic tasks as well, would at the same time give a powerful impetus to the international socialist revolution. Only the victory of the proletariat in the West could protect Russia from bourgeois restoration and assure it the possibility of rounding out the establishment of socialism.

That compact formula discloses with equal distinctness the similarity of the latter two concepts in their irreconcilable differentiation from the liberal Menshevik perspective as well as their extremely essential distinction from each other on the question of the social character and the tasks of the "dictatorship" which must grow out of the revolution. The not infrequent complaint in the writings of the present Moscow theoreticians that the program of the dictatorship of the proletariat was "premature" in 1905 is beside the point. In an empirical sense the program of the democratic dictatorship of the proletariat and the peasantry proved equally "premature." The unfavorable combination of forces at the time of the First Revolution did not so much preclude the dictatorship of the proletariat as the victory of the revolution in general. Yet all the revolutionary groups were based on the hope of complete victory; the supreme revolutionary struggle would have been impossible without such a hope. The differences of opinion dealt with the general perspective of the revolution and the strategy arising from that. The perspective of Menshevism was false to the core: it pointed out the wrong road to the proletariat. The perspective of Bolshevism was not complete: it correctly pointed out the general direction of the struggle, but characterized its stages incorrectly. The insufficiency in the perspective of Bolshevism did not become apparent in 1905 only because the revolution itself did not undergo further development. But then at the beginning of 1917 Lenin was obliged to alter his perspective, in direct conflict with the old cadres of his party.

No political prognosis can pretend to be mathematically exact; suffice it if it correctly indicates the general line of development and helps to orient the actual course of events, which inevitably bends the main line right and left. In that sense it is impossible not to see that the concept of permanent revolution has completely passed the test of history. During the initial years of the Soviet regime no one denied that; on the contrary, that fact found acknowledgment in a number of official publications. But when the bureaucratic reaction against October opened up in the calmed and cooled upper crust of Soviet society, it was at once directed against the theory which reflected the first proletarian revolution more completely than anything else while at the same time openly exposing its unfinished, limited, and partial character. Thus, by way of repulsion, originated the theory of socialism in a separate country, the basic dogma of Stalinism.

The Red Terror and the Freedom of the Press

From *Terrorism and Communism* (1922).

The problem of revolution, as of war, consists in breaking the will of the foe, forcing him to capitulate and to accept the conditions of the conqueror. The will, of course, is a fact of the physical world, but in contradistinction to a meeting, a dispute, or a congress, the revolution carries out its object by means of the employment of material resources—though to a lesser degree than war. The bourgeoisie itself conquered power by means of revolts, and consolidated it by the civil war. In the peaceful period, it retains power by means of a system of repression. As long as class society, founded on the most deep-rooted antagonisms, continues to exist, repression remains a necessary means of breaking the will of the opposing side.

Even if, in one country or another, the dictatorship of the proletariat grew up within the external framework of democracy, this would by no means avert the civil war. The question as to who is to rule the country, i.e., of the life or death of the bourgeoisie, will be decided on either side, not by references to the paragraphs of the constitution, but by the employment of all forms of violence. However deeply Kautsky goes into the question of the food of the anthropopithecus (see page 122 *et seq.* of his book) and other immediate and remote conditions which determine the cause of human cruelty, he will find in history no other way of breaking the class will of the enemy except the systematic and energetic use of violence.

The degree of ferocity of the struggle depends on a series of internal and international circumstances. The more ferocious and dangerous is the resistance of the class enemy who have been overthrown, the more inevitably does the system of repression take the form of a system of terror.

But here Kautsky unexpectedly takes up a new position in his struggle with Soviet terrorism. He simply waves aside all reference to the ferocity of the counterrevolutionary opposition of the Russian bourgeoisie.

"Such ferocity," he says, "could not be noticed in October, 1917, in Petrograd and Moscow, and still less, more recently, in Budapest." (Page 149.) With such a happy formulation of the question, revolutionary terrorism merely proves to be a product of the bloodthirstiness of the Bolsheviks, who simultaneously abandoned the traditions of the vegetarian anthropopithecus and the moral lessons of Kautsky.

The first conquest of power by the Soviets at the beginning of October, 1917, was actually accomplished with insignificant sacrifices. The Russian bourgeoisie found itself to such a degree estranged from the masses of the people, so internally helpless, so compromised by the course and the result of the war, so demoralized by the regime of Kerensky, that it scarcely dared show any resistance. In Petrograd the power of Kerensky was overthrown almost without a fight. In Moscow its resistance was dragged out, mainly owing to the indecisive character of our own actions. In the majority of the provincial towns, power was transferred to the Soviet on the mere receipt of a telegram from Petrograd or Moscow. If the matter had ended there, there would have been no word of the Red Terror. But in October, 1917, there was already evidence of the beginning of the resistance of the propertied classes. True, there was required the intervention of the imperialist governments of the West in order to give the Russian counterrevolution faith in itself, and to add ever-increasing power to its resistance. This can be shown from facts, both important and insignificant, day by day during the whole epoch of the Soviet revolution.

Kerensky's "Staff" felt no support forthcoming from the mass of the soldiery, and was inclined to recognize the Soviet government, which had begun negotiations for an armistice with the Germans. But there followed the protest of the military missions of the Entente, followed by open threats. The Staff was frightened; incited by "Allied" officers, it entered the path of opposition. This led to armed conflict and to the murder of the chief of the field staff, General Dukhonin, by a group of revolutionary sailors.

In Petrograd, the official agents of the Entente, especially the French Military Mission, hand in hand with the S.R.'s and the Mensheviks, openly organized the opposition, mobilizing, arming, inciting against us the *Kadets,* and the bourgeois youth generally, from the second day of the Soviet revolution. The rising of the Junkers on October 28 brought about a hundred times more victims than the revolution of October 25. The campaign of the adventurers Kerensky and Krasnov against Petrograd, organized at the same time by the Entente, naturally introduced into the struggle the first elements of savagery. Nevertheless, General Krasnov was set free on his word of honor. The Yaroslav rising (in the summer of 1918), which involved so many victims, was organized by Savinkov on the instructions of the French Embassy, and with its resources. Archangel was captured according to the plans of British naval agents, with the help of British warships and airplanes. The beginning of the empire of Kolchak, the nominee of the American Stock Exchange, was brought about by the foreign Czechoslovak Corps maintained by the resources of the French government. Kaledin and Krasnov (liberated by us), the first leaders of the counterrevolution on the Don, could enjoy partial success only thanks to the open military and financial aid of Germany. In the Ukraine the Soviet power was overthrown in the beginning of 1918 by German militarism. The Volunteer Army of Denikin was created with the financial and technical help of Great Britain and France. Only in the hope of British intervention and of British military support was Yudenich's army created. The politicians, the diplomats, and the journalists of the Entente have for two years on end been debating with complete frankness the question of whether the financing of the civil war in Russia is a sufficiently profitable enterprise. In such circumstances, one needs truly a brazen forehead to seek the reason for the sanguinary character of the civil war in Russia in the malevolence of the Bolsheviks, and not in the international situation.

The Russian proletariat was the first to enter the path of the social revolution, and the Russian bourgeoisie, politically helpless, was emboldened to struggle against its political and economic expropriation only because it saw its elder sister in all countries still in power, and still maintaining economic, political, and, to a certain extent, military supremacy.

If our October Revolution had taken place a few months, or even a few weeks, after the establishment of the rule of the proletariat in Germany, France, and England, there can be no doubt that our revolution would have been the most "peaceful," the most "bloodless" of all possible revolutions on this sinful earth. But this historical sequence—the most "natural" at the first glance, and, in any case, the most beneficial for the Russian working class—found itself infringed: not through our fault, but through the will of events. Instead of being the last, the Russian proletariat proved to be the first. It was just this circumstance, after the first period of confusion, that imparted desperation to the character of the resistance of the classes which had ruled in Russia previously, and forced the Russian proletariat, in a moment of the greatest peril, foreign attacks, and internal plots and insurrections, to have recourse to severe measures of State terror. No one will now say that those measures proved futile. But, perhaps, we are expected to consider them "intolerable"?

The working class, which seized power in battle, had as its object and its duty to establish that power unshakably, to guarantee its own supremacy beyond question, to destroy its enemies' hankering for a new revolution, and thereby to make sure of carrying out socialist reforms. Otherwise there would be no point in seizing power.

The revolution "logically" does not demand terrorism, just as "logically" it does not demand an armed insurrection. What a profound commonplace! But the revolution does require of the revolutionary class that it should attain its end by all methods at its disposal—if necessary, by an armed rising; if required, by terrorism. A revolutionary class which has conquered power with arms in its hands is bound to, and will, suppress, rifle in hand, all attempts to tear the power out of its hands. Where it has against it a hostile army, it will oppose to it its own army. Where it is confronted with armed conspiracy, attempt at murder, or rising, it will hurl at the heads of its enemies an unsparing penalty. Perhaps Kautsky has invented other methods? Or does he reduce the whole question to the *degree* of repression, and recommend in all circumstances imprisonment instead of execution?

The question of the form of repression, or of its degree, of course, is not one of "principle." It is a question of expediency. In a revolutionary period, the party which has been thrown from power, which does not reconcile itself with the stability of the ruling class, and which proves this by its desperate struggle against the latter, cannot be terrorized by the threat of imprisonment, as it does not believe in its duration. It is just this simple but decisive fact that explains the widespread recourse to shooting in a civil war.

Or, perhaps, Kautsky wishes to say that execution is not expedient, that "classes cannot be cowed." This is untrue. Terror is helpless—and then only "in the long run"—if it is employed by reaction against a historically rising class. But terror can be very efficient against a reactionary class which does not want to leave the scene of operations. *Intimidation* is a powerful weapon of policy, both internationally and internally. War, like revolution, is founded upon intimidation. A victorious war, generally speaking, destroys only an insignificant part of the conquered army, intimidating the remainder and breaking their will. The revolution works in the same way: it kills individuals, and intimidates thousands. In this sense, the Red Terror is not distinguishable from the armed insurrection, the direct continuation of which it represents. The State terror of a revolutionary class can be condemned "morally" only by a man who, as a principle, rejects (in words) every form of violence whatsoever—consequently, every war and every rising. For this one has to be merely and simply a hypocritical Quaker.

"But, in that case, in what do your tactics differ from the tactics of Czarism?" we are asked, by the high priests of Liberalism and Kautskianism.

You do not understand this, holy man? We shall explain to you. The terror of Czarism was directed against the proletariat. The *gendarmerie* of Czarism throttled the workers who were fighting for the socialist order. Our Extraordinary Commissions shoot landlords, capitalists, and generals who are striving to restore the capitalist order. Do you grasp this . . . distinction? Yes? For us communists it is quite sufficient.

"FREEDOM OF THE PRESS"

One point particularly worries Kautsky, the author of a great many books and articles—the freedom of the press. Is it permissible to suppress newspapers?

During war all institutions and organs of the State and of public opinion become, directly or indirectly, weapons of warfare. This is particularly true of the press. No government carrying on a serious war will allow publications to exist on its territory which, openly or indirectly, support the enemy. Still more so in a civil war. The nature of the latter is such that each of the struggling sides has in the rear of its armies considerable circles of the population on the side of the enemy. In war, where both success and failure are repaid by death, hostile agents who penetrate into the rear are subject to execution. This is inhumane, but no one ever considered war a school of humanity—still less civil war. Can it be seriously demanded that, during a civil war with the White Guards of Denikin, the publications of parties supporting Denikin should come out unhindered in Moscow and Petrograd? To propose this in the name of the "freedom" of the press is just the same as, in the name of open dealing, to demand the publication of military secrets. "A besieged city," wrote a Communard, Arthur Arnould of Paris, "cannot permit within its midst that hopes for its fall should openly be expressed, that the fighters defending it should be incited to treason, that the movements of its troops should be communicated to the enemy. Such was the position of Paris under the Commune." Such is the position of the Soviet Republic during the two years of its existence.

Let us, however, listen to what Kautsky has to say in this connection.

> The justification of this system [i.e., repressions in connection with the press] is reduced to the naïve idea that an absolute truth [!] exists, and that only the communists possess it [!]. Similarly, it reduces itself to another point of view, that all writers are by nature liars [!] and that only communists are fanatics for truth[!]. In reality, liars and fanatics for what they consider truth are to be found in all camps. [Page 176.]

In this way, in Kautsky's eyes, the revolution, in its most acute phase, when it is a question of the life and death of classes, continues as hitherto to be a literary discussion with the object of establishing—the truth. What profundity! Our "truth," of course, is not absolute. But as in its name we are, at the present moment, shedding our blood, we have neither cause nor possibility to carry on a literary discussion as to the relativity of truth with those who "criticize" us with the help of all forms of arms. Similarly, our problem is not to punish liars and to encourage just men among journalists of all shades of opinion, but to throttle the class lie of the bourgeoisie and to achieve the class truth of the proletariat, irrespective of the fact that in both camps there are fanatics and liars.

> The Soviet government [Kautsky thunders] has destroyed the sole remedy that might militate against corruption: the freedom of the press. Control by means of unlimited freedom of the press alone could have restrained those bandits and adventurers who will inevitably cling like

leeches to every unlimited, uncontrolled power. [Page 188.]

The press as a trusty weapon of the struggle with corruption! This liberal recipe sounds particularly pitiful when one remembers the two countries with the greatest "freedom" of the press—North America and France—which, at the same time, are countries of the most highly developed state of capitalist corruption.

Feeding on the old scandal of the political anterooms of the Russian Revolution, Kautsky imagines that without *Kadet* and Menshevik freedom the Soviet apparatus is honeycombed with "bandits" and "adventurers." Such was the voice of the Mensheviks a year or eighteen months ago. Now even they will not dare to repeat this. With the help of Soviet control and party selection, the Soviet government, in the intense atmosphere of the struggle, has dealt with the bandits and adventurers who appeared on the surface at the moment of the revolution incomparably better than any government whatsoever at any time whatsoever.

We are fighting. We are fighting a life-and-death struggle. The press is a weapon not of an abstract society, but of two irreconcilable, armed and contending sides. We are destroying the press of the counterrevolution, just as we destroyed its fortified positions, it stores, its communications, and its intelligence system. Are we depriving ourselves of *Kadet* and Menshevik criticisms of the corruption of the working class? In return we are victoriously destroying the very foundations of capitalist corruption.

But Kautsky goes further to develop this theme. He complains that we suppress the newspapers of the S.R.'s and the Mensheviks, and even—such things have been known—arrest their leaders. Are we not dealing here with "shades of opinion" in the proletarian or the socialist movement? The scholastic pedant does not see facts beyond his accustomed words. The Mensheviks and S.R.'s for him are simply tendencies in socialism, whereas, in the course of the revolution, they have been transformed into an organization which works in active cooperation with the counterrevolution and carries on against us an open war. The army of Kolchak was organized by Social Revolutionaries (how that name savors today of the charlatan!), and was supported by Mensheviks. Both carried on—and carry on—against us, for a year and a half, a war on the northern front. The Mensheviks who rule the Caucasus, formerly the allies of Hohenzollern, and today the allies of Lloyd George, arrested and shot Bolsheviks hand in hand with German and British officers. The Mensheviks and S.R.'s of the Kuban Rada organized the army of Denikin. The Estonian Mensheviks who participate in their government were directly concerned in the last advance of Yudenich against Petrograd. Such are these "tendencies" in the socialist movement. Kautsky considers that one can be in a state of open and civil war with the Mensheviks and S.R.'s, who, with the help of the troops they themselves have organized for Yudenich, Kolchak and Denikin, are fighting for their "shades of opinion" in socialism, and at the same time to allow those innocent "shades of opinion" freedom of the press in our rear. If the dispute with the S.R.'s, and the Mensheviks could be settled by means of persuasion and voting—that is, if there were not behind their backs the Russian and foreign imperialists—there would be no civil war.

Kautsky, of course, is ready to "condemn"—an extra drop of ink—the blockade, and the Entente support of Denikin, and the White Terror. But in his high impartiality he cannot deny the latter certain extenuating circumstances. The White Terror, you see, does not infringe their own principles, while the Bolsheviks, making use of the Red Terror, betray the principle of "the sacredness of human life which they themselves proclaimed." (Page 210.)

The meaning of the principle of the sacredness of human life in practice, and in what it differs from the commandment, "Thou shalt not kill," Kautsky does not explain. When a murderer raises his knife over a child, may one kill the murderer to save the child? Will not thereby the principle of the "sacredness of human life" be infringed? May one kill the murderer to save oneself? Is an insurrection of oppressed slaves against their masters permissible? Is it permissible to purchase one's freedom at the cost of the life of one's jailer? If human life in general is sacred and inviolable, we must deny ourselves not only the use of terror, not only war, but also revolution itself. Kautsky simply does not realize the counterrevolutionary meaning of the "principle" which he attempts to force upon us. Elsewhere we shall see that Kautsky accuses us of concluding the Brest-Litovsk peace: in his opinion we ought to have continued war. But what then becomes of the sacredness of human life? Does life cease to be sacred when it is a question of people talking another language, or does Kautsky consider that mass murders organized on principles of strategy and tactics are not murders at all? Truly it is difficult to put forward in our age a principle more hypocritical and more stupid. As long as human labor power, and, consequently, life itself, remain articles of sale and purchase, of exploitation and robbery, the principle of the "sacredness of human life" remains a shameful lie, uttered with the object of keeping the oppressed slaves in their chains.

We used to fight against the death penalty introduced by Kerensky, because that penalty was inflicted by the courts-martial of the old army on soldiers who refused to continue the imperialist war. We tore this weapon out of the hands of the old courts-martial, destroyed the courts-martial themselves, and demobilized the old army which had brought them forth. Destroying in the Red Army, and generally throughout the country, counterrevolutionary conspirators who strive by means of insurrections, murders, and disorganization to restore the old regime, we are acting in accordance with the iron laws of a war in which we desire to guarantee our victory.

If it is a question of seeking formal contradictions, then obviously we must do so on the side of the White Terror, which is the weapon of classes which consider themselves "Christian," patronize idealist philosophy, and are firmly convinced that the individuality (their own) is an end-in-itself. As for us, we were never concerned with the Kantian-priestly and vegetarian-Quaker prattle about the "sacredness of human life." We were revolutionaries in opposition, and have remained revolutionaries in power. To make the individual sacred we must destroy the social order which crucifies him. And this problem can be solved only by blood and iron.

There is another difference between the White Terror and the Red, which Kautsky today ignores, but which in the eyes of a Marxist is of decisive significance. The White Terror is the weapon of the historically reactionary class. When we exposed the futility of the repressions of the bourgeois state against the proletariat, we never denied that by arrests and executions the ruling class, under certain conditions, might temporarily retard the development of the social revolution. But we were convinced that they would not be able to bring it to a halt. We relied on the fact that the proletariat is the historically rising class, and that bourgeois society could not develop without increasing the forces of the proletariat. The bourgeoisie today is a falling class. It not only no longer plays an essential part in production, but by its imperialist methods of appropriation is destroying the economic structure of the world and human culture generally. Nevertheless, the historical persistence of the bourgeoisie is colossal. It holds to power, and does not wish to abandon it. Thereby it threatens to drag after it into the abyss the whole of society. We are forced to tear it off, to chop it away. The Red Terror is a weapon utilized against a class doomed to destruction, not wishing to perish. If the White Terror can only retard the historical rise of the proletariat, the Red Terror hastens the destruction of the bourgeoisie. This hastening—a pure question of acceleration—is at certain periods of decisive importance. Without the Red Terror, the Russian bourgeoisie, together with the world bourgeoisie would throttle us long before the coming of the revolution in Europe. One must be blind not to see this, or a swindler to deny it.

The man who recognizes the revolutionary historic importance of the very fact of the existence of the Soviet system must also sanction the Red Terror. Kautsky, who during the last two years has covered mountains of paper with polemics against communism and terrorism, is obliged, at the end of his pamphlet, to recognize the facts, and unexpectedly to admit that the Russian Soviet government is today the most important factor in the world revolution. He writes:

However one regards the Bolshevik methods, the fact that a proletarian government in a large country has not only reached power, but has retained it for two years up to the present time, amidst great difficulties, extraordinarily increases the sense of power amongst the proletariat of all countries. For the actual revolution the Bolsheviks have thereby accomplished a great work—*grosses geleistet*. [Page 233.]

This announcement stuns us as a completely unexpected recognition of historical truth from a quarter whence we had long since ceased to await it. The Bolsheviks have accomplished a great historical task by existing for two years against the united capitalist world. But the Bolsheviks held out not only by ideas, but by the sword. Kautsky's admission is an involuntary sanctioning of the methods of the Red Terror, and at the same time the most effective condemnation of his own critical concoction.

10

The Metaphysics of Democracy

From *Terrorism and Communism* (1922).

Feeling the historical ground shaking under his feet on the question of democracy, Kautsky crosses to the ground of metaphysics. Instead of inquiring into what is, he deliberates about what ought to be.

The principles of democracy—the sovereignty of the people, universal and equal suffrage, personal liberties—appear, as presented to him, in a halo of moral duty. They are turned from their historical meaning and presented as unalterable and sacred things-in-themselves. This metaphysical fall from grace is not accidental. It is instructive that the late Plekhanov, a merciless enemy of Kantism at the best period of his activity, attempted at the end of his life, when the wave of patriotism had washed over him, to clutch at the straw of the categorical imperative.

That real democracy with which the German people is now

making practical acquaintance Kautsky confronts with a kind of ideal democracy, as he would confront a common phenomenon with the thing-in-itself. Kautsky indicates with certitude not one country in which democracy is really capable of guaranteeing a painless transition to socialism. But he does know and firmly, that such democracy ought to exist. The present German National Assembly, that organ of helplessness, reactionary malice and degraded solicitations, is confronted by Kautsky with a different, real, true National Assembly, which possesses all virtues—excepting the small virtue of reality.

The doctrine of formal democracy is not scientific socialism, but the theory of so-called natural law. The essence of the latter consists in the recognition of eternal and unchanging standards of law, which among different peoples and at different periods find a different, more or less limited and distorted expression. The natural law of the latest history—i.e., as it emerged from the middle ages—included first of all a protest against class privileges, the abuse of despotic legislation, and the other "artificial" products of feudal positive law. The theoreticians of the, as yet, weak Third Estate expressed its class interests in a few ideal standards, which later on developed into the teaching of democracy, acquiring at the same time an individualist character. The individual is absolute; all persons have the right of expressing their thoughts in speech and print; every man must enjoy equal electoral rights. As a battle cry against feudalism, the demand for democracy had a progressive character. As time went on, however, the metaphysics of natural law (the theory of formal democracy) began to show its reactionary side—the establishment of an ideal standard to control the real demands of the laboring masses and the revolutionary parties.

If we look back to the historical sequence of world concepts, the theory of natural law will prove to be a paraphrase of Christian spiritualism freed from its crude mysticism. The Gospels proclaimed to the slave that he had just the same soul as the slaveowner, and in this way established the equality of all men before the heavenly tribunal. In reality, the slave remained a slave, and obedience became for him a religious duty.

In the teaching of Christianity, the slave found an expression for his own ignorant protest against his degraded condition. Side by side with the protest was also the consolation. Christianity told him: "You have an immortal soul, although you resemble a pack-horse." Here sounded the note of indignation. But the same Christianity said: "Although you are like a pack-horse, yet your immortal soul has in store for it an eternal reward." Here is the voice of consolation. These two notes were found in historical Christianity in different proportions at different periods and amongst different classes. But as a whole, Christianity, like all other religions, became a method of deadening the consciousness of the oppressed masses.

Natural law, which developed into the theory of democracy, said to the worker: "All men are equal before the law, independently of their origin, their property, and their position; every man has an equal right in determining the fate of the people." This ideal criterion revolutionized the consciousness of the masses insofar as it was a condemnation of absolutism, aristocratic privileges, and the property qualification. But the longer it went on, the more it sent the consciousness to sleep, legalizing poverty, slavery and degradation: for how could one revolt against slavery when every man has an equal right in determining the fate of the nation?

Rothschild, who has coined the blood and tears of the world into the gold napoleons of his income, has one vote at the parliamentary elections. The ignorant tiller of the soil who cannot sign his name, sleeps all his life without taking his clothes off, and wanders through society like an underground mole, plays his part, however, as a trustee of the nation's sovereignty, and is equal to Rothschild in the courts and at the elections. In the real conditions of life, in the economic process, in social relations, in their way of life, people become more and more unequal; dazzling luxury was accumulated at one pole, poverty and hopelessness at the other. But in the sphere of the legal edifice of the state, these glaring contradictions disappeared, and there penetrated thither only unsubstantial legal shadows. The landlord, the laborer, the capitalist, the proletarian, the minister, the bootblack—all are equal as "citizens" and as "legislators." The mystic equality of Christianity has taken one step down from the heavens in the shape of the "natural," "legal" equality of democracy. But it has not yet reached earth, where lie the economic foundations of society. For the ignorant day-laborer, who all his life remains a beast of burden in the service of the bourgeoisie, the ideal right to influence the fate of the nations by means of the parliamentary elections remained little more real than the palace which he was promised in the kingdom of heaven.

In the practical interests of the development of the working class, the Socialist Party took its stand at a certain period on the path of parliamentarism. But this did not mean in the slightest that it accepted in principle the metaphysical theory of democracy, based on extra-historical, super-class rights. The proletarian doctrines examined democracy as the instrument of bourgeois society entirely adapted to the problems and requirements of the ruling classes; but as bourgeois society lived by the labor of the proletariat and could not deny it the legalization of a certain part of its class struggle without destroying itself, this gave the Socialist Party the possibility of utilizing, at a certain period, and within certain limits, the mechanism of democracy, without taking an oath to do so as an unshakable principle.

The root problem of the party, at all periods of its struggle, was to create the conditions for real, economic, living equality for mankind as members of a united human commonwealth. It was just for this reason that the theoreticians of the proletariat had to expose the metaphysics of democracy as a philosophic mask for political mystification.

The democratic party at the period of its revolutionary enthusiasm, when exposing the enslaving and stupefying lie of church dogma, preached to the masses: "You are lulled to sleep by promises of eternal bliss at the end of your life, while here you have no rights and you are bound with the chains of tyranny." The Socialist Party, a few decades later, said to the same masses with no less right: "You are lulled to sleep with the fiction of civic equality and political rights, but you are deprived of the possibility of realizing those rights.

Conditional and shadowy legal equality has been transformed into the convicts' chain with which each of you is fastened to the chariot of capitalism."

In the name of its fundamental task, the Socialist Party mobilized the masses on the parliamentary ground as well as on others; but nowhere and at no time did any party bind itself to bring the masses to socialism only through the gates of democracy. In adapting ourselves to the parliamentary regime, we stopped at a theoretical exposure of democracy, because we were still too weak to overcome it in practice. But the path of socialist ideas which is visible through all deviations, and even betrayals, foreshadows no other outcome but this: to throw democracy aside and replace it by the mechanism of the proletariat, at the moment when the latter is strong enough to carry out such a task.

We shall bring one piece of evidence, albeit a sufficiently striking one.

> Parliamentarism [wrote Paul Lafargue in the Russian review *Sozialdemokrat* in 1888] is a system of government in which the people acquire the illusion that it is controlling the forces of the country itself, when, in reality, the actual power is concentrated in the hands of the bourgeoisie—and not even of the whole bourgeoisie, but only of certain sections of that class. In the first period of its supremacy the bourgeoisie does not understand, or, more correctly, does not feel, the necessity for making the people believe in the illusion of self-government. Hence it was that all the parliamentary countries of Europe began with a limited franchise. Everywhere the right of influencing the policy of the country by means of the election of deputies belonged at first only to more or less large property holders, and was only gradually extended to less substantial citizens, until finally in some countries it became, not a privilege, but the universal right of all and sundry.
>
> In bourgeois society, the more considerable becomes the amount of social wealth, the smaller becomes the number of individuals by whom it is appropriated. The same takes

The Metaphysics of Democracy

place with power: in proportion as the mass of citizens who possess political rights increases, and the number of elected rulers increases, the actual power is concentrated and becomes the monopoly of a smaller and smaller group of individuals.

Such is the secret of the majority.

For the Marxist Lafargue, parliamentarism remains as long as the supremacy of the bourgeoisie remains.

On the day when the proletariat of Europe and America seizes the state, it will have to organize a revolutionary government, and govern society as a dictatorship, until the bourgeoisie has disappeared as a class.

Kautsky in his time knew this Marxist estimate of parliamentarism, and more than once repeated it himself, although with no such Gallic sharpness and lucidity. The theoretical apostasy of Kautsky lies just in this point: having recognized the principle of democracy as absolute and eternal, he has stepped back from materialist dialectics to natural law. That which was exposed by Marxism as the passing mechanism of the bourgeoisie, and was subjected only to temporary utilization with the object of preparing the proletarian revolution, has been newly sanctified by Kautsky as the supreme principle standing above classes, and unconditionally subordinating to itself the methods of the proletarian struggle. The counter-revolutionary degeneration of parliamentarism finds its most perfect expression in the deification of democracy by the decaying theoreticians of the Second International.

II

"War Communism," The New Economic Policy (NEP), and The Course Toward the Kulak

TRANSLATED BY MAX EASTMAN
from *The Revolution Betrayed* (1937).

The line of development of the Soviet economy is far from being an uninterrupted and evenly rising curve. In the first eighteen years of the new regime you can clearly distinguish several stages marked by sharp cries. A short outline of the economic history of the Soviet Union in connection with the policy of the government is absolutely necessary both for diagnosis and prognosis.

The first three years after the revolution were a period of overt and cruel civil war. Economic life was wholly subjected to the needs of the front. Cultural life lurked in corners and was characterized by a bold range of creative thought, above all the personal thought of Lenin, with an extraordinary scarcity of material means. That was the period of so-called "war communism" (1918-21), which forms an heroic parallel to the "war socialism" of the capitalist countries. The economic problems of the Soviet government in those years came down chiefly to supporting the war industries, and using the scanty resources left from the past for military purposes and to keep the city populations alive. War communism was, in essence, the systematic regimentation of consumption in a besieged fortress.

It is necessary to acknowledge, however, that in its original conception it pursued broader aims. The Soviet government hoped and strove to develop these methods of regimentation directly into a system of planned economy in distribution as well as production. In other words, from "war communism" it hoped gradually, but without destroying the system, to arrive at genuine communism. The program of the Bolshevik party adopted in March, 1919, said: "In the sphere of distribution the present task of the Soviet government is unwaveringly to continue on a planned, organized and state-wide scale to replace trade by the distribution of products."

Reality, however, came into increasing conflict with the program of "war communism." Production continually declined, and not only because of the destructive action of the war, but also because of the quenching of the stimulus of personal interest among the producers. The city demanded grain and raw materials from the rural districts, giving nothing in exchange except varicolored pieces of paper, named, according to ancient memory, money. And the *muzhik* buried his stores in the ground. The government sent out armed workers' detachments for grain. The *muzhik* cut down his sowings. Industrial production for 1921, immediately after the end of the civil war, amounted at most to one fifth of the prewar level. The production of steel fell from 4.2 million tons to 183 thousand tons—that is, to 1/23 of what it had been. The total harvest of grain decreased from 801 million hundredweight to 503 million in 1922. That was a year of terrible hunger. Foreign trade at the same time plunged from 2.9 billion rubles to 30 million. The collapse of the productive forces surpassed anything of the kind that history had ever seen. The country, and the government with it, were at the very edge of the abyss.

The utopian hopes of the epoch of war communism came in

later for a cruel, and in many respects just, criticism. The theoretical mistake of the ruling party remains inexplicable, however, only if you leave out of account the fact that all calculations at that time were based on the hope of an early victory of the revolution in the West. It was considered self-evident that the victorious German proletariat would supply Soviet Russia, on credit against future food and raw materials, not only with machines and articles of manufacture, but also with tens of thousands of highly skilled workers, engineers and organizers. And there is no doubt that if the proletarian revolution had triumphed in Germany—a thing that was prevented solely and exclusively by the Social Democrats—the economic development of the Soviet Union as well as of Germany would have advanced with such gigantic strides that the fate of Europe and the world would today have been incomparably more auspicious. It can be said with certainty, however, that even in that happy event it would still have been necessary to renounce the direct state distribution of products in favor of the methods of commerce.

Lenin explained the necessity of restoring the market by the existence in the country of millions of isolated peasant enterprises, unaccustomed to defining their economic relations with the outside world except through trade. Trade circulation would establish a "connection," as it was called, between the peasant and the nationalized industries. The theoretical formula for this "connection" is very simple: industry should supply the rural districts with necessary goods at such prices as would enable the state to forego forcible collection of the products of peasant labor.

To mend economic relations with the rural districts was undoubtedly the most critical and urgent task of the NEP. A brief experiment showed, however, that industry itself, in spite of its socialized character, had need of the methods of money payment worked out by capitalism. A planned economy cannot rest merely on intellectual data. The play of supply and demand remains for a long period a necessary material basis and indispensable corrective.

The market legalized by the NEP began, with the help of an organized currency, to do its work. As early as 1923, thanks to an initial stimulus from the rural districts, industry began to revive. And moreover it immediately hit a high tempo. It is sufficient to say that production doubled in 1922 and 1923, and by 1926 had already reached the prewar level—that is, had grown more than five times its size in 1921. At the same time, although at a much more modest tempo, the harvests were increasing.

Beginning with the critical year 1923, the disagreements observed earlier in the ruling party on the relation between industry and agriculture began to grow sharp. In a country which had completely exhausted its stores and reserves, industry could not develop except by borrowing grain and raw material from the peasants. Too heavy "forced loans" of products, however, would destroy the stimulus to labor. Not believing in the future prosperity, the peasant would answer the grain expeditions from the city by a sowing strike. Too light collections, on the other hand, threatened a standstill. Not receiving industrial products, the peasants would turn to industrial labor to satisfy their own needs, and revive the old home crafts. The disagreements in the party began about the question how much to take from the villages for industry, in order to hasten the period of dynamic equilibrium between them. The dispute was immediately complicated by the question of the social structure of the village itself.

In the spring of 1923, at a congress of the party, a representative of the "Left Opposition"—not yet, however, known by that name—demonstrated the divergence of industrial and agricultural prices in the form of an ominous diagram. This phenomenon was then first called "the scissors," a term which has since become almost international. If the further lagging of industry—said the speaker—continues to open these scissors, then a break between city and country is inevitable.

The peasants made a sharp distinction between the democratic and agrarian revolution which the Bolshevik party had carried through, and its policy directed toward laying the foundations of socialism. The expropriation of the landlords and the state lands brought the peasants upwards of half a billion gold rubles a year. In the prices of state products, however, the peasants were paying out a much larger sum. So long as the net result of the two revolutions, democratic and socialistic, bound together by the firm knot of October, reduced itself for the peasantry to a loss of hundreds of millions, a union of the two classes remained dubious.

The scattered character of the peasant economy, inherited from the past, was aggravated by the results of the October Revolution. The number of independent farms rose during the subsequent decade from sixteen to twenty-five million, which naturally strengthened the purely consummatory character of the majority of peasant enterprises. That was one of the causes of the lack of agricultural products.

A small commodity economy inevitably produces exploiters. In proportion as the villages recovered, the differentiation within the peasant mass began to grow. This development fell into the old well-trodden ruts. The growth of the *kulak*[1] far outstripped the general growth of agriculture. The policy of the government under the slogan "face to the country" was actually a turning of its face to the *kulak*. Agricultural taxes fell upon the poor far more heavily than upon the well-to-do, who moreover skimmed the cream of the state credits. The surplus grain, chiefly in possession of the upper strata of the village, was used to enslave the poor and for speculative selling to the bourgeois elements of the cities. Bukharin, the theoretician of the ruling faction at that time, tossed to the peasantry his famous slogan, "Get rich!" In the language of theory, that was supposed to mean a gradual growing of the *kulaks* into socialism. In practice, it meant the enrichment of the minority at the expense of the overwhelming majority.

Captive to its own policy, the government was compelled to retreat step by step before the demands of a rural petty bourgeoisie. In 1925 the hiring of labor power and the renting of land were legalized for agriculture. The peasantry was becoming polarized between the small capitalist on one side and the hired hand on the other. At the same time, lacking industrial commodities, the state was crowded out of the rural market. Between the *kulak* and the petty home craftsman there appeared, as though from under the earth, the middleman. The state enterprises themselves, in search of raw ma-

[1] Well-off peasant, employing labor.

terial, were more and more compelled to deal with the private trader. The rising tide of capitalism was visible everywhere. Thinking people saw plainly that a revolution in the forms of property does not solve the problem of socialism, but only raises it.

In 1925, when the course toward the *kulak* was in full swing, Stalin began to prepare for the denationalization of the land. To a question asked at his suggestion by a Soviet journalist: "Would it not be expedient in the interest of agriculture to deed over to each peasant for ten years the parcel of land tilled by him?" Stalin answered: "Yes, and even for forty years." The People's Commissar of Agriculture of Georgia, upon Stalin's own initiative, introduced the draft of a law denationalizing the land. The aim was to give the farmer confidence in his own future. While this was going on in the spring of 1926, almost sixty per cent of the grain destined for sale was in the hands of six per cent of the peasant proprietors! The state lacked grain not only for foreign trade, but even for domestic needs. The insignificance of exports made it necessary to forego bringing in articles of manufacture, and cut down to the limit the import of machinery and raw materials.

Retarding industrialization and striking a blow at the general mass of the peasants, this policy of banking on the well-to-do farmer revealed unequivocally inside of two years, 1924-26, its political consequences. It brought about an extraordinary increase of self-consciousness in the petty bourgeoisie of both city and village, a capture by them of many of the lower Soviets, an increase of the power and self-confidence of the bureaucracy, a growing pressure upon the workers, and the complete suppression of party and Soviet democracy. The growth of the *kulaks* alarmed two eminent members of the ruling group, Zinoviev and Kamenev, who were, significantly, presidents of the Soviets of the two chief proletarian centers, Leningrad and Moscow. But the provinces, and still more the bureaucracy, stood firm for Stalin. The course toward the well-to-do farmer won out. In 1926 Zinoviev and Kamenev with their adherents joined the Opposition of 1923 (the "Trotskyists").

Of course "in principle" the ruling group did not even then

renounce the collectivization of agriculture. They merely put it off a few decades in their perspective. The future People's Commissar of Agriculture, Yakovlev, wrote in 1927 that, although the socialist reconstruction of the village can be accomplished only through collectivization, still "this obviously cannot be done in one, two or three years, and maybe not in one decade." "The collective farms and communes," he continued, " . . . are now, and will for a long time undoubtedly remain, only small islands in a sea of individual peasant holdings." And in truth at that period only eight per cent of the peasant families belonged to collectives.

The struggle in the party about the so-called general line, which had come to the surface in 1923, became especially intense and passionate in 1926. In its extended platform, which took up all the problems of industry and economy, the Left Opposition wrote:

> The party ought to resist and crush all tendencies directed to the annulment or undermining of the nationalization of land, one of the pillars of the proletarian dictatorship.

On that question the Opposition gained the day; direct attempts against nationalization were abandoned. But the problem, of course, involved more than forms of property in land.

> To the growth of individual farming[2] in the country we must oppose a swifter growth of the collective farms. It is necessary to set aside systematically, year by year, a considerable sum to aid the poor peasants organized in collectives. The whole work of the co-operatives ought to be imbued with the purpose of converting small production into a vast collectivized production.

But this broad program of collectivization was stubbornly regarded as utopian for the coming years. During the preparations for the Fifteenth Party Congress, whose task was to expel the Left Opposition, Molotov, the future president of the Soviet of People's Commissars, said repeatedly: "We must

[2] *Fermerstvo.*

not slip down (!) into poor peasant illusions about the collectivization of the broad peasant masses. In the present circumstances it is no longer possible." It was then, according to the calendar, the end of 1927. So far was the ruling group at that time from its own future policy toward the peasants!

Those same years (1923-28) were passed in a struggle of the ruling coalition, Stalin, Molotov, Rykov, Tomsky, Bukharin (Zinoviev and Kamenev went over to the Opposition in the beginning of 1926), against the advocates of "super-industrialization" and planned leadership. The future historian will re-establish with no small surprise the moods of spiteful disbelief in bold economic initiative with which the government of the socialist state was wholly imbued. An acceleration of the tempo of industrialization took place empirically, under impulses from without, with a crude smashing of all calculations and an extraordinary increase of overhead expenses. The demand for a Five Year Plan, when advanced by the Opposition in 1923, was met with mockery, in the spirit of the petty bourgeois who fears "a leap into the unknown." As late as April, 1927, Stalin asserted at a plenary meeting of the Central Committee that to attempt to build the Dnieperstroy hydroelectric station would be the same thing for us as for the *muzhik* to buy a gramophone instead of a cow. This winged aphorism summed up the whole program. It is worth noting that during those years the bourgeois press of the whole world, and the social-democratic press after it, repeated with sympathy the official attribution to the "Left Opposition" of industrial romanticism.

Amid the noise of party discussions the peasants were replying to the lack of industrial goods with a more and more stubborn strike. They would not take their grain to market, nor increase their sowings. The Right wing (Rykov, Tomsky, Bukharin), who were setting the tone at that period, demanded a broader scope for capitalist tendencies in the village through a raising of the price of grain, even at the cost of a lowered tempo in industry. The sole possible way out under such a policy would have been to import articles of manufacture in exchange for exported agricultural raw materials. But this would have meant to form a "connection" not between the peasant economy and the socialist industries, but between the *kulak* and world capitalism. It was not worthwhile to make the October revolution for that.

Answered the representative of the Opposition at the Party Conference of 1926:

> To accelerate industrialization, in particular by way of increased taxation on the *kulak*, will produce a large mass of goods and lower market prices, and this will be to the advantage both of the worker and of the majority of the peasants. . . . *Face to the village* does not mean turn your back to industry; it means *industry to the village*. For the "face" of the state, if it does not include industry, is of no use to the village.

In answer Stalin thundered against the "fantastic plans" of the Opposition. Industry must not "rush ahead, breaking away from agriculture and abandoning the tempo of accumulation in our country." The party decisions continued to repeat these maxims of passive accommodation to the well-off upper circles of the peasantry. The Fifteenth Party Congress, meeting in December, 1927, for the final smashing of the "super-industrializers," gave warning of "the danger of a too great involvement of state capital in big construction." The ruling faction at that time still refused to see any other dangers.

In the economic year 1927-28, the so-called restoration period in which industry worked chiefly with pre-revolutionary machinery, and agriculture with the old tools, was coming to an end. For any further advance independent industrial construction on a large scale was necessary. It was impossible to lead any further gropingly and without plan.

The hypothetical possibilities of socialist industrialization had been analyzed by the Opposition as early as 1923-25. Their general conclusion was that, after exhausting the equipment inherited from the bourgeoisie, the Soviet industries might, on the basis of socialist accumulation, achieve a rhythm of growth wholly impossible under capitalism. The leaders of the ruling faction openly ridiculed our cautious coefficients in the vicinity of fifteen to eighteen per cent as the fantastic music of an unknown future. This constituted at that time the essence of the struggle against "Trotskyism."

The first official draft of the Five Year Plan, prepared at last in 1927, was completely saturated with the spirit of stingy tinkering. The growth of industrial production was projected with a tempo declining yearly from nine to four per cent. Consumption per person was to increase during the whole five years twelve per cent! The incredible timidity of thought in this first plan comes out clearly in the fact that the state budget at the end of the five years was to constitute in all sixteen per cent of the national income, whereas the budget of Czarist Russia, which had no intention of creating a socialist society, had swallowed eighteen per cent! It is perhaps worth adding that the engineers and economists who drew up this plan were some years later severely judged and punished by law as conscious saboteurs acting under the direction of foreign powers. The accused might have answered, had they dared, that their planning work corresponded perfectly to the "general line" of the Politburo at that time and was carried out under its orders.

The struggle of tendencies was now translated into arithmetical language. "To present on the tenth anniversary of the October revolution such a piddling and completely pessimistic plan," said the platform of the Opposition, "means in reality to work against socialism." A year later the Politburo adopted a new Five Year Plan with an average yearly increase of production amounting to nine per cent. The actual course of the development, however, revealed a stubborn tendency to approach the coefficients of the "supper-industrializers." After another year, when the governmental policy had radically changed, the State Planning Commission drew up a third Five Year Plan, whose rate of growth came far nearer than could have been expected to the hypothetical prognosis made by the Opposition in 1925.

The real history of the economic policy of the Soviet Union, as we thus see, is very different from the official legend. Unfortunately such pious investigators as the Webbs pay not the slightest attention to this.

12

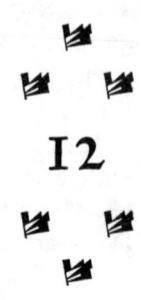

Bureaucratism and the Revolution

TRANSLATED BY MAX SHACHTMAN
from *The New Course* (1943).

(OUTLINE OF A REPORT THAT THE AUTHOR COULD NOT DELIVER)

1. The essential conditions which not only prevent the realization of the socialist ideal but are, in addition, sometimes a source of painful tests and grave dangers to the revolution, are well enough known. They are: a) the internal social contradictions of the revolution which were automatically compressed under war communism but which, under the NEP, unfold unfailingly and seek to find political expression; b) the protracted counterrevolutionary threat to the Soviet republic represented by the imperialist states.

2. The social contradictions of the revolution are class contradictions. What are the fundamental classes of our country? a) the proletariat, b) the peasantry, c) the new bourgeoisie with the layer of bourgeois intellectuals that covers it.

From the standpoint of economic role and political significance, first place belongs to the proletariat organized in the state and to the peasantry that provides the agricultural products dominant in our economy. The new bourgeoisie plays principally the role of intermediary between Soviet industry and agriculture, as well as between the different parts of Soviet industry and the different spheres of rural economy. But it does not confine itself to being a commerical intermediary; in part, it also assumes the role of organizer of production.

3. Putting aside for the moment the question of the tempo of the development of the proletarian revolution in the West, the course of our revolution will be determined by the comparative growth of the three fundamental elements of our economy: state industry, agriculture, and private commercial-industrial capital.

4. Historical analogies with the Great French Revolution (the fall of the Jacobins) made by liberalism and Menshevism for their own nourishment and consolation are superficial and inconsistent. The fall of the Jacobins was predetermined by the lack of maturity of the social relationships: the left (ruined artisans and merchants), deprived of the possibility of economic development, could not be a firm support for the revolution; the right (bourgeoisie) grew irresistibly; finally, Europe, economically and politically more backward, prevented the revolution from spreading beyond the limits of France.

In all these respects our situation is incomparably more favorable. With us, the nucleus as well as the Left wing of the revolution is the proletariat, whose tasks and objectives coincide entirely with the tasks of socialist construction. The proletariat is politically so strong that while permitting, within certain limits, the formation by its side of a new bourgeoisie, it has the peasantry participate in the state power, not through the intermediary of the bourgeoisie and the petty bourgeois parties, but directly, thus barring to the bourgeoisie any access to political life. The economic and political situation of Europe not only does not exclude but makes inevitable the extension of the revolution over its territory.

So that if, in France, even the most clairvoyant policy of the

Jacobins would have been powerless to alter radically the course of events, with us, whose situation is infinitely more favorable, the correctness of a political line drawn according to the methods of Marxism will be for a considerable period of time a decisive factor in safeguarding the revolution.

5. Let us take the historical hypothesis more unfavorable to us. The rapid development of private capital, if it should take place, would signify that Soviet industry and commerce, including the co-operatives, do not assure the satisfaction of the needs of peasant economy. In addition it would show that private capital is interposing itself more and more between the workers' state and the peasantry, is acquiring an economic and therefore a political influence over the latter. It goes without saying that such a rupture between Soviet industry and agriculture, between the proletariat and the peasantry, would constitute a grave danger for the proletarian revolution, a symptom of the possibility of the triumph of the counterrevolution.

6. What are the *political* paths by which the victory of the counterrevolution might come if the *economic* hypothesis just set forth were to be realized? There could be many: either the direct overthrow of the workers' party, or its progressive degeneration, or finally, the conjunction of a partial degeneration, splits, and counterrevolutionary upheavals.

The realization of one or the other of these eventualities would depend above all on the *tempo* of the economic development. In case private capital succeeded, little by little, slowly, in dominating state capital, the political process would assume in the main the character of the degeneration of the state apparatus in a bourgeois direction, with the consequences that this would involve for the party. If private capital increased rapidly and succeeded in fusing with the peasantry, the active counterrevolutionary tendencies directed against the Communist Party would then probably prevail.

If we set forth these hypotheses bluntly, it is of course not because we consider them historically probable (on the contrary, their probability is at a minimum), but because only such a way of putting the question makes possible a more correct and complete historical orientation and, consequently, the adoption of all possible preventive measures. The superiority of us Marxists is in distinguishing and grasping the new tendencies and the new dangers even when they are still only in an embryonic stage.

7. The conclusion from what we have already said in the economic domain brings us to the problem of the "scissors," that is, to the rational organization of industry and to its co-ordination with the peasant market. To lose time in this connection is to slow down our struggle against private capital. That is where the principal task is, the essential key to the problem of the revolution and of socialism.

8. If the counterrevolutionary danger arises, as we have said, out of certain social relationships, this in no wise means that by a rational policy it is not possible to parry this danger (even under economic conditions unfavorable for the revolution), to reduce it, to remove it, to postpone it. Such a postponement is in turn apt to save the revolution by assuring it either a favorable economic shift at home or contact with the victorious revolution in Europe.

That is why, on the basis of the economic policy indicated above, we must have a definite state and party policy (including a definite policy inside the party), aimed at counteracting the accumulation and consolidation of the tendencies directed against the dictatorship of the working class and nurtured by the difficulties and failures of the economic development.

9. The heterogeneity of the social composition of our party reflects the objective contradictions of the development of the revolution, along with the tendencies and dangers flowing from it:

The factory nuclei which assure the contact of the party with the essential class of the revolution now represent one-sixth of the membership of the party.

In spite of all their negative sides, the cells of the Soviet institutions assure the party its leadership of the state apparatus; which also determines the great specific weight of these cells. A large percentage of old militants take part in the life of the party through the medium of these Soviet cells.

The rural cells give the party a certain contact (still very weak) with the countryside.

The military cells effect the contact of the party with the army, and by means of the latter, with the countryside too (above all).

Finally, in the cells of the educational institutions, all these tendencies and influences mingle and cross.

10. By their class composition, the factory cells are, it goes without saying, fundamental. But inasmuch as they constitute only one-sixth of the party and their most active elements are taken away to be assigned to the party or the state apparatus, the party cannot yet, unfortunately, lean exclusively or even principally upon them.

Their growth will be the surest gauge of the success of the party in industry, in economy in general, and at the same time the best guarantee that it will retain its proletarian character. But it is hardly possible to expect their speedy growth in the immediate future. As a result, the party will be obliged in the next period to assure its internal equilibrium and its revolutionary line by leaning on cells of a *heterogeneous* social composition.

11. The counterrevolutionary tendencies can find a support among the *kulaks*, the middlemen, the retailers, the concessionaries, in a word, among elements much more capable of surrounding the state apparatus than the party itself. Only the peasant and the military cells might be threatened by a more direct influence and even a penetration by the *kulaks*.

Nevertheless, the differentiation of the peasantry represents a factor which will be of help to us. The exclusion of *kulaks* from the army (including the territorial divisions) should not only remain an untouchable rule but what is more, become an important measure for the political education of the rural youth, the military units and particularly the military cells.

The workers will assure their leading role in the military cells by counterposing politically the rural working masses of the army to the renascent stratum of the *kulaks*. In the rural cells, too, this counterposition applies. The success of the work will naturally depend, in the long run, upon the extent to which state industry succeeds in satisfying the needs of the countryside.

But whatever the speed of our economic successes may be, our fundamental political line in the military cells must be directed not simply against the Nepmen, but primarily against the renascent *kulak* stratum, the only historically conceivable and serious support for any and all counterrevolutionary attempts. In this respect, we need more minute analysis of the various components of the army from the standpoint of their social composition.

12. It is beyond doubt that through the medium of the rural and military cells, tendencies reflecting more or less the countryside, with the special traits that distinguish it from the town, filter and will continue to filter into the party. If that were not the case, the rural cells would have no value for the party.

The changes in mood that manifest themselves in the cells are a reminder or a warning to the party. The possibility of directing these cells according to the party line depends on the correctness of the general direction of the party as well as upon its internal regime and, in the last analysis, on whether we come closer to solving or attenuating the problem of the "scissors."

13. The state apparatus is the most important source of bureaucratism. On the one hand, it absorbs an enormous quantity of the most active party elements and it teaches the most capable of them the methods of administration of men and things, instead of political leadership of the masses. On the other hand, it preoccupies largely the attention of the party apparatus over which it exerts influence by its methods of administration.

Thence, in large measure, the bureaucratization of the apparatus, which threatens to separate the party from the masses. This is precisely the danger that is now most obvious and direct. The struggle against the other dangers must under present conditions begin with the struggle against bureaucratism.

14. It is unworthy of a Marxist to consider that bureaucratism is only the aggregate of the bad habits of office holders. Bureaucratism is a social phenomenon in that it is a definite system of administration of men and things. Its profound causes lie in the heterogeneity of society, the difference be-

tween the daily and the fundamental interests of various groups of the population. Bureaucratism is complicated by the fact of the lack of culture of the broad masses. With us, the essential source of bureaucratism resides in the necessity of creating and sustaining a state apparatus that unites the interests of the proletariat and those of the peasantry in a perfect economic harmony, from which we are still far removed. The necessity of maintaining a permanent army is likewise another important source of bureaucratism.

It is quite plain that precisely the negative social phenomena we have just enumerated and which now nurture bureaucratism could place the revolution in peril should they continue to develop. We have mentioned above this hypothesis: the growing discord between state and peasant economy, the growth of the *kulaks* in the country, their alliance with private commercial-industrial capital: these would be—given the low cultural level of the toiling masses of the countryside and in part of the towns—the causes of the eventual counterrevolutionary dangers.

In other words, bureaucratism in the state and party apparatus is the expression of the most vexatious tendencies inherent in our situation, of the defects and deviations in our work which, under certain social conditions, might sap the basis of the revolution. And, in this case as in many others, quantity will at a certain stage be transformed into quality.

15. The struggle against the bureaucratism of the state apparatus is an exceptionally important but prolonged task, one that runs more or less parallel to our other fundamental tasks: economic reconstruction and the elevation of the cultural level of the masses.

The most important historical instrument for the accomplishment of all these tasks is the party. Naturally, not even the party can tear itself away from the social and cultural conditions of the country. But as the voluntary organization of the vanguard, of the best, the most active and the most conscious elements of the working class, it is able to preserve itself much better than can the state apparatus from the tendencies of bureaucratism. For that, it must see the danger clearly and combat it without let-up.

Thence the immense importance of the education of the party youth, based upon personal initiative, in order to serve the state apparatus in a new manner and to transform it completely.

13

"Five Year Plan in Four Years" and "Complete Collectivization"

TRANSLATED BY MAX EASTMAN
from *The Revolution Betrayed* (1937).

Irresoluteness before the individual peasant enterprises, distrust of large plans, defense of a minimum tempo, neglect of international problems—all this taken together formed the essence of the theory of "socialism in one country," first put forward by Stalin in the autumn of 1924 after the defeat of the proletariat in Germany. Not to hurry with industrialization, not to quarrel with the *muzhik*, not to count on world revolution, and above all to protect the power of the party bureaucracy from criticism! The differentiation of the peasantry was denounced as an invention of the Opposition. The above-mentioned Yakovlev dismissed the Central Statistical Bureau, whose records gave the *kulak* a greater place than was satisfactory to the authorities, while the leaders tranquilly asserted that the goods famine was outliving itself, that "a peaceful tempo in economic development was at hand," that the grain collections would in the future be carried on more "evenly," etc. The strengthened *kulak* carried with him the middle peasant and subjected the cities to a grain blockade. In January, 1928, the working class stood face to face with the shadow of an advancing famine. History knows how to play spiteful jokes. In that very month, when the *kulaks* were taking the revolution by the throat, the representatives of the Left Opposition were thrown into prison or banished to different parts of Siberia in punishment for their "panic" before the specter of the *kulak*.

The government tried to pretend that the grain strike was caused by the naked hostility of the *kulak* (where did he come from?) to the socialist state—that is, by ordinary political motives. But the *kulak* is little inclined to that kind of "idealism." If he hid his grain, it was because the bargain offered him was unprofitable. For the very same reason he managed to bring under his influence wide sections of the peasantry. Mere repressions against *kulak* sabotage were obviously inadequate. It was necessary to change the policy. Even yet, however, no little time was spent in vacillation.

Rykov, then still head of the government, announced in July, 1928: "To develop individual farms is . . . the chief task of the party." And Stalin seconded him: "There are people who think that individual farms have exhausted their usefulness, that we should not support them. . . . These people have nothing in common with the line of our party." Less than a year later, the line of the party had nothing in common with those words. The dawn of "complete collectivization" was on the horizon.

The new orientation was arrived at just as empirically as the preceding, and by way of a hidden struggle within the governmental bloc. "The groups of the Right and Center are united by a general hostility to the Opposition"—thus the platform of the Left gave warning a year before—"and the cutting off of the latter will inevitably accelerate the coming struggle between these two." And so it happened. The leaders of the disintegrating bloc would not for anything, of course, admit that this prognosis of the left wing, like many others, had come true. As late as the nineteenth of October, 1928, Stalin announced publicly: "It is time to stop gossiping about the existence of a Right deviation and a conciliatory attitude towards it in the Politburo of our Central Committee." Both groups at that time were feeling out the party machine. The repressed party was living on dark rumors and guesses. But in just a few months the official press, with its usual freedom from embarrassment, announced that the head of the government, Rykov, "had speculated on the economic difficulties of the Soviet power"; that the head of the Communist International, Bukharin, was "a conducting wire of bourgeois-liberal influences"; that Tomsky, president of the all-Russian Central Council of Trade Unions, was nothing but a miserable trade-unionist. All three, Rykov, Bukharin and Tomsky were members of the Politburo. Whereas the whole preceding struggle against the Left Opposition had taken its weapons from the right groups, Bukharin was now able, without sinning against the truth, to accuse Stalin of using in his struggle with the Right a part of the condemned Left Opposition platform.

In one way or another the change was made. The slogan "Get rich!" together with the theory of the *kulak*'s growing painlessly into socialism, was belatedly, but all the more decisively, condemned. Industrialization was put upon the order of the day. Self-satisfied quietism was replaced by a panic of haste. The half-forgotten slogan of Lenin, "catch up with and outstrip," was filled out with the words, "in the shortest possible time." The minimalist Five Year Plan, already confirmed in principle by a congress of the party, gave place to a new plan, the fundamental elements of which were borrowed *in toto* from the platform of the shattered Left Opposition. Dnieperstroy, only yesterday likened to a gramophone, today occupied the center of attention.

After the first new successes the slogan was advanced: "Achieve the Five Year Plan in Four Years." The startled empiricists now decided that everything was possible. Opportunism, as has often happened in history, turned into its opposite, adventurism. Whereas from 1923 to 1928 the Politburo had been ready to accept Bukharin's philosophy of a "tortoise tempo," it now lightly jumped from a twenty to a thirty per cent yearly growth, trying to convert every partial and temporary achievement into a norm, and losing sight of the conditioning interrelation of the different branches of industry. The financial holes in the plan were stopped up with printed paper. During the years of the first plan the number of bank notes in circulation rose from 1.7 billion to 5.5, and by the beginning of the second Five Year Plan had reached 8.4 billion rubles. The bureaucracy not only freed itself from the political control of the masses, upon whom this forced industrialization was laying an unbearable burden, but also from the automatic control exercised by the chervonetz.[1] The currency system, put on a solid basis at the beginning of the NEP, was now again shaken to its roots.

The chief danger, however, and that not only for the fulfillment of the plan but for the regime itself, appeared from the side of the peasants.

On February 15, 1928, the population of the country learned with surprise from an editorial in *Pravda* that the villages looked not at all the way they had been portrayed up to that moment by the authorities, but on the contrary very much as the expelled Left Opposition had presented them. The press which only yesterday had been denying the existence of the *kulaks*, today, on a signal from above, discovered them not only in the villages, but in the party itself. It was revealed that the communist nuclei were frequently dominated by rich peasants possessing complicated machinery, employing hired labor, concealing from the government hundreds and thousands of poods[2] of grain, and implacably denouncing the "Trotskyist" policy. The newspapers vied with each other in printing sensational exposures of how *kulaks* in the position of local secretaries were denying admission to the party to poor peasants and hired hands. All the old criteria were turned upside down; minuses and pluses changed places.

In order to feed the cities, it was necessary immediately to take from the *kulak* the daily bread. This could be achieved only by force. The expropriation of the grain reserve, and that not only of the *kulak* but of the middle peasant, was called, in the official language, "extraordinary measures." This phrase

[1] [Theoretical par = $5.00.—Tr.]
[2] [One pood = approximately 36 pounds.—Tr.]

is supposed to mean that tomorrow everything will fall back into the old rut. But the peasants did not believe these fine words, and they were right. The violent seizures of grain deprived the well-off peasants of their motive to increased sowings. The hired hands and the poor peasants found themselves without work. Agriculture again arrived in a blind alley, and with it the state. It was necessary at any cost to reform the "general line."

Stalin and Molotov, still giving individual farming the chief place, began to emphasize the necessity of a swifter development of the Soviet and collective farms. But since the bitter need of food did not permit a cessation of military expeditions into the country, the program of promoting individual farms was left hanging in the air. It was necessary to "slip down" to collectivization. The temporary "extraordinary measures" for the collection of grain developed unexpectedly into a program of "liquidation of the *kulaks* as a class." From the shower of contradictory commands, more copious than food rations, it became evident that on the peasant question the government had not only no Five Year Plan, but not even a five months' program.

According to the new plan, drawn up under the spur of a food crisis, collective farms were at the end of five years to comprise about twenty per cent of the peasant holdings. This program—whose immensity will be clear when you consider that during the preceding ten years collectivization had affected less than one per cent of the country—was nevertheless by the middle of the five years left far behind. In November, 1929, Stalin, abandoning his own vacillations, announced the end of individual farming. The peasants, he said, are entering the collective farms "in whole villages, counties and even provinces." Yakovlev, who two years before had insisted that the collectives would for many years remain only "islands in a sea of peasant holdings," now received an order as People's Commissar of Agriculture to "liquidate the *kulaks* as a class," and establish complete collectivization at "the earliest possible date." In the year 1929, the proportion of collective farms rose from 1.7 per cent to 3.9 per cent. In 1930 it rose to 23.6, in 1931 to 52.7, in 1932 to 61.5 per cent.

At the present time hardly anybody would be foolish enough to repeat the twaddle of liberals to the effect that collectivization as a whole was accomplished by naked force. In former historical epochs the peasants in their struggle for land have at one time raised an insurrection against the landlords, at another sent a stream of colonizers into untilled regions, at still another rushed into all kinds of sects which promised to reward the *muzhik* with heaven's vacancies for his narrow quarters on earth. Now, after the expropriation of the great estates and the extreme parcelation of the land, the union of these small parcels into big tracts had become a question of life and death for the peasants, for agriculture, and for society as a whole.

The problem, however, is far from settled by these general historic considerations. The real possibilities of collectivization are determined, not by the depth of the impasse in the villages and not by the administrative energy of the government, but primarily by the existing productive resources—that is, the ability of the industries to furnish large-scale agriculture with the requisite machinery. These material conditions were lacking. The collective farms were set up with an equipment suitable in the main only for small-scale farming. In these conditions an exaggeratedly swift collectivization took the character of an economic adventure.

Caught unawares by the radicalism of its own shift of policy, the government did not and could not make even an elementary political preparation for the new course. Not only the peasant masses, but even the local organs of power were ignorant of what was being demanded of them. The peasants were heated white-hot by rumors that their cattle and property were to be seized by the state. This rumor, too, was not so far from the truth. Actually realizing their own former caricature of the Left Opposition, the bureaucracy "robbed the villages." Collectivization appeared to the peasant primarily in the form of an expropriation of all his belongings. They collectivized not only horses, cows, sheep, pigs, but even new-born chickens. They "dekulakized," as one foreign observer wrote, "down to the felt shoes, which they draggged from the feet of little children." As a result there was an epidemic selling of cattle for a song by the peasants, or a slaughter of cattle for meat and hides.

In January, 1930, at a Moscow congress, a member of the Central Committee, Andreyev, drew a two-sided picture of collectivization: On the one side he asserted that a collective movement powerfully developing throughout the whole country "will now destroy upon its road each and every obstacle"; on the other, a predatory sale by the peasants of their own implements, stock and even seeds before entering the collectives "is assuming positively menacing proportions." However contradictory those two generalizations may be, they show correctly from opposite sides the epidemic character of collectivization as a measure of despair. "Complete collectivization," wrote the same foreign critic, "plunged the national economy into a condition of ruin almost without precedent, as though a three years' war had passed over."

Twenty-five million isolated peasant egos, which yesterday had been the sole motive force of agriculture—weak as an old farmer's nag, but nevertheless forces—the bureaucracy tried to replace at one gesture by the commands of two thousand collective farm administrative offices, lacking technical equipment, agronomic knowledge and the support of the peasants themselves. The dire consequences of this adventurism soon followed, and they lasted for a number of years. The total harvest of grain, which had risen in 1930 to 835 million hundredweight, fell in the next two years below 700 million. The difference does not seem catastrophic in itself, but it meant a loss of just that quantity of grain needed to keep the towns even at their customary hunger norm. In technical culture the results were still worse. On the eve of collectivization the production of sugar had reached almost 109 million poods, and at the height of complete collectivization it had fallen, owing to a lack of beets, to 48 million poods—that is, to half of what it had been. But the most devastating hurricane hit the animal kingdom. The number of horses fell fifty-five per cent —from 34.6 million in 1929 to 15.6 million in 1934. The number of horned cattle fell from 30.7 million to 19.5 million—that is, forty per cent. The number of pigs, fifty-five per cent; sheep, sixty-six per cent. The destruction of people—by hunger, cold, epidemics and measures of repression—is unfortunately less accurately tabulated than the slaughter of stock, but it also mounts up to millions. The blame for these sacrifices lies not upon collectivization, but upon the blind, violent, gambling methods with which it was carried through. The bureaucracy foresaw nothing. Even the constitutions of the collectives, which made an attempt to bind up the personal interests of the peasants with the welfare of the farm, were not published until after the unhappy villages had been thus cruelly laid waste.

The forced character of this new course rose from the necessity of finding some salvation from the consequences of the policy of 1923-28. But even so, collectivization could and should have assumed a more reasonable tempo and more deliberated forms. Having in its hands both the power and the industries, the bureaucracy could have regulated the process without carrying the nation to the edge of disaster. They could have, and should have, adopted tempos better corresponding to the material and moral resources of the country.

> Under favorable circumstances, external and internal, [wrote the émigré organ of the Left Opposition in 1930] the material-technical conditions of agriculture can in the course of some ten or fifteen years be transformed to the bottom, and provide the productive basis for collectivization. However, during the intervening years there would be time to overthrow the Soviet power more than once.

This warning was not exaggerated. Never before had the breath of destruction hung so directly above the territory of the October revolution as in the years of complete collectivization. Discontent, a distrust, bitterness were corroding the country. The disturbance of the currency, the mounting up of stable, "conventional," and free market prices, the transition from a simulacrum of *trade* between the state and the peasants to a grain, meat and milk *levy*, the life-and-death struggle with mass plunderings of the collective property and mass concealment of these plunderings, the purely military mobilization of the party for the struggle against *kulak* sabotage (after the "liquidation" of the *kulaks* as a class); together with this, a return to food cards and hunger rations, and finally a restoration of the passport system—all these measures revived throughout the country the atmosphere of the seemingly so long ended civil war.

The supply to the factories of food and raw materials grew worse from season to season. Unbearable working conditions caused a migration of labor power, malingering, careless work, breakdown of machines, a high percentage of trashy products and general low quality. The average productivity of labor declined 11.7 per cent in 1931. According to an incidental acknowledgment of Molotov, printed in the whole Soviet press, industrial production in 1932 rose only 8.5 per cent, instead of the 36 per cent indicated by the year's plan. To be sure, the world was informed soon after this that the Five Year Plan had been fulfilled in four years and three months. But that means only that the cynicism of the bureaucracy in its manipulation of statistics and public opinion is without limit. That, however, is not the chief thing. Not the fate of the Five Year Plan, but the fate of the regime was at stake.

The regime survived.

But that is the merit of the regime itself, which had put down deep roots in the popular soil. It is in no less degree due to favorable external circumstances. In those years of economic chaos and civil war in the villages, the Soviet Union was essentially paralyzed in the face of a foreign enemy. The discontent of the peasantry swept through the army. Mistrust and vacillation demoralized the bureaucratic machine and the commanding cadres. A blow either from the East or West at that period might have had fatal consequences.

Fortunately, the first years of a crisis in trade and industry had created throughout the capitalist world moods of bewildered watchful waiting. Nobody was ready for war; nobody dared attempt it. Moreover, in no one of the hostile countries was there an adequate realization of the acuteness of these social convulsions which were shaking the land of Soviets under the roar of the official music in honor of the "general line."

The zigzags of the governmental course have reflected not only the objective contradictions of the situation, but also the inadequate ability of the leaders to understand these contradictions in season and react prophylactically against them. It is not easy to express the mistakes of the leadership in bookkeeper's magnitudes, but our schematic exposition of the history of these zigzags permits the conclusion that they have imposed upon the Soviet economy an immense burden of overhead expenses.

It remains of course incomprehensible—at least with a rational approach to history—how and why a faction the least rich of all in ideas, and the most burdened with mistakes, should have gained the upper hand over all other groups, and concentrated an unlimited power in its hands. Our further analysis will give us a key to this problem too. We shall see, at the same time, how the bureaucratic methods of autocratic leadership are coming into sharper and sharper conflict with the demands of economy and culture, and with what inevitable necessity new crises and disturbances arise in the development of the Soviet Union.

However, before taking up the dual role of the "socialist" bureaucracy, we must answer the question: What is the net result of the preceding successes? Is socialism really achieved in the Soviet Union? Or, more cautiously: Do the present economic and cultural achievements constitute a guarantee against the danger of capitalist restoration—just as bourgeois society at a certain stage of its development became insured by its own successes against a restoration of serfdom and feudalism?

14

The Degeneration of the Bolshevik Party

TRANSLATED BY MAX EASTMAN
from *The Revolution Betrayed* (1937).

The Bolshevik party prepared and insured the October victory. It also created the Soviet state, supplying it with a sturdy skeleton. The degeneration of the party became both cause and consequence of the bureaucratization of the state. It is necessary to show at least briefly how this happened.

The inner regime of the Bolshevik party was characterized by the method of *democratic centralism*. The combination of these two concepts, democracy and centralism, is not in the least contradictory. The party took watchful care not only that its boundaries should always be strictly defined, but also that all those who entered these boundaries should enjoy the actual right to define the direction of the party policy. Freedom of criticism and intellectual struggle was an irrevocable content of the party democracy. The present doctrine that Bolshevism does not tolerate factions is a myth of the epoch of decline. In reality the history of Bolshevism is a history of the struggle of factions. And, indeed, how could a genuinely revolutionary organization, setting itself the task of overthrowing the world and uniting under its banner the most audacious iconoclasts, fighters and insurgents, live and develop without intellectual conflicts, without groupings and temporary factional formations? The farsightedness of the Bolshevik leadership often made it possible to soften conflicts and shorten the duration of factional struggle, but no more than that. The Central Committee relied upon this seething democratic support. From this it derived the audacity to make decisions and give orders. The obvious correctness of the leadership at all critical stages gave it that high authority which is the priceless moral capital of centralism.

The regime of the Bolshevik party, especially before it came to power, stood thus in complete contradiction to the regime of the present sections of the Communist International, with their "leaders" appointed from above, making complete changes of policy at a word of command, with their uncontrolled apparatus, haughty in its attitude to the rank and file, servile in its attitude to the Kremlin. But in the first years after the conquest of power also, even when the administrative rust was already visible on the party, every Bolshevik, not excluding Stalin, would have denounced as a malicious slanderer anyone who should have shown him on a screen the image of the party ten or fifteen years later.

The very center of Lenin's attention and that of his colleagues was occupied by a continual concern with protecting the Bolshevik ranks from the vices of those in power. However, the extraordinary closeness and at times actual merging of the party with the state apparatus had already in those first years done indubitable harm to the freedom and elasticity of the party regime. Democracy had been narrowed in proportion as difficulties increased. In the beginning, the party had wished and hoped to preserve freedom of political struggle within the framework of the Soviets. The civil war introduced stern amendments into this calculation. The Opposition parties were forbidden one after the other. This measure, obviously in conflict with the spirit of Soviet democracy, the leaders of Bolshevism regarded not as a principle, but as an episodic act of self-defense.

The swift growth of the ruling party, with the novelty and immensity of its tasks, inevitably gave rise to inner disagreements. The underground oppositional currents in the country exerted a pressure through various channels upon the sole legal political organization, increasing the acuteness of the factional struggle. At the moment of completion of the civil war, this struggle took such sharp forms as to threaten to unsettle the state power. In March, 1921, in the days of the Kronstadt revolt, which attracted into its ranks no small number of Bolsheviks, the tenth congress of the party thought it necessary to resort to a prohibition of factions—that is, to transfer the political regime prevailing in the state to the inner life of the ruling party. This forbidding of factions was again regarded as an exceptional measure to be abandoned at the first serious improvement in the situation. At the same time, the Central Committee was extremely cautious in applying the new law, concerning itself most of all lest it lead to a strangling of the inner life of the party.

However, what was in its original design merely a necessary concession to a difficult situation proved perfectly suited to the taste of the bureaucracy, which had then begun to approach the inner life of the party exclusively from the viewpoint of convenience in administration. Already in 1922, during a brief improvement in his health, Lenin, horrified at the threatening growth of bureaucratism, was preparing a struggle against the faction of Stalin, which had made itself the axis of the party machine as a first step toward capturing the machinery of state. A second stroke and then death prevented him from measuring forces with this internal reaction.

The entire effort of Stalin, with whom at that time Zinoviev and Kamenev were working hand in hand, was thenceforth directed to freeing the party machine from the control of the rank-and-file members of the party. In this struggle for "stability" of the Central Committee, Stalin proved the most consistent and reliable among his colleagues. He had no need to tear himself away from international problems; he had never been concerned with them. The petty-bourgeois outlook of the new ruling stratum was his own outlook. He profoundly believed that the task of creating socialism was national and administrative in its nature. He looked upon the Communist International as a necessary evil which should be used so far as possible for the purposes of foreign policy. His own party kept a value in his eyes merely as a submissive support for the machine.

Together with the theory of socialism in one country, there was put into circulation by the bureaucracy a theory that in Bolshevism the Central Committee is everything and the party nothing. This second theory was in any case realized with more success than the first. Availing itself of the death of Lenin, the ruling group announced a "Leninist levy." The gates of the party, always carefully guarded, were now thrown wide open. Workers, clerks, petty officials, flocked through in crowds. The political aim of this maneuver was to dissolve the revolutionary vanguard in raw human material, without experience, without independence, and yet with the old habit of submitting to the authorities. The scheme was successful. By freeing the bureaucracy from the control of the proletarian vanguard, the "Leninist levy" dealt a deathblow to the party of Lenin. The machine had won the necessary independence. Democratic centralism gave place to bureaucratic centralism. In the party apparatus itself there now took place a radical reshuffling of personnel from top to bottom. The chief merit of a Bolshevik was declared to be obedience. Under the guise of a struggle with the Opposition, there occurred a sweeping replacement of revolutionists with *chinovniks*.[1] The history of the Bolshevik party became a history of its rapid degeneration.

The political meaning of the developing struggle was darkened for many by the circumstance that the leaders of all three groupings, Left, Center and Right, belonged to one and the same staff in the Kremlin, the Politburo. To superficial minds it seemed to be a mere matter of personal rivalry, a struggle for the "heritage" of Lenin. But in the conditions of iron dictatorship social antagonisms could not show themselves at first except through the institutions of the ruling party. Many Thermidorians emerged in their day from the circle of

[1] [Professional governmental functionaries.—Tr.]

the Jacobins. Bonaparte himself belonged to that circle in his early years, and subsequently it was from among former Jacobins that the First Consul and Emperor of France selected his most faithful servants. Times change and the Jacobins with them, not excluding the Jacobins of the twentieth century.

Of the Politburo of Lenin's epoch there now remains only Stalin. Two of its members, Zinoviev and Kamenev, collaborators of Lenin throughout many years as émigrés, are enduring ten-year prison terms for a crime which they did not commit. Three other members, Rykov, Bukharin and Tomsky, are completely removed from the leadership, but as a reward for submission occupy secondary posts. And, finally, the author of these lines is in exile. The widow of Lenin, Krupskaya, is also under the ban, having proved unable with all her efforts to adjust herself completely to the Thermidor.

The members of the present Politburo occupied secondary posts throughout the history of the Bolshevik party. If anybody in the first years of the revolution had predicted their future elevation, they would have been the first in surprise, and there would have been no false modesty in their surprise. For this very reason, the rule is more stern at present that the Politburo is always right, and in any case that no man can be right against the Politburo. But, moreover, the Politburo cannot be right against Stalin, who is unable to make mistakes and consequently cannot be right against himself.

Demands for party democracy were through all this time the slogans of all the oppositional groups, as insistent as they were hopeless. The above-mentioned platform of the Left Opposition demanded in 1927 that a special law be written into the Criminal Code "punishing as a serious state crime every direct or indirect persecution of a worker for criticism." Instead of this, there was introduced into the Criminal Code an article against the Left Opposition itself.

Of party democracy there remained only recollections in the memory of the older generation. And together with it had disappeared the democracy of the Soviets, the trade unions, the co-operatives, the cultural and athletic organizations. Above each and every one of them there reigns an unlimited hierarchy of party secretaries. The regime had become "totalitarian" in character several years before this word arrived from Germany. Rakovsky wrote in 1928:

> By means of demoralizing methods, which convert thinking communists into machines, destroying will, character and human dignity, the ruling circles have succeeded in converting themselves into an unremovable and inviolate oligarchy, which replaces the class and the party.

Since those indignant lines were written, the degeneration of the regime has gone immeasurably further. The GPU has become the decisive factor in the inner life of the party. If Molotov in March, 1936, was able to boast to a French journalist that the ruling party no longer contains any factional struggle, it is only because disagreements are now settled by the automatic intervention of the political police. The old Bolshevik party is dead, and no force will resurrect it.

Parallel with the political degeneration of the party, there occurred a moral decay of the uncontrolled apparatus. The word "sovbour"—Soviet bourgeois—as applied to a privileged dignitary, appeared very early in the workers' vocabulary. With the transfer to the NEP, bourgeois tendencies received a more copious field of action. At the Eleventh Party Congress, in March, 1922, Lenin gave warning of the danger of a degeneration of the ruling stratum. It has occurred more than once in history, he said, that the conqueror took over the culture of the conquered, when the latter stood on a higher level. The culture of the Russian bourgeoisie and the old bureaucracy was, to be sure, miserable, but, alas, the new ruling stratum must often take off its hat to that culture. "Four thousand seven hundred responsible communists" in Moscow administer the state machine. "Who is leading whom? I doubt very much whether you can say that the communists are in the lead. . . ." In subsequent congresses, Lenin could not speak. But all his thoughts in the last months of his active life were of warning and arming the workers against the oppression, caprice and decay of the bureaucracy. He, however, saw only the first symptoms of the disease.

Christian Rakovsky, former president of the Soviet of People's Commissars of the Ukraine, and later Soviet Ambassador in London and Paris, sent to his friends in 1928, when already in exile, a brief inquiry into the Soviet bureaucracy, which still remains the best that has been written on this subject:

> In the mind of Lenin, and in all our minds, the task of the party leadership was to protect both the party and the working class from the corrupting action of privilege, place and patronage on the part of those in power, from *rapprochement* with the relics of the old nobility and burgherdom, from the corrupting influence of the NEP, from the temptation of bourgeois morals and ideologies. . . . We must say frankly, definitely and loudly that the party apparatus has not fulfilled this task, that it has revealed a complete incapacity for its double role of protector and educator. It has failed. It is bankrupt.

It is true that Rakovsky himself, broken by the bureaucratic repressions, subsequently repudiated his own critical judgments. But the seventy-year-old Galileo, too, caught in the vise of the Holy Inquisition, found himself compelled to repudiate the system of Copernicus—which did not prevent the earth from continuing to revolve around the sun. We do not believe in the recantation of the sixty-year-old Rakovsky, for he himself has more than once made a withering analysis of such recantations. As to his political criticisms, they have found in the facts of the objective development a far more reliable support than in the subjective stout-heartedness of their author.

The conquest of power changes not only the relations of the proletariat to other classes, but also its own inner structure. The wielding of power becomes the specialty of a definite social group, which is the more impatient to solve its own "social problem," the higher its opinion of its own mission.

> In a proletarian state, where capitalist accumulation is forbidden to the members of the ruling party, the differ-

entiation is at first functional, but afterward becomes social. I do not say it becomes a class differentiation, but a social one. . . .

Rakovsky further explains:

The social situation of the communist who has at his disposition an automobile, a good apartment, regular vacations, and receives the party maximum of salary, differs from the situation of the communist who works in the coal mines, where he receives from fifty to sixty rubles a month.

Counting over the causes of the degeneration of the Jacobins when in power—the chase after wealth, participation in government contracts, supplies, etc., Rakovsky cites a curious remark of Babeuf to the effect that the degeneration of the new ruling stratum was helped along not a little by the former young ladies of the aristocracy, toward whom the Jacobins were very friendly. "What are you doing, small-hearted plebeian?" cries Babeuf. "Today they are embracing you and tomorrow they will strangle you." A census of the wives of the ruling stratum in the Soviet Union would show a similar picture. The well-known Soviet journalist, Sosnovsky, pointed out the special role played by the "automobile-harem factor" in forming the morals of the Soviet bureaucracy. It is true that Sosnovsky, too, following Rakovsky, recanted and was returned from Siberia. But that did not improve the morals of the bureaucracy. On the contrary, that very recantation is proof of a progressing demoralization.

The old articles of Sosnovsky, passed about in manuscript from hand to hand, were sprinkled with unforgettable episodes from the life of the new ruling stratum, plainly showing to what vast degree the conquerors have assimilated the morals of the conquered. Not to return, however, to past years—for Sosnovsky finally exchanged his whip for a lyre in 1934—we will confine ourselves to wholly fresh examples from the Soviet press. And we will not select the abuses and so-called excesses, either, but everyday phenomena legalized by official social opinion.

The director of a Moscow factory, a prominent communist,

boasts in *Pravda* of the cultural growth of the enterprise directed by him.

A mechanic telephones: "What is your order, sir, check the furnace immediately or wait?" I answer: "Wait."

The mechanic addresses the director with extreme respect, using the second person plural, while the director answers him in the second person singular.[2] And this disgraceful dialogue, impossible in any cultured capitalist country, is related by the director himself on the pages of *Pravda* as something entirely normal! The editor does not object because he does not notice it. The readers do not object because they are accustomed to it. We also are not surprised, for at solemn sessions in the Kremlin, the "leaders" and People's Commissars address in the second person singular directors of factories subordinate to them, presidents of collective farms, shop foremen and working women, especially invited to receive decorations. How can they fail to remember that one of the most popular revolutionary slogans in Czarist Russia was the demand for the abolition of the use of the second person singular by bosses in addressing their subordinates!

These Kremlin dialogues of the authorities with "the people," astonishing in their lordly ungraciousness, unmistakably testify that, in spite of the October revolution, the nationalization of the means of production, collectivization, and "the liquidation of the *kulaks* as a class," the relations among men, and that at the very height of the Soviet pyramid, have not only not yet risen to socialism, but in many respects are still lagging behind a cultured capitalism. In recent years enormous backward steps have been taken in this very important sphere. And the source of this revival of genuine Russian barbarism is indubitably the Soviet Thermidor, which has given complete independence and freedom from control to a bureaucracy possessing little culture, and has given to the masses the well-known gospel of obedience and silence.

We are far from intending to contrast the abstraction of dic-

---

[2] [It is impossible to convey the flavor of this dialogue in English. The second person singular is used either with intimates in token of affection, or with children, servants and animals in token of superiority.—Tr.]

tatorship with the abstraction of democracy, and weigh their merits on the scales of pure reason. Everything is relative in this world, where change alone endures. The dictatorship of the Bolshevik party proved one of the most powerful instruments of progress in history. But here too, in the words of the poet, "Reason becomes unreason, kindness a pest." The prohibition of oppositional parties brought after it the prohibition of factions. The prohibition of factions ended in a prohibition to think otherwise than the infallible leaders. The police-manufactured monolithism of the party resulted in a bureaucratic impunity which has become the source of all kinds of wantonness and corruption.

THE SOCIAL ROOTS OF THERMIDOR

We have defined the Soviet Thermidor as a triumph of the bureaucracy over the masses. We have tried to disclose the historic conditions of this triumph. The revolutionary vanguard of the proletariat was in part devoured and gradually demoralized by the administrative apparatus, in part annihilated in the civil war, and in part thrown out and crushed. The tired and disappointed masses were indifferent to what was happening on the summits. These conditions, however, important as they may have been in themselves, are inadequate to explain why the bureaucracy succeeded in raising itself above society and getting its fate firmly into its own hands. Its own will to this would in any case be inadequate; the arising of a new ruling stratum must have deep social causes.

The victory of the Thermidorians over the Jacobins in the eighteenth century was also aided by the weariness of the masses and the demoralization of the leading cadres, but beneath these essentially incidental phenomena a deep organic process was taking place. The Jacobins rested upon the lower petty bourgeoisie lifted by the great wave. The revolution of the eighteenth century, however, corresponding to the course of development of the productive forces, could not but bring the great bourgeoisie to political ascendancy in the long run. The Thermidor was only one of the stages in this inevitable process. What similar social necessity found expression in the

Soviet Thermidor? We have tried already in one of the preceding chapters to make a preliminary answer to the question why the gendarme triumphed. We must now prolong our analysis of the conditions of the transition from capitalism to socialism, and the role of the state in this process. Let us again compare theoretic prophecy with reality.

> It is still necessary to suppress the bourgeoisie and its resistance, [wrote Lenin in 1917, speaking of the period which should begin immediately after the conquest of power] but the organ of suppression here is now the majority of the population, and not the minority as has heretofore always been the case. . . . In that sense the state *is beginning to die away.*

In what does this dying away express itself? Primarily in the fact that "in place of special institutions of a privileged minority (privileged officials, commanders of a standing army), the majority itself can directly carry out" the functions of suppression. Lenin follows this with a statement axiomatic and unanswerable:

> The more universal becomes the very fulfillment of the functions of the state power, the less need is there of this power.

The annulment of private property in the means of production removes the principal task of the historic state—defense of the proprietary privileges of the minority against the overwhelming majority.

The dying away of the state begins, then, according to Lenin, on the very day after the expropriation of the expropriators—that is, before the new regime has had time to take up its economic and cultural problems. Every success in the solution of these problems means a further step in the liquidation of the state, its dissolution in the socialist society. The degree of this dissolution is the best index of the depth and efficacy of the socialist structure. We may lay down approximately this sociological theorem: The strength of the compulsion exercised by the masses in a workers' state is directly proportional to the strength of the exploitive tendencies, or the danger of a restoration of capitalism, and inversely proportional to the strength of the social solidarity and the general loyalty to the new regime. Thus the bureaucracy—that is, the "privileged officials and commanders of a standing army"—represents a special kind of compulsion which the masses cannot or do not wish to exercise, and which, one way or another, is directed against the masses themselves.

If the democratic soviets had preserved to this day their original strength and independence, and yet were compelled to resort to repressions and compulsions on the scale of the first years, this circumstance might of itself give rise to serious anxiety. How much greater must be the alarm in view of the fact that the mass soviets have entirely disappeared from the scene, having turned over the function of compulsion to Stalin, Yagoda and company. And what forms of compulsion! First of all we must ask ourselves: What social cause stands behind this stubborn virility of the state and especially behind its policification? The importance of this question is obvious. In dependence upon the answer, we must either radically revise our traditional views of the socialist society in general, or as radically reject the official estimates of the Soviet Union.

Let us now take from the latest number of a Moscow newspaper a stereotyped characterization of the present Soviet regime, one of those which are repeated throughout the country from day to day and which school children learn by heart:

> In the Soviet Union the parasitical classes of capitalists, landlords and *kulaks* are completely liquidated, and thus is forever ended the exploitation of man by man. The whole national economy has become socialistic, and the growing Stakhanov movement is preparing the conditions for a transition from socialism to communism. [*Pravda*, April 4, 1936.]

The world press of the Communist International, it goes without saying, has no other thing to say on this subject. But if exploitation is "ended forever," if the country is really now on the road from socialism, that is, the lowest stage of communism, to its higher stage, then there remains nothing for society to do but to throw off at last the straitjacket of the state. In place of this—it is hard even to grasp this contrast with the mind!—the Soviet state has acquired a totalitarian-bureaucratic character.

The same fatal contradiction finds illustration in the fate of the party. Here the problem may be formulated approximately thus: Why, from 1917 to 1921, when the old ruling classes were still fighting with weapons in their hands, when they were actively supported by the imperialists of the whole world, when the *kulaks* in arms were sabotaging the army and food supplies of the country—why was it possible to dispute openly and fearlessly in the party about the most critical questions of policy? Why now, after the cessation of intervention, after the shattering of the exploiting classes, after the indubitable successes of industrialization, after the collectivization of the overwhelming majority of the peasants, is it impossible to permit the slightest word of criticism of the unremovable leaders? Why is it that any Bolshevik who should demand a calling of the congress of the party in accordance with its constitution would be immediately expelled, any citizen who expressed out loud a doubt of the infallibility of Stalin would be tried and convicted almost as though a participant in a terrorist plot? Whence this terrible, monstrous and unbearable intensity of repression and of the police apparatus?

Theory is not a note which you can present at any moment to reality for payment. If a theory proves mistaken we must revise it or fill out its gaps. We must find out those real social forces which have given rise to the contrast between Soviet reality and the traditional Marxian conception. In any case we must not wander in the dark, repeating ritual phases, useful for the prestige of the leaders, but which nevertheless slap the living reality in the face. We shall now see a convincing example of this.

In a speech at a session of the Central Executive Committee in January, 1936, Molotov, the president of the Council of People's Commissars, declared:

> The national economy of the country has become socialistic (applause). In that sense [?] we have solved the problem of the liquidation of classes (applause).

However, there still remain from the past "elements in their nature hostile to us," fragments of the former ruling classes. Moreover, among the collectivized farmers, state employees and sometimes also the workers, "petty speculators" [*spekulantiki*] are discovered, "grafters in relation to the collective and state wealth, anti-Soviet gossips, etc." And hence results the necessity of a further reinforcement of the dictatorship. In opposition to Engels, the workers' state must not "fall asleep," but on the contrary become more and more vigilant.

The picture drawn by the head of the Soviet government would be reassuring in the highest degree, were it not murderously self-contradictory. Socialism completely reigns in the country: "in that sense" classes are abolished. (If they are abolished in that sense, then they are in every other.) To be sure, the social harmony is broken here and there by fragments and remnants of the past, but it is impossible to think that scattered dreamers of a restoration of capitalism, deprived of power and property, together with "petty speculators" (not even *speculators!*) and "gossips" are capable of overthrowing the classless society. Everything is getting along, it seems, the very best you can imagine. But what is the use then of the iron dictatorship of the bureaucracy?

Those reactionary dreamers, we must believe, will gradually die out. The "petty speculators" and "gossips" might be disposed of with a laugh by the super-democratic Soviets.

> We are not utopians, [responded Lenin in 1917 to the bourgeois and reformist theoreticians of the bureaucratic state, and] by no means deny the possibility and inevitability of excesses on the part of *individual persons,* and likewise the necessity for suppressing *such* excesses. But . . . for this there is no need of a special machine, a special apparatus of repression. This will be done by the armed people themselves, with the same simplicity and ease with which any crowd of civilized people even in contemporary society separate a couple of fighters or stop an act of violence against a woman.

Those words sound as though the author had especially foreseen the remarks of one of his successors at the head of the government. Lenin is taught in the public schools of the Soviet Union, but apparently not in the Council of People's Commissars. Otherwise it would be impossible to explain Molotov's daring to resort without reflection to the very construction against which Lenin directed his well-sharpened weapons. The flagrant contradiction between the founder and his Epigoni is before us! Whereas Lenin judged that even the liquidation of the exploiting classes might be accomplished without a bureaucratic apparatus, Molotov, in explaining why *after* the liquidation of classes the bureaucratic machine has strangled the independence of the people, finds no better pretext than a reference to the "remnants" of the liquidated classes.

To live on these "remnants" becomes, however, rather difficult since, according to the confession of authoritative representatives of the bureaucracy itself, yesterday's class enemies are being successfully assimilated by the Soviet society. Thus Postyshev, one of the secretaries of the Central Committee of the party, said in April, 1936, at a congress of the League of Communist Youth: "Many of the saboteurs . . . have sincerely repented and joined the ranks of the Soviet people." In view of the successful carrying out of collectivization, "the children of *kulaks* are not to be held responsible for their parents." And yet more: "The *kulak* himself now hardly believes in the possibility of a return to his former position of exploiter in the village." Not without reason did the government annul the limitations connected with social origin! But if Postyshev's assertion, wholly agreed to by Molotov, makes any sense it is only this: Not only has the bureaucracy become a monstrous anachronism, but state compulsion in general has nothing whatever to do in the land of the Soviets. However, neither Molotov nor Postyshev agrees with that immutable inference. They prefer to hold the power even at the price of self-contradiction.

In reality, too, they cannot reject the power. Or, to translate this into objective language: The present Soviet society cannot get along without a state, nor even—within limits—without a bureaucracy. But the cause of this is by no means the pitiful remnants of the past, but the mighty forces and tendencies of the present. The justification for the existence of a Soviet state as an apparatus of compulsion lies in the fact that the present transitional structure is still full of social contradictions, which in the sphere of *consumption*—closest to everyone, and most sensitively felt—are extremely tense, and forever threaten to break over into the sphere of production. The triumph of socialism cannot be called either final or irrevocable.

The basis of bureaucratic rule is the poverty of society in objects of consumption, with the resulting struggle of each against all. When there are enough goods in a store, the purchasers can come whenever they want to. When there are few goods, the purchasers are compelled to stand in line. When the lines are very long, it is necessary to appoint a policeman to keep order. Such is the starting point of the power of the Soviet bureaucracy. It "knows" who is to get something and who has to wait.

A raising of the material and cultural level ought, at first glance, to lessen the necessity of privileges, narrow the sphere of application of "bourgeois law," and thereby undermine the standing ground of its defenders, the bureaucracy. In reality the opposite thing has happened: the growth of the productive forces has been so far accompanied by an extreme development of all forms of inequality, privilege and advantage, and therewith of bureaucratism. That too is not accidental.

In its first period, the Soviet regime was undoubtedly far more equalitarian and less bureaucratic than now. But that was an equality of general poverty. The resources of the country were so scant that there was no opportunity to separate out from the masses of the population any broad privileged strata. At the same time the "equalizing" character of wages, destroying personal interestedness, became a brake upon the development of the productive forces. Soviet economy had to lift itself from its poverty to a somewhat higher level before fat deposits of privilege became possible. The present state of production is still far from guaranteeing all necessities to everybody. But it is already adequate to give significant privileges to a minority, and convert inequality into a whip for the spurring on of the majority. That is the first reason why the growth of production has so far strengthened not the socialist, but the bourgeois, features of the state.

But that is not the sole reason. Alongside the economic factor dictating capitalistic methods of payment at the present stage, there operates a parallel political factor in the person of the bureaucracy itself. In its very essence it is the planter and protector of inequality. It arose in the beginning as the bourgeois organ of a workers' state. In establishing and defending the advantages of a minority, it of course draws off the cream for its own use. Nobody who has wealth to distribute ever omits himself. Thus out of a social necessity there has developed an organ which has far outgrown its socially necessary function, and become an independent factor and therewith the source of great danger for the whole social organism.

The social meaning of the Soviet Thermidor now begins to take form before us. The poverty and cultural backwardness of the masses has again become incarnate in the malignant figure of the ruler with a great club in his hand. The deposed and abused bureaucracy, from being a servant of society, has again become its lord. On this road it has attained such a degree of social and moral alienation from the popular masses, that it cannot now permit any control over either its activities or its income.

The bureaucracy's seemingly mystical fear of "petty speculators, grafters, and gossips" thus finds a wholly natural explanation. Not yet able to satisfy the elementary needs of the population, the Soviet economy creates and resurrects at every step tendencies to graft and speculation. On the other side, the privileges of the new aristocracy awaken in the masses of the population a tendency to listen to anti-Soviet "gossips"—that is, to anyone who, albeit in a whisper, criticizes the greedy and capricious bosses. It is a question, therefore, not of specters of the past, not of the remnants of what no longer exists, not, in short, of the snows of yesteryear, but of new, mighty and continually reborn tendencies to personal accumulation. The first still very meager wave of prosperity in the country, just because of its meagerness, has not weakened, but strengthened, these centrifugal tendencies. On the other hand, there has developed simultaneously a desire of the unprivileged to slap the grasping hands of the new gentry. The social struggle again grows sharp. Such are the sources of the power of the bureaucracy. But from those same sources comes also a threat to its power.

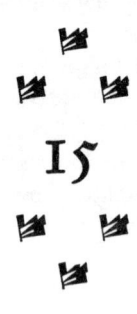

Thermidor
and Anti-Semitism

TRANSLATED BY FREDDIE JAMES
(1937).

At the time of the last Moscow trial I remarked in one of my statements that Stalin, in the struggle with the Opposition, exploited the anti-Semitic tendencies in the country. On this subject I received a series of letters and questions which were, by and large—there is no reason to hide the truth—very naïve. "How can one accuse the Soviet Union of anti-Semitism?" "If the USSR is an anti-Semitic country, is there anything left at all?" That was the dominant note of these letters. These people raise objections and are perplexed because they are accustomed to counterpose fascist anti-Semitism with the emancipation of the Jews accomplished by the October revolution. To these people it now appears that I am wresting from their hands a magic charm. Such a method of reasoning is typical of those who are accustomed to vulgar, non-dialectical thinking. They live in a world of immutable abstractions. They recognize only that which suits them: the Germany of Hitler is the absolutist kingdom of anti-Semitism; the USSR, on the contrary, is the kingdom of national harmony. Vital contradictions, changes, transitions from one condition to another, in a word, the actual historical processes escape their lackadaisical attention.

It has not yet been forgotten, I trust, that anti-Semitism was quite widespread in Czarist Russia among the peasants, the petty bourgeoisie of the city, the intelligentsia and the more backward strata of the working class. "Mother" Russia was renowned not only for her periodic Jewish pogroms but also for the existence of a considerable number of anti-Semitic publications which, in that day, enjoyed a wide circulation. The October revolution abolished the outlawed status against the Jews. That, however, does not at all mean that with one blow it swept out anti-Semitism. A long and persistent struggle against religion has failed to prevent suppliants even today from crowding thousands and thousands of churches, mosques and synagogues. The same situation prevails in the sphere of national prejudices. Legislation alone does not change people. Their thoughts, emotions, outlook depend upon tradition, material conditions of life, cultural level, etc. The Soviet regime is not yet twenty years old. The older half of the population was educated under Czarism. The younger half has inherited a great deal from the older. These general historical conditions in themselves should make any thinking person realize that, despite the model legislation of the October revolution, it is impossible that national and chauvinist prejudices, particularly anti-Semitism, should not have persisted strongly among the backward layers of the population.

But this is by no means all. The Soviet regime, in actuality, initiated a series of new phenomena which, because of the poverty and low cultural level of the population, were capable of generating anew, and did in fact generate, anti-Semitic moods. The Jews are a typical city population. They comprise a considerable percentage of the city population in the Ukraine, in White Russia and even in Great Russia. The Soviet, more than any other regime in the world, needs a very great number of civil servants. Civil servants are recruited from the more cultured city population. Naturally the Jews occupied a disproportionately large place among the bureaucracy and particularly so in its lower and middle levels. Of course we can close our eyes to that fact and limit ourselves to vague generalities about the equality and brotherhood of all races. But an ostrich policy will not advance us a single step. *The hatred of the peasants and the workers for the bureaucracy is a fundamental fact in Soviet life.* The despotism of the regime, the persecution of every critic, the stifling of every living thought, finally, the judicial frame-ups are merely the reflection of this basic fact. Even by *a priori* reasoning it is impossible not to conclude that the hatred for the bureaucracy would assume an anti-Semitic color, at least in those places where the Jewish functionaries compose a significant percentage of the population and are thrown into relief against the broad background of the peasant masses. In 1923 I proposed to the party conference of the Bolsheviks of the Ukraine that functionaries should be able to speak and write the idiom of the surrounding population. How many ironical remarks were made about this proposal, in the main by the Jewish intelligentsia who spoke and read Russian and did not wish to learn the Ukrainian language! It must be admitted that in that respect the situation has changed considerably for the better. But the national composition of the bureaucracy changed little, and what is immeasurably more important, the antagonism between the population and the bureaucracy has grown monstrously during the past ten to twelve years. All serious and honest observers, especially those who have lived among the toiling masses for a long time, bear witness to the existence of anti-Semitism, not only of the old and hereditary, but also of the new, "Soviet" variety.

The Soviet bureaucrat feels himself morally in a beleaguered camp. He attempts with all his strength to break through from his isolation. The politics of Stalin, at least to the extent of fifty per cent, is dictated by this urge. To wit: (1) the pseudo-socialist demagogy ("Socialism is already accomplished," "Stalin gave, gives and will give the people a happy life," etc.); (2) political and economic measures designed to build around the bureaucracy a broad layer of a new aristocracy (the disproportionately high wages of the Stakhanovites, military ranks, honorary orders, the new "nobility," etc.); and (3) catering to the national feelings and prejudices of the backward layers of the population.

The Ukrainian bureaucrat, if he himself is an indigenous Ukrainian, will, at the critical moment, inevitably try to emphasize that he is a brother to the *muzhik* and the peasant—not some sort of foreigner and under no circumstances a Jew. Of course there is not—alas!—a grain of "socialism" or even of elementary democracy in such an attitude. But that's precisely the nub of the question. The privileged bureaucracy, fearful of its privileges, and consequently completely demoralized, represents at present *the most anti-socialist and most anti-democratic stratum of Soviet society*. In the struggle for its self-preservation it exploits the most ingrained prejudices and the most benighted instincts. If in Moscow, Stalin stages trials which accuse the Trotskyites of plotting to poison the workers, then it is not difficult to imagine to what foul depths the bureaucracy can resort in some Ukrainian or central Asiatic hovel!

He who attentively observes Soviet life, even if only through official publications, will from time to time see bared in various parts of the country hideous bureaucratic abscesses: bribery, corruption, embezzlement, murder of persons whose existence is embarrassing to the bureaucracy, violation of women and the like. Were we to slash vertically through, we would see that every such abscess resulted from the bureaucratic stratum. Sometimes Moscow is constrained to resort to demonstration trials. In all such trials the Jews inevitably comprise a significant percentage, in part because, as was already stated, they make up a great part of the bureaucracy and are branded with its odium, partly because, impelled by the instinct for self preservation, the leading cadre of the bureaucracy at the center and in the provinces strives to divert the indignation of the working masses from itself to the Jews. This fact was known to every critical observer in the USSR as far back as ten years ago, when the Stalin regime had hardly as yet revealed its basic features.

The struggle against the Opposition was for the ruling clique a question of life and death. The program, principles, ties with the masses, everything was rooted out and cast aside because of the anxiety of the new ruling clique for its self-preservation. These people stop at nothing in order to guard their privileges and power. Recently an announcement was released to the whole world, to the effect that my youngest son, Sergei Sedov, was under indictment for plotting a mass poisoning of the workers. Every normal person will conclude: people capable of preferring such a charge have reached the last degree of moral degradation. Is it possible in that case to doubt even for a moment that these same accusers are capable of fostering the anti-Semitic prejudices of the masses? Precisely in the case of my son, both these depravities are united. It is worthwhile to consider this case. From the day of their birth, my sons bore the name of their mother (Sedov). They never used any other name—neither at elementary school, nor at the university, nor in their later life. As for me, during the past thirty-four years I have borne the name of Trotsky. During the Soviet period no one ever called me by the name of my father (Bronstein), just as no one ever called Stalin Dzhugashvili. In order not to oblige my sons to change their name, I, for "citizenship" requirements, took on the name of my wife (which, according to the Soviet law, is fully permissible). However, after my son, Sergei Sedov, was charged with the utterly incredible accusation of plotting to poison workers, the GPU announced in the Soviet and foreign press that the "real" (!) name of my son is not Sedov but Bronstein. If these falsifiers wished to emphasize the connection of the accused with me, they would have called him Trotsky since politically the name Bronstein means nothing at all to anyone. But they were out for other game; that is, they wished to emphasize my Jewish origin and the semi-Jewish origin of my son. I paused at this episode because it has a vital and yet not at all exceptional character. The whole struggle against the Opposition is full of such episodes.

Between 1923 and 1926, when Stalin, with Zinoviev and Kamenev, was still a member of the "Troika," the play on the strings of anti-Semitism bore a very cautious and masked character. Especially schooled orators (Stalin already then led an underhanded struggle against his associates) said that the followers of Trotsky are petty bourgeois from "small towns," without defining their race. Actually that was untrue. The percentage of Jewish intellectuals in the Opposition was in no case any greater than that in the party and in the bureaucracy. It is sufficient to name the leaders of the Opposition for the years 1923-25: I. N. Smirnov, Serebryakov, Rakovsky, Piatakov, Preobrazhensky, Krestinsky, Muralov, Beloborodov, Mrachkovsky, V. Yakolev, Sapronov, V. M. Smirnov, Ishtchenko—fully indigenous Russians. Radek at that time was only half-sympathetic. But, as in the trials of the grafters and other scoundrels, so at the time of the expulsions of the Opposition from the party, the bureaucracy purposely emphasized the names of Jewish members of casual and secondary importance. This was quite openly discussed in the party and, back in 1925, the Opposition saw in this situation the unmistakable symptom of the decay of the ruling clique.

After Zinoviev and Kamenev joined the Opposition the situation changed radically for the worse. At this point there opened wide a perfect chance to say to the workers that at the head of the Opposition stand three "dissatisfied Jewish intellectuals." Under the direction of Stalin, Uglanov in Moscow and Kirov in Leningrad carried through this line systematically and almost fully in the open. In order the more sharply to demonstrate to the workers the differences between the "old" course and the "new," the Jews, even when unreservedly devoted to the general line, were removed from responsible party and Soviet posts. Not only in the country but even in Moscow factories the baiting of the Opposition back in 1926 often assumed a thoroughly obvious anti-Semitic character. Many agitators spoke brazenly: "The Jews are rioting." I received hundreds of letters deploring the anti-Semitic methods in the struggle with the Opposition. At one of the sessions of the Politburo I wrote Bukharin a note: "You cannot help knowing that even in Moscow in the struggle against the Opposition, methods of Black Hundred demagogues (anti-Semitism, etc.) are utilized." Bukharin answered me evasively on that same piece of paper: "Individual instances, of course, are possible." I again wrote: "I have in mind not individual instances but a systematic agitation among the party secretaries at large Moscow enterprises. Will you agree to come with me to investigate an example of this at the factory 'Skorokhod' (I know of a number of other such examples)." Bukharin answered, "All right, we can go." In vain I tried to make him carry out the promise. Stalin most categorically forbade him to do so. In the months of preparations for the expulsions of the Opposition from the party, the arrests, the exiles (in the second half of 1927), the anti-Semitic agitation assumed a thoroughly unbridled character. The slogan, "Beat the Opposition," often took on the complexion of the old slogan "Beat the Jews and save Russia." The matter went so far that Stalin was constrained to come out with a printed statement which declared: "We fight against Trotsky, Zinoviev and Kamenev not because they are Jews but because they are Oppositionists," etc. To every politically thinking person it was completely clear that this consciously equivocal declaration, directed against "excesses" of anti-Semitism, did at the same time with complete premeditation nourish it. "Do not forget that the leaders of the Opposition are—Jews." That was the *meaning* of the statement of Stalin, published in all Soviet journals.

When the Opposition, to meet the repressions, proceeded with a more decisive and open struggle, Stalin, in the form of a very significant "jest," told Piatakov and Preobrazhensky: "You at least are fighting against the C.E., openly brandishing your axes. That proves *your 'orthodox'* action.[1] Trotsky works slyly and not with a hatchet." Preobrazhensky and Piatakov related this conversation to me with strong revulsion. Dozens of times Stalin attempted to counterpose the "orthodox" core of the Opposition to me.

The well-known German radical journalist, the former editor of *Aktion*, Franz Pfemfert, at present in exile, wrote me in August, 1936:

> Perhaps you remember that several years ago in *Aktion* I declared that many actions of Stalin can be explained by his anti-Semitic tendencies. The fact that in this monstrous trial he, through *Tass*, managed to "correct" the names of Zinoviev and Kamenev represents, by itself, a gesture in typical Streicher style. In this manner Stalin

[1] [The word used by Stalin in Russian refers to the Greek Orthodox Church.—Tr.]

gave the "Go" sign to all anti-Semitic, unscrupulous elements.

In fact the names, Zinoviev and Kamenev, it would seem, are more famous than the names of Radomislyski and Rozenfeld. What other motive could Stalin have had to make known the "real" names of his victims, except to play with anti-Semitic moods? Such an act, and without the slightest legal justification, was, as we have seen, likewise committed over the name of my son. But, undoubtedly, the most astonishing thing is the fact that all four "terrorists" allegedly sent by me from abroad turned out to be Jews and—at the same time—agents of the anti-Semitic Gestapo! Inasmuch as I have never actually seen any of these unfortunates, it is clear that the GPU deliberately selected them because of their racial origin. And the GPU does not function by virtue of its own inspiration!

Again: if such methods are practiced at the very top where the personal responsibility of Stalin is absolutely unquestionable, then it is not hard to imagine what transpires in the ranks, at the factories, and especially at the *kolkhozes.* And how can it be otherwise? The physical extermination of the older generation of the Bolsheviks is, for every person who can think, an incontrovertible expression of Thermidorian reaction, and in its most advanced stage at that. History has never yet seen an example when the reaction following the revolutionary upsurge was not accompanied by the most unbridled chauvinistic passions, anti-Semitism among them.

In the opinion of some "Friends of the USSR," my reference to the exploitation of anti-Semitic tendencies by a considerable part of the present bureaucracy represents a malicious invention for the purpose of a struggle against Stalin. It is difficult to argue with professional "friends" of the bureaucracy. These people deny the existence of a Thermidorian reaction. They accept even the Moscow trials at face value. There are "friends" who visit the USSR with special intention of not seeing the spots on the sun. Not a few of these receive special pay for their readiness to see only what is pointed out to them by the finger of the bureaucracy. But woe to those workers, revolutionists, socialists, democrats who, in the words of Pushkin, prefer "a delusion which exalts us" to the bitter truth. A healthy revolutionary optimism has no need for illusions. One must face life as it is. It is necessary to find in reality itself the force to overcome its reactionary and barbaric features. That is what Marxism teaches us.

Some would-be "pundits" have even accused me of "suddenly" raising the "Jewish question" and of intending to create some kind of ghetto for the Jews. I can only shrug my shoulders in pity. I have lived my whole life outside of Jewish circles. I have always worked in the Russian workers' movement. My native tongue is Russian. Unfortunately, I have not even learned to read Jewish. The Jewish question therefore has never occupied the center of my attention. But that does not mean that I have the right to be blind to the Jewish problem which exists and demands solution. "The Friends of the USSR" are satisfied with the creation of Biro-Bidjan. I will not stop at this point to consider whether it was built on a sound foundation, and what type of regime exists there. (Biro-Bidjan cannot help reflecting all the vices of bureaucratic despotism.) But not a single progressive, thinking individual will object to the USSR designating a special territory for those of its citizens who feel themselves to be Jews, who use the Jewish language in preference to all others and who wish to live as a compact mass. Is this or is this not a ghetto? During the period of Soviet democracy, of completely *voluntary* migrations, there could be no talk about ghettos. But the Jewish question, by the very manner in which settlements of Jews occurred, assumes an international aspect. Are we not correct in saying that a world socialist federation would have to make possible the creation of a "Biro-Bidjan" for those Jews who wish to have their own autonomous republic as the arena for their own culture? It may be presumed that a socialist democracy will not resort to compulsory assimilation. It may very well be that within two or three generations the boundaries of an independent Jewish republic, as of many other national regions, will be erased. I have neither time nor desire to meditate on this. Our descendants will know better than we what to do. I have in mind a transitional historical period when the Jewish question, as such, is still acute and demands adequate measures from a world federation of workers' states. The very same methods of solving the Jewish question which under decaying capitalism have a utopian and reactionary character (Zionism), will, under the regime of a socialist federation, take on a real and salutary meaning. This is what I wanted to point out. How could any Marxist, or even any consistent democrat, object to this?

16

Is the Bureaucracy a Ruling Class?

TRANSLATED BY MAX EASTMAN
from *The Revolution Betrayed* (1937).

Classes are characterized by their economic position within the social system, and primarily by their relation to the means of production. In civilized societies, property relations are validated by laws. The nationalization of the land, the means of industrial production, transport and exchange, together with the monopoly of foreign trade, constitute the basis of the Soviet social structure. Through these relations, established by the proletarian revolution, the nature of the Soviet Union as a proletarian state is for us basically defined.

In its intermediary and regulating function, its concern with maintaining social ranks, and its exploitation of the state apparatus for personal goals, the Soviet bureaucracy is similar to every other bureaucracy, especially the fascist. But it is also vastly different. In no other regime has a bureaucracy ever achieved such a degree of independence from the dominating class. In bourgeois society, the bureaucracy represents the interests of a possessing and educated class, which has at its disposal innumerable means of everyday control over its administration of affairs. The Soviet bureaucracy has risen above a class which is hardly emerging from destitution and darkness, and has no tradition of dominion or command. Whereas the fascists, when they find themselves in power, are united with the big bourgeoisie by bonds of common interest, friendship, marriage, etc., the Soviet bureaucracy takes on bourgeois customs without having beside it a national bourgeoisie. In this sense we cannot deny that it is something more than a bureaucracy. It is in the full sense of the word the sole privileged and commanding stratum in the Soviet society.

Another difference is no less important. The Soviet bureaucracy has expropriated the proletariat politically, in order by methods *of its own* to defend the social conquests. But the very fact of its appropriation of political power in a country where the principal means of production are in the hands of the state, creates a new and hitherto unknown relation between the bureaucracy and the riches of the nation. The means of production belong to the state. But the state, so to speak, "belongs" to the bureaucracy. If these as yet wholly new relations should solidify, become the norm and be legalized, whether with or without resistance from the workers, they would, in the long run, lead to a complete liquidation of the social conquests of the proletarian revolution. But to speak of that now is at least premature. The proletariat has not yet said its last word. The bureaucracy has not yet created social supports for its dominion in the form of special types of property. It is compelled to defend state property as the source of its power and its income. In this aspect of its activity it still remains a weapon of proletarian dictatorship.

The attempt to represent the Soviet bureaucracy as a class of "state capitalists" will obviously not withstand criticism. The bureaucracy has neither stocks nor bonds. It is recruited, supplemented and renewed in the manner of an administrative hierarchy, independently of any special property relations of its own. The individual bureaucrat cannot transmit to his heirs his rights in the exploitation of the state apparatus. The bureaucracy enjoys its privileges under the form of an abuse of power. It conceals its income; it pretends that as a special social group it does not even exist. Its appropriation of a vast share of the national income has the character of social parasitism. All this makes the position of the commanding Soviet stratum in the highest degree contradictory, equivocal and undignified, notwithstanding the completeness of its power and the smoke screen of flattery that conceals it.

Bourgeois society has in the course of its history displaced many political regimes and bureaucratic castes, without changing its social foundations. It has preserved itself against the restoration of feudal and guild relations by the superiority of its productive methods. The state power has been able either to co-operate with capitalist development, or put brakes on it. But in general the productive forces, upon a basis of private property and competition, have been working out their own destiny. In contrast to this, the property relations which issued from the socialist revolution are indivisibly bound up with the new state as their repository. The predominance of socialist over petty-bourgeois tendencies is guaranteed, not by the automatism of the economy—we are still far from that— but by political measures taken by the dictatorship. The character of the economy as a whole thus depends upon the character of the state power.

A collapse of the Soviet regime would lead inevitably to the collapse of the planned economy, and thus to the abolition of state property. The bond of compulsion between the trusts and the factories within them would fall away. The more successful enterprises would succeed in coming out on the road of independence. They might convert themselves into stock companies, or they might find some other transitional form of property—one, for example, in which the workers should participate in the profits. The collective farms would disintegrate at the same time, and far more easily. The fall of the present bureaucratic dictatorship, if it were not replaced by a new socialist power, would thus mean a return to capitalist relations with a catastrophic decline of industry and culture.

But if a socialist government is still absolutely necessary for the preservation and development of the planned economy,

Is the Bureaucracy a Ruling Class?

the question—upon whom the present Soviet government relies, and in what measure the socialist character of its policy is guaranteed—is all the more important. At the Eleventh Party Congress in March, 1922, Lenin, in practically bidding farewell to the party, addressed these words to the commanding group:

> History knows transformations of all sorts. To rely upon conviction, devotion, and other excellent spiritual qualities—that is not to be taken seriously in politics.

Being determines consciousness. During the last fifteen years the government has changed its social composition even more deeply than its ideas. Since of all the strata of Soviet society the bureaucracy has best solved its own social problem, and is fully content with the existing situation, it has ceased to offer any subjective guarantee whatever of the socialist direction of its policy. It continues to preserve state property only to the extent that it fears the proletariat. This saving fear is nourished and supported by the illegal party of Bolshevik-Leninists, which is the most conscious expression of the socialist tendencies opposing that bourgeois reaction with which the Thermidorian bureaucracy is completely saturated. As a conscious political force the bureaucracy has betrayed the revolution. But a victorious revolution is fortunately not only a program and a banner, not only political institutions, but also a system of social relations. To betray it is not enough. You have to overthrow it. The October revolution has been betrayed by the ruling stratum, but not yet overthrown. It has a great power of resistance, coinciding with the established property relations, with the living force of the proletariat, the consciousness of its best elements, the impasse of world capitalism, and the inevitability of world revolution.

THE CHARACTER OF THE SOVIET UNION

In order better to understand the character of the present Soviet Union, let us make two different hypotheses about its future. Let us assume first that the Soviet bureaucracy is overthrown by a revolutionary party having all the attributes of the old Bolshevism, enriched moreover by the world experience of the recent period. Such a party would begin with the restoration of democracy in the trade unions and the Soviets. It would be able to, and would have to, restore freedom of Soviet parties. Together with the masses, and at their head, it would carry out a ruthless purgation of the state apparatus. It would abolish ranks and decorations, all kinds of privileges, and would limit inequality in the payment of labor to the life necessities of the economy and the state apparatus. It would give the youth free opportunity to think independently, learn, criticize and grow. It would introduce profound changes in the distribution of the national income in correspondence with the interests and will of the worker and peasant masses. But so far as concerns property relations, the new power would not have to resort to revolutionary measures. It would retain and further develop the experiment of planned economy. After the political revolution—that is, the deposing of the bureaucracy—the proletariat would have to introduce into the economy a series of very important reforms, but not another social revolution.

If—to adopt a second hypothesis—a bourgeois party were to overthrow the ruling Soviet caste, it would find no small number of ready servants among the present bureaucrats, administrators, technicians, directors, party secretaries and privileged upper circles in general. A purgation of the state apparatus would, of course, be necessary in this case too. But a bourgeois restoration would probably have to clean out fewer people than a revolutionary party. The chief task of the new power would be to restore private property in the means of production. First of all, it would be necessary to create conditions for the development of strong farmers from the weak collective farms, and for converting the strong collectives into producers' co-operatives of the bourgeois type—into agricultural stock companies. In the sphere of industry, denationalization would begin with the light industries and those producing food. The planning principle would be converted for the transitional period into a series of compromises between state power and individual "corporations"—potential proprietors, that is, among the Soviet captains of industry, the émigré former proprietors and foreign capitalists. Notwithstanding that the Soviet bureaucracy has gone far toward preparing a bourgeois restoration, the new regime would have to introduce, in the matter of forms of property and methods of industry, not a reform, but a social revolution.

Let us assume—to take a third variant—that neither a revolutionary nor a counterrevolutionary party seizes power. The bureaucracy continues at the head of the state. Even under these conditions social relations will not jell. We cannot count upon the bureaucracy's peacefully and voluntarily renouncing itself in behalf of socialist equality. If at the present time, notwithstanding the too obvious inconveniences of such an operation, it has considered it possible to introduce ranks and decorations, it must inevitably in future stages seek supports for itself in property relations. One may argue that the big bureaucrat cares little what are the prevailing forms of property, provided only they guarantee him the necessary income. This argument ignores not only the instability of the bureaucrat's own rights, but also the question of his descendants. The new cult of the family has not fallen out of the clouds. Privileges have only half their worth, if they cannot be transmitted to one's children. But the right of testament is inseparable from the right of property. It is not enough to be the director of a trust; it is necessary to be a stockholder. The victory of the bureaucracy in this decisive sphere would mean its conversion into a new possessing class. On the other hand, the victory of the proletariat over the bureaucracy would insure a revival of the socialist revolution. The third variant consequently brings us back to the two first, with which, in the interests of clarity and simplicity, we set out.

To define the Soviet regime as transitional, or intermediate, means to abandon such finished social categories as *capitalism* (and therewith "state capitalism") and also *socialism*. But besides being completely inadequate in itself, such a definition is capable of producing the mistaken idea that from the present Soviet regime *only* a transition to socialism is possible. In reality a backslide to capitalism is wholly possible. A more complete definition will of necessity be complicated and ponderous.

The Soviet Union is a contradictory society halfway between capitalism and socialism, in which: (a) the productive forces are still far from adequate to give the state property a socialist character; (b) the tendency toward primitive accumulation created by want breaks out through innumerable pores of the planned economy; (c) norms of distribution preserving a bourgeois character lie at the basis of a new differentiation of society; (d) the economic growth, while slowly bettering the situation of the toilers, promotes a swift formation of privileged strata; (e) exploiting the social antagonisms, a bureaucracy has converted itself into an uncontrolled caste alien to socialism; (f) the social revolution, betrayed by the ruling party, still exists in property relations and in the consciousness of the toiling masses; (g) a further development of the accumulating contradictions can as well lead to socialism as back to capitalism; (h) on the road to capitalism the counterrevolution would have to break the resistance of the workers; (i) on the road to socialism the workers would have to overthrow the bureaucracy. In the last analysis, the question will be decided by a struggle of living social forces, on both the national and the world arenas.

Doctrinaires will doubtless not be satisfied with this hypothetical definition. They would like categorical formulae: yes —yes, and no—no. Sociological problems would certainly be simpler, if social phenomena had always a finished character. There is nothing more dangerous, however, than to throw out of reality, for the sake of logical completeness, elements which today violate your scheme and tomorrow may wholly overturn it. In our analysis, we have above all avoided doing violence to dynamic social formations which have had no precedent and have no analogies. The scientific task, as well as the political, is not to give a finished definition to an unfinished process, but to follow all its stages, separate its progressive from its reactionary tendencies, expose their mutual relations, foresee possible variants of development, and find in this foresight a basis for action.

17

The Revolution in Spain

TRANSLATED BY MORRIS LEWITT
from *The Revolution in Spain* (1931).

OLD SPAIN

The capitalist chain is again threatening to break at the weakest link: Spain is next in order. The revolutionary movement is developing in that country with such vigor that world reaction is deprived in advance of the possibility of believing in a speedy restoration of order on the Iberian peninsula.

Spain belongs unmistakably to the group of the most backward countries of Europe. But its backwardness has a singular character, weighed down by the great historic past of the country. While the Russia of the Czars always remained far behind its western neighbors and advanced slowly under their pressure, Spain knew periods of great bloom, of superiority over the rest of Europe and of domination over South America. The mighty development of domestic and world commerce surmounted more and more the feudal dismemberment of the provinces and the particularism of the national parts of the country. The growth of the power and significance of the Spanish monarchy was inextricably bound up in those centuries with the centralizing role of mercantile capital, and with the gradual formation of the *Spanish nation.*

The discovery of America, which at first enriched and elevated Spain, was subsequently directed against it. The great routes of commerce were diverted from the Iberian peninsula. Holland, which had grown rich, broke away from Spain. Following Holland, England rose to great heights over Europe, and for a long time. Beginning with the second half of the sixteenth century, Spain had already begun to decline. With the destruction of the Great Armada (1588), this decline assumed, so to speak, an official character. The condition which Marx called "inglorious and slow decay" settled down upon feudal-bourgeois Spain.

The old and new ruling classes—the landed nobility, the Catholic clergy with its monarchy, the bourgeois classes with their *intelligenzia,* stubbornly attempted to preserve the old pretensions, but alas! without the old resources. In 1820, the South American colonies finally broke away. With the loss of Cuba in 1898, Spain was almost completely deprived of colonial possessions. The adventures in Morocco only ruined the country, adding fuel to the already deep dissatisfaction of the people.

The retardation of the economic development of Spain inevitably weakened the centralist tendencies inherent in capitalism. The decline of the commercial and industrial life in the cities and of the economic ties between them inevitably led to the decline in the dependence of individual provinces upon each other. This is the chief reason why bourgeois Spain has not succeeded to this day in eliminating the centrifugal tendencies of its historic provinces. The meagerness of the resources of national economy and the feeling of indisposition in all parts of the country could only foster the separatist tendencies. Particularism appears in Spain with unusual force, especially alongside of neighboring France, where the Great Revolution finally established the bourgeois nation, united and inseparable, over the old feudal provinces.

Not permitting the formation of a new bourgeois society, the economic stagnation also decomposed the old ruling classes. The proud noblemen often cloaked their haughtiness in rags. The church robbed the peasantry, but from time to time it was compelled to submit to robbery by the monarchy. The latter, in the words of Marx, had more features of resemblance to Asiatic despotism than to European absolutism. How is this thought to be construed? The comparison of Czarism to Asiatic despotism, which has been made more than once, seems much more natural geographically and historically. But with regard to Spain, as well, this comparison retains all its force. The difference is only in the fact that Czarism as constituted on the basis of an *extremely slow development* of the nobility and of the primitive urban centers. But the Spanish monarchy was constituted under the conditions of the *decline* of the country and the *decay* of the ruling classes. If European absolutism generally could rise only thanks to the struggle of the strengthened cities against the old privileged estates, then the Spanish monarchy, like Russian Czarism, drew its relative strength from the impotence of the old estates and the cities. In this lies its indubitable proximity to Asiatic despotism.

The predominance of the centrifugal tendency over the centripetal, in economy as well as in politics, undermined the ground beneath Spanish parliamentarism. The pressure of the government upon the electorate had a decisive character: during the last century elections unfailingly gave the government a majority. Because the *Cortes* [the Spanish Assembly] found itself dependent upon the alternating ministries, the ministries themselves naturally fell into dependence upon the monarchy. Madrid made the elections but the power appeared in the hands of the king. The monarchy was doubly necessary to the disconnected and decentralized ruling classes, incapable of governing the country in their own name. And this monarchy, reflecting the weakness of the whole state, was—between two overturns—strong enough to impose its will upon the country. In general the state system of Spain can be called degenerated absolutism, limited by periodic *pronunciamentos*.[1] The figure of Alfonso XIII expresses the system very well: from the point

[1] [Military plots, military coups d'état.—Tr.]

of view of degeneracy and absolutist tendencies, and from the point of view of fear of *pronunciamentos*. The king's playing to windward, his betrayals, his treason, and his victory over the temporary combinations hostile to him are not at all rooted in the character of Alfonso XIII himself, but in the character of the whole governmental system: under new circumstances, Alfonso XIII repeats the inglorious history of his great-grandfather, Ferdinand VII.

Alongside of the monarchy, and in union with it, the clergy still represents a centralized force. Catholicism, to this day, continues to remain a state religion. The clergy, being the firmest axis of reaction, plays a big role in the life of the country. The state spends many tens of millions of pesetas annually for the support of the clergy. The religious orders are extremely numerous, possessing great wealth and still greater influence. The number of monks and nuns is close to 70,000, equaling the number of high school students and exceeding double the number of college students. Is it a wonder that under these conditions forty-five per cent of the population can neither read nor write? The main mass of illiterates is concentrated, it is understood, in the village.

If the peasantry in the epoch of Charles V (Carlos I) gained little from the might of the Spanish empire, it was subsequently burdened with the heaviest consequences of its decline. For centuries it led a miserable, and in many provinces a famished, existence. Making up even now more than seventy per cent of the population, the peasantry bears on its back the main burden of the state structure. The lack of land, the lack of water, high rents, antiquated implements, primitive tilling of the soil, high taxes, the requisitions of the church, high prices of industrial products, a surplus of rural population, a great number of tramps, paupers, friars—that is the picture of the Spanish village. The condition of the peasantry has for a long time made it a participant in the numerous uprisings. But these sanguinary outbursts proceeded not along national but along local radii, dyed in the most multicolored and most often reactionary colors. Just as the Spanish revolutions as a whole were small revolutions, so the peasant uprisings assumed the form of small wars. Spain is a classic country of "guerilla warfare."

THE SPANISH ARMY IN POLITICS

Following the war with Napoleon, a new force was created in Spain—officers in politics, the younger generation of the ruling classes who inherited from their fathers the ruins of the once great empire and were in a considerable measure declassed. In the country of particularism and separatism, the army of necessity assumed great significance as a centralized force. It not only became a prop of the monarchy but also the vehicle of dissatisfaction of all the sections of the ruling classes, and primarily, of its own: like the bureaucracy, the officers are recruited from those elements, extremely numerous in Spain, which demand of the state first of all their means of livelihood. And as the appetites of the different groups of "cultured" society are far in excess of the state, parliamentary and other positions available, the dissatisfaction of those remaining unattached nurtures the republican party, which is just as unstable as all the other groups in Spain. But insofar as genuine and sharp revolt is often concealed under this instability, the republican movement from time to time produces resolute and courageous revolutionary groups to whom the republic appears as a magic slogan of salvation.

The total number of the Spanish army is nearly 170,000. Over 13,000 of them are officers. 15,000 marines should be added to this. Because it is the weapon of the ruling classes of the country, the commanding staff also drags the ranks of the army into its plots. This creates the conditions for the independent movement of the soldiers. Already in the past, noncommissioned officers have burst into politics, without their officers and against them. In 1836, the noncommissioned officers of the Madrid garrison, in an uprising, compelled the queen to promulgate a constitution; in 1866, the artillery sergeants, dissatisfied with the aristocratic orders in the army, rose in insurrection. Nevertheless, the leading role in the past has remained with the officers. The soldiers followed their dissatisfied commanders even though the dissatisfaction of the soldiers, politically helpless, was fostered by other, deeper social forces.

The contradictions in the army usually correspond to the branch of service. The more advanced the type of arms, that is, the more intelligence it requires on the part of the soldiers and officers, the more susceptible they are, generally speaking, to revolutionary ideas. While the cavalry is usually inclined to the monarchy, the artillerists furnish a big percentage of the republicans. No wonder that the fliers, piloting the modern type of war machine, appeared on the side of the revolution and brought into it elements of the individualist adventurism of their profession. The decisive word remains with the infantry.

The history of Spain is the history of continuous revolutionary convulsions. *Pronunciamentos* and palace revolutions follow one another. During the nineteenth century and the first third of the twentieth, a continuous change of political regime occurred and within each one of them—a kaleidoscopic change of ministries. Not finding sufficiently stable support in any one of the propertied classes—even though they were all in need of it—the Spanish monarchy more than once fell into dependence upon its own army. But the provincial dismemberment of Spain put its stamp on the character of the military plots. The petty rivalry of the *juntas* was only the external expression of the fact that the Spanish revolutions did not have a leading class. Precisely because of this the monarchy repeatedly triumphed over each new revolution. However, some time after the triumph of order, the chronic crisis once more broke through with an acute revolt. Not one of the regimes that supplanted each other sank deep enough into the soil. Every one of them wore off quickly in the struggle with the difficulties growing out of the meagerness of the national income, which is incommensurate with the appetites and pretensions of the ruling classes. We saw in particular how shamefully the last military dictatorship came to the end of its days. The stern Primo de Rivera fell even without a new *pronunciamento:* the air simply went out of him like out of a tire that runs over a nail.

All the Spanish revolutions were the movement of a minority against another minority: the ruling and semi-ruling classes impatiently snatching the state pie out of each other's hands.

If by the permanent revolution we are to understand the accumulation of social revolutions, transferring power into the hands of the most resolute class, which afterwards applies this power for the abolition of all classes, and subsequently the very possibility of new revolutions, we would then have to state that in spite of the "uninterruptedness" of the Spanish revolutions there is nothing in them that resembles the *permanent* revolution: they are rather the chronic convulsions in which the senile disease of a nation thrown backward is expressed.

It is true that the Left wing of the bourgeoisie, particularly personified by the young intellectuals, has long ago set itself the task of converting Spain into a republic. The Spanish students who, for the same general reasons as the officers, were recruited primarily from the dissatisfied youth, became accustomed to playing a role in the country altogether out of proportion to their numbers. The domination of the Catholic reaction fed the flames of the opposition in the universities, investing it with an anticlerical character. However, students do not create a regime. In their leading summits, the Spanish republicans are distinguished by an extremely conservative social program: they see their ideal in present-day reactionary France, calculating that along with the republic they will also acquire wealth; they do not at all expect, and are not even able, to march the road of the French Jacobins: their fear of the masses is greater than their hostility to the monarchy. If the cracks and gaps of bourgeois society are filled in Spain with declassed elements of the ruling classes, the numerous seekers of positions and income, then at the bottom, in the cracks of the foundation, this place is occupied by the numerous slum proletarians, declassed elements of the toiling classes. Loafers with cravats as well as loafers in rags form the quicksands of society. They are all the more dangerous for the revolution, the less it finds its genuine motive support and its political leadership.

Six years of the dictatorship of Primo de Rivera leveled and compressed all the forms of dissatisfaction and rebellion. But the dictatorship bore within it the incurable vice of the Spanish monarchy: strong towards each of the separate classes, it remained impotent in relation to the historic needs of the country. This brought about the wreck of the dictatorship on the submarine reefs of financial and other difficulties before the first revolutionary wave had a chance to reach it. The fall of Primo de Rivera aroused all the forms of dissatisfaction and all hopes. Thus, General Berenguer has become the gateman of the revolution.

THE SPANISH PROLETARIAT AND THE NEW REVOLUTION

In this new revolution, we meet at first view the same elements we found in a series of previous revolutions: the perfidious monarchy; the split-up factions of the conservatives and liberals who despise the king and crawl on their bellies before him; the Right republicans, always ready to betray, and the Left republicans, always ready for adventure; the plotting officers, some of whom want a republic and others of whom a promotion in position; the dissatisfied students, whom their fathers view with alarm; finally, the striking workers, scattered among the different organizations, and the peasants, stretching out their hands for pitchforks and even for guns.

It would, however, be a grave error to assume that the present crisis is unfolding according to and in the image of all those that preceded it. The last decades, particularly the years of the world war, produced important changes in the economy of the country and in the social structure of the nation. Of course, even today Spain remains at the tail end of Europe. Nevertheless, the country has experienced the development of its own industry, on the one hand, extractive, on the other, light. During the war, coal mining, textile, the construction of hydroelectric stations, etc., were greatly developed. Industrial centers and regions sprouted all over the country. This creates a new relation of forces and opens up new perspectives.

The successes of industrialization did not at all mitigate the internal contradictions. On the contrary, the circumstance that the industry of Spain, as a neutral country, bloomed under the golden rain of the war, was transformed at the end of the war, when the increased foreign demand disappeared, into a source of new difficulties. Not only did the foreign markets disappear —the share of Spain in world commerce is now even smaller than it was prior to the war (1.1. per cent as against 1.2 per cent)—but the dictatorship was compelled, with the aid of the highest tariff walls in Europe, to defend its domestic market from the influx of foreign commodities. The high tariff led to high prices, which diminished the already low purchasing power of the people. That is why industry after the war does not rise out of its lethargy, which is expressed by chronic unemployment on the one hand and the sharp outbursts of the class struggle on the other.

Even less now than in the nineteenth century can the Spanish bourgeoisie lay claim to that historic role which the British or French bourgeoisie once played. Appearing too late, depending on foreign capital, the big industrial bourgeoisie of Spain, which has dug like a vampire into the body of the people, is incapable of coming forward as the leader of the "nation" against the old estates even for a brief period. The magnates of Spanish industry face the people hostilely, forming one of the most reactionary groups in the bloc of the bankers, the industrialists, the large landowners, the monarchy, its generals and its officials, corroded by internal antagonisms. It is sufficient to refer to the fact that the most important supporters of the dictatorship of Primo de Rivera were the manufacturers of Catalonia.

But the industrial development raised to its feet and strengthened the proletariat. Out of a population of twenty-three million—it would be considerably greater were it not for emigration—there are nearly a million and a half industrial, commercial and transportation workers. To them should be added an approximately equal number of agricultural workers. Social life in Spain was condemned to revolve in a vicious circle so long as there was no class capable of taking the solution of the revolutionary problem into its own hands. The appearance of the Spanish proletariat on the historic arena radically changes the situation and opens up new perspectives. In order to grasp this properly it must first be understood that the establishment of the economic dominance of the big bourgeoisie, and the growth of the political significance of the proletariat, definitely deprive the petty bourgeoisie of the possibility of occupying a leading position in the political life of the country. The question of whether the present revolutionary convulsions can produce a genuine revolution, capable of reconstructing the very basis of national existence, is consequently reduced to whether the Spanish proletariat is capable of taking into its hands the leadership of the national life. There is no other claimant to this role in the composition of the Spanish nation. Moreover, the historic experience of Russia succeeded in showing with sufficient clarity the specific gravity of the proletariat, united by big industry in a country with a backward argiculture and enmeshed in a net of semi-feudal relations.

The Spanish workers, it is true, already took a militant part in the revolutions of the nineteenth century: but always on the leading string of the bourgeoisie, always in the second rank, as a subsidiary force. The independent revolutionary role of the workers was reinforced in the first quarter of the twentieth century. The uprising in Barcelona in 1909 showed what power was pent up in the young proletariat of Catalonia. Numerous strikes, turning themselves into direct uprisings, broke out in other parts of the country too. In 1912, a strike of the railroad workers took place. The industrial regions became fields of valiant proletarian struggles. The Spanish workers revealed a complete emancipation from routine, an ability to respond quickly to events and to mobilize their ranks, and their courage, in the offensive.

The first postwar years, or more correctly, the first years after the Russian Revolution (1917-1920), were years of great battles for the Spanish proletariat. The year 1917 witnessed a general revolutionary strike. Its defeat, and the defeat of a number of subsequent movements, prepared the conditions for the dictatorship of Primo de Rivera. When the collapse of the latter once more posed in all its magnitude the question of the further destiny of the Spanish people, when the cowardly search for old cliques and the impotent lamentations of the petty-bourgeois radicals showed clearly that salvation cannot be expected from this source, the workers, by a series of courageous strikes, cried out to the people: *We are here!*

The "Left" European bourgeois journalists with pretensions to learning, and, following them, the Social Democrats, philosophize on the theme that Spain is simply about to reproduce the Great French Revolution, after a delay of almost a hundred and fifty years. To expound revolution to these people is equivalent to arguing with a blind man about colors. With all its backwardness, Spain has passed far beyond eighteenth-century France. Big industrial enterprises, 10,000 miles of railway, 30,000 miles of telegraph, represent a more important factor of revolution than historical reminiscences.

Endeavoring to take a step forward, a certain English weekly, *The Economist*, says with regard to the Spanish events: "We have here the influence of Paris of '48 and '71 rather than the influence of Moscow of 1917." [2] But Paris of '71 is a step from '48 towards 1917. The comparison is an empty one.

L. Tarquin wrote last year in *La Lutte de Classes* infinitely more seriously and profoundly:

> The proletariat [of Spain], supporting itself on the peasant masses, is the only force capable of seizing power.

The perspective in connection with this is depicted as follows:

> The revolution must bring about the dictatorship of the proletariat which would carry out the bourgeois revolution and would courageously open the road to socialist transformation.

This is the way—the only way—the question can now be posed.

[2] [Retranslated from the Russian.—Tr.]

18

Democracy and Fascism

TRANSLATED BY JOSEPH VANZLER
from *What Next?* (1932).

The Eleventh Plenum of the ECCI [Executive Committee of the Communist International] came to the decision that it was imperative to put an end to those erroneous views which originate in "the liberal interpretation of the contradictions between fascism and bourgeois democracy and the outright fascist forms." The gist of this Stalinist philosophy is quite plain: from the Marxist denial of the *absolute* contradiction it deduces the *general* negation of the contradiction, even of the *relative* contradiction. This error is typical of vulgar radicalism. For if there be no contradiction *whatsoever* between democracy and Fascism—even in the sphere of the *form* of the rule of the bourgeoisie—then these two regimes obviously enough must be equivalent. Whence the conclusion: social democracy = fascism. For some reason, however, social democracy is dubbed *social* fascism. And the meaning of the term "social" in this connection has been left unexplained to this very moment.[1]

Nevertheless, the nature of things does not change in accordance with the decisions of the ECCI plenums. A contradiction does exist between democracy and fascism. It is not at all "absolute," or, putting it in the language of Marxism, it doesn't at all denote the rule of two irreconcilable classes. But it does denote different systems of the domination of one and the same class. These two systems—the one parliamentary-democratic, the other fascist—derive their support from different combinations of the oppressed and exploited classes; and they unavoidably come to a sharp clash with each other.

The social democracy, which is today the chief representative of the parliamentary-bourgeois regime, derives its support from the workers. Fascism is supported by the petty bourgeoisie. The social democracy without the mass organizations of the workers can have no influence. Fascism cannot entrench itself in power without annihilating the workers' organizations. The parliament is the main arena of the social democracy. The system of fascism is based upon the destruction of parliamentarism. For the monopolistic bourgeoisie, the parliamentary and fascist regimes represent only different vehicles of dominion; it has recourse to one or the other, depending upon the historical conditions. But for both the social democracy and fascism, the choice of one or the other vehicle has an independent significance, more than that: for them it is a question of political life or death.

---

[1] Metaphysicians (people who do not reason dialectically) assign to one and the same abstraction two, three or more designations, often directly contradictory. "Democracy" in general and "fascism" in general, so we are told, are in no way distinguished from one another. But in addition there must also exist in the world, on this account, "the dictatorship of workers and peasants" (for China, India, Spain). Proletarian dictatorship? No! Capitalist dictatorship, perhaps? No! What then? A democratic one! Somewhere in the universe, it appears, there exists a pure classless democracy. Yet according to the Eleventh Plenum of the ECCI, democracy differs in no wise from fascism. That being so, wherein does "the democratic dictatorship" differ from . . . the fascist dictatorship?

Only a person utterly naïve will expect to get a serious and an honest answer to this fundamental question from the Stalinists: they'll let loose a few more choice epithets—and that's all. And meanwhile the fate of the revolutions in the Orient is tied up with this question.

At the moment that the "normal" police and military resources of the bourgeois dictatorship, together with their parliamentary screens, no longer suffice to hold society in a state of equilibrium—the turn of the fascist regime arrives. Through the fascist agency, capitalism sets in motion the masses of the crazed petty bourgeoisie, and bands of the declassed and demoralized *Lumpenproletariat;* all the countless human beings from finance capital itself has brought to desperation and frenzy. From fascism the bourgeoisie demands a thorough job; once it has resorted to methods of civil war, it insists on having peace for a period of years. And the fascist agency by utilizing the petty bourgeoisie as a battering ram, by overwhelming all obstacles in its path, does a thorough job. After fascism is victorious, finance capital gathers into its hands, as in a vise of steel, directly and immediately, all the organs and institutions of sovereignty, the executive, administrative and educational powers of the state: the entire state apparatus together with the army, the municipalities, the universities, the schools, the press, the trade unions, and the co-operatives. When a state turns fascist, it doesn't only mean that the forms and methods of government are changed in accordance with the patterns set by Mussolini—the changes in this sphere ultimately play a minor role—but it means, first of all for the most part, that the workers' organizations are annihilated; that the proletariat is reduced to an amorphous state; and that a system of administration is created which penetrates deeply into the masses and which serves to frustrate the independent crystallization of the proletariat. Therein precisely is the gist of fascism.

The above is not at all contradicted by the fact that, during a given period, between the democratic and the fascist systems, a transitional regime, which combines the features of both, is established: such, in general, is the law that governs the displacement of one social system by another, even though they are irreconcilably inimical to each other. There are periods during which the bourgeoisie leans upon both the social democracy and fascism, that is, during which it manipulates simultaneously its electoral and terroristic agencies. Such, in a certain sense, was the government of Kerensky during the last months of its existence, when it leaned partly on the Soviets and at the same time conspired with Kornilov. Such is the government of Brüning as it dances on a tightrope between two irreconcilable camps, balancing itself with the emergency decrees instead of a pole. But such a condition of the state and of the administration is temporary in character. It signalizes the transition period, during which the social democracy is on the verge of exhausting its mission, while, in that same period, neither communism nor fascism is ready as yet to seize power.

The Italian communists, who have had to study the problems of fascism for a long time, have protested time and again against the widespread abuse of these concepts. Formerly, at the Sixth Congress of the Comintern, Ercoli was still formulating views on the question of fascism which are now credited as "Trotskyist." Ercoli at that time defined fascism as being the most thorough and uncompromising system of reaction, and he explained: "this administration supports itself not by the cruelty of its terroristic acts, not by murdering large numbers of workers and peasants, not by applying on a large scale varied methods of brutal torture, not by the severity of its law courts; but it depends upon the systematic annihilation of each and every form of the independent organization of the masses." In this Ercoli is absolutely correct: the gist and task of fascism consist in a complete suppression of all workers' organizations and in the prevention of their revival. In a developed capitalist society this goal cannot be achieved by police methods alone. There is only one method for it, and that is by directly opposing the pressure of the proletariat—the moment it weakens—by the pressure of the desperate masses of the petty bourgeoisie. It is this particular system of capitalist reaction that has entered history under the name of fascism.

> All questions as to the relation between fascism and social democracy [wrote Ercoli] belong to the same sphere [the irreconcilability of fascism with the existence of workers' organizations]. It is in this relation that fascism clearly differentiates itself from all other reactionary regimes established hitherto in the contemporary capitalist world. It rejects all compromise with the social democ-

racy; it persecutes it relentlessly; it deprives it of all legal means of existence; it forces it to emigrate.

So reads an article published in the leading organs of the Comintern! Subsequently, Manuilsky buzzed in Molotov's ear the great idea of "the third period." France, Germany and Poland were assigned to "the front rank of the revolutionary offensive." The seizure of power was proclaimed to be the immediate task. And since, in the face of the uprising of the proletariat, all parties, except the Communist, are counterrevolutionary, it was no longer necessary to distinguish between fascism and social democracy. The theory of social fascism was ordained. And the functionaries of the Comintern lost no time in realigning themselves. Ercoli made haste to prove that precious as truth was to him, Molotov was more precious, and he . . . wrote a report in defense of the theory of social fascism. "The Italian social democracy," he announced in February, 1930, "turns fascist with the greatest readiness." Alas, the functionaries of official communism turn flunkies even more readily.

As was to be expected, our criticism of the theory and application of "the third period" was decreed counterrevolutionary. Nevertheless, the cruel experiences that cost the proletarian vanguard dearly, forced an about-face in this sphere also. "The third period" was pensioned off, and so was Molotov himself—from the Comintern. But the theory of social fascism remained behind as the lone ripe fruit of the third period. No changes could take place here: only Molotov was tied up with the third period; but Stalin himself was enmeshed in social fascism.

Die Rote Fahne begins its researches into social fascism with Stalin's words:

> Fascism is the military organization of the bourgeoisie which leans upon the social democracy for active support. The social democracy, objectively speaking, is the moderate wing of fascism.

Objectively speaking, it is a habit with Stalin, when he attempts to generalize, to contradict the first phrase by the second and to conclude in the second what doesn't at all follow from the first. There is no debating that the bourgeoisie leans on the social democracy, and that fascism is a military organization of the bourgeoisie; and this has been remarked upon a long time ago. The only conclusion which follows from this is that the social democracy as well as fascism are the tools of the big bourgeoisie. How the social democracy becomes thereby also a "wing" of fascism is incomprehensible. Equally profound is another observation by the same author: fascism and social democracy are not enemies; they are twins. Now twins may be the bitterest enemies: while on the other hand allies need not be born necessarily on one and the same day and from identical parents. Stalin's constructions lack even formal logic, to say nothing of dialectics. Their strength lies in the fact that none dares challenge them.

"As regards 'the class content' there are no distinctions between democracy and fascism," lectures Werner Hirsch, echoing Stalin (*Die Internationale*, January, 1932). The transition from democracy to fascism may take the character of "an organic process," that is, it may occur "gradually" and "bloodlessly." Such reasoning might dumfound anyone, but the epigoni have inured us to becoming dumfounded.

There are no "class distinctions" between democracy and fascism. Obviously this must mean that democracy as well as fascism is bourgeois in character. We guessed as much even prior to January, 1932. The ruling class, however, does not inhabit a vacuum. It stands in definite relations to other classes. In a developed capitalist society, during a "democratic" regime, the bourgeoisie leans for support primarily upon the working classes which are held in check by the reformists. In its most finished form, this system finds its expression in England during the administration of the Labor government as well as during that of the Conservatives. In a fascist regime, at least during its first phase, capital leans on the petty bourgeoisie, which destroys the organizations of the proletariat. Italy, for instance! Is there a difference in the "class content" of these two regimes? If the question is posed only as regards the *ruling class,* then there is no difference. If one takes into account the position and the interrelations of *all* classes, from the angle of the proletariat, then the difference appears to be quite enormous.

In the course of many decades, the workers have built up within the bourgeois democracy, by utilizing it, by fighting against it, their own strongholds and bases of *proletarian democracy:* the trade unions, the political parties, the educational and sport clubs, the co-operatives, etc. The proletariat cannot attain power within the formal limits of bourgeois democracy, but can do so only by taking the road of revolution: this has been proved both by theory and experience. And these bulwarks of workers' democracy within the bourgeois state are absolutely essential for the taking of the revolutionary road. The work of the Second International consisted in creating just such bulwarks during the epoch when it was still fulfilling its progressive historic labor.

Fascism has for its basic and only task the razing to their foundation of all institutions of proletarian democracy. Has this, or has it not, any "class meaning" for the proletariat? The lofty theoreticians had better ponder over this. After pronouncing the regime to be bourgeois—which no one questions—Hirsch, together with his masters, overlooks a mere trifle: the position of the proletariat in this regime. In place of the historical process they substitute a bald sociological abstraction. But the class war takes place on the soil of history, and not in the stratosphere of sociology. The point of departure in the struggle against fascism is not the abstraction of the democratic state, but the living organizations of the proletariat, which concentrate all its past experience, and which prepare it for the future.

The statement that the transition from democracy to fascism may take on an "organic" and a "gradual" character can mean one thing and one thing only, and that is: without any fuss, without a fight, the proletariat may be deprived not only of all its material conquests—not only of its given standard of living, of its social legislation, of its civil and political rights—but also even of the basic weapon whereby these were achieved, that is, its organizations. The "bloodless" transition to fascism implies under this terminology the most frightful capitulation of the proletariat that can be conceived.

Werner Hirsch's theoretical discussions are not accidental; while they serve to develop still further the theoretical soothsayings of Stalin, they also serve to generalize the entire present agitation of the Communist Party. The party's chief resources are in fact being strained only to prove that there is no difference between Brüning's regime and Hitler's regime. Thälmann and Remmele see in this the quintessence of Bolshevist policy.

Nor is the matter restricted to Germany only. The notion that nothing new will be added by the victory of fascists is being zealously propagated now in all sections of the Comintern. In the January issue of the French periodical *Cahiers du Bolchevisme*, we read:

> The Trotskyists behave in practice like Breitscheid; they accept the famous social-democratic theory of the "lesser evil," according to which *Brüning is not as bad as Hitler*, according to which it is not so unpleasant to starve under Brüning as under Hitler, and infinitely more preferable to be shot down by Gröner than by Frick.

This is not the most stupid passage, although—to give it due credit—stupid enough. Unfortunately, however, it expresses the gist of the political philosophy of the leaders of the Comintern.

The fact of the matter is that the Stalinists compare the two regimes from the point of view of vulgar democracy. And indeed, were one to consider Brüning's regime from the criterion of "formal" democracy, one would arrive at a conclusion which is beyond argument: nothing is left of the proud Weimar constitution save the skin and bones. But this does not settle the question so far as we are concerned. The question must be approached from the angle of *proletarian* democracy. This criterion is also the only reliable one on which to consider the question as to when and where the "normal" police methods of reaction under decay capitalism are replaced by the fascist regime.

Whether Brüning is "better" than Hitler (better-looking, perhaps?) is a question which, we confess, doesn't interest us at all. But one need only glance at the list of workers' organizations to assert: fascism has not conquered yet in Germany. In the way of its victory there still remain gigantic obstacles and forces.

The present Brüning regime is the regime of bureaucratic dictatorship, or more definitely, the dictatorship of the bourgeoisie enforced by means of the army and the police. The fascist petty bourgeoisie and the proletarian organizations seem to counterbalance one another. Were the workers united by Soviets; were factory committees fighting for the control of production, then one could speak of *dual power*. Because of the split within the proletariat, because of the tactical helplessness of its vanguard, *dual power* does not exist as yet. But the very fact that mighty organizations of workers do exist, which *under certain conditions* are capable of repelling fascism with crushing force—that is what keeps Hitler from seizing power and imparts a certain "independence" to the bureaucratic apparatus.

Brüning's dictatorship is a caricature of bonapartism. His dictatorship is unstable, unreliable, short-lived. It signalizes not the initiation of a new social equilibrium, but the early crash of the old one. Directly supported only by a small minority of the bourgeoisie, tolerated by the social democracy against the will of the workers, threatened by fascism, Brüning can bring down the thunder of paper decrees but not real thunderbolts. Brüning is fit for dissolving parliament with its own assent; he'll do to promulgate a few decrees against the workers; to proclaim a Christmas truce and to make a few deals under its cover; to break up a hundred meetings, close down a dozen papers, exchange letters with Hitler worthy of a village druggist—that is all. But for greater things his hands are too short.

Brüning is compelled to tolerate the existence of workers' organizations because to this very day he hasn't decided to hand the power over to Hitler, and because he himself has no independent means of liquidating them. Brüning is compelled to tolerate the fascists and to patronize them inasmuch as he mortally fears the victory of the workers. Brüning's regime is a transitional, short-lived regime, preceding the catastrophe. The present administration holds on only because the chief camps have not as yet pitted their strength. The real battle hasn't begun. It is still to come. The dictatorship of bureaucratic impotence fills in the lull before the battle, before the forces are openly matched.

The wiseacres who boast that they do not recognize any difference "between Brüning and Hitler" are saying in reality: it makes no difference whether our organizations exist, or whether they are already destroyed. Beneath this pseudo-radical phraseology there hides the most sordid passivity; we can't escape defeat anyway! Read over carefully the quotation from the French Stalinist periodical. They reduce the question to whether it is better to starve under Hitler or Brüning. To them it is a question of under whom to starve. To us, on the contrary, it is not a question of under which conditions it is better to die. We raise the question of how to fight and win. And we conclude thus, the major offensive must be begun before the bureaucratic dictatorship is replaced by the fascist regime, that is, before the workers' organizations are crushed. The general offensive should be prepared for by deploying, extending, and sharpening the sectional clashes. But for this one must have a correct perspective; and first of all, one should not proclaim victorious the enemy who is still a long way from victory.

Herein is the crux of the problem; herein is the strategic key to the background; herein is the operating base from which the battle must be waged. Every thinking worker, the more so every communist, must give himself an accounting and plumb to the bottom the empty and rotten talk of the Stalinist bureaucracy about Brüning and Hitler being one and the same thing. You are muddling! we say in answer. You muddle disgracefully because you are afraid of the difficulties that lie ahead, because you are terrified by the great problems that lie ahead; you throw in the sponge before the fighting is begun, you proclaim that we have already suffered defeat. You are lying! The working class is split; it is weakened by the reformists and disorientated by the vacillations of its own vanguard, but it is not yet annihilated, its forces are not yet exhausted. No. The proletariat of Germany is powerful. The most optimistic estimates will be infinitely surpassed once its revolutionary energy will clear the way for it to the arena of action.

Brüning's regime is the preparatory regime. Preparatory to what? Either to the victory of fascism, or to the victory of the proletariat. This regime is preparatory because both camps are only preparing for the decisive battle. If you identify Brüning with Hitler, you identify the conditions before the battle with the conditions after defeat; it means that you admit defeat beforehand; it means that you appeal for surrender without a battle.

The overwhelming majority of the workers, particularly the communists, does not want this. The Stalinist bureaucracy, of course, does not want it either. But one must take into account not one's good intentions, with which Hitler will pave the road to his Hell, but the objective meaning of one's policies, of their direction and their tendencies. We must disclose in its entirety the passive, timidly hesitant, capitulating and declamatory character of the politics of Stalin-Manuilsky-Thälmann-Remmele. We must teach the revolutionary workers to understand that the key to the situation is in the hands of the Communist Party; but the Stalinist bureaucracy attempts to use this key to lock the gates to revolutionary action.

19

For a Workers' United Front Against Fascism

TRANSLATED BY MORRIS LEWITT
from *Germany: The Key to the International Situation* (1932).

At the present moment Germany is passing through one of those great historic hours upon which the fate of the German people, the fate of Europe and in an important measure, the fate of all humanity will depend for decades. If you place a ball on top of a pyramid, the slightest impact can cause it to roll down either to the left or to the right. That is the situation approaching with every hour in Germany today. There are forces which would like the ball to roll down towards the right and break the back of the working class. There are forces which would like the ball to remain at the top. That is a utopia. The ball cannot remain at the top of the pyramid. The communists want the ball to roll down toward the left and break the back of capitalism. But it is not enough to want, one must know how. Let us calmly reflect once more: Is the policy carried on at present by the Central Committee of the Communist Party of Germany correct or incorrect?

WHAT DOES HITLER WANT?

The Fascists are growing very rapidly. The communists are also growing, but much more slowly. The growth at the extreme poles shows that the ball cannot maintain itself at the top of the pyramid. The rapid growth of the Fascists signifies the danger that the ball *may* roll down toward the right. Therein lies an enormous danger.

Hitler emphasizes that he is against a coup d'état. In order to strangle democracy once and for all, he wants to gain power in no other way, so to speak, than by the democratic road. Can we seriously believe this?

Of course, if the Fascists could figure on obtaining an absolute majority of the votes at the next elections in a peaceful way, then they would perhaps even prefer this road. In reality, however, this road is unthinkable for them. It is stupid to believe that the Nazis would grow uninterruptedly, as they do now, for an unlimited period of time. Sooner or later they will drain their social reservoir. Fascism has introduced into its own ranks such terrific contradictions, that the moment must come in which the flow ceases to replace the ebb. This moment can arrive long before the Fascists have united about them even half of the votes. They will not be able to halt, for they will have nothing more to look for here. They will be forced to resort to an overturn.

But even apart from all this, the Fascists are cut off from the democratic road. The immense growth of the political contradictions in the country, the stark brigands' agitation of the Fascists will inevitably lead to a situation in which the closer the Fascists approach a majority, the more heated the atmosphere will become and the more extensive the unfolding of the conflicts and struggles will be. With this perspective, civil war is absolutely inevitable. Consequently, the question of the seizure of power by the Fascists will be decided not by vote, but by civil war, which the Fascists are preparing and provoking.

Can we assume even for one minute that Hitler and his councilors do not realize and foresee this? That would be to consider them blockheads. There is no greater crime in politics than that of hoping for stupidities on the part of a strong enemy. But if Hitler is not unaware that the road to power leads through the most gruesome civil war, then it means that his speeches about the peaceful democratic road are only a cloak, that is, a stratagem. In that case, it is all the more necessary to keep one's eyes open.

WHAT IS CONCEALED BEHIND HITLER'S STRATAGEM?

His calculations are quite simple and obvious: He wants to lull his antagonists with the long-run perspective of the parliamentary growth of the Nazis in order to catch them napping and to deal them a deathblow at the right moment. It is quite possible that Hitler's courtesies to democratic parliamentarism may, moreover, help to set up some sort of coalition in the immediate future in which the Fascists will obtain the most important posts and employ them in turn for their coup d'état. For it is entirely clear that the coalition, let us assume, between the Center and the Fascists will not be a stage in the "democratic" solution of the question, but a step closer to the coup d'état under conditions most favorable to the Fascists.

WE MUST PLAN ACCORDING TO THE SHORTER PERSPECTIVE

All this means that, even independently of the desires of the fascist general staff, the solution can intervene in the course of the next few months, if not weeks. This circumstance is of tremendous importance in elaborating a correct policy. If we allow the Fascists to seize power in two or three months, then the struggle against them next year will be much harder than in this. All revolutionary plans laid out in advance of two, three or five years will prove to be only wretched and disgraceful twaddle, if the working class allows the Fascists to gain power in the course of the next two, three or five months.

In the polity of revolutionary crises, the calculation of time is of just as decisive importance as it is in war operations. . . .

Yes, should the Fascists really conquer power, that would mean not only the physical destruction of the Communist Party, but veritable political bankruptcy for it. An ignominious defeat in a struggle against bands of human rubbish would never be forgiven the Communist International and its German section by the many-millioned German proletariat. The seizure of power by the Facists would therefore most probably signify the necessity of creating a new revolutionary party, and in all likelihood also a new International. That would be a frightful historical catastrophe. But to assume today that all this is *unavoidable* can be done only by genuine liquidators, those who under the mantle of hollow phrases are really hastening to capitulate like cravens in the face of the struggle, and without a struggle. With this conception we Bolshevik-Leninists who are called "Trotskyists" by the Stalinists have nothing in common.

We are unshakably convinced that the victory over the Fascists is possible—not after their coming to power, not after five, ten or twenty years of their rule, but now, under the given conditions, in the coming months and weeks.

THÄLMANN CONSIDERS THE VICTORY OF FASCISM INEVITABLE

A correct policy is necessary in order to achieve victory. That is, we need a policy appropriate to the present situation, to the present relationship of forces, and not to the situation that may develop in one, two or three years, when the question of power will already have been decided for a long time.

The whole misfortune lies in the fact that the policy of the Central Committee of the German Communist party, in part consciously and in part unconsciously, proceeds from the recognition of the inevitability of a fascist victory. In fact, in the appeal for the "Red United Front" published on November 29, 1931, the Central Committee of the Communist Party of Germany proceeds from the idea that it is impossible to defeat fascism without first defeating the social democracy. The same idea is repeated in all possible shades in Thälmann's article. Is this idea correct? On the historical scale it is unconditionally correct. But that does not at all mean that with its aid, that is, by simple repetition, one can solve the *questions of the day*. An idea, correct from the point of view of revolutionary *strategy* as a whole, is converted into a lie and at that into a reactionary lie, if it is not translated into the language of *tactics*. Is it correct that in order to destroy unemployment and misery it is first necessary to destroy capitalism? It is correct. But only the biggest blockhead can conclude from all this that we do not have to fight this very day, with all of our forces, against the measures with whose aid capitalism is increasing the misery of the workers.

Can we expect that in the course of the next few months the Communist Party will defeat both the social democracy and fascism? No normal-thinking person who can read and calculate would risk such a contention. Politically, the question stands like this: can we successfully repel fascism now, in the course of the next few months, that is, with the existence of a greatly weakened, but still (unfortunately) very strong social democracy? The Central Committee replies in the negative. In other words, Thälmann considers the victory of fascism inevitable.

ONCE AGAIN: THE RUSSIAN EXPERIENCE

In order to express my thought as clearly and as concretely as possible I will come back once more to the experience with the Kornilov uprising. On August 26, 1917, General Kornilov led his Cossack corps and one irregular division against Petrograd. At the helm of power stood Kerensky, lackey of the bourgeoisie and three-quarters a confederate of Kornilov. Lenin was still in hiding because of the accusation that he was in the service of the Hohenzollerns. For the same accusation, I was at that time incarcerated in solitary confinement in Kresty Prison. How did the Bolsheviks proceed in this question? They also had a right to say: "In order to defeat the Korniloviad—we must first defeat the Kerenskiad." They said this more than once, for it was correct and necessary for all the subsequent propaganda. But that was entirely inadequate for offering resistance to Kornilov on August 26, and on the days that followed, and for preventing him from butchering the Petrograd proletariat. That is why the Bolsheviks did not content themselves with a general appeal to the workers and soldiers to break with the conciliators and to support the Red united front of the Bolsheviks. No, the Bolsheviks proposed the united front struggle to the Mensheviks and the Social Revolutionaries and created together with them joint organizations of struggle. Was this correct or incorrect? Let Thälmann answer that. In order to show even more vividly how matters stood with the united front, I will cite the following incident: Immediately upon my release after the trade unions had put up bail for me, I went directly to the Committee for National Defense, where I discussed and adopted decisions regarding the struggle against Kornilov, with the Menshevik Dan and the Social Revolutionist Gotz—allies of Kerensky, who had kept me in prison. Was this right or wrong? Let Remmele answer that.

IS BRÜNING THE "LESSER EVIL"?

The social democracy supports Brüning, votes for him, assumes responsibility for him before the masses—on the grounds that the Brüning government is the "lesser evil." The *Rote Fahne* attempts to ascribe the same view to me—on the grounds that I expressed myself against the stupid and shameful participation of the communists in the Hitler referendum. But has the German Left Opposition, and myself in particular, demanded that the communists vote for and support Brüning? We Marxists regard Brüning and Hitler, Braun included, as component parts of one and the same system. The question as to which one of them is the "lesser evil" has no sense, for the system we are fighting against needs all these elements. But these elements are momentarily involved in conflicts with one another, and the party of the proletariat must take advantage of these conflicts in the interest of the revolution.

There are seven keys in the musical scale. The question as to which of these keys is "better," Do, Re, or Sol, is a nonsensical question. But the musician must know when to strike and what keys to strike. The abstract question of who is the lesser evil, Brüning or Hitler, is just as nonsensical. It is necessary to know which of these keys to strike. Is that clear? For the feeble-minded let us cite another example. When one of my enemies sets before me small daily portions of poison and the second, on the other hand, is about to shoot straight at me, then I will first knock the revolver out of the hand of my second enemy, for this gives me an opportunity to get rid of my first enemy. But that does not at all mean that the poison is a "lesser evil" in comparison with the revolver.

The misfortune consists precisely of the fact that the leaders of the German Communist Party have placed themselves on the same ground as the social democracy, only with inverted prefixes: the social democracy votes for Brüning, recognizing in him the lesser evil. The communists, on the other hand, who refuse to trust either Braun or Brüning in any way (and that is absolutely the right way to act), go into the streets to support Hitler's referendum, that is, the attempt of the Fascists to overthrow Brüning. But by this they themselves have recognized in Hitler the lesser evil, for the victory of the referendum would not have brought the proletariat into power, but Hitler. To be sure, it is painful to have to argue over such ABC questions. It is sad, very sad indeed, when musicians like Remmele, instead of distinguishing between the keys, stamp with their boots on the keyboard.

IT IS NOT A QUESTION OF THE WORKERS WHO HAVE ALREADY LEFT THE SOCIAL DEMOCRACY BUT OF THOSE WHO STILL REMAIN WITH IT

The thousands upon thousands of Noskes, Welses and Hilferdings prefer, *in the last analysis*, fascism to communism. But for that they must once and for all tear themselves loose from the workers. Today this is not yet the case. Today the social democracy as a whole, with all its internal antagonisms, is forced into sharp conflict with the Fascists. It is our task to take advantage of this conflict and not to unite the antagonists against us.

The front must now be directed against fascism. And this

common front of direct struggle against fascism, embracing the entire proletariat, must be utilized in the struggle against the social democracy directed as a flank attack but no less effective for all that.

It is necessary to show by deeds a complete readiness to make a bloc with the social democrats against the Fascists in all cases in which they will accept a bloc. To say to the social democratic workers: "Cast your leaders aside and join our 'non-party' united front," means to add just one more hollow phrase to a thousand others. We must understand how to tear the workers away from their leaders in reality. But reality today is—the struggle against fascism. There are and doubtless will be social democratic workers who are prepared to fight hand in hand with the communist workers against the Fascists, regardless of the desires or even against the desires of the social democratic organizations. With such progressive elements it is obviously necessary to establish the closest possible contact. At the present time, however, they are not great in number. The German worker has been raised in the spirit of organization and of discipline. This has its strong as well as its weak sides. The overwhelming majority of the social democratic workers will fight against the Fascists, but—for the present at least—only together with their organizations. This stage cannot be skipped. We must help the social democratic workers in action—in this new and extraordinary situation—to test the value of their organizations and leaders at this time, when it is a matter of life and death for the working class.

WE MUST FORCE THE SOCIAL DEMOCRACY INTO A BLOC AGAINST THE FASCISTS

The trouble is that in the Central Committee of the Communist Party there are many frightened opportunists. They have heard that opportunism consists of a love for blocs, and that is why they are against blocs. They do not understand the difference between, let us say, a parliamentary agreement and an-ever-so modest agreement for struggle in a strike or in defense of workers' printshops against fascist bands.

Election agreements and parliamentary compromises concluded between the revolutionary party and the social democracy serve, as a rule, to the advantage of the social democracy. Practical agreements for mass action, for purposes of struggle are always useful to the revolutionary party. The Anglo-Russian Committee was an impermissible type of bloc of two leaderships on one common political platform, vague, deceptive, binding no one to any action at all. The maintenance of this bloc at the time of the General Strike, when the General Council assumed the role of strike-breaker, signified, on the part of the Stalinists, a policy of betrayal.

No common platform with the social democracy, or with the leaders of the German trade unions; no common publications, banners, placards! March separately, but strike unitedly! Agree only how to strike, whom to strike, and when to strike! Such an agreement can be concluded even with the devil himself, with his grandmother and even with Noske and Grzezinsky. On one condition: not to bind one's own hands.

It is necessary, without any delay, finally to elaborate a practical system of measures—not with the aim of merely "exposing" the social democracy (before the Communists), but with the aim of actual struggle against fascism. The question of factory defense organizations, of unhampered activity on the part of the factory councils, the inviolability of the workers' organizations and institutions, the question of arsenals that may be seized by the Fascists, the question of measures in the case of an emergency, that is, of the co-ordination of the actions of the Communist and the social democratic divisions in the struggle, etc., etc., must be dealt with in this program.

In the struggle against fascism, the factory councils occupy a tremendously important position. Here a particularly precise program of action is necessary. Every factory must become an anti-fascist bulwark, with its own commandants and its own battalions. It is necessary to have a map of the fascist barracks and all other fascist strongholds, in every city and in every district. The Fascists are attempting to encircle the revolutionary strongholds. The encirclers must be encircled. On this basis, an agreement with the social democratic and trade union organizations is not only permissible, but a duty. To reject this for reasons of "principle" (in reality because of bureaucratic stupidity, or what is still worse, because of cowardice) is to give direct and immediate aid to fascism.

A practical program of agreements with the social democratic workers was proposed by us as far back as September, 1930 ("The Turn in the Comintern and the Situation in Germany," published by *The Militant*), that is, a year and a quarter ago. What has the leadership undertaken in this direction? Next to nothing. The Central Committee of the Communist Party has taken up everything except that which constitutes its direct task. How much valuable, irretrievable time has been lost! As a matter of fact, not much time is left. The program of action must be strictly practical, strictly objective, to the point, without any of those artificial "claims," without any reservations, so that every average social democratic worker can say to himself: What the communists propose is completely indispensable for the struggle against fascism. On this basis, we must pull the social democratic workers along with us by our example, and criticize their leaders, who will inevitably serve as a check and a brake. Only in this way is victory possible.

A GOOD QUOTATION FROM LENIN

The present-day Epigoni, that is, the thoroughly bad disciples of Lenin, like to cover up their shortcomings on every occasion that offers itself with quotations—often entirely irrelevant. For Marxists, the question is decided not by a quotation but by means of the correct method. If one is guided by correct methods, it is not hard also to find suitable quotations. After I had drawn the above analogy with the Kornilov insurrection, I said to myself: We can probably find in Lenin a theoretical elucidation of our bloc with the conciliators in the struggle against Kornilov. And here is what I actually found in the second part of Volume XIV of the Russian edition, in a letter of Lenin to the Central Committee, written at the beginning of September, 1917:

> Even at the present time, we are not duty-bound to support the Kerensky government. That would be unprin-

cipled. It is asked: then we are not to fight against Kornilov? Of course we are. But that is not one and the same thing. There is a limit to this; it is being transgressed by many Bolsheviks who fall into "conciliationism" and allow themselves to be driven by the current of events.

We shall fight, we are fighting against Kornilov but we do not support Kerensky; we are uncovering his weaknesses. The distinction is rather delicate, but highly important, and must not be forgotten.

What does the change of our tactics consist of after the Kornilov insurrection?

In this: that we are *varying the forms of struggle against Kerensky*. Without diminishing our hostility to him even by one single note, without taking back one word from what we have said against him, without giving up the task of overthrowing Kerensky, we say: *We must calculate the moment, we will not overthrow Kerensky at present*. We approach the question of the struggle against him differently: *by explaining the weaknesses and vacillations of Kerensky to the people* (who are fighting against Kornilov).

We are proposing nothing different. Complete independence of the Communist organization and press, complete freedom of Communist criticism, the same for the social democracy and the trade unions. Only contemptible opportunists can allow the freedom of the Communist Party to be limited (for example, like entrance into the Kuomintang). We are not of their number.

No retraction of our criticism of the social democracy. No forgetting of all that has been. The whole historical reckoning, including the reckoning for Karl Liebknecht and Rosa Luxemburg will be presented at the proper time, just as the Russian Bolsheviks finally presented a general reckoning to the Mensheviks and Social Revolutionaries for the baiting, calumny, imprisonment and murder of workers, soldiers and peasants.

But we presented our general reckoning to them two months after we had utilized the partial reckoning between Kerensky and Kornilov, between the "democrats" and the Fascists—

in order to drive back the Fascists all the more certainly. Only thanks to this circumstance were we victorious.

When the Central Committee of the Communist Party of Germany adopts the position expressed in the quotation from Lenin cited above, the entire approach to the social democratic masses and the trade union organizations will change at once: instead of the articles and speeches which are convincing only to those people who are already convinced without them, the agitators will find a common language with new hundreds of thousands and millions of workers. The differentiation within the social democracy will proceed at an increased pace. The Fascists will soon feel that their task does not at all consist merely of defeating Brüning, Braun and Wels, but of taking up the open struggle against the whole working class. On this plane, a profound differentiation will inevitably be produced within fascism. Only by this road is victory possible.

But it is necessary to *desire* this victory. In the meantime, there are among the Communist officials not a few cowardly careerists and fakers whose little posts, whose incomes and more than that, whose hides, are dear to them. These creatures are very much inclined to spout ultra-radical phrases, beneath which is concealed a wretched and contemptible fatalism. "Without a victory over the social democracy, we cannot battle against fascism!" say such terrible revolutionists, and for this reason . . . they get their passports ready.

Worker-Communists, you are hundreds of thousands, millions; you cannot leave for any place; there are not enough passports for you. Should fascism come to power, it will ride over your skulls and spines like a terrific tank. Your salvation lies in merciless struggle. And only a fighting unity with the social democratic workers can bring victory. Make haste, worker-communists, you have very little time left!

20

The German Catastrophe

TRANSLATED BY MAX SHACHTMAN
(1933).

The imperialist epoch, in Europe at least, has been one of sharp turns, in which politics has acquired an extremely mobile character. At each turn the stakes have been, not some partial reform or other, but the fate of the regime. On this fact the exceptional role of the revolutionary party and of its leadership is based. If, in the good old days when the social democracy grew regularly and uninterruptedly, like the capitalism which nourished it, the leadership of Bebel resembled a general staff tranquilly elaborating plans for a war in the indefinite future (a war that perhaps might not come after all), under present conditions the Central Committee of a revolutionary party resembles the field headquarters of an army in action. The strategy of the study has been replaced by the strategy of the battle field.

The struggle against a centralized enemy demands centralization. Trained in a spirit of strict discipline, the German workers assimilated this idea with renewed vigor during the war and the political convulsions which followed it. The workers are not blind to the defects of their leadership, but none of them as an individual is able to shake off the grip of the organization. The workers as a whole consider it better to have a strong leadership, even if a faulty one, than to pull in different directions or to resort to "free-lance" activities. Never before in the history of humanity has a political staff played so important a role or borne such responsibility as in the present epoch.

The unparalleled defeat of the German proletariat is the most important event since the conquest of power by the Russian proletariat. The first task on the morrow of the defeat is to analyze the policy of the leadership. The most responsible leaders (who are, heaven be praised, safe and sound) point with pathos to the imprisoned rank-and-file executors of their policies in order to suppress all criticism. We can only meet such a spuriously sentimental argument with contempt. Our solidarity with those whom Hitler has imprisoned is unassailable, but this solidarity does not extend to accepting the mistakes of the leaders. The losses sustained will be justified only if the ideas of the vanquished are advanced. The preliminary condition for this is courageous criticism.

For a whole month not a single communist organ, the Moscow *Pravda* not excepted, uttered a word on the catastrophe of March 5. They all waited to hear what the Praesidium of the Executive Committee of the Communist International would say. For its part the Praesidium oscillated between two contradictory variants: "The German Central Committee led us astray," and "The German Central Committee pursued a correct policy." The first variant was ruled out: the preparation of the catastrophe had taken place under the eyes of everybody, and the controversy with the Left opposition that preceded the catastrophe had too clearly committed the leaders of the Communist International. At last, on April 7, the decision was announced:

> The political line ... of the Central Committee, with Thälmann at its head, was completely correct up to and during Hitler's coup d'état.

It is only to be regretted that all those who were dispatched into the beyond by the Fascists did not learn of this consoling affirmation before they died.

The resolution of the Praesidium does not attempt to analyze the policy of the German Communist Party—which was, above all else, to have been expected—but constitutes another in the long series of indictments against the social democracy. It preferred, we are told, a coalition with the bourgeoisie to a coalition with the communists; it evaded a real struggle against fascism; it fettered the initiative of the masses; and as it had in its hands the "leadership of the mass labor organizations," it succeeded in preventing a general strike. All this is true. But it is nothing new. The social democracy, as the party of social reform, exhausted the progressiveness of its mission, as capitalism was transforming itself into imperialism. During the war the social democracy functioned as a direct instrument of imperialism. After the war it hired itself out officially as the family doctor of capitalism. The Communist Party strove to be its grave-digger. On whose side was the whole course of development? The chaotic state of international relations, the collapse of pacifist illusions, the unparalleled crisis which is tantamount to a great war with its aftermath of epidemics—all this, it would seem, revealed the decadent character of European capitalism and the hopelessness of reformism.

Then what happened to the Communist Party? In reality the Communist International is ignoring one of its own sections, even though that section rallied some six million votes in the election. That is no longer a mere vanguard; it is a great independent army. Why, then, did it take part in the events only as a victim of repression and pogroms? Why, at the decisive hour, did it prove to be stricken with paralysis? There are circumstances under which one cannot withdraw without giving battle. A defeat may result from the superiority of the enemy forces; after defeat one may recover. The passive surrender of all the decisive positions reveals an organic incapacity to fight which does not go unpunished.

The Praesidium tells us that the policy of the Communist International was correct "before as well as during the coup d'état." A correct policy, however, begins with a correct appraisal of the situation. Yet, for the last four years, in fact up to March 5, 1933, we heard day in and day out that a mighty anti-fascist front was growing uninterruptedly in Germany, that National Socialism was retreating and disintegrating, that the whole situation was under the aegis of the revolutionary offensive. *How could a policy have been correct when the whole analysis on which it was based was knocked over like a house of cards?*

The Praesidium justifies the passive retreat by the fact that the Communist Party, "lacking the support of the majority of the working class," could not engage in a decisive battle without committing a crime. Nevertheless, the same resolution considers the July 20 call for a general political strike as deserving special praise, though for some unknown reason it neglects to mention an identical call of March 5. Is not the general strike a "decisive struggle"? The two strike calls wholly corresponded to the obligations of a "leading role" in the "anti-fascist united front" under the conditions of the "revolutionary offensive." Unfortunately, the strike calls fell on deaf ears; nobody came out and answered them. But if, between the official interpretation of events and the strike calls on the one hand, and the facts and deeds on the other, there arises such a crying contradiction, it is hard to understand wherein a correct policy can be distinguished from a disastrous one. In any case, the Praesidium has forgotten to explain which was correct—the two strike calls or the indifference of the workers to them.

But perhaps the division in the ranks of the proletariat was the cause for the defeat? Such an explanation is created especially for lazy minds. The unity of the proletariat, as a universal slogan, is a myth. The proletariat is not homogeneous. The split begins with the political awakening of the proletariat, and constitutes the mechanics of its growth. Only under the conditions of a ripened social crisis, when it is faced with the seizure of power as an immediate task, can the vanguard of the proletariat, provided with a correct policy, rally around itself the overwhelming majority of its class. But the rise to this revolutionary peak is accomplished on the steps of successive splits.

It was not Lenin who invented the policy of the united front; like the split within the proletariat, it is imposed by the dialectics of the class struggle. No successes would be possible without temporary agreements, for the sake of fulfilling immediate tasks, among various sections, organizations and groups of the proletariat. Strikes, trade unions, journals, parliamentary elections, street demonstrations demand that the split be bridged in practice from time to time as the need arises; that is, they demand a united front *ad hoc,* even if it does not always take on the form of one. In the first stages of a movement, unity arises episodically and spontaneously from below, but when the masses are accustomed to fighting through their organizations, unity must also be established at the top. Under the conditions existing in advanced capitalist countries, the slogan of "only from below" is a gross anachronism, fostered by memories of the first stages of the revolutionary movement, especially in Czarist Russia.

At a certain level, the struggle for unity of action is converted from an elementary fact into a tactical task. The simple formula of the united front solves nothing. It is not only communists who appeal for unity, but also reformists, and even Fascists. The tactical application of the united front is subordinated, in every given period, to a definite strategic conception. In preparing the revolutionary unification of the workers, without and against reformism, a long, persistent and patient experience in applying the united front with the reformists is necessary; always, of course, from the point of view of the final revolutionary goal. It is precisely in this field that Lenin gave us incomparable examples.

The strategic conception of the Communist International was false from beginning to end. The point of departure of the German Communist Party was that there is nothing but a mere division of labor between the social democracy and fascism, that their interests are similar if not identical. Instead of helping to aggravate the discord between Communism's principal political adversary and its mortal foe—for which it would have been sufficient to proclaim the truth aloud instead of violating it—the Communist International convinced the reformists and the Fascists that they were twins; it predicted their conciliation, embittered and repulsed the Social Democratic workers and consolidated their reformist leaders. Worse yet: in every case where, despite the obstacles presented by the leadership, local unity committees for workers' defense were created, the bureaucracy forced its representatives to withdraw under threat of expulsion. It displayed persistency and perseverance only in sabotaging the united front, from above as well as from below. All this it did, to be sure, with the best of intentions.

No policy of the Communist Party could, of course, have transformed the social democracy into a party of the revolution. But neither was that the aim. It was necessary to exploit to the limit the contradiction between reformism and fascism —in order to weaken fascism, at the same time weakening reformism by exposing to the workers the incapacity of the social democratic leadership. These two tasks fused naturally into one. The policy of the Communist International bureaucracy led to the opposite result: the capitulation of the reformists served the interests of fascism and not of Communism; the social democratic workers remained with their leaders; the Communist workers lost faith in themselves and in the leadership.

The masses wanted to fight, but they were obstinately prevented from doing so by the leaders. Tension, uneasiness and finally disorientation disrupted the proletariat from within. It is dangerous to keep molten metal too long on the fire; it is still more dangerous to keep society too long in a state of revolutionary crisis. The petty bourgeoisie swung over in its overwhelming majority to the side of National Socialism only because the proletariat, paralyzed from above, proved powerless to lead it along a different road. The absence of resistance on the part of the workers heightened the self-assurance of fascism and diminished the fear of the big bourgeoisie confronted by the risk of civil war. The inevitable demoralization of the communist detachment, increasingly isolated from the proletariat, rendered impossible even a partial resistance. Thus the triumphal procession of Hitler over the bones of the proletarian organizations was assured.

The false strategic conceptions of the Communist International collided with reality at every stage, thereby leading to a course of incomprehensible and inexplicable zigzags. The fundamental principle of the Communist International was: *a united front with the reformist leaders cannot be permitted!* Then, at the most critical hour, the Central Committee of the German Communist Party, without explanation or preparation, appealed to the leaders of the social democracy, proposing the united front as an ultimatum: today or never! Both leaders and workers in the reformist camp interpreted this step, not as the product of fear, but, on the contrary, as a diabolical trap. After the inevitable failure of an attempt at compromise, the Communist International ordered that the appeal be ignored and the very idea of a united front was once more proclaimed counterrevolutionary. Such an insult to the political consciousness of the masses could not pass with impunity. If up to March 5 one could, with some difficulty, still imagine that the Communist International, in its fear of the enemy, might possibly call upon the social democracy, at the last moment, under the club of the enemy—then the appeal of the Praesidium on March 5 proposing joint action to the social democratic parties of the entire world, independent of the internal conditions of each country, made even this explanation impossible. In this belated and world-wide proposal for a united front, when Germany was revealed by the flames of the Reichstag fire, there was no longer a word about social fascism. The Communist International was even prepared—it is hard to believe this, but it was printed in black and white!—*to refrain from criticism of the social democracy* during the whole period of the joint struggle.

The waves of this panic-stricken capitulation to reformism had hardly had time to subside when Wels swore fealty to Hitler, and Leipart offered fascism his assistance and support. "The communists," immediately declared the Praesidium of the Communist International, "were right in calling the Social Democrats social fascists." These people are always right.

Then why did they themselves abandon the theory of social fascism a few days before this unmistakable confirmation of it? Luckily, nobody dares to put embarrassing questions to the leaders. But the misfortunes do not stop there: the bureaucracy thinks too slowly to keep pace with the present tempo of events. Hardly had the Praesidium fallen back upon the famous revelation, "fascism and social democracy are twins," when Hitler accomplished the complete destruction of the free trade unions and, incidentally, arrested Leipart and company. The relations between the twin brothers are not entirely brotherly.

Instead of taking reformism as an historical reality, with its interests and its contradictions, with all its oscillations to the right and left, the bureaucracy operates with mechanical models. Leipart's readiness to crawl on all fours *after* the defeat is offered as an argument against the united front *before* the defeat, *for the purpose of avoiding* the defeat. As if the policy of making fighting agreements with the reformists were based upon the valor of the reformist leaders and not upon the incompatibility of the organs of the proletarian democracy and the fascist bands.

In August, 1932, when Germany was still ruled by the "social General," von Schleicher, who was supposed to assure the union of Hitler with Wels, announced by the Communist International, I wrote:

> Everything goes to show that the Wels-von Schleicher-Hitler triangle will fall apart before it has really been put together. But perhaps it will be replaced by a Hitler-Wels combination? . . . Let us assume that the Social Democracy, without being afraid of its own workers, would seek to sell Hitler its toleration. Fascism, however, does not need this commodity, it is not the toleration of the Social Democracy which it needs but its abolition. The Hitler government can realize its task only when it has broken the resistance of the proletariat and all the possible organs of such a resistance. Therein lies the historical role of fascism. ("The Only Road," p. 31.)

That the reformists, after the defeat, would be happy if Hitler were to permit them to vegetate legally until better times return cannot be doubted. But unfortunately for them, Hitler —the experience of Italy has not been in vain for him— realizes that the labor organizations, even if their leaders accept a muzzle, would inevitably become a threatening danger at the first political crisis.

Doctor Ley, the corporal of the present "labor front," has determined, with much more logic than the Praesidium of the Communist International, the relationship between the so-called twins.

> Marxism is playing dead, [he said on May 2] in order to rise again at a more favorable opportunity. . . . The sly fox does not deceive us! It is better for us to deal him the final blow rather than to tolerate him until he recovers. The Leiparts and the Grossmanns may feign all sorts of devotion to Hitler—but it is better to keep them under lock and key. That is why we are striking out of the hands of the Marxist rabble its principal weapon (the trade unions) and are thus depriving it of the last possibility of arming itself again.

If the bureaucracy of the Communist International were not so infallible and if it listened to criticism, it would not have made additional mistakes between March 22, when Leipart swore fealty to Hitler, and May 2, when Hitler, in spite of the oath, arrested him.

Essentially the theory of "social fascism" could have been refuted even if the Fascists had not done such a thorough job of forcing themselves into the trade unions. Even if Hitler had found it necessary, as a result of the relationship of forces, to leave Leipart temporarily and nominally at the head of the trade unions, the agreement would not have eliminated the incompatibility of the fundamental interests. Even though tolerated by fascism, the reformists would remember the flesh-pots of the Weimar democracy, and that alone would make them concealed enemies. How can one fail to see that the interests of the Social Democracy and of fascism are incompatible when even the independent existence of the Steel Helmets is impossible in the Third Reich? Mussolini tolerated the Social Democracy and even the Communist Party for some time, only to destroy them all the more mercilessly later on. The vote of the Social Democratic deputies in the Reichstag for the foreign policy of Hitler, covering this party with fresh dishonor, will not ameliorate its fate by one iota.

As one of the main causes for the victory of fascism, the luckless leaders refer—in secret, to be sure—to the "genius" of Hitler, who foresaw everything and neglected nothing. It would be fruitless now to submit the fascist policy to a retrospective criticism. One need only remember that Hitler, during the summer of last year, allowed the high peak of the fascist tide to escape him. But even the gross loss of rhythm—a colossal mistake—did not have fatal results. The burning of the Reichstag by Göring, even if this act of provocation was crudely executed, did, however, yield the necessary result. The same must be said of the fascist policy as a whole, for it led to victory. One cannot, unfortunately, deny the superiority of the fascist over the proletarian leadership. But it is only out of an unbecoming modesty that the beaten chiefs keep silent about their own part in the victory of Hitler. There is the game of checkers and there is also the game of losers-win. The game that was played in Germany has this singular feature, that Hitler played checkers and his opponents played to lose. As for political genius, Hitler has no need for it. The strategy of his enemy compensated largely for anything his own strategy lacked.

21

The Popular Front in France

TRANSLATED BY HAROLD ISAACS AND JOHN G. WRIGHT

from *Whither France?* (1936).

Parliamentary cretins who consider themselves connoisseurs of the people like to repeat: "One must not frighten the middle classes with revolution. They do not like extremes." In this general form this affirmation is absolutely false. Naturally, the petty proprietor prefers order so long as business is going well and so long as he hopes that tomorrow it will go better.

But when this hope is lost, he is easily enraged and is ready to give himself over to the most extreme measures. Otherwise, how could he have overthrown the democratic state and brought fascism to power in Italy and Germany? The despair-

[Trotsky distinguished sharply between the united front, which he approved of on particular occasions, and the Popular Front, to which he was opposed in principle. Thus, he advocated a united front of the working-class parties in pre-Hitler Germany but attacked the French Popular Front in 1936.

As Trotsky saw it, the united front involved temporary cooperation being petty bourgeois sees in fascism, above all, a fighting force against big capital, and believes that, unlike the working class parties which deal only in words, fascism will use force to establish more "justice." The peasant and the artisan are in their manner realists. They understand that one cannot forego the use of force.

It is false, thrice false, to affirm that the present petty bourgeoisie is not going to the working class parties because it fears "extreme measures." Quite the contrary. The lower petty bourgeoisie, its great masses, see in the working class parties only parliamentary machines. They do not believe in their strength, nor in their capacity to struggle, nor in their readiness this time to conduct the struggle to the end.

And if this is so, is it worth the trouble to replace radicalism by its parliamentary confrères on the Left? That is how the semi-expropriated, ruined, and discontented proprietor reasons or feels. Without an understanding of this psychology of the peasants, the artisans, the employees, the petty functionaries, etc.—a psychology which flows from the social crisis—it is impossible to elaborate a correct policy. The petty bourgeoisie is economically dependent and politically atomized. That is why it cannot conduct an independent policy. It needs a "leader" who inspires it with confidence. This individual or collective leadership, i.e., a personage or party, can be given to it by one or the other of the fundamental classes—either the big bourgeoisie or the proletariat. Fascism unites and arms the scattered masses. Out of human dust it organizes combat detachments. It thus gives the petty bourgeoisie the illusion of being an independent force. It begins to imagine that it will

---

tween working-class parties, directed toward specific, limited ends (e.g., the defense of Left wing meetings against fascist raids); it did not mean programmatic compromises, and it left each participating party free to advance its own political line. The Popular Front he saw as a variation upon the "class collaboration" policies of the European Social Democrats, who in the twenties had joined in governments with bourgeois parties and had therefore come under heavy criticism from the communists. In France, said Trotsky, the Popular Front meant a programmatic alliance between working-class parties and a bourgeois party (the misnamed Radical Socialists) within the confines of bourgeois parliamentarism.—Ed.]

really command the state. It is not surprising that these illusions and hopes turn the head of the petty bourgeoisie!

But the petty bourgeoisie can also find a leader in the proletariat. This was demonstrated in Russia and partially in Spain. In Italy, in Germany, and in Austria the petty bourgeosie gravitated in this direction. But the parties of the proletariat did not rise to their historic task.

To bring the petty bourgeoisie to its side, the proletariat must win its confidence. And for that it must have confidence in its own strength.

It must have a clear program of action and must be ready to struggle for power by all possible means. Tempered by its revolutionary party for a decisive and pitiless struggle, the proletariat says to the peasants and petty bourgeoisie of the cities: "We are struggling for power. Here is our program. We are ready to discuss with you changes in this program. We will employ violence only against big capital and its lackeys, but with you toilers, we desire to conclude an alliance on the basis of a given program." The peasants will understand such language. Only, they must have faith in the capacity of the proletariat to seize power.

But for that it is necessary to purge the united front of all equivocation, of all indecision, of all hollow phrases. It is necessary to understand the situation and to place oneself seriously on the revolutionary road.

AN ALLIANCE WITH THE RADICALS WOULD BE AN ALLIANCE AGAINST THE MIDDLE CLASSES

Renaudel, Frossard and their like seriously imagine that an alliance with the Radicals is an alliance with the "middle classes" and consequently a barrier against fascism. These men see nothing but parliamentary shadows. They ignore the real evolution of the masses and chase after the "Radical Party," which has outlived itself and which in the meantime turns its back on them. They think that in an era of great social crisis an alliance of classes set in motion can be replaced by a bloc with a parliamentary clique that is compromised and doomed to extinction. A real alliance of the proletariat and the middle classes is not a question of parliamentary statistics but of revolutionary dynamics.

This alliance must be created and forged in the struggle. The whole meaning of the present political situation resides in the fact that the despairing petty bourgeoisie is beginning to break from the yoke of parliamentary discipline and from the tutelage of the conservative "radical" clique which has always fooled the people, and which has now definitely betrayed it. To join in this situation with the Radicals means to condemn oneself to the scorn of the masses, and to push the petty bourgeoisie into the embrace of fascism as the sole savior.

The working class party must not occupy itself with a hopeless effort to save the party of the bankrupts. It must, on the contrary, with all its strength, accelerate the process of liberation of the masses from radical influence. The more zeal and the more boldness it applies to this task, the more surely and rapidly will it prepare a real alliance of the working class with the petty bourgeoisie. It is necessary to approach the classes in motion. It is necessary to place oneself at their head and not at their tail. History is working quickly. Woe to him who lags behind!

When Frossard denies the right of the Socialist Party to expose, weaken and speed the disintegration of the Radical Party, he comes forward not as a socialist but as a conservative radical. Only that party has the right to historical existence which believes in its own program and strives to rally the whole people to its banner. Otherwise it is not a party but a parliamentary coterie, a clique of careerists. It is not only the right but the elementary duty of the proletarian party to free the toiling masses from the fatal influence of the bourgeoisie. This historic task takes on a particular sharpness at the present time, for the Radicals are more than ever striving to cover up the reaction, to lull and dupe the people and in this way prepare for the victory of fascism. And the Left Radicals? They capitulate to Herriot, just as Herriot capitulates to Tardieu.

Frossard would have the alliance of the Socialists and the Radicals end in a government of the "Left" which will dissolve the fascist organizations and save the republic. It is difficult to imagine a more monstrous amalgam of democratic illusions and police cynicism. When we say—we speak of this in more detail below—that *what is needed is a workers' militia,* Frossard and his satellites object: "Against fascism one must fight not with physical but with ideological means." When we say only a bold mobilization of the masses, which is only possible in a struggle against radicalism, is capable of undermining fascism, the same gentlemen reply to us: "No, only the police government of Daladier-Frossard can save us."

What pitiful prattle! For the Radicals have held the power, and if they voluntarily ceded it to Doumergue, it was not because they lacked the aid of Frossard but because they feared fascism, because they feared the big bourgeoisie which threatened it with royalist razors and because they feared still more the proletariat, which was beginning to marshal itself against fascism. To cap it all, Frossard himself, taking fright at the alarm of the Radicals, advised Daladier to capitulate.

If one supposes for an instant—an obviously unlikely hypothesis—that the Radicals had consented to break the alliance with Doumergue for the alliance with Frossard, the fascist bands, this time with the direct collaboration of the police, would have come into the streets trebly numerous, and the Radicals, together with Frossard, would have immediately crawled under the tables or hidden themselves in their ministerial toilets.

But let us make one more fantastic hypothesis: the police of Daladier-Frossard "disarm the Fascists." Does that settle the question? And who will disarm the same police, who with the right hand will give back to the Fascists what they will have taken from them with the left? The comedy of disarmament by the police will only have caused the authority of the Fascists to increase as fighters against the capitalist state. Blows against the fascist gangs can prove effective only to the extent that these gangs are at the same time politically isolated.

Meanwhile, the hypothetical government of Daladier-Frossard would give nothing either to the workers or to the petty bourgeois masses because it would be unable to attack the foundations of private property; and without expropriation of the banks, the great commercial enterprises, the key branches of industry and transport, without foreign trade monopoly, and without a series of other profound measures, there is no possible way of coming to the aid of the peasant, the artisan, the petty merchant. By its passivity, its impotence, its lies, the government of Daladier-Frossard would provoke a tempest of revolt in the petty bourgeoisie, and would push it definitely on the road to fascism, if—if this government were possible. It is necessary to recognize, however, that Frossard is not alone. The same day (October 24) on which the moderate Zyromski came out in *Le Populaire* against the attempt of Frossard to revive the cartel, Cachin spoke up in *L'Humanité* to defend the idea of a bloc with the Radical Socialists. He, Cachin, greeted with enthusiasm the fact that the Radicals had declared for the "disarmament of the Fascists."

Certainly, the Radicals declared themselves for the disarmament of everyone—workers' organizations included. Certainly, in the hands of a bonapartist state, such a measure would be directed especially against the workers. Certainly, the "disarmed" Fascists would receive on the morrow double their arms, not without the aid of the police. But why bother with somber reflections? Every man needs to hope. So there is Cachin traveling in the footsteps of Wels and Otto Bauer, who also in their time sought salvation in the disarmament to be effected by the police of Brüning and Dollfuss.

Executing the latest turn of 180 degrees, Cachin identifies the Radicals with the middle classes. He sees oppressed peasants only through the prism of radicalism. The alliance with the petty toiling proprietors is represented by him only in the form of a bloc with the parliamentary careerists who are at last beginning to lose the confidence of the petty proprietors.

Instead of nourishing and fanning the nascent revolt of the peasant and the artisan against the "democratic" exploiters and guiding this revolt in the direction of an alliance with the proletariat, Cachin is preparing to support the bankrupt Radicals with the authority of the "common front," and thus to drive the revolt of the most exploited petty bourgeois along the road of fascism.

Theoretical sloppiness always takes cruel vengeance in revolutionary politics. "Anti-fascism" and fascism alike are for the

Stalinists not concrete conceptions but two great empty sacks into which they stuff anything that comes into their hands. For them Doumergue is a Fascist just as before that Daladier was also for them a Fascist. In point of fact, Doumergue is a capitalist exploiter of the fascist wing of the petty bourgeoisie just as Herriot is an exploiter of the Radical petty bourgeoisie. At the present time these two systems combine in the Bonapartist regime. Doumergue is also, after his fashion, an "anti-fascist," since he prefers a military and police dictatorship of big capital to a civil war whose issue is always uncertain. For fear of fascism and still more for fear of the proletariat, the "anti-fascist" Daladier joins with Doumergue. But the regime of Doumergue is inconceivable without the existence of the fascist gangs. An elementary Marxian analysis thus shows the utter futility of the idea of an alliance with the Radicals against fascism!

The Radicals themselves will take pains to show in action how fantastic and reactionary are the political day dreams of Frossard and Cachin.

THE ARMING OF THE PROLETARIAT

A strike is inconceivable without propaganda and without agitation. It is also inconceivable without pickets who, when they can, use persuasion, but when obliged, use force. The strike is the most elementary form of the class struggle, which always combines, in varying proportions, "ideological" methods with physical ones. The struggle against fascism is basically a political struggle, which needs a militia just as the strike needs pickets. Basically, the picket is the embryo of the workers' militia. He who thinks of renouncing "physical" struggle must renounce all struggle, for the spirit does not live without flesh.

Following the splendid phrase of the great military theoretician Clausewitz, war is the continuation of politics by other means. This definition also fully applies to civil war. Physical struggle is only "another means" of political struggle. It is impermissible to oppose one to the other since it is impossible to check at will the political struggle when it transforms itself, by force of inner necessity, into a physical struggle.

The duty of a revolutionary party is to foresee in time the inescapability of the transformation of politics into open armed conflict, and with all its forces to prepare for that moment just as the ruling classes are preparing.

The militia detachments for defense against fascism are the first step on the road to the arming of the proletariat, not the last. Our slogan is:

Arm the proletariat and the revolutionary peasants.

The workers' militia must in the final analysis embrace all the toilers. To fulfill this program *completely* would be possible only in a workers' state, into whose hands would pass all the means of production and consequently also all the means of destruction, i.e., all the arms and the factories which produce them.

However, it is impossible to arrive at a workers' state with empty hands. Only political invalids like Renaudel can speak of a peaceful, constitutional road to socialism. The constitutional road is cut by trenches held by the fascist bands. There are not a few trenches before us. The bourgeoisie will not hesitate to resort to a dozen coups d'état aided by the police and the army, to prevent the proletariat from coming to power.

A workers' socialist state can be created only by a victorious revolution.

Every revolution is prepared by the march of economic and political development, but it is always decided by open armed conflicts between hostile classes. A revolutionary victory can become possible only as a result of long political agitation, a lengthy period of education and organization of the masses.

But the armed conflict itself must likewise be prepared long in advance.

The advanced workers must know that they will have to fight and win a death struggle. They must reach out for arms, as a guarantee of their emancipation.

In an era as critical as the present, the party of the revolution must unceasingly preach to the workers the need for arming themselves and must do everything to assure the arming, at least, of the proletarian vanguard. Without this, victory is impossible.

The most recent electoral victories of the British Labor Party do not at all invalidate what is said above. Even if we were to allow that the next parliamentary elections will give the Labor Party an absolute majority, which is not assured in any case; if we were further to allow that the party would actually take the road of socialist transformations—which is scarcely probable—it would immediately meet with such fierce resistance from the House of Lords, the king, the banks, the stockmarket, the bureaucracy, the press, that a split in its ranks would become inevitable, and the Left, more radical wing would become a parliamentary minority. Simultaneously the fascist movement would acquire an unprecedented sweep. Alarmed by the municipal elections, the British bourgeoisie is no doubt already actively preparing for an extra-parliamentary struggle while the tops of the Labor Party lull the proletariat with the successes and are compelled, unfortunately, to see the British events through the rosy spectacles of Jean Longuet. In point of fact, the less the leaders of the Labor Party prepare for it, the more cruel will be the civil war forced upon the proletariat by the British bourgeoisie.

"But where will you get arms for the whole proletariat?" object once more the skeptics who mistake their own inner futility for an objective impossibility. They forget that the same question has been posed before every revolution in history. And despite everything, victorious revolutions mark important stages in the development of humanity.

The proletariat produces arms, transports them, erects the buildings in which they are kept, defends these buildings against itself, serves in the army, and creates all its equipment. It is neither locks nor walls which separate the proletariat from arms, but the habit of submission, the hypnosis of class domination, and nationalist poison.

It is sufficient to destroy these psychological walls—and no wall of stone will stand in the way. It is enough that the proletariat should want arms—and it will find them. The task of the revolutionary party is to awaken his desire and to facilitate its realization.

But here Frossard and hundreds of frightened parliamentarians, journalists and trade union officials, advance their last argument, the weightiest: "Can serious men in general place their hopes in the success of physical struggle after the recent tragic experiences in Austria and Spain? Think of present-day techniques, tanks, gas, airplanes! !" This argument only shows that a number of "serious men" not only want to learn nothing but in their fear even forget what little they ever learned.

The history of the last twenty years demonstrates with particular clarity that the fundamental problems in the relations among classes, as among nations, are settled by physical force. The pacifists have long hoped that the growth of military technique would make war impossible. The philistines have repeated for decades that the growth of military technique would make revolution impossible. However, wars and revolutions continue. Never have there been so many revolutions, including victorious revolutions, as there have been since the last war, which uncovered all the might of military technique.

Frossard and Company offer old clichés as though they were the latest discoveries, invoking, instead of automatic rifles and machine guns, tanks and bombing planes. We reply: behind each machine there are men who are linked not only by technical but by social and political bonds. When historical development poses before society an unpostponable revolutionary task as a question of life or death, when there exists a progressive class with whose victory is joined the salvation of society —then the very development of the political struggle opens up before the revolutionary class the most varied possibilities—as much to paralyze the military force of the enemy as to win it over, at least partially. In the mind of a philistine these possibilities always appear as "lucky accidents" which will never be repeated. In fact, in the most unexpected but fundamentally natural combinations, possibilities of every sort open up in every great, i.e., truly popular, revolution. But despite everything victory does not come of itself.

To utilize the favorable possibilities it is necessary to have a revolutionary will, an iron determination to conquer, a bold and perspicacious leadership. *L'Humanité* agrees in words with the slogan of "arming the workers," only to renounce it in deeds. At the present time, according to this paper, it is inadmissible to advance a slogan which is only opportune "in a full revolutionary crisis." It is dangerous to load your rifle, says the "too-prudent" hunter, so long as the game remains invisible. But when the game puts in an appearance it is a little too late to load the rifle. Do the strategists of *L'Humanité* really think that in "the full revolutionary crisis" they will be able without any preparation to mobilize and arm the proletariat? To secure a large quantity of arms, one needs a certain quantity on hand. One needs military cadres. One needs the invincible desire of the masses to secure arms. One needs uninterrupted preparatory work not only in the gymnasiums but in indissoluble connection with the daily struggle of the masses. This means:

It is necessary immediately to build the militia and at the same time to carry on propaganda for the general armament of the revolutionary workers and peasants.

22

I Stake My Life!

(1937)

Dear Listeners, Comrades and Friends:
My first word is one of apology for my impossible English. My second word is one of thanks to the Committee, which has made it possible for me to address your meeting. The theme of my address is the Moscow trials. I do not intend for an instant to overstep the limits of this theme, which even in itself is much too vast. I will appeal not to the passions, not to your nerves, but to reason. I do not doubt that *reason* will be found on the side of *truth*.

The Zinoviev-Kamenev trial has provoked, in public opinion, terror, agitation, indignation, distrust, or at least, perplexity. The trial of Piatakov-Radek has once more enhanced these sentiments. Such is the incontestable fact. A doubt of justice signifies, in this case, a suspicion of frame-up. Can one find a more humiliating suspicion against a government which appears under the banner of socialism? Where do the interests of the Soviet government itself lie? In dispelling these suspicions. What is the duty of the true friends of the Soviet Union? To say firmly to the Soviet government: it is necessary at all costs to dispel the distrust of the Western world for Soviet justice.

To answer to this demand: "We have our justice, the rest does not concern us much," is to occupy oneself, not with the socialist enlightenment of the masses, but with the policies of inflated prestige, in the style of Hitler or Mussolini.

Even the "Friends of the USSR," who are convinced in their own hearts of the justice of the Moscow trials (and how many are there? What a pity that one cannot take a census of consciences!), even these unshakable friends of the bureaucracy are duty-bound to demand with us the creation of an authorized commission of inquiry. The Moscow authorities must present to such a commission all the necessary testimonies. There can evidently be no lack of them, since it was on the basis of those given that forty-nine persons were shot in the "Kirov" trials, without counting the 150 who were shot without trial.

Let us recall that by way of guarantees for the justice of the Moscow verdicts before world public opinion, two lawyers present themselves: Pritt from London and Rosenmark from Paris, not to mention the American journalist Duranty. But who gives guarantee for these guarantees? The two lawyers Pritt and Rosenmark acknowledge gratefully that the Soviet government placed at their disposal all the necessary explanations. Let us add that the "King's Counselor" Pritt was invited to Moscow at a fortunate time, since the date of the trial was carefully concealed from the entire world until the last moment. The Soviet government did not thus count on humiliating the dignity of its justice by having recourse behind the scenes to the assistance of foreign lawyers and journalists. But when the Socialist and Trade Union Internationals demanded the opportunity to send their lawyers to Moscow, they were treated—no more and no less—as defenders of assassins and of the Gestapo! You know, of course, that I am not a partisan of the Second International or of the Trade Union International. But is it not clear that their moral authority is incomparably above the authority of lawyers with supple spines? Have we not the right to say: the Moscow government forgets its "prestige" before authorities and experts, whose approbation is assured to them in advance; it is cheerfully willing to make the "King's Counselor" Pritt a counselor of the GPU. But, on the other hand, it has up to now brutally rejected every examination which would carry with it guarantees of objectivity and impartiality. Such is the incontestable and deadly fact! Perhaps, however, this conclusion is inaccurate? There is nothing easier than to refute it: let the Moscow government present to an international commission of inquiry serious, precise, and concrete explanations regarding all the obscure spots of the Kirov trials. And apart from these obscure spots there is—alas! —nothing! That is precisely why Moscow resorts to all kinds of measures to force me, the principal accused, to keep my silence. Under Moscow's terrible economic pressure the Norwegian government placed me under lock and key. What good fortune that the magnanimous hospitality of Mexico permitted myself and my wife to meet the new trial, not under imprisonment, but in freedom! But all the wheels to force me once more into silence have again been set into motion. Why does Moscow so fear the voice of a single man? Only because I know the truth, the whole truth. Only because I have nothing to hide. Only because I am ready to appear before a public and impartial commission of inquiry with documents, facts and testimonies in my hands, and to disclose the truth to the very end. *I declare: if this commission decides that I am guilty in the slightest degree of the crimes which Stalin imputes to me, I pledge in advance to place myself voluntarily in the hands of the executioners of the GPU.* That, I hope, is clear Have you all heard? I make this declaration before the entire world. I ask the press to publish my words in the farthest corners of our planet. But if the commission establishes—do you hear me?—that the Moscow trials are a conscious and premeditated frame-up, constructed with the bones and nerves of human beings, I will not ask my accusers to place themselves voluntarily before a firing-squad. No, the eternal disgrace in the memory of human generations will be sufficient for them! Do the accusers of the Kremlin hear me? I throw my defiance in their faces. And I await their reply!

. . .

Through this declaration I reply in passing to the frequent objections of superficial skeptics: "Why must we believe Trotsky and not Stalin?" It is absurd to busy oneself with psychological divinations. It is not a question of personal confidence. It is a question of *verification!* I propose a verification! I demand the verification!

Listeners and friends! Today you expect from me neither a refutation of the "proofs," which do not exist in this affair, nor a detailed analysis of the "confessions," those *unnatural,* artificial, inhuman monologues which carry in themselves their own refutation. I would need more time than the prosecutor for a concrete analysis of the trials, because it is more difficult to disentangle than to entangle. This work I will accomplish in the press and before the future commission. My task today is to unmask the *fundamental, original* viciousness of the Moscow trials, to show the motive forces of the frame-up, its true political aims, the psychology of its participants and of its victims.

The trial of Zinoviev-Kamenev was concentrated upon "terrorism." The trial of Piatakov-Radek placed in the center of the stage, no longer terror, but the alliance of the Trotskyists with Germany and Japan for the preparation of war, the dismemberment of the USSR, the sabotage of industry and the extermination of workers. How to explain this crying discrepancy? For after the execution of the sixteen we were told that the depositions of Zinoviev, Kamenev and the others were voluntary, sincere, and corresponded to the facts. Moreover, Zinoviev and Kamenev demanded the death penalty for themselves! Why then did they not say a word about the most important thing: the alliance of the Trotskyists with Germany and Japan and the plot to dismember the USSR? Could they have forgotten such "details" of the plot? Could they themselves, the leaders of the so-called *center,* not have known what was known by the accused in the last trial, people of a secondary category? The enigma is easily explained: the new amalgam was constructed *after* the execution of the sixteen, during the course of the last five months, as an answer to unfavorable echoes in the world press.

The most feeble part of the trial of the sixteen is the accusation against old Bolsheviks of an alliance with the secret police of Hitler, the Gestapo. Neither Zinoviev, nor Kamenev, nor Smirnov, nor in general any one of the accused with political names confessed to this liaison; they stopped short before this extreme of self-abasement! It follows that I, through obscure, unknown intermediaries such as Olberg, Berman, Fritz David and others, had entered into an alliance with the Gestapo for such grand purposes as the obtaining of a Honduran passport for Olberg. The whole thing was too foolish. No one wanted to believe it. The whole trial was discredited. It was necessary to correct the gross error of the stage managers at all costs. It was necessary to fill up the hole. Yagoda was replaced by Yezhov. A new trial was placed on the order of the day. Stalin decided to answer his critics in this way: "You don't believe that Trotsky is capable of entering into alliance with the Gestapo for the sake of an Olberg and a passport from Honduras? Very well, I will show you that the purpose of his alliance with Hitler was to provoke war and partition out the world." However, for this second, more grandiose production, Stalin lacked the principal actors: he had shot them. In the principal roles of the principal presentation he could place only secondary actors! It is not superfluous to note that Stalin attached much value to Piatakov and Radek as collaborators. But he had no other people with well-known names, who, if only because of their distant pasts, could pass as "Trotskyists." That is why fate descended sternly upon Radek and Piatakov. The version about my meetings with the rotten trash of the Gestapo through unknown, occasional intermediaries was dropped. The matter was suddenly raised to the heights of the world stage! It was no longer a question of a Honduran passport, but of the parceling of the USSR and even the defeat of the United States of America. With the aid of a gigantic elevator the plot ascends during a period of five months from the dirty police dregs to the heights on which are decided the destinies of nations. Zinoviev, Kamenev, Smirnov, Mrachkovsky, went to their graves without knowing of these grandiose schemes, alliances, and perspectives. Such is the *fundamental falsehood* of the last amalgam!

In order to hide, even if only slightly, the glaring contradiction between the two trials, Piatakov and Radek testified, under the dictation of the GPU, that they had formed a *"parallel"* center, in view of Trotsky's lack of confidence in Zinoviev and Kamenev. It is difficult to imagine a more stupid and deceitful explanation! I really did not have confidence in Zinoviev and Kamenev after their capitulation, and I have had no connection with them since 1927. But I had still less confidence in Radek and Piatakov! Already in 1929 Radek delivered into the hands of the GPU the oppositionist Blumkin, who was shot silently and without trial. Here is what I wrote then in the *Bulletin of the Russian Opposition,* which appears abroad:

After having lost the last remnants of moral equilibrium, Radek does not stop at any objection.

It is outrageous to be forced to cite such harsh statements about the unfortunate victims of Stalin. But it would be criminal to hide the truth out of sentimental considerations. . . . Radek and Piatakov themselves regarded Zinoviev and Kamenev with haughty superiority, and in this self-appreciation they were not mistaken. But more than that. At the time of the trial of the sixteen, the prosecutor named Smirnov as the "leader of the Trotskyists in the USSR." The accused Mrachkovsky, as a proof of his proximity to me, declared that I was accessible only through his intermediation, and the prosecutor in his turn emphasized this fact. How then was it possible that not only Zinoviev and Kamenev, but Smirnov, the "leader of the Trotskyists in the USSR," and Mrachkovsky as well, knew nothing of the plans about which I had instructed Radek, openly branded by me as a traitor? Such is the primary falsehood of the last trial. It appears by itself in broad daylight. We know its source. We see the strings offstage. We see the brutal hand which pulls them.

Radek and Piatakov confessed to frightful crimes. But their crimes, from the point of view of the accused and not of the accusers, *do not make sense.* With the aid of terror, sabotage and alliance with the imperialists, they would have liked to re-establish capitalism in the Soviet Union. Why? Throughout their entire lives they struggled against capitalism. Perhaps they were guided by personal motives: the lust for power? the thirst for gain? Under any other regime Piatakov and Radek could not hope to occupy higher positions than those which they occupied before their arrest. Perhaps they were so stupidly sacrificing themselves out of friendship for me? An absurd hypothesis! By their actions, speeches, and articles during the last eight years, Radek and Piatakov demonstrated that they were my bitter enemies.

Terror? But is it possible that the oppositionists, after all the revolutionary experience in Russia, could not have foreseen that this would only serve as a pretext for the extermination of the best fighters? No, they knew that, they foresaw it, they stated it hundreds of times. No, terror was not necessary for us. On the other hand it was absolutely necessary for the ruling clique. On the fourth of March, 1929, eight years ago, I wrote:

> Only one thing is left for Stalin: to attempt to draw a line of blood between the official party and the opposition. He absolutely must *connect the opposition with attempts at assassination, the preparation of armed insurrection, etc.*

Remember: bonapartism has never existed in history without police fabrication of plots!

The Opposition would have to be composed of cretins to think that an alliance with Hitler or the Mikado, both of whom are doomed to defeat in the next war, that such an absurd, inconceivable, senseless alliance could yield to revolutionary Marxists anything but disgrace and ruin. On the other hand, such an alliance—of the Trotskyists with Hitler—was most necessary for Stalin. Voltaire says: "If God did not exist, it would be necessary to invent him." The GPU says: "If the alliance does not exist, it is necessary to fabricate it."

At the heart of the Moscow trials is an absurdity. According to the official version, the Trotskyists had been organizing the most monstrous plot since 1931. However, all of them, as if by command, spoke and wrote in one way but acted in another. In spite of the hundreds of persons implicated in the plot, over a period of five years, not a trace of it was revealed: no splits, no denunciations, no confiscated letters, until the hour of the general confessions arrived! Then a new miracle came to pass. People who had organized assassinations, prepared war, divided the Soviet Union, these hardened criminals suddenly confessed in August, 1936, not under the pressure of proofs—no, because there were no proofs—but for certain mysterious reasons, which hypocritical psychologists declare are peculiar attributes of the "Russian soul." Just think: yesterday they carried out railroad wrecking and poisoning of workers—by unseen order of Trotsky. Today they are Trotsky's accusers and heap upon him their pseudo-crimes. Yesterday they dreamed only of killing Stalin. Today they all sing hymns of praise to him. What is it: a madhouse? No, the Messieurs Duranty tell us, it is not a madhouse, but the "Russian soul." You lie, gentlemen, about the Russian soul. You lie about the human soul in general.

The miracle consists not only in the simultaneity and the universality of the confessions. The miracle, above all, is that, according to the general confessions, the conspirators did something which was fatal precisely to their own political interests, but extremely useful to the leading clique. Once more the conspirators before the tribunal said just what the most servile agents of Stalin would have said. Normal people, following the dictates of their own will, would never have been able to conduct themselves as Zinoviev, Kamenev, Radek, Piatakov and the others did. Devotion to their ideas, political dignity, the simple instinct of self-preservation would force them to struggle for themselves, for their personalities, for their interests, for their lives. The only reasonable and fitting question is this: *Who led these people into a state in which all human reflexes are destroyed, and how did he do it?* There is a very simple principle in jurisprudence, which holds the key to many secrets: *is fecti cui prodest;* he who benefits by it, he is the guilty one. The entire conduct of the accused has been dictated from beginning to end, not by their own ideas and interests, but by the interests of the ruling clique. And the pseudo-plot, and the confessions, the theatrical judgment and the entirely real executions, all were arranged by one and the same hand. Whose? *Cui prodest?* Who benefits? The hand of Stalin! The rest is deceit, falsehood, and idle babbling about the "Russian soul"! In the trials there did not figure fighters, nor conspirators, but puppets in the hands of the GPU. They play assigned roles. The aim of the disgraceful performance: to eliminate the whole opposition, to poison the very source of critical thought, to definitively ensconce the totalitarian regime of Stalin.

We repeat: The accusation is a premeditated frame-up. This frame-up must inevitably appear in each of the defendants' confessions, if they are examined alongside the facts. The prosecutor Vyshinsky knows this very well. That is why he did not address a single concrete question to the accused, which would have embarrassed them considerably. The names, documents, dates, places, means of transportation, circumstances of the meetings—around these decisive facts Vyshinsky has placed a cloak of shame, or to be more exact, a shameless cloak. Vyshinsky dealt with the accused, not in the language of the jurist, but in the conventional language of the past master of frame-up, in the jargon of the thief. The insinuating character of Vyshinsky's questions—along with the complete absence of material proofs—this represents the *second crushing evidence against Stalin*. . . .

But already what has been said by me permits, I hope, a forecast of the future development of the investigation. On the one hand, an accusation which is fantastic to its very core; the entire old generation of Bolsheviks is accused of an abominable treason, devoid of sense or purpose. To establish this accusation the prosecutor does not have at his command any material proofs, in spite of the thousands and thousands of arrests and searchings. *The complete absence of evidence is the most terrible evidence against Stalin!* The executions are based exclusively on forced confessions. And when facts are mentioned in these confessions, they crumble to dust at the first contact with critical examination.

The GPU is guilty not only of frame-up. It is guilty of concocting a rotten, gross, foolish frame-up. Impunity is depraving. The absence of control paralyzes criticism. The falsifiers carry out their work no matter how. They rely on the sum-total effect of confessions and executions. If one carefully compares the fantastic nature of the accusation in its entirety with the manifest falsehood of the factual depositions, what is left of all these monotonous confessions? The suffocating odor of the inquisitorial tribunal, and nothing more!

But there is another kind of evidence which seems to me no less important. In the year of my deportation and the eight years of my emigration I wrote to close and distant friends about two thousand letters, dedicated to the most vital questions of current politics. The letters received by me and the copies of my replies exist. Thanks to their continuity, these letters reveal, above all, the profound contradictions, anachronisms and direct absurdities of the accusation, not only insofar as myself and my son are concerned, but also as regards the other accused. However, the importance of these letters extends beyond that fact. All of my theoretical and political activity during these years is reflected without a gap in these letters. The letters supplement my books and articles. The examination of my correspondence, it seems to me, is of decisive importance for the characterization of the political and moral personality—not only of myself, but also of my correspondents. Vyshinsky has not been able to present a single letter to the tribunal. I will present to the commission or to a tribunal thousands of letters, addressed, moreover, to the people who are closest to me and from whom I had nothing to hide, particularly to my son, Leon. This correspondence alone by its internal force of conviction nips the Stalinist amalgam in the bud. The prosecutor with his subterfuges and his insults and the accused with their confessional monologues are left suspended in thin air. Such is the significance of my correspondence. Such is the content of my archives. I do not ask anybody's confidence. I make an appeal to reason, to logic, to criticism. I present facts and documents. I demand a verification!

Among you, dear listeners, there must be not a few people who freely say: "The confessions of the accused are false, that is clear; but how was Stalin able to obtain such confessions? Therein lies the secret!" In reality the secret is not so profound. The Inquisition, with a much more simple technique, extorted all sorts of confessions from its victims. That is why the democratic penal law renounced the methods of the Middle Ages, because they led not to the establishment of the truth, but to a simple confirmation of the accusations dictated by the inquiring judge. The GPU trials have a thoroughly inquisitorial character: that is the simple secret of the confessions!

The whole political atmosphere of the Soviet Union is impregnated with the spirit of the Inquisition. Have you read André Gide's little book, *Return from the USSR?* Gide is a friend of the Soviet Union, but not a lackey of the bureaucracy. Moreover, this artist has eyes. A little episode in Gide's book is of incalculable aid in understanding the Moscow trials. At the end of his trip Gide wished to send a telegram to Stalin, but not having received the inquisitorial education, he referred to Stalin with the simple democratic word "you." They refused to accept the telegram! The representatives of authority explained to Gide: "When writing to Stalin one must say: 'leader of the workers' or 'chieftain of the people,' not the simple democratic word 'you.'" Gide tried to argue: "Isn't Stalin above such flattery?" It was no use. They still refused to accept his telegram without the Byzantine flattery. At the very end Gide declared: "I submit in this wearisome battle, but disclaim all responsibility. . . ." Thus a universally recognized writer and honored guest was worn out in a few minutes and forced to sign not the telegram which he himself wanted to send, but that which was dictated to him by petty inquisitors. Let him who has a particle of imagination picture to himself, not a well-known traveler but an unfortunate Soviet citizen, an Oppositionist, isolated and persecuted, a pariah, who is constrained to write, not telegrams of salutation to Stalin, but dozens and scores of confessions of his crimes. Perhaps in this world there are many heroes who are capable of bearing all kinds of tortures, physical or moral, which are inflicted on themselves, their wives, their children. I do not know. . . . My personal observations inform me that the capacities of the human nervous system are limited. Through the GPU Stalin can trap his victim in an abyss of black despair, humiliation, infamy, in such a manner that he takes upon himself the most monstrous crimes, with the prospect of imminent death or a feeble ray of hope for the future as the sole outcome. If, indeed, he does not contemplate suicide, which Tomsky preferred! Joffe earlier found the same way out, as well as two members of my military secretariat, Glazman and Boutov, Zinoviev's secretary, Bogdan, my daughter Zinaida, and many dozens of others. Suicide or moral prostration: there is no other choice! But do not forget that in the prisons of the GPU even suicide is often an inaccessible luxury!

The Moscow trials do not dishonor the revolution, because they are the progeny of reaction. The Moscow trials do not dishonor the old generation of Bolsheviks; they only demonstrate that even Bolsheviks are made of flesh and blood, and that they do not resist endlessly when over their heads swings the pendulum of death. The Moscow trials dishonor the political regime which has conceived them: the regime of bonapartism, without honor and without conscience! All of the executed died with curses on their lips for this regime.

Let him who wishes weep bitter tears because history moves ahead so perplexingly: two steps forward, one step back. But tears are of no avail. It is necessary, according to Spinoza's advice, not to laugh, not to weep, but to understand!

[An address written in 1936 to be delivered by radio from Mexico to a meeting held in New York City under the auspices of the American Committee for the Defense of Leon Trotsky.—Ed.]

23

The Moscow Trials and Terrorism

From *The Case of Leon Trotsky* (1938).

If terror is feasible for one side, why should it be considered as excluded for the other? For all its seductive symmetry, this reasoning is corrupt to the core. It is altogether inadmissible to place the terror of a dictatorship against an opposition on the same plane with the terror of an opposition against a dictatorship. To the ruling clique, the preparation of murders through the medium of a court or from behind an ambush is purely and simply a question of police technique. In the event of a failure, some second-rank agents can always be sacrificed. On the part of an opposition, terror presupposes the concentration of all forces upon preparing acts of terror, with the foreknowledge that every one of such acts, whether successful or unsuccessful, will evoke in reply the destruction of scores of its best men. An opposition could by no means permit itself such an insane squandering of its forces. It is precisely for this, and for no other reason, that the Comintern does not resort to terroristic attempts in the countries of fascist dictatorships. The [Trotskyist] Opposition is as little inclined to the policy of suicide as the Comintern.

According to the indictment, which banks on ignorance and mental laziness, the "Trotskyists" resolved to destroy the ruling group in order in this way to clear for themselves the path to power. The average philistine, especially if he wears the badge of a "Friend of the USSR," reasons as follows: "The Oppositionists could not but strive for power, and could not but hate the ruling group. Why, then, shouldn't they really resort to terror?" In other words, for the philistine the matter ends where in reality it only begins. The leaders of the Opposition are neither upstarts nor novices. It is not at all a question of whether they were striving for power. Every serious political tendency strives to conquer power. The question is: Could the Oppositionists, educated upon the enormous experience of the revolutionary movement, have entertained even a moment's belief that terror is capable of bringing them closer to power? Russian history, Marxist theory, political psychology reply: No, they could not!

At this point, the problem of terror requires clarification, even though briefly, from the standpoint of history and theory. In so far as I am delineated as the initiator of the "anti-Soviet terror," I am compelled to invest my exposition with an autobiographic character. In 1902, I had no sooner arrived in London from Siberia, after almost five years of prison and exile, than I had the occasion, in a memorial article devoted to the bicentennial of the fortress of Schlüsselburg, with its hard-labor prison, to enumerate the revolutionists there tortured to death. "The shades of these martyrs clamor for vengeance. . . ." But immediately thereafter I added: "Not for a personal, but for a revolutionary vengeance. Not for the execution of ministers, but for the execution of the autocracy." These lines were directed wholly against individual terror. Their author was twenty-three years of age. From the earliest days of his revolutionary activity he was already an opponent of terror. From 1902 to 1905 I delivered, in various cities in Europe, before Russian students and émigrés, scores of political reports against terrorist ideology, which at the beginning of the century was once again spreading among the Russian youth.

Beginning with the eighties of the past century, two generations of Russian Marxists in their personal experience lived through the era of terror, learned from its tragic lessons, and organically instilled in themselves a negative attitude toward the heroic adventurism of lone individuals, Plekhanov, the founder of Russian Marxism; Lenin, the leader of Bolshevism; Martov, the most eminent representative of Menshevism; all dedicated thousands of pages and hundreds of speeches to the struggle against the tactic of terror.

The ideological inspiration emanating from these senior Marxists nourished my attitude toward the revolutionary alchemy of the shut-in intellectual circles during my adolescence. For us, the Russian revolutionists, the problem of terror was a life-and-death matter in the political as well as the personal meaning of the term. For us, a terrorist was not a character from a novel, but a living and familiar being. In exile we lived for years side by side with the terrorists of the older generation. In prisons and in police custody we met with terrorists of our own age. We tapped out messages back and forth, in the Peter and Paul fortress, with terrorists condemned to death. How many hours, how many days, were spent in passionate discussion! How many times did we break personal relationships on this most burning of all questions! The Russian literature on terrorism, nourished by and reflecting these debates, would fill a large library.

Isolated terroristic explosions are inevitable whenever political oppression transgresses certain boundaries. Such acts almost always have a symptomatic character. But politics that sanctifies terror, raising it into a system—that is a different thing. I wrote in 1909:

> Terrorist work, in its very essence demands such a concentration of energy upon "the supreme moment," such an overestimation of personal heroism and, lastly, such a hermetically concealed conspiracy as . . . excludes completely any agitational and organizational activity among

the masses. . . . Struggling against terrorism, the Marxian intelligentsia defended their right or their duty not to withdraw from the working-class districts for the sake of tunneling mines underneath the Grand Ducal and Czarist palaces.

It is impossible to fool or outwit history. In the long run, history puts everybody in his place. The basic property of terror as a system is to destroy that organization which by means of chemical compounds seeks to compensate for its own lack of political strength. There are, of course, historical conditions where terror can introduce confusion among the governing ranks. But in that case who is it that can reap the fruits? At all events, not the terrorist organization itself, and not the masses behind whose backs the duel takes place. Thus, the liberal Russian bourgeois, in their day, invariably sympathized with terrorism. The reason is plain. In 1909 I wrote:

> Insofar as terror introduces disorganization and demoralization into the ranks of the government (at the price of disorganizing and demoralizing the ranks of the revolutionists), to that extent it plays into the hands of none other than the liberals themselves.

The very same idea, expressed in virtually the same words, we meet a quarter of a century later in connection with the Kirov assassination.

The very fact of individual acts of terror is an infallible token of the political backwardness of a country and the feebleness of the progressive forces there. The Revolution of 1905, which disclosed the vast strength of the proletariat, put an end to the romanticism of the single combat between a handful of intellectuals and Czarism. "Terrorism in Russia is dead," I reiterated in a number of articles.

> Terror has migrated far to the East—to the provinces of Punjab and Bengal. . . . It may be that in other countries of the Orient terrorism is still destined to pass through an epoch of flowering. But in Russia it is already a part of the heritage of history.

In 1907 I found myself again in exile. The whip of counter-revolution was savagely at work, and the Russian colonies in European cities became very numerous. The entire period of my second emigration was devoted to reports and articles against the terror of vengeance and despair. In 1909 it was revealed that at the head of the terrorist organization of the so-called Social Revolutionists stood an *agent provocateur,* Azef. "In the blind alley of terrorism," I wrote, "the hand of provocation rules with assurance" (January, 1910). Terrorism has always remained for me nothing but a "blind alley."

During the same period I wrote:

> The irreconcilable attitude of the Russian social democracy towards the bureaucratized terror of the revolution as a means of struggle against the terrorist bureaucracy of Czarism has met with bewilderment and condemnation not only among the Russian liberals but also among the European socialists.

Both the latter and the former accused us of "doctrinairism." On our part, we, the Russian Marxists, attributed this sympathy for Russian terrorism to the opportunism of the leaders of European Social Democracy, who had become accustomed to transferring their hopes from the masses to the ruling summits.

> Whoever stalks a ministerial portfolio . . . as well as those who, clasping an infernal machine beneath a cloak, stalk the Minister himself, must equally *overestimate* the Minister—his personality and his post. For them the *system* itself disappears or recedes far away, and there remains only the *individual* invested with power.

We shall presently, in connection with the Kirov assassination, meet once again with this thought, which runs through the decades of my activity.

In 1911 terrorist moods arose among certain groups of Austrian workers. Upon the request of Friedrich Adler, editor of *Der Kampf,* the theoretical monthly of the Austrian Social Democracy, I wrote in November, 1911, an article on terrorism for this publication.

Whether or not a terrorist attempt, even if "successful," introduces confusion in the ruling circles depends upon the concrete political circumstances. In any case this confusion can be of only short duration. The capitalist state does not rest upon ministers and cannot be destroyed together with them. The classes whom the state serves will always find new men—the mechanism remains intact and continues to function. But much deeper is that confusion which the terrorist attempts introduce into the ranks of the working masses. If it is enough to arm oneself with a revolver to reach the goal, then to what end are the endeavors of the class struggle? If a pinch of powder and a slug of lead are ample to shoot the enemy through the neck, where is the need of a class organization? If there is any rhyme or reason in scaring titled personages with the noise of an explosion, what need is there for a party? What is the need of meetings, mass agitation, elections, when it is so easy to take aim at the Ministerial bench from the Parliamentary gallery? Individual terrorism in our eyes is inadmissible precisely for the reason that it *lowers the masses in their own consciousness*, reconciles them to importance, and directs their glances and hopes towards the great avenger and emancipator who will some day come and accomplish his mission.

Five years later, in the heat of the imperialist war, Friedrich Adler, who had spurred me to write this article, killed the Austrian Minister-President Stuergkh in a Vienna restaurant. The heroic skeptic and opportunist was unable to find any other outlet for his indignation and despair. My sympathies were, naturally, not on the side of the Hapsburg dignitary. However, to the individualist action of Friedrich Adler I counterposed the form of activity of Karl Liebknecht who, during wartime, went out into a Berlin square to distribute a revolutionary manifesto to the workers.

On December 28, 1934, four weeks after the Kirov assassination, at a time when the Stalinist judiciary did not know as yet in which direction to aim the barb of their "justice," I wrote in the *Bulletin of the Opposition:*

... If Marxists have categorically condemned individual terrorism ... even when the shots were directed against the agents of the Czarist government and of capitalist exploitation, then all the more relentlessly will they condemn and reject the criminal adventurism of terrorist acts directed against the bureaucratic representatives of the first workers' state in history. The subjective motivations of Nikolayev and his associates are a matter of indifference to us. The road to hell is paved with good intentions. So long as the Soviet bureaucracy has not been removed by the proletariat—a task which will eventually be accomplished—it fulfills a necessary function in the defense of the workers' state. Should terrorism of the Nikolayev type spread, it could, given other unfavorable circumstances, render service only to the fascist counter-revolution.

Only political fakers who bank on imbeciles would endeavor to lay Nikolayev at the door of the Left Opposition, even if only in the guise of the Zinoviev group as it existed in 1926-27. The terrorist organization of the Communist youth is fostered not by the Left Opposition but by the bureaucracy, by its internal decomposition. *Individual terrorism in its very essence is bureaucratism turned inside out.* For Marxists this law was not discovered yesterday. Bureaucratism has no confidence in the masses, and endeavors to substitute itself for the masses. Terrorism behaves in the same manner; it wants to make the masses happy without asking their participation. The Stalinist bureaucracy has created a revolting leader-cult, endowing leaders with divine attributes. The "hero" cult is also the religion of terrorism, only with a minus sign. The Nikolayevs imagine that all that is necessary is to remove a few leaders by means of revolvers, in order for history to take another course. Communist-terrorists, as an ideological grouping, are of the same flesh and blood as the Stalinist bureaucracy. [January, 1935, No. 41.]

These lines, as you have had the opportunity to convince yourselves, were not written *ad hoc*. They summarize the experience of a whole lifetime, which was in turn fed by the experience of two generations.

Already in the epoch of Czarism, a young Marxist who went over to the ranks of the terrorist party was a comparatively rare phenomenon—rare enough to cause people to point their fingers. But at that time there was at least taking place an unceasing theoretical struggle between two tendencies; the publications of the two parties were waging a bitter polemic; public disputes did not cease for a single day. Now, on the other hand, they want to force us to believe that not young revolutionists, but old leaders of Russian Marxism, with the tradition of three revolutions behind them, have suddenly, without criticism, without discussion, without a single word of explanation, turned their faces toward the terrorism that they had always rejected as a method of political suicide. The very possibility of such an accusation shows to what depths of debasement the Stalinist bureaucracy has dragged the official theoretical and political thought, not to mention Soviet justice. To political convictions gained through experience, sealed by theory, tempered in the white heat of the history of mankind, the falsifiers counterpose inchoate, contradictory, and utterly unsubstantiated testimonies of suspicious nonentities.

"Yes," said Stalin and his agents, "we cannot deny that Trotsky did warn with the very same insistence against terrorist adventurism, not only in Russia but also in other countries in various stages of political development and under different conditions. But we have discovered in his lifetime a few instances which constitute an exception to the rule: In a conspiratorial letter he wrote to one Dreitzer [and which nobody ever saw]; in a conversation with Holtzman who was brought to Trotsky in Copenhagen by his son [who was at the time in Berlin]; in a conversation with Berman-Yurin and David [of whom I never heard prior to the first reports of the court proceedings], in these four or five instances Trotsky issued to his followers [who were in reality my bitterest opponents] terrorist instructions [without making any attempt either to justify them or to tie them up with the cause to which my entire life has been devoted]. If Trotsky had imparted his programmatic views on terror orally and in writing to hundreds of thousands and millions in the course of forty years, it was only in order to deceive them. His real views he expounded in strictest secrecy to the Bermans and the Davids." And then a miracle came to pass! These inarticulate "instructions," which rest wholly on the mental level of the Messrs. Vyshinsky, proved sufficient for this: That hundreds of old Marxists—automatically, without any objections, without uttering a syllable—turned to the path of terror. Such is the political basis of the trial of the sixteen (Zinoviev, et al.). In other words, the trial of the sixteen completely lacks a political basis.

24

Why and Wherefore These Trials?

From *The Case of Leon Trotsky* (1938).

An American writer complained to me in a conversation: "It is difficult for me to believe," he said, "that you entered into an alliance with fascism; but it is equally difficult for me to believe that Stalin carried out such horrible frame-ups." I can only pity the author of this remark. It is, in fact, difficult to find a solution if one approaches the question exclusively from an individual psychological, not a political, viewpoint. I do not wish to deny by this the importance of the individual element in history. Neither Stalin nor I find ourselves in our present positions by accident. But we did not create these positions. Each of us is drawn into this drama as the representative of definite ideas and principles. In their turn, the ideas and principles do not fall from the sky, but have profound social roots. That is why one must take, not the psychological abstraction of Stalin as a "man," but his concrete, historical personality as leader of the

Soviet bureaucracy. One can understand the acts of Stalin only by starting from the conditions of existence of the new privileged stratum, greedy for power, greedy for material comforts, apprehensive for its positions, fearing the masses, and mortally hating all opposition.

The position of a privileged bureaucracy in a society which that bureaucracy itself calls socialist is not only contradictory, but also false. The more precipitous the jump from the October overturn—which laid bare all social falsehood—to the present situation, in which a caste of upstarts is forced to cover up its social ulcers, the cruder the Thermidorian lies. It is, consequently, a question not simply of the individual depravity of this or that person, but of the corruption lodged in the position of a whole social group for whom lying has become a vital political necessity. In the struggle for its newly gained positions, this caste has re-educated itself and simultaneously re-educated—or rather, demoralized—its leaders. It raised upon its shoulders the man who best, most resolutely and most ruthlessly expresses its interests. Thus Stalin, who was once a revolutionist, became the leader of the Thermidorian caste.

The formulas of Marxism, expressing the interests of the masses, more and more inconvenienced the bureaucracy, insofar as they were inevitably directed against its interests. From the time that I entered into opposition to the bureaucracy, its courtier-theoreticians began to call the revolutionary essence of Marxism: *"Trotskyism."* At the same time, the official conception of *Leninism* changed from year to year, becoming more and more adapted to the needs of the ruling caste. Books devoted to party history, to the October revolution, or to the theory of Leninism, were revised annually. I have adduced an example from the literary activity of Stalin himself. In 1918 he wrote that the victory of the October insurrection was "principally and above all" assured by Trotsky's leadership. In 1924 Stalin wrote that Trotsky could not have played any special role in the October revolution. To this tune the whole historiography was adjusted. This signifies in practice that hundreds of young scholars and thousands of journalists were systematically trained in the spirit of falsification. Whoever resisted was stifled. This applies in a still greater measure to the propagandists, functionaries, judges, not to speak of the examining magistrates of the GPU. The incessant party purges were directed above all toward the uprooting of "Trotskyism," and during these purges not only discontented workers were called "Trotskyists," but also all writers who honestly presented historical facts or citations which contradicted the latest official standardization. Novelists and artists were subject to the same regime. The spiritual atmosphere of the country became completely impregnated with the poison of conventionalities, lies and direct frame-ups.

All the possibilities along this road were soon exhausted. The theoretical and historical falsifications no longer attained their aims—people grew too accustomed to them. It was necessary to give to bureaucratic repression a more massive foundation. To bolster up the literary falsifications, accusations of a criminal character were brought in.

My exile from the USSR was officially motivated by the allegation that I had prepared an "armed insurrection." However, the accusation launched against me was not even published in the press. Today it may seem incredible, but already in 1929 we were confronted with accusations against the Trotskyists of "sabotage," "espionage," "preparation of railroad wrecks," etc., in the Soviet press. However, there was not a single trial involving these accusations. The matter was limited to a literary calumny which represented, nevertheless, the first link in the preparation of the future judicial frame-ups. To justify the repressions, it was necessary to have framed accusations. To give weight to the false accusations, it was necessary to reinforce them with more brutal repressions. Thus the logic of the struggle drove Stalin along the road of gigantic judicial amalgams.

They also became necessary to him for international reasons. If the Soviet bureaucracy does not want revolutions and fears them, it cannot, at the same time, openly renounce the revolutionary traditions without definitely undermining its prestige within the USSR. However, the obvious bankruptcy of the Comintern opens the way for a new International. Since 1933, the idea of new revolutionary parties under the banner of the Fourth International has met with great success in the Old and

New Worlds. Only with difficulty can an outside observer appreciate the real dimensions of this success. It cannot be measured by membership statistics alone. The general tendency of development is of much greater importance. Deep internal fissures are spreading throughout all the sections of the Comintern, which at the first historic shock will result in splits and debacles. If Stalin fears the little *Bulletin of the Opposition* and punishes its introduction into the USSR with death, it is not difficult to understand what fright seizes the bureaucracy at the possibility that news of the self-sacrificing work of the Fourth International in the service of the working class may penetrate into the USSR.

The moral authority of the leaders of the bureaucracy and above all, of Stalin, rests in large measure upon the Tower of Babel of slanders and falsifications erected over a period of thirteen years. The moral authority of the Soviet bureaucracy. In its turn, the authority of the Comintern, as well as its support, is necessary for Stalin, before the Russian workers. This Tower of Babel, which frightens its own builders, is maintained inside the USSR with the aid of more and more terrible repressions, and outside the USSR with the aid of a gigantic apparatus which, through resources drawn from the labor of the Soviet workers and peasants, poisons world public opinion with the virus of lies, falsifications, and blackmail. Millions of people throughout the world identify the October revolution with the Thermidorian bureaucracy, the Soviet Union with Stalin's clique, the revolutionary workers with the utterly demoralized Comintern apparatus.

The first great breach in this Tower of Babel will necessarily cause it to collapse entirely, and bury beneath its debris the authority of the Thermidorian chiefs. That is why it is for Stalin a life-and-death question to kill the Fourth International while it is still in embryo! Now, as we are here examining the Moscow trials, the Executive Committee of the Comintern, according to information in the press, is sitting in Moscow. Its agenda is: *The struggle against world Trotskyism.* The session of the Executive Committee of the Comintern is not only a link in the long chain of the Moscow frame-ups, but also the projection of the latter on the world arena. Tomorrow we shall hear about new misdeeds of the Trotskyists in Spain, of their direct or indirect support of the Fascists. Echoes of this base calumny, indeed, have already been heard in this room. Tomorrow we shall hear how the Trotskyists in the United States are preparing railroad wrecks and the obstruction of the Panama Canal, in the interests of Japan. We shall learn the day after tomorrow how the Trotskyists in Mexico are preparing measures for the restoration of Porfirio Díaz. You say Díaz died a long time ago? The Moscow creators of amalgams do not stop before such trifles. They stop before nothing—nothing at all. Politically and morally, it is a question of life and death for them. Emissaries of the GPU are prowling in all countries of the Old and the New World. They do not lack money. What does it mean to the ruling clique to spend twenty or fifty millions of dollars more or less, to sustain its authority and its power? These gentlemen buy human consciences like sacks of potatoes. We shall see this in many instances.

Fortunately, not everybody can be bought. Otherwise humanity would have rotted away a long time ago. Here, in the person of the Commission, we have a precious cell of unmarketable public conscience. All those who thirst for purification of the social atmosphere will turn instinctively toward the Commission. In spite of intrigues, bribes and calumny, it will be rapidly protected by the armor of the sympathy of broad, popular masses.

Ladies and gentlemen of the Commission! Already for five years—I repeat, five years!—I have incessantly demanded the creation of an international commission of inquiry. The day I received the telegram about the creation of your sub-commission was a great holiday in my life. Some friends anxiously asked me: Will not the Stalinists penetrate into the Commission, as they at first penetrated into the Committee for the Defense of Trotsky? I answered: Dragged into the light of day, the Stalinists are not fearsome. On the contrary, I will welcome the most venomous questions from the Stalinists; to break them down I have only to tell what actually happened. The world press will give the necessary publicity to my replies. I knew in advance that the GPU would bribe individual journalists and whole newspapers. But I did not doubt for one moment that the conscience of the world cannot be bribed and that it will score, in this case as well, one of its most splendid victories.

Esteemed Commissioners! The experience of my life, in which there has been no lack either of successes or of failures, has not only not destroyed my faith in the clear, bright future of mankind, but, on the contrary, has given it an indestructible temper. This faith in reason, in truth, in human solidarity, which at the age of eighteen I took with me into the workers' quarters of the provincial Russian town of Nikolayev—this faith I have preserved fully and completely. It has become more mature, but no less ardent. In the very fact of your Commission's formation—in the fact that, at its head, is a man of unshakable moral authority, a man who by virtue of his age should have the right to remain outside of the skirmishes in the political arena—in this fact I see a new and truly magnificent reinforcement of the revolutionary optimism which constitutes the fundamental element of my life.

[The two selections from *The Case of Leon Trotsky* are taken from Trotsky's concluding speech before the hearings, held in Coyoacan, Mexico, during April 1937, of the Preliminary Commission of Inquiry into the Charges Made Against Leon Trotsky in the Moscow Trials.—Ed.]

25

The USSR in War

(1939)

THE GERMAN-SOVIET PACT AND THE CHARACTER OF THE USSR

Is it possible after the conclusion of the German-Soviet pact to consider the USSR a workers' state? The future of the Soviet state has again and again aroused discussion in our midst. Small wonder; we have before us the first experiment in the workers' state in history. Never before and nowhere else has this phenomenon been available for analysis. In the question of the social character of the USSR, mistakes commonly flow, as we have previously stated, from replacing the historical fact with the programmatic norm. Concrete fact departs from the norm. This does not signify, however, that it has overthrown the norm; on the contrary, it has reaffirmed it, from the negative side. The degeneration of the first workers' state, ascertained and explained by us, has only the more graphically shown what the workers' state should be, what it could and would be under certain historical conditions. The contradiction between the concrete fact and the norm constrains us not to reject the norm but, on the contrary, to fight for it by means of the revolutionary road. The program of the approaching revolution in the USSR is determined on the one hand by our appraisal of the USSR as an objective historical *fact,* and on the other hand, by a *norm* of the workers' state. We do not say: "Everything is lost, we must begin all over again." We clearly indicate those elements of the workers' state which at the given stage can be salvaged, preserved, and further developed.

Those who seek nowadays to prove that the Soviet-German pact changes our appraisal of the Soviet state take their stand, in essence, on the position of the Comintern—to put it more correctly, on yesterday's position of the Comintern. According to this logic, the historical mission of the workers' state is the struggle for imperialist democracy. The "betrayal" of the democracies in favor of fascism divests the USSR of its being considered a workers' state. In point of fact, the signing of the treaty with Hitler supplies only an extra gauge with which to measure the degree of degeneration of the Soviet bureaucracy, and its contempt for the international working class, including the Comintern, but it does not provide any basis whatsoever for a re-evaluation of the sociological appraisal of the USSR.

ARE THE DIFFERENCES POLITICAL OR TERMINOLOGICAL?

Let us begin by posing the question of the nature of the Soviet state not on the abstract sociological plane but on the plane of concrete political tasks. Let us concede for the moment that the bureaucracy is a new "class" and that the present regime in the USSR is a special system of class exploitation. What new political conclusions follow for us from these definitions? The Fourth International long ago recognized the necessity of overthrowing the bureaucracy by means of revolutionary uprising of the toilers. Nothing else is proposed or can be proposed by those who proclaim the bureaucracy to be an exploiting "class." The goal to be attained by the overthrow of the bureaucracy is the re-establishment of the rule of the Soviets, expelling from them the present bureaucracy. Nothing different can be proposed or is proposed by the leftist critics.[1] It is the task of the regenerated Soviets to collaborate with the world revolution and the building of a socialist society. The overthrow of the bureaucracy therefore presupposes the preservation of state property and of planned economy. Herein is the nub of the whole problem.

Needless to say, the distribution of productive forces among the various branches of the economy, and generally the entire content of the plan, will be drastically changed when this plan is determined by the interests not of the bureaucracy but of the producers themselves. But inasmuch as the question of overthrowing the parasitic oligarchy still remains linked with that of preserving the nationalized (state) property, we called the future revolution *political*. Certain of our critics (Ciliga, Bruno and others) want, come what may, to call the future revolution *social*. Let us grant this definition. What does it alter in essence? To those tasks of the revolution which we have enumerated it adds nothing whatsoever.

Our critics as a rule take the facts as we long ago established them. They add absolutely nothing essential to the appraisal either of the position of the bureaucracy and the toilers, or of the role of the Kremlin on the international arena. In all these spheres, not only do they fail to challenge our analysis, but on the contrary they themselves lean completely upon it and even restrict themselves entirely to it. The sole accusation they bring against us is that we do not draw the necessary "conclusions." Upon analysis it turns out, however, that these conclusions are of a purely terminological character. Our critics refuse to call the degenerated workers' state—a workers' state. They demand that the totalitarian bureaucracy be called a ruling class. The revolution against this bureaucracy they propose to consider not political but social. Were we then to make these terminological concessions, we would place our ʼcritics in a

[1] We recollect that some of those comrades who are inclined to consider the bureaucracy a new class, at the same time objected strenuously to the exclusion of the bureaucracy from the Soviets.

very difficult position, inasmuch as they themselves would not know what to do with their purely verbal victory.

LET US CHECK OURSELVES ONCE AGAIN

It would therefore be a piece of monstrous nonsense to split with comrades who on the question of the sociological nature of the USSR have an opinion different from ours, insofar as they agree with us in regard to the political tasks. But on the other hand, it would be blindness on our part to ignore purely theoretical and even terminological differences, because in the course of further development they may acquire flesh and blood and lead to diametrically opposite political conclusions. Just as a tidy housewife never permits an accumulation of cobwebs and garbage, so a revolutionary party cannot tolerate unclearness, confusion, and equivocation. Our house must be kept clean!

Let me recall for the sake of illustration the question of Thermidor. For a long time we asserted that Thermidor in the USSR was only being prepared but had not yet been consummated. Later, investing the analogy to Thermidor with a more precise and well-deliberated character, we came to the conclusion that Thermidor had already taken place long ago. This open rectification of our own mistake did not introduce the slightest consternation in our ranks. Why? Because the *essence* of the processes in the Soviet Union was appraised identically by all of us, as day by day we jointly studied the growth of reaction. For us it was only a question of rendering more precise an historical analogy, nothing more. I hope that still today despite the attempt of some comrades to uncover differences on the question of the "defense of the USSR"—with which we shall deal presently—we shall succeed by means of simply rendering our own ideas more precise to preserve unanimity on the basis of the program of the Fourth International.

IS IT A CANCEROUS GROWTH OR A NEW ORGAN?

Our critics have more than once argued that the present Soviet bureaucracy bears very little resemblance to either the bourgeois or labor bureaucracy in capitalist society; that, to a far greater degree than does fascist bureaucracy, it represents a new and much more powerful social formation. This is quite correct and we have never closed our eyes to it. But if we consider the Soviet bureaucracy a "class," then we are compelled to state immediately that this class does not at all resemble any of those propertied classes known to us in the past; our gain consequently is not great. We frequently call the Soviet bureaucracy a caste, underscoring thereby its shut-in character, its arbitrary rule, and the haughtiness of the ruling stratum, which considers that its progenitors issued from the divine lips of Brahma whereas the popular masses originated from the grosser portions of his anatomy. But even this definition does not of course possess a strictly scientific character. Its relative superiority lies in this, that the makeshift character of the term is clear to everybody, since it would enter nobody's mind to identify the Moscow oligarchy with the Hindu caste of Brahmins. The old sociological terminology did not and could not prepare a name for a new social event which is in process of evolution (degeneration) and which has not assumed stable forms. All of us, however, continue to call the Soviet bureaucracy a bureaucracy, not being unmindful of its historical peculiarities. In our opinion this should suffice for the time being.

Scientifically and politically—and not purely terminologically—the question poses itself as follows: Does the bureaucracy represent a temporary growth on a social organism or has this growth already become transformed into an historically indispensable organ? Social excrescences can be the product of an "accidental" (i.e., temporary and extraordinary) enmeshing of historical circumstances. A social organ (and such is every class, including an exploiting class) can take shape only as a result of the deeply rooted inner needs of production itself. If we do not answer this question, then the entire controversy will degenerate into sterile toying with words.

THE EARLY DEGENERATION OF THE BUREAUCRACY

The historical justification for every ruling class consists in this—that the system of exploitation it headed raised the development of the productive forces to a new level. Beyond the shadow of a doubt, the Soviet regime gave a mighty impulse to economy. But the source of this impulse was the nationalization of the means of production and the planned beginnings, and by no means the fact that the bureaucracy usurped command over the economy. On the contrary, bureaucratism, as a system, became the worst brake on the technical and cultural development of the country. This was veiled for a certain time by the fact that the Soviet economy was occupied for two decades with transplanting and assimilating the technology and organization of production in advanced capitalist countries. The period of borrowing and imitation still could, for better or for worse, be accommodated to bureaucratic automatism, i.e., the suffocation of all initiative and all creative urge. But the higher the economy rose, the more complex its requirements became, all the more unbearable became the obstacle of the bureaucratic regime. The constantly sharpening contradiction between them leads to uninterrupted political convulsions, to systematic annihilation of the most outstanding creative elements in all spheres of activity. Thus, before the bureaucracy could succeed in exuding from itself a "ruling class," it came into irreconcilable contradiction with the demands of development. The explanation for this is to be found precisely in the fact that the bureaucracy is not the bearer of a new system of economy peculiar to itself and impossible without itself, but is a parasitic growth on a workers' state.

THE CONDITIONS FOR THE OMNIPOTENCE AND FALL OF THE BUREAUCRACY

The Soviet oligarchy possesses all the vices of the old ruling classes but lacks their historical mission. In the bureaucratic degeneration of the Soviet state it is not the general laws of modern society from capitalism to socialism which find expression but a special, exceptional and temporary refraction of these laws under the conditions of a backward revolutionary country in a capitalist environment. The scarcity of consumer goods and the universal struggle to obtain them generate a policeman who arrogates to himself the function of distribution. Hostile pressure from without imposes on the policeman the role of "defender" of the country, endows him with national authority, and permits him doubly to plunder the country.

Both conditions for the omnipotence of the bureaucracy—the backwardness of the country and the imperialist environment—bear, however, a temporary and transitional character and must disappear with the victory of the world revolution. Even bourgeois economists have calculated that with a planned economy it would be possible to raise the national income of the United States rapidly to two hundred billion dollars a year and thus assure the entire population not only the satisfaction of its primary needs but real comforts. On the other hand, the world revolution would do away with the danger from without as a supplementary cause of bureaucratization. The elimination of the need to expend an enormous share of the national income on armaments would raise even higher the living and cultural level of the masses. In these conditions the need for a policeman-distributor would fall away by itself. Administration as a gigantic co-operative would very quickly supplant state power. There would be no room for a new ruling class or for a new exploiting regime, located between capitalism and socialism.

AND WHAT IF THE SOCIALIST REVOLUTION
IS NOT ACCOMPLISHED?

The disintegration of capitalism has reached extreme limits; likewise the disintegration of the old ruling class. The further existence of this system is impossible. The productive forces must be organized in accordance with a plan. But who will accomplish this task: the proletariat, or a new ruling class of "commissars"—politicians, administrators, and technicians? Historical experience bears witness, in the opinion of certain rationalizers, that one cannot entertain hope in the proletariat. The proletariat proved "incapable" of averting the last imperialist war although the material prerequisites for a socialist revolution already existed at that time. The successes of fascism after the war were once again the consequence of the "incapacity" of the proletariat to lead capitalist society out of the blind alley. The bureaucratization of the Soviet state was in its turn the consequence of the "incapacity" of the proletariat itself to regulate society through the democratic mechanism. The Spanish Revolution was strangled by the fascist and Stalinist bureaucracies before the very eyes of the world proletariat. Finally, last link in this chain is the new imperialist war, the preparation of which took place quite openly, with complete impotence on the part of the world proletariat. If this conception is adopted, that is, if it is acknowledged that the proletariat does not have the forces to accomplish the socialist revolution, then the urgent task of the statification of the productive forces will obviously be accomplished by somebody else. By whom? By a new bureaucracy, which will replace the decayed bourgeoisie as a new ruling class on a world scale. That is how the question is beginning to be posed by those "Leftists" who do not rest content with debating over words.

THE PRESENT WAR AND THE FATE OF MODERN SOCIETY

By the very march of events this question is now posed very concretely. The Second World War has begun. It attests incontrovertibly to the fact that society can no longer live on the basis of capitalism. Thereby it subjects the proletariat to a new and perhaps decisive test.

If this war provokes, as we firmly believe, a proletarian revolution, it must inevitably lead to the overthrow of the bureaucracy in the USSR and regeneration of Soviet democracy on a far higher economic and cultural basis than in 1918. In that case the question as to whether the Stalinist bureaucracy was a "class" or a growth on the workers' state will be automatically solved. To every single person it will become clear that in the process of the development of the world revolution the Soviet bureaucracy was only an *episodic* relapse.

If, however, it is conceded that the present war will provoke not revolution but a decline of the proletariat, then there remains another alternative: the further decay of monopoly capitalism, its further fusion with the state and the replacement of democracy wherever it still remains by a totalitarian regime. The inability of the proletariat to take into its hands the leadership of society could actually lead under these conditions to the growth of a new exploiting class from the bonapartist fascist bureaucracy. This would be, according to all indications, a regime of decline, signalizing the eclipse of civilization.

An analogous result might occur in the event that the proletariat of advanced capitalist countries, having conquered power, should prove incapable of holding it and surrender it, as in the USSR, to a privileged bureaucracy. Then we would be compelled to acknowledge that the reason for the bureaucratic relapse is rooted not in the backwardness of the country and not in the imperialist environment, but in the congenital incapacity of the proletariat to become a ruling class. Then it would be necessary in retrospect to establish that in its fundamental traits the present USSR was the precursor of a new exploiting regime on an international scale.

We have diverged very far from the terminological controversy over the nomenclature of the Soviet state. But let our critics not protest; only by taking the necessary historical perspective can one provide oneself with a correct judgment upon such a question as the replacement of one social regime by another. The historical alternative, carried to the end, is as follows: either the Stalin regime is an abhorrent relapse in the process of transforming a bourgeois society into a socialist society, or the Stalin regime is the first stage of a new exploiting society. If the second prognosis proves to be correct, then, of course, the bureaucracy will become a new exploiting class. However onerous the second perspective may be, if the world proletariat should actually prove incapable of fulfilling the mission placed upon it by the course of development, nothing else would remain except only to recognize that the socialist program, based on the internal contradictions of capitalist society, ended as a utopia. It is self-evident that a new "minimum" program would be required—for the defense of the interests of the slaves of the totalitarian bureaucratic society. . . .

PART TWO
Samples of Opinion

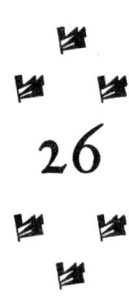

Gogol:
An Anniversary Tribute

TRANSLATED BY I. A. LANGNAS
(previously untranslated, written in 1902).

Gogol was born in 1809 and died in 1852. His life spanned forty-three years, considerably fewer than were required by the interests of literature. Yet in this brief and tragic life, Gogol's achievement was immense.

Before his appearance, Russian literature merely tried to exist. After him, it exists. By linking it forever with the course of Russian life, he brought our literature into being, and it is in this sense that he was the father of the realistic or naturalistic school, of which Belinsky was the intellectual godfather.

Before Gogol and Belinsky, our life and the convictions aroused by it went one way, our poetry another. The link between the writer and the man was feeble. The most vital men, when they took up their pens to write, concerned themselves mainly with theories of taste and not with the meaning of their work. "This defect—the absence of a link between the convictions of the writer and his writings—characterized all our literature," declares Chernyshevsky, "until the time when Gogol and Belinsky transformed it."

For entirely understandable reasons, satire has always been the most lively and honest element in Russian literature. Even before Gogol, vital social thought embodied in more or less artistic form had made its appearance: in the comedies of Fonvizin, the fables of Krylov, the plays of Griboyedov. But it is in the work of Gogol, in his great poem about "the poverty and imperfection of our life," that this satirical tendency achieved its profoundest depth.

Before Gogol we had a Russian Theocritus and a Russian Aristophanes, a native Corneille and a native Racine, a northern Goethe and a northern Shakespeare; but we had no truly national writers. Even Pushkin, as his title of the "Russian Byron" suggests, was not free of the impulse toward imitation.

But Gogol was entirely himself, simply Gogol. After him, our writers ceased to be mere duplicates of European genius. Now we have "simply" Grigoriev, "simply" Goncharov, Saltykov, Tolstoy, Dostoevsky, Ostrovsky. . . . All derive from Gogol, the father of Russian comedy and the Russian novel.

Having now achieved a national character, our literature abandoned its phase of schoolboy imitation, especially its reliance upon "local color," which in practice often resembled a masquerade. To distract attention from its imitative character, Russian literature before Gogol had donned peasant smocks, coats and mittens. But with Gogol, the novel—"that episode from the endless poem of human fates"—began to dominate our writing. Until then we could produce odes, tragedies, fantasies, idylls, whatever we pleased. Nor did it trouble us that life yielded no material for tragedies or odes. Letters were dissociated from life; literature created its works from itself, in obedience to the laws of poetry. But Gogol in his fiction, and Belinsky in his criticism, put an end to this stifling autonomy.

Reality began to live a second life in Russia, in both the realistic novel and comedy. Most of all, however, in the novel, for as Belinsky remarked, "the novel is our daily bread, our bedside book, which we read when we shut our eyes at night and when we open them in the morning."

. . .

How much abuse Gogol had to take because he portrayed the "poverty and imperfection of our life"! Had Gogol been fully aware of the meaning and value of his creative work, he would not have yielded to this abuse. On the contrary, he would have found greater strength and self-confidence with which to confront it. He would have said, "How am I to be blamed if the slavish atmosphere of serfdom and of bureaucratic arbitrariness yield only 'poverty and imperfection' ?" But Gogol did not succeed in reaching a full critical view of the social structure of his day. He did not rebel against the foundations of Russian life, and to the end of his days he held its principles to be sacred. That these foundations and principles could produce only imperfection and poverty, poverty and imperfection—should not this, however, have troubled him?

Perhaps it is this dilemma which lies behind the strange lyrical outburst at the end of the first volume of *Dead Souls,* where Russia is likened to a madly-driven troika, or behind Gogol's stillborn plan for presenting in fiction a heroic Russian man and a sublime Slav maiden.

As a realist to the core of his being, Gogol could not successfully create "positive" characters any more than the life of his time could. Wasn't he then doomed to failure when he decided, after suffering the torments of the stupidity he saw all about him, to create through sheer will a great hero and a sublime maiden such as no other nation could boast? Alas, it was not to be. The Chichikovs, the Manilovs, the Pyushkins, and even the Tentetnikovs stood shoulder to shoulder, leg to leg, refusing to give way either in life or literature. . . . And from whose lineage could Gogol's great man arise? From the lineage of a Chichikov, or a Manilov? What air could Gogol's projected hero breathe? The air of serfdom?

Gogol started his great service to Russian literature with *Evenings on a Farm,* those pure and unclouded works of a young spirit, clear as a spring morning, those "gay songs at the banquet of unconsumed life." He then rose to write the great comedy of aristocratic and bureaucratic Russia—and ended with the narrow-spirited moralizing of *Correspondence with Friends*. Between the poles of this career there would seem hardly to be a connection.

From the young "bee-keeper" of *Evenings on a Farm* to the creator of *Dead Souls*, one can discern a transition in accordance with the successive stages of normal psychology. These two phases of Gogol's career are related to one another as the youth and maturity of poetic genius. But how are we to account for the further transition, from Gogol the realist to Gogol the mystic, from the deeply human poet to the narrowly ascetic moralist? How are we to explain the fact that Gogol, who had so completely mastered the psychological mechanism of dreamy apathy and sentimental provincialism, above all in the character of Manilov—that Gogol who had, in Orest Miller's phrase, "liquidated Manilovism in Russian literature once and for all"—should now preach a mystical and moralistic Manilovism in *Correspondence with Friends?*

Consider the late Gogol who, in tones of earnest conviction, begins to offer everyone his dull and empty advice. To the governor's wife: on how to regenerate society by modesty of dress. To the governor: on the necessity of having right-minded officials in the provincial administration. To the landlord: on how to establish idyllic relations with his peasants upon the inviolable foundations of . . . serfdom. Is it really possible that Gogol the searcher of hearts, Gogol the humorist, Gogol the realist who led Russian meanness, narrowness and apathy to the executioner's block, should now indulge in such narrow-minded and quietistic homilies?

Attempts have been made to explain the split between Gogol the artist and Gogol the moralist on psychiatric grounds. Gogol himself expressed regret that, after the publication of *Correspondence with Friends*, "people began to say, almost to the author's face, that he had lost his mind and even offered him remedies for mental disorder." In our own day, too, efforts have been made to diagnose the spiritual illness of this martyr-writer and assimilate the oddity of his writing, his melancholy disposition and obtrusively mystical ideas into a clinical scheme of "depressive psychosis."

Such descriptions lie outside the problem of literary history with which we are here concerned, and quite apart from whether the soul of the late Gogol belongs to the sphere of psychopathology, they are irrelevant to the question: How and why did this realistic artist become a didactic mystic? Not psychopathology but social history will enable us to answer this question.

By the power of his artistic intuition Gogol stormed the fortress of barbarism, daily brutality, common crime and invincible meanness—meanness, endless Russian meanness. He took everything accumulated by history, consolidated by custom, covered by the dust of centuries, and crowned by mystical sanction and proceeded to shake it, lift it, lay it bare, and make it into a problem for our thought, a question for our conscience. All this he did without the aid of systematic reason: his creative genius came to grips with reality through the use, so to speak, of its bare hands. Belinsky understood this well:

> The power of *direct creation*, amazing though it was, also did Gogol a lot of harm. One might say that it averted his eyes from the ideas and moral problems that excited his contemporaries, and made him concentrate on facts and be satisfied with the objective representation of facts.

Indeed, whatever else he may have seen as problematic, Gogol saw serfdom, the breeding ground of all the horrors, monstrosities and brutalities of Russian life, not as a problem but simply as another fact of human existence.

We must remember that Gogol lived at a time when our society did not yet enjoy a coherent intellectual atmosphere. Questions of political ideology were not yet accessible to literature; indeed, they were barely discussed. In the 1820's, when Gogol was a provincial youth, the best circles of Petersburg "society" began to work out a political creed which, in the jargon of the day, could be called "a leading social ideology." But in the middle of the decade [through the repressive measures of Nicholas I after his ascent to the throne in 1825] this process was cut off. In the 1830's, oases of thinking intelligentsia began to appear, and the best leaders of the following decades came from among them. But before Gogol could encounter such groups, he became famous as the author of *Evenings on a Farm*. He entered Pushkin's circle, from which he received a great deal of support as an artist but very little that could broaden his political horizons. And then add to this the fact that from 1836 Gogol lived almost entirely abroad, led a very secluded life, and met only a few people, whose views were as uncritical as his own.

The unarmed and undefended mind of Gogol had to contend with a mass of related questions that his artistic creation threw up. His tender conscience left him no peace. He had to find solutions, as best he could, with the aid of the sorry patterns of thought that tradition had yielded him and taught him to regard as complete, absolute and beyond the touch of doubt.

Now a mind which lacked internal support needed some kind of external authority by means of which to confront the destructive work of artistic creation, to cope with the troubling materials it forced him to see. And Gogol found such an authority in his inherited moral codes, linked as these were with childhood impressions and sanctified by memories.

The mystical and moralizing mood of the great writer's closing years was a development of assumptions he had acquired through a traditional upbringing. His activity as an artist created in him a need to find some meaning in life, and toward this end he fell back upon the archaic principles he had inherited, principles that in Russia are transmitted from generation to generation. It is not hard to imagine the false judgments that these decrepit moral codes would encourage in regard to the problems thrown up by Gogol's artistic intuition, or the narrow and childishly naïve solutions they would lead to concerning problems of social life.

Take for example *The Inspector General*, a comedy that is a kind of poem of provincial bureaucracy. Skvoznik-Dmukhanovsky is a rogue, an embezzler, a bribe-taker, an utterly servile creature. The most horrible thing about him, as Belinsky remarks, is that his character is "not a corruption, but a development of his morality, his own exalted view of his duties." His moral deformity is a simple conclusion from well-known social premises. And here lies the "pathos" of this figure, to employ a term much favored in Gogol's day.

For it is clear that the comedy requires a conclusion going far beyond the strictures of civic decency, far beyond such rules as those forbidding us to take bribes and rob public funds. But Gogol, given the nature of his ideas, was quite unable to grasp the social value and historical meaning of such conclusions. And so he evaded them, with the result that he ended by trying to give a mystical and moralistic explanation of his deeply realistic social comedy. From this explanation it would appear that the city in which the comedy occurs is finally nothing but our corrupted human soul, the crooked officials are merely our cunning passions, while the gendarme, that Russian *deus ex machina,* is merely the agent of our true and inexorable conscience.

This dull and didactic explanation was unable, however, to decrease by one iota the subversive power of Gogol's comedy. All of Gogol's creative work produced in the public conscience a coherent body of thought which went far beyond the limitations of Gogol's own social outlook. "Behind these monstrous and deformed figures," wrote Belinsky, "thinking readers perceive other and worthier faces; the squalid reality makes them contemplate an ideal reality and *that which is* clarifies for them *that which should be.*"

Where does Belinsky—and with him the better part of our society—find the "pathos" of *Dead Souls,* the basic idea of the work?

> In the contradiction between the social forms of Russian life and its deep substantial beginning, which is still a secret, has not yet revealed itself to the public consciousness, and cannot as yet be grasped by any definition.

Freed from the shackles of Hegelian phraseology, this sentence yields a simple but profound thought: the basic idea of Gogol's poem is the contradition between the rigid *forms* of Russian life and its fluid *content.*

. . .

Yes, Gogol made many blunders. His *Correspondence with Friends* failed to provide a new overcoat for any of the innumerable Akakii Akakyeviches . . . and yet they needed them so badly!

But who would dare now to throw a stone at the martyr who sought so passionately for truth and paid for his errors with such enormous suffering? If he tried to weaken the social meaning of his own books by the explanations he provided for them, let this not be held against him! If he seduced some small-souled creature through his publicistic work, let him be forgiven! And for his great service to our literature, for the elevating and humane influence of his work, eternal and undying glory!

The Young Lenin

TRANSLATED from *Vie de Lenine: Jeunesse* (French edition, 1936) BY I. A. LANGNAS (previously untranslated).

The numerous insults which Lenin hurled against his personal enemies and later against whole social classes have inspired many writers, of both the journalistic and the more serious variety, to present him even in his young days as a kind of red-haired monster of cruelty, vanity, and vindictiveness. Eugene Chirikov, expelled at the same time as Ulianov[1] from the University of Kazan, did so in a novel he wrote after the October revolution as a White émigré. The young Vladimir is characterized there by "unhealthy pride and great touchiness." And the populist Vodovozov relates that

> Vladimir's outbursts and coarse gestures and his rude and brutal remarks—of which there were many—deeply shocked Maria Alexandrovna [Lenin's mother]. She was

[1] [Lenin's family name was Vladimir Ilyich Ulianov.—Ed.]

often moved to retort: "Really, Volodia, do you think this is the right way to behave?"

Actually, Lenin was too clearly aware of his own worth to fall into an unhealthy pride. And there was no need for him to be touchy, if only because there was then no one who was likely to offend him. Still, there is no doubt that Lenin's intractable harshness did not always spare the self-respect of others. According to Yasneva, some of his adversaries "bore him a grudge from the very first," a grudge that was to be expressed as long as they remained alive.

The late Vodovozov was among those whom Lenin hurt for life. When he arrived at Samara, Vladimir received him warmly, and helped him to get settled. But he soon appraised Vodovozov as a man of sterile eclecticism who could neither be counted upon to become a supporter nor be taken seriously as an enemy. Aid to famine victims and a petition to the governor led to clashes between the two men which left a lasting mark. Vodovozov's resentment against the young Ulianov vented itself in his memoirs, which include some pages in which the author said more than he intended—to the ultimate benefit to the reader.

> Vodovozov wrote on Vladimir's external appearance: The face as a whole struck one by its mixture of intelligence and coarseness, I might even say bestiality. And one was surprised by the forehead, intelligent though receding. The fleshy nose. . . . There was a stubborn and cruel quality in these traits, combined with undoubted intelligence.

Chirikov, in his pamphlet-novel, makes the youth of Simbirsk say this about Vladimir Ulianov:

> His hands are always clammy! And yesterday he killed a little cat with a shot from his rifle. . . . Then he took it by the tail and threw it over the fence. . . .

Kuprin, another fairly well-known Russian writer, discovered —more recently, to be sure—that Lenin had the green eyes of a monkey. Thus, even Lenin's external appearance, which would seem to be a man's least controversial aspect, has been subjected to a tendentious transformation through memory and imagination.

A photograph made in 1890 has preserved the figure of a cool young man[2] whose composure points to a reserved disposition. The stubborn forehead has not yet been extended by baldness. The small eyes look piercingly from under Asiatic eyelids. The firm lips under the large nose and the solid jaw are covered by a downy growth as yet untouched by scissors or razor. Definitely not a pretty face. But these rough and unrefined traits are so animated by a high spiritual discipline that one simply cannot think of them as bestial. Vladimir's hands were dry, plebeian, with short fingers; hot and masculine hands. And as for little cats, he loved them, as he loved anything weak and defenseless, with the affectionate indulgence of a strong man. The literary gentlemen have obviously slandered him.

"The moral personality of Vladimir Ilyich," Vodovozov went on, "was clearly marked by some kind of amoralism. It is my belief that this was an organic trait of his nature." This amoralism happened to consist in accepting as admissible any means as long as it led to the end. To be sure, Ulianov didn't admire the morality of the Russian priests, or that of Kant, which pretends to regulate our lives from starry heights. The aims he pursued were so great and suprapersonal that he openly subordinated his moral criteria to them. He viewed with indifferent irony, if not with repugnance, the cowards and hypocrites who camouflage the insignificance of their ambitions or the villainy of their methods by superior norms, which they present as absolute but which are actually very flexible.

"I know of no concrete facts which prove Lenin's amoralism," says Vodovozov, reproving himself unwittingly. But after searching his memory he manages to recall how his delicate conscience "was hurt because Lenin was inclined to encourage tittle-tattle." On one occasion, in a small group of people, says Vodovozov, Lenin felt no scruples about using notoriously mendacious arguments "as long as they brought him . . . suc-

[2] [Lenin was born on April 22, 1870.—Ed.]

cess among the listeners who failed to understand him completely." It seems, however, that Vodovozov himself felt that his own story was "quite unimportant" and soon paid a visit to the Ulianovs as if nothing had happened. But Vladimir, whom a friend had told of the visitor's scurrilous judgment, asked him for an explanation. In reply, Vodovozov "tried to attenuate the meaning of his words." The conversation led to a formal reconciliation; but, towards the spring of 1892, the relations between the two deteriorated so badly that they hardly ever met.

For all its banality, this is a truly remarkable episode. The moralist accuses the amoralist, within their circle, of consciously using dishonest arguments. Having done this, he regards his insinuation as "quite unimportant" and pays a friendly visit to the person he slandered. The amoralist, to whom his own words matter, openly asks for an explanation. The moralist, with his back to the wall, wriggles, retreats and finally repudiates his words. One cannot but conclude from Vodovozov's own narrative that the moralist is altogether like a cowardly detractor, while the amoralist shows no propensity whatsoever "to encourage tittle-tattle." We may add that Vodovozov also disproves, with his own words, the gist of his accusation—the use of notoriously lying arguments. On another occasion he writes of Ulianov: "All his speeches manifested his deep faith in his truthfulness." All of us should bear this episode in mind: it will serve us on many future occasions as a key to conflicts in which the sanctimonious will launch the charge of moral indifference against the revolutionary.

No letter of or about Vladimir has been preserved from the Samara period, nor any other testimony. The judgments of both friends and enemies are all retrospective and inevitably colored by the powerful influences of the Soviet period. Still, by employing the method of approximation and—often—that of opposition, they can be used to reconstruct, at least in part, the personality of Lenin at the dawn of his revolutionary activity.

It should be noted, first of all, that Lenin in no way resembled the classical stereotype of the Russian nihilist, which existed not only in reactionary novels but sometimes in real life as well: a rebellious mop of uncombed hair, rumpled clothes, a knotty stick. "His hairline had begun to recede noticeably in those years," Semyonov recalled. There was nothing striking or provocative about his clothes or his manners. Sergeyevsky, who belonged to more or less the same Marxist generation, gives a description of Vladimir towards the end of the Samara period, which is not devoid of interest:

> A modest man carefully and, as they say, respectfully dressed, but quite without pretention and with nothing that would make him attract attention amid ordinary people. This protective coloring pleased me . . . I didn't notice at the time the tricky expression of his face which drew my attention later, after the deportation. . . . He was prudent, looked around circumspectly, observant, calm, self-contained and had all the temperament that his letters had made me attribute to him. . . .

Semyonov gives, in passing, a little picture of the manners of Samara's radical youth. When he came to the Sklyarenkos, Lenin would stretch out on his back on his host's bed "after first putting a newspaper under his feet," and start listening to the conversations around the samovar. Some opinion or other would make him raise his voice. "Nonsense!" would then be heard from the bed, and the word would be followed by a systematic demolition job. This not very laudable habit of sitting or lying on other people's beds was common in all the groups of young men of that day; it was due to their simple manners, and also to the lack of chairs. If anything distinguished Vladimir from the others, it was his putting a newspaper under his feet. The harshness of his retorts expressed an intransigent resistance and was also a way of compelling his adversary to show himself in his true light.

After Ulianov had read that polemical encyclopedia of Marxism, the *Anti-Duehring,* he was indefatigable in sweeping young brains clean of metaphysical values during conversations held around the samovar. Justice? A myth that conceals the right of the stronger. Absolute norms? Morality is the servant of material interests. The government? An excessive committee of the exploiters. The revolution? Don't forget to add the adjective "bourgeois." It is aphorisms of this kind, shattering the beautiful porcelain of idealism, that probably explain his precocious reputation as an "amoralist." Lifted above the level of their exercise books, his listeners were dumfounded and tried to protest. This was just what the young intellectual athlete wanted. "Sophisms?" "Paradoxes?" The bruises were amicably distributed to the right and to the left. Taken by surprise, the opponent would fall silent—sometimes even forgetting to shut his mouth—would try to find the books from which Ulianov quoted and then, one fine day, would proclaim himself a Marxist.

Vladimir, coryphée of the growing Marxist clan, used the socratic method in his debates with the Jacobins and the militants of *Narodnaya Volya*. "All right, so you take power. And then what?" he would ask his opponent. "Decrees." "And your support?" "The people." "But what is this 'people'?" This question would be followed by an analysis of antagonisms between the classes. Toward the end of the Samara period, a manuscript work of Ulianov, "Discussion Between a Social Democrat and a Populist," circulated among the youth. Unfortunately, it has been lost, but it must have been a summary of the Samara controversies in dialogue form.

Vladimir debated with passion—he did everything with passion—but not in a disorderly or haphazard manner. He did not rush into the fray, did not interrupt nor try to outshout the others. He let his opponent have his say, even when indignation choked him; pounced upon his weak points; and then launched his marvelously spirited attack. But even the most furious blows of the young polemicist were not of a personal nature. He attacked ideas and slovenly ways of dealing with them; he hit the man only by the way. It was now his opponent's turn to be silent. Just as he did not interrupt others, Vladimir did not let others interrupt him. And as in his chess games, he never gave up a game or freely yielded a piece.

Maria Ulianova's affirmation that Vladimir's timidity was a family trait seems strange. The numerous testimonies of the younger sister are characterized by an insufficient degree of psychological insight; therefore, prudence is all the more necessary, the greater our desire—a natural one here—to locate in Lenin as many family traits as possible. True, the 1890 photograph mentioned above seems indeed to point to a struggle between timidity and self-assurance, a struggle that had not yet come out into the open. One might say that the young man felt awkward facing the photographer and yielded to him only reluctantly—just as it embarrassed him thirty years later to dictate his letters and articles to a stenographer. If this is, indeed, timidity, it by no means implies a feeling of weakness or an excessive sensitivity; rather, it conceals strength. Its aim is to shelter the inner core from contacts that are too direct, and from acts of indiscreet familiarity. The same trait may assume very different forms among members of the same family; it may even turn into its opposite. The timidity of Alexander [Lenin's older brother], noticed by all who came into contact with him, fully accords with his reticent and self-contained personality. Alexander was clearly embarrassed by his superiority whenever he became aware of it. But it was precisely this trait which set him apart from his younger brother, who unhesitatingly demonstrated his superiority over others. One might even say that Vladimir's aggressive character, given his complete subordination to ideas and lack of personal vanity, freed him in some way from the restraints of timidity. In any case, if he was sometimes seized, especially in his younger days, by an inhibiting embarrassment, it was not for himself that he felt embarrassed, but for others—the banality of their interests, the vulgarity of their jokes, or simply their stupidity. Samoilov shows us Lenin among people he met only recently: "He spoke little; but hardly because he felt ill at ease among people he didn't know well." On the contrary, his presence put others on their guard, and people usually free and easy became prudent or even embarrassed.

The elder sister has told us at the time how Alexander's friends restrained themselves in his presence: "They didn't feel like telling him their silly views, turned towards him and waited for him to have his say." However much the two brothers may have differed in character, in this respect at least Vladimir affected others "like Sasha": he forced them to rise above themselves. Semyonov writes:

Vladimir was, from his youth, a stranger to all bohemianism . . . and all of us who belonged to Sklyarenko's circle restrained ourselves in his presence. . . . A frivolous conversation, a coarse joke were out of the question in his presence.

This is a testimony of inestimable value. Vladimir may have used a vulgar word in the heat of a dispute or in judging an enemy; but he never permitted himself a vile allusion, a trivial witticism or a pornographic anecdote—the common indulgences of young men. He did not put himself under any kind of ascetic rules to that effect; this "amoralist" didn't need any such transcendental *knut* [whip]. Neither was he indifferent by nature to aspects of life outside politics. No, nothing human was alien to him. True, we have no account of young Ulianov's attitude towards women. He surely fell in love and courted; it is certainly no accident that he sang *Charming Little Eyes* with an irony which merely masked his emotions. But even if we remain in ignorance of the details, we can firmly assert that Vladimir maintained, from his youth and all through his life, a pure attitude towards women. The almost Spartan cast of his moral personality was not due to any coldness of temperament; on the contrary, he was basically passionate by nature. But this trait was supplemented by another, for which there can be no other word but "chastity." The organic combination of these two elements, a passionate temper and chastity, made cynicism quite out of the question. Vladimir needed no moral restraints to be superior to others; it was enough that he was organically repelled by anything base or trivial.

Vodovozov himself testifies that in the Marxist circle of Samara, Vladimir "exercized an uncontested authority; he was looked up to almost as much as in his family," even though some members of the circle were older than he. "His authority in the circle was uncontested," Semyonov confirms. The old Bolshevik Lalayants says that Ulianov, whom he met a year after the break with Vodovozov, conquered him at once.

This young man of twenty-three astonishingly combined in his manner, on the one hand, simplicity, delicacy, the joy of living and a taste for teasing, and on the other, solidity and depth of knowledge, a logic implacable in discussions. . . .

After the very first meeting, Lalayants congratulated himself for having chosen Samara as his place of exile.

It is the privilege of the superior person to inspire such contradictory judgments. Even in his younger years Ulianov was by no means inclined to complain about the prejudices of others. And, indeed, the sentiments which he inspired in others were all too much like induction currents generated by his own opinions. Man was for him not an aim but a means.

His attitudes towards other people, [writes Semyonov,] differed very markedly. With friends whom he felt to be on his side, he argued pleasantly and engaged in quite easy-going banter. . . . But as soon as he noted that an opponent represented a differing tendency . . . his polemical fire was inexorable. He hit his adversaries at their most sensitive points and put few restrictions on his language.

This evidence of a companion of his youth is of first-rate importance for our understanding of Lenin.

He was "partial" because his utilitarian attitude towards people came from the deepest mainsprings of his nature, which was completely turned towards the reconstruction of the world. If it still contained an element of calculation—as it did, and that element became more subtle and cautious as time went on—calculation was inseparable from genuine feeling. Lenin very easily "became fond" of people, if they turned out to be valuable and useful to him. But no personal quality could sway him in the case of an adversary. His attitude towards the same person changed abruptly according to whether he happened to be, at any given moment, in one camp or another. But in these "passing fancies," as in the periods of hostility which followed them, there was no trace of impressionability, caprice or personal ambition. The laws of struggle were his code of justice. This explains why his published judgments on various people are often full of striking contradictions, and also why Lenin always remained true to himself in spite of these contradictions.

Our individualist friends tell us that personality is an end in itself; but in their practical relations with other people, they are guided by their personal tastes or even by the state of their liver. The great historical task which our "amoralist" chose to serve ennobled his attitude towards people; in his practical dealings with them he measured them by the same standard that he used for himself. His partiality, dictated by the interests of the cause he served, became in the end a superior kind of impartiality. This rare quality, the true attribute of a leader, gave Lenin, from his early years, an unmatched authority.

Semyonov, who was three years older than Vladimir, once remarked in the course of a general conversation that he and his friends found Marxism so difficult because their knowledge of the history of bourgeois economy was so poor. Vladimir replied briefly and severely: "If *that* is bad, then everything is bad. You must study. . . ." When great questions were at issue, that plain and merry young man spoke like a man who held power. And the others fell silent, felt uneasy, and searched their consciences.

Semyonov also tells how firmly and confidently Lenin rejected some ill-chosen arguments of his brother-in-law Elizarov, who had tried to support him in a dispute with Vodovozov. No, he was by no means timid. We must remember, moreover, that both Elizarov, who idolized Vladimir, and Vodovozov, who was no longer fond of him, were at least six years older than he. Where revolutionary ideas were at stake, Vladimir took no notice of friendship or kinship; still less could he respect superior age.

At twenty-two, Lenin produced, according to Vodovozov, "the impression of a man fully grown and, as far as his politics were concerned, fully shaped." To which Semyonov adds: "Already at that time, Vladimir seemed a man of fully formed opinions. In gatherings of various circles, he behaved with independence and complete self-assurance." The student P. P. Maslov, the future Menshevik economist, learned from some friends in a village of the Ufa province, to which he was confined under police surveillance, that there lived in

Samara a certain Vladimir Ulianov, "who was also interested in economics and who was, besides, "a man of a very distinguished intelligence and education." Ulianov sent him a manuscript—the printing press was still out of reach for Russian Marxists—and, in reading it, Maslov was struck by "the neat and trenchant formulations" which showed that the author "was a man of fully formed opinions."

The phrase "Old Man," later to become Lenin's nickname, became strangely associated with the person of young Vladimir in the Samara period. And there was nothing senile about him in those days or, for that matter, to the end of his life, with the possible exception of his baldness. The striking things about the young men were the maturity of his thought, the balance of his mental powers, the sureness of his thrusts. "Of course," wrote Vodovozov, "I could not foresee the role he was destined to play; but I felt already then—and I said so openly —that Ulianov's role would be great."

The heretical doctrine [Marxism], managed in those days to acquire adherents in the youth circles of Samara. It also obtained something like an official recognition in the radical milieu. Populism, which remained the dominant current of thought, had to give way to it somewhat. The chief propagandist of Social Democracy among the students was Sklyarenko, a gifted but not very diligent man. In March, 1893, a student of Kazan University arrived in Samara, to which he had been exiled under police supervision. It was Lalayants, who soon became a close friend of Ulianov and Sklyarenko. These three men were the Marxist general staff of Samara, for a few months only, of course. Vladimir did not take part in propaganda work. The testimony of Lalayants is clear: "In Samara, in my time at least, he belonged to no circle and led no study group." On the other hand, he exercised an uncontested general leadership. The "trio" met frequently; sometimes at Sklyarenko's lodgings and sometimes at a Samara beer hall, for which Sklyarenko showed an excessive partiality. Ulianov reported to his friends on his activities and they, in turn, told him the latest news of the Samara circles. They frequently fell into theoretical discussions, but even by then

Ulianov always had the last word. In the summer Sklyarenko made a trip to Alakayevka, where he was welcomed for his sociability and his joviality. He carried a supply of new ideas for the students at the seminary and the medical school. Both Sklyarenko and Lalayants later became prominent Bolsheviks.

About that time, Vladimir made the definite conquest of a former organizer of a land commune, Preobrazhensky, with whom he conversed while walking the *verst*[3] and a half which separated the two farms. Preobrazhensky became a member of the Social Democratic organization of Samara and, many years later, managed the famous Gorki estate, on which the head of the Soviet state rested, was ill and died. The friendships of his youth generally played a notable part in Lenin's life.

Vladimir had taken from the provincial life on the banks of the Volga all that it could offer him. According to Elizareva, towards the end of the 1892-93 winter "he already felt bored on occasions and longed to be in a livelier place." But since there was no point quitting Alakayevka in the summer, his departure was delayed till fall. The younger brother was finishing his studies at the *gymnasium* and was preparing to go to Moscow University. Maria Alexandrovna wanted to accompany Dmitri to Moscow, just as she had accompanied Vladimir to Kazan six years earlier. The time had come to detach himself from his family. Petersburg, the most European of Russian cities, attracted Vladimir more than the Moscow of those days, "the great village." Moreover, by living apart from his kin, he lessened the risk of getting his brother and sisters into difficulties by his revolutionary activities.

The last months at Samara and Alakayevka were devoted to preparations for a rapid departure. Vladimir prepares summaries of books and articles, puts together his most important conclusions, outlines his polemical studies. He tests, cleans and sharpens the weapon he will soon wield. The critical movement in the brains of the intelligentsia and the deeper movement in the industrial classes require a doctrine, a program, a teacher. The pace of Russian history begins to quicken. It is time to say good-by to Samara, to Alakayevka, to the avenue

[3] [About two-thirds of a mile.—Tr.]

of lindens! Vladimir Ulianov leaves his remote provincial refuge for the capital city where, soon after his arrival, he stands head and shoulders above his generation.

Thus—in the short and long six years of strenuous work which passed between the execution of his brother and his move to Petersburg—was formed the future Lenin. He still has to take off on great flights, internal as well as external; and one can see several clearly marked stages in his later development. But the essential traits of his character, of his worldview, and of his style of conduct were definitely fixed between his seventeenth and twenty-second years.

28

The Family and Ceremony

TRANSLATED BY Z. VENGEROVNA
from *Problems of Life* (1924).

Church ceremonial enslaves even the worker of little or no religious belief in the three great moments of the life of man—birth, marriage, and death. The workers' state has rejected Church ceremony, and informed its citizens that they have the right to be born, to marry and to die without the mysterious gestures and exhortations of persons clad in cassocks, gowns and other ecclesiastical vestments. But custom finds it harder to discard ceremony than does the state. The life of the working family is too monotonous, and it is this monotony that wears out the nervous system. Hence comes the desire for alcohol—a small flask containing a whole world of images. Hence comes the need for the Church and her ritual. How is a marriage to be celebrated, or the birth of a child in a family? How is one to pay the tribute of affection to the beloved dead?

The Family and Ceremony

It is on this need of marking and decorating the principal signposts along the road of life that Church ritual depends.

What can we set against it? Superstition, which lies at the room of ritual, must, of course, be opposed by rationalistic criticism, by an atheistic, realistic attitude to Nature and her forces. But this question of scientific, critical propaganda does not exhaust the subject; in the first place it appeals only to a minority, while even this minority feels the need of enriching, improving and ennobling its individual life, or at any rate, the more salient events of it.

The workers' state already has its festivals, processions, reviews and parades, symbolic spectacles—the new theatrical ceremonies of state. It is true that in the main they are too closely allied to the old forms, which they imitate and perpetuate. But on the whole, the revolutionary symbolism of the workers' state is novel, distinct and forcible—the red flag, red star, worker, peasant, comrade, International. But within the shut cages of family life the new has not penetrated, or at least, has done so but little, while individual life is closely bound up with the family. This explains why in the matter of ikons, christenings, Church funerals, etc., the balance is in favor of custom. The revolutionary members of the family have nothing to offer in place of them. Theoretical argument acts on the mind only. Spectacular ceremony acts on the senses and imagination. The influence of the latter, consequently, is much more widespread. In the most communistic of circles a need has arisen to oppose old practices by new forms, new symbols, not merely in the domain of State life, where this has largely been done, but in the domain of the family.

There is a tendency among workers to celebrate the birthday instead of the patron saint's day, and to name newborn infants by some name symbolizing new and intimate events and ideas, rather than by the name of a saint. At the deliberations of the Moscow Propagandists I first learnt that the novel girls' name of Octobrina has come to be associated with the right of citizenship.

There is the name Ninel (Lenin spelt backward) and Rem (Revolution, Electrification, *Mir* [peace]). Infants, too, are given the Christian name of Vladimir, Ilyich and even Lenin, also Rosa (in honor of Rosa Luxemburg) and so on, showing a desire to link up with the revolution.

There have been cases where the birth of a child has been celebrated by a mock ceremonial "inspection" in Fabzavkom, with a special protocol decree adding the infant's name to the list of RSFP citizens. This was followed by a feast. In a working family the apprenticeship of a boy is also celebrated as a festival. It is an event of real importance, bearing as it does on the choice of a trade, a course of life. This is a fitting occasion for the intervention of the trade union. On the whole, the trade unions ought to play a more important part in the creation of the forms of the new life. The guilds of the Middle Ages were powerful because they hemmed in the life of the apprentice, laborer, and mechanic on all sides. They greeted the child on the day of its birth, led it to the school door, and to church when it married, and buried it when it had fulfilled the duties of its calling. The guilds were not merely trade federations; they were the organized life of the community. It is on these lines that our industrial unions are largely developing, with this difference, certainly, that in opposition to the medieval, the forms of the new life will be free from the Church and her superstition and imbued with an aspiration to utilize every conquest of science and machinery for the enrichment and beautifying of life.

Marriage, if you like, more easily dispenses with ceremonial. Though, even in this respect, how many "misunderstandings" and exclusions from the party have there been on account of Church weddings? Custom refuses to be reconciled to the mere marriage, unbeatified by a spectacular ceremony.

The question of burial is an infinitely more difficult one. To be laid in the ground without the due funeral service is as unusual, disgraceful and monstrous as to grow up without baptism. In cases where the standing of the dead has called for a funeral of a political character, the stage has been set for the new spectacular ceremony, imbued with the symbolism of the revolution—the red flag, the revolutionary Dead March, the farewell rifle salute. Some of the members of the Moscow conference emphasized the need for a speedy adoption of cremation, proposing to set an example by cremating the bodies of prominent revolutionary workers. They justly regarded this as a powerful weapon to be used for anti-Church and anti-religious propaganda. But cremation, which it is high time we adopted, does not mean the giving up of processions, speech-making, marches, the rifle salute. The need for an outer manifestation of emotion is strong and legitimate. If the spectacular has in the past been closely connected with the Church, there is no reason, as we have already said, why it cannot be separated from her. The theater separated earlier from the Church than the Church from the state. In early days the Church fought very much against the "worldly" theater, fully realizing that it was a dangerous rival in the matter of spectacular sights. The theater died except as a special spectacle shut within four walls. But daily custom, which used the spectacular form, was instrumental in preserving the Church. The Church had other rivals in this respect, in the form of secret societies like the Freemasons. But they were permeated through and through with a worldly priesthood. The creation of the revolutionary "ceremonial" of custom (we use the word "ceremonial" for want of a better), set against the "ceremonial" of the Church, is possible not only on public or state occasions, but in the relationships of family life. Even now a band playing a funeral march competes successfully with the Church funeral music. And we must, of course, make an ally of the band in the struggle against Church ritual, which is based on a slavish belief in another world, where you will be repaid a hundredfold for the miseries and evils of this. A still more powerful ally is the cinema.

The creation of new forms of life and new spectacular customs will move apace with the spread of education and the growth of economic security. We have every cause to watch this process with the utmost care. There cannot, of course, be any question of compulsion from above, i.e., the bureaucratizing of newborn customs. It is only by the creativeness of the general masses of the population, assisted by creative imagination and artistic initiative, that we can, in the course of years and decades, come out on the road of spiritualized, ennobled forms of life. Without regulating this creative process, we must, nevertheless, help it in every way. For this purpose, first of all, the tendency to blindness must give place to sight. We must carefully watch all that happens in the working family in this respect, and the Soviet family in general. Every new form, whether abortive or a mere approach to one, must be recorded in the press and brought to the knowledge of the general public, in order to stimulate imagination and interest, and give the impulse to further collective creation of new customs.

Komsomol has an honorable place in this work. Not every invention is successful, not every project takes on. What does it matter? The proper choice will come in due course. The new life will adopt the forms most after its own heart. In the result life will be richer, broader, more full of color and harmony. This is the essence of the problem.

Céline: Novelist and Politician

(1935)

Louis-Ferdinand Céline walked into great literature as other men walk into their own homes. A mature man, with a colossal stock of observations as physician and artist, with a sovereign indifference toward academism, with an extraordinary instinct for intonations of life and language, Céline has written a book which will survive, independently of whether he writes other books, and whether they attain to the level of his first. *Journey to the End of the Night* is a novel of pessimism, a book dedicated by terror in the face of life, and weariness of it, rather than by indignation. Active indignation is linked up with hope. In Céline's book there is no hope.

A Parisian student, who comes from a family of little men, a rationalist, an anti-patriot, and a semi-anarchist—the cafés of the Latin quarter swarm with such types—enlists, to his own astonishment, at the very first trumpet call, as a volunteer in the army; he is sent to the front, and in the mechanized slaughter finds himself envying the horses who perish as men do, but without mouthing false phrases; after being wounded and bemedaled, he wanders through the hospitals where successful doctors exhort him to speed his return to the "flaming cemetery of battles"; as an invalid, he is discharged from the army; he departs for an African colony and there pines away from human baseness, from the heat and the malaria of the tropics; he makes his way illegally into the United States, and finds employment in Ford's plant; he finds a true mate in a prostitute (these are the genuinely tender pages in the book); he returns to France, becomes a physician to the poor, and, soul-sick, wanders through the night of life among the sick and the hearty, all equally pathetic, depraved, and miserable.

Céline does not at all set himself the goal of exposing social conditions in France. True, in passing, he spares neither priests nor generals nor ministers, nor the President of the Republic. But all the while the warp of his tale extends considerably below the level of the ruling classes, cutting across the milieu of little men, functionaries, students, traders, artisans, and concierges; and in addition, on two occasions, it transports itself beyond the boundaries of France. The present social system is as rotten as every other, whether past or future. Céline, in general, is dissatisfied with men and their affairs.

The novel is conceived and executed as a panorama of life's meaninglessness, with its cruelties, conflicts, and lies, with no issue, and no light flickering. A noncommissioned officer torturing the soldiers just before he perishes together with them; an American coupon clipper airing her emptiness in European hotels; French colonial functionaries brutalized by greed and failure; New York, with its automatic unconcern for the man without a checkbook, technically perfected to suck the marrow from human bones; then Paris again; the petty and envious little universe of scholars; the protracted and docile death of a seven-year-old boy; the rape of a little girl; the little virtuous rentiers who murder their mother in order to economize; the priest in Paris and the priest in darkest Africa, both equally alert to sell a man for a few hundred francs, the one an accomplice of civilized rentiers, the other in cahoots with cannibals . . . from chapter to chapter, from one page to the next, the slivers of life compose themselves into a mud-caked, bloody nightmare of meaninglessness. Receptivity which is passive, with its nerves sliced open, without the will straining toward the future—that is the psychological base of despair, sincere in the convulsions of its cynicism.

Céline the moralist follows the footsteps of the artist, and step by step he rips away the halo from all those social values which have become highly acclaimed through custom, from patriotism and personal ties down to love. Is the Fatherland in danger? "No great loss, when the landlord's house burns down. . . . There will be rent to pay just the same." He has no use for historical criteria. Danton's war is not superior to Poincaré's: in both instances the "patriotic function" was paid in the coin of blood. Love is poisoned by selfishness and vanity. All forms of idealism are merely "petty instincts draped in highfaluting phrases." Even the image of the mother is not spared: on meeting her wounded son

> "she squealed like a bitch whose pup had been restored. But she was beneath a bitch because she had faith in those syllables she was told in order to deprive her of her son."

Céline's style is subordinated to his receptivity of the objective world. In his seemingly careless, ungrammatical, passionately condensed language there lives, beats, and vibrates the genuine wealth of French culture, the entire emotional and mental experience of a great nation, in its living content, in its keenest tints.

And, concurrently, Céline writes like a man who has stumbled across human language for the first time. The artist has newly threshed the dictionary of French literature. Pat expressions fly off like chaff. And, instead, words that have been excluded from circulation by academic aesthetic and morality become irreplaceable to give expression to life in its crudeness and abjectness. Erotic terms serve Céline only to rip the glamour from eroticism. He operates with them in the same manner in which he utilizes the names of other physiological functions which do not meet with recognition on the part of art.

On the very first page of the novel the reader unexpectedly runs across the name of Poincaré, the President of the Republic, who, as the latest issue of *Le Temps* reports, hies himself in the morning to open a lap-dog show.

This detail is not a piece of fiction. Evidently this is one of the duties of the President of the Republic, and personally we see no ground for objecting to it. But the mischievous newspaper quotation obviously is not intended to serve the ends of glorifying the head of the state.

Yet, ex-President Poincaré, the most prosaic of all outstanding personalities of the Republic, happens to be its most authoritative political figure. Since his illness he has become an ikon. Not only the Rights, but the Radicals deem it impossible to mention his name without pronouncing a few words in pathetic avowal of love. Poincaré is, incontestably, the purest distillate of a bourgeois culture such as the French nation is—the most bourgeois of all nations, pickled in the consciousness of its bourgeoisdom, and proud of it as the mainspring of its providential role toward the rest of mankind.

The national conceit of the French bourgeoisie, cloaked in exquisite forms, is the crystallized precipitate of the ages. The past, the time when their forefathers had a great historic mission to perform, has left the descendants a rich wardrobe which serves as a cloak for the most hidebound conservatism. The entire political and cultural life of France is staged in the costumes of the past.

Just as in countries whose currency is fixed, so in French life fictitious values have a compulsory circulation. The formulas of liberationist messianism, which have long since gone off the parity of objective reality, still preserve their high compulsory rate. Conventionalities seem to have taken on flesh and blood, attaining an independent existence. Powder and rouge might still be considered fraudulent; but a mask ceases to be a forgery: it is simply a technical instrument. It exists apart from the flesh, and it subordinates gestures and intonations to its own self.

Poincaré is almost a social symbol. His supreme representativeness molds his individuality. He has no other. Just as in the youthful verses of this man—he did have a youth—so in his senile memoirs there is not to be found a single original note. The interests of the bourgeoisie form his genuine moral shell, the source of his icy pathos. The conventional values of French politics have entered into his marrow and blood. "I am a bourgeois, and nothing bourgeois is alien to me." The political mask has fused with the face. Hypocrisy, attaining the character of the absolute, becomes a sincerity of its own sort.

So peaceloving is the French government, according to Poincaré, that it is incapable even of presupposing any mental reservations on the part of the enemy. "Beautiful is the trust of the people always endowing others with its own virtues." This is not hypocrisy any longer, no subjective falsehood, but a compulsory element in a ritual, like a postscript vowing eternal faithfulness appended to a perfidious letter.

Emil Ludwig put a question to Poincaré, at the time of the occupation of the Ruhr: "In your opinion, is it that we don't want to pay, or that we are unable to pay?" And Poincaré replied: "No one likes to pay of his own accord."

In July, 1931, Brüning asked Poincaré by telegraph for cooperation, and he received for an answer, "Learn to suffer."

But just as personal egoism, when it transcends a certain limit, begins to devour itself, so too does the egoism of a conservative class. Poincaré wished to crucify Germany so as to free France from anxiety once and for all. Meantime, the chauvinistic distillations of the Versailles peace, criminally mild in the eyes of Poincaré, condensed in Germany into the ominous visage of Hitler. Without the Ruhr occupation, the Nazis would not have come to power so easily. And Hitler in power opens up the prospect of new wars.

The national French ideology is built upon the cult of lucidity—that is, logic. It is not the logic of the eighteenth century, wined by an audacity that overthrew the entire world, but the niggardly, cautious, and ready-for-any-compromise logic of the Third Republic. With the condescending sense of superiority with which an old master explains the precepts of his craft, Poincaré speaks in his memoirs of these difficult operations of the mind: selection, classification, co-ordination.

Unquestionably, difficult operations. But Poincaré himself performs them not within the three-dimensional space of the historical process, but in the two-dimensional plane of documents. To him truth is merely the product of law proceedings, the rational interpretation of treaties and laws. The conservative rationalism of ruling France bears the same relation to Descartes as does, say, medieval scholasticism to Aristotle.

The much-trumpeted "sense of proportion" has become the sense of *petty* proportions. It endows the mind with a tendency toward mosaics. With what loving care does Poincaré depict the most insignificant episodes of statecraft! He copies the order of the White Elephant, bestowed upon him by the Danish king, as if it were a priceless miniature: its dimensions, shape, pattern, and the coloring of the stupid fingle-fangle— nothing is left out in his memoirs.

Words serve him either to define the size of the reparations or to figure as rhetorical decorations. He compares his sojourn in the Élysée palace with the incarceration of Silvio Pellico in the dungeons of the Austrian monarchy!

In these salons of gilded banality nothing struck a responsive chord in my imagination.

Gilded banality, however, is the official style of the Third Republic. And Poincaré's imagination is the sublimation of this style.

On the very eve of the impending war, Poincaré was making a maritime journey between Petersburg and France: he does not miss the opportunity to insert an oil landscape into the anxious chronicle of his journey: "the pale, almost deserted sea, indifferent to human conflicts." Word for word, precisely what he had written in his matriculating examination at the Lycée! When he dilates upon his patriotic worries, he lists, in passing, every kind of flower that decorated his summer retreat: between a code telegram and a telephone conversation —a scrupulous catalogue of a florist shop! At the most critical moments, the Siamese cat also intrudes, as the symbol of family intimacy. It is impossible to read without a feeling of suffocation this autobiographic protocol, lacking a single living image, lacking human feeling even, but replete instead with "indifferent" seas, ferns, garlands, hyacinths, doves, and the all-pervading odor of a Siamese cat.

There are two spheres in life: the one public and official, which is passed off for the whole of life, the other secret and most important. This dualism cuts across personal relationships, as well as social: across the intimate family circle, the school, the courtroom, parliament, and the diplomatic service. It is lodged in the conditions of the contradictory development of human society, and it is peculiar to all civilized countries and peoples. But the forms, the scope, and the masks of this dualism are luminously tinted with national colorations.

In Anglo-Saxon countries religion enters as an important element into the system of moral dualism. Official France has deprived itself of this important resource. While the British masonry is incapable of comprehending a universe without God, and, similarily, a parliament without a king, or property without the proprietor, the French masons have deleted "the great architect of the Universe" from their statutes. In political deals the wider the couches are, the better the service: to sacrifice earthly interests for the sake of heavenly problematics would imply going headlong against Latin lucidity. Politicians, however, like Archimedes, require a fulcrum; the will of the Great Architect had to be supplanted by values on this side of the great divide. The first of these is—France.

Nowhere is the "religion of patriotism" spoken of so readily as in the secular republic. All the attributes with which human imagination has endowed the Father, the Son, and the Holy Ghost have been transferred to his own nation by the freethinking French bourgeois. And since France is an image female in gender, she has had conferred upon her the traits of the Virgin Mary as well. The politician steps forward as the lay priest of a secular divinity. The liturgy of patriotism worked out in elaborate detail forms a necessary part of the political ritual. Words and expressions obtain which automatically engender their echo of applause in parliament, just as certain church words are cued to call forth kneeling or tears on the part of the believers.

However, there is a difference. By its very nature the sphere of true religion is removed from daily practice; given the necessary delimitation of jurisdiction, collisions are as little likely as the crash between an automobile and an airplane. The secular religion of patriotism, on the contrary, impinges directly upon day-to-day politics. Personal appetite and class interests rise up in hostility at every step against the formulas of pure patriotism. Fortunately the antagonists are so well educated, and above all so bound by mutual pledges, that they turn their eyes aside on all ticklish occasions. The governmental majority and the responsible opposition adhere voluntarily to the rules of the political game. The chief of these reads: "Just as the movement of physical bodies is subject to the laws of gravity, so the actions of politicians are subject to the love of the Fatherland."

Yet even the sun of patriotism has its spots. A surfeit of mutual indulgence is inconvenient in that it engenders the feeling of impunity and erases the boundary between what is laudable and what is reprehensible. Thus political gases accumulate which explode from time to time and poison the atmosphere. The Union-General crash, Panama, the Dreyfus case, the Roschette case, the Stavisky crash—these are landmarks on the road of the Third Republic familiar to all. Clemenceau was nicked by Panama. Poincaré personally always remained on the side lines. But his politics fed from the very same sources. Not without cause does he proclaim his teacher in morality to be Marcus Aurelius, whose Stoic virtues managed to abide quite well with the morals of the imperial throne in decaying Rome.

> In his memoirs Poincaré laments that during the first six months of 1914 . . . the abject spectacle of parliamentary intrigues and financial scandals passed before my eyes.

But war, of course, with a single swoop swept away all selfish motives. *Union sacrée* cleansed the souls. This is to say: the intrigues and the rascalities swung inward behind the patriotic scenes, there to assume unheard-of proportions. As Céline relates, the more drawn out the critical resolution at the front, the more depraved the rear became. The picture of Paris in wartime is depicted in the novel by the hand of a merciless master. There is almost no politics. But there is something more: the living substratum out of which it takes form.

In all court, parliamentary, and financial scandals of France, what hits one between the eyes is their organic character. From the industry and thriftiness of the peasant and the artisan, from the wariness of the merchant and the industrialist, from the blind greed of the rentier, the courtesy of the parliamentarian, and the patriotism of the press, the numberless threads lead to the ganglia which bear the generic name of Panama. In the web of connections, favors, mediations, masked semi-bribes, there are thousands of transitional forms between civic virtue and capital crime. No sooner does an unfortunate incident shrivel the irreproachable veils, exposing to view the anatomy of politics—at any time, in any place—than it becomes immediately necessary to appoint a parliamentary or judicial committee of investigation.

But precisely here arises the difficulty: What to begin with, and where to end?

Only because Stavisky went bankrupt at an inopportune moment was it revealed that this Argonaut among small saloonkeepers had, as his errand boys, deputies and journalists, ex-ministers and ambassadors, some denoted by initials, others by their full names; that papers profitable to the banker passed through the ministries like lightning, while the harmful ones were held up until rendered harmless. Using the resources of his fancy, salon ties, and printing paper, the financial magus created wealth, played with the lives of thousands of people, bribed—what a coarse and an impermissibly precise word!—rewarded, supported, and encouraged the press, the officials, and the parliamentarians. And almost always in a nonincriminating manner!

As the scope of the work of the investigating committee grew wider, the more obviously hopeless the investigation became. Where one was prepared to unearth crime, one revealed only the usual reciprocity between politics and finance. Where the source of the disease was sought, the normal tissue of the organism was found.

As attorney, X was the guardian of the interests of Stavisky's enterprises; as journalist, he supported the tariff system which happened to coincide with Stavisky's interests; as people's representative, he specialized in revamping tariff duties. And as Minister? The committee was endlessly occupied with the question whether X, while holding the post of Minister, continued to receive his attorney's fee, or whether in the interval between two ministerial crises his conscience had remained as clear as crystal.

What a load of moral pedantry is there injected into hypocrisy! Raoul Perez, former chairman of the Chamber of Deputies, candidate for President of the Republic, turned out to be a candidate for capital criminal. Yet, according to his profound conviction, he had acted "like everybody else," perhaps only a trifle less carefully—at any rate, not so fortunately.

Against the background of the "abject spectacle of parliamentary intrigues and financial scandals—to use Poincaré's expression—Céline's novel attains a twofold significance. Not without cause did the well-meaning press, which in its own time was wroth with the public investigation, immediately damn Céline for calumniating the "nation." The parliamentary committee had, at any rate, carried on its investigation in the courteous language of the initiated, from which neither the accusers nor the accused departed. But Céline is not bound by convention. He rudely discards the gratuitous colors of the political palette. He has his own colors. These he has ripped from life, with the artist's privilege.

True, he takes life not in its parliamentary cross-section, not on the ruling heights, but in its most prosaic manifestations. But this does not ease matters any. He bares the roots. From underneath the veils of decorum he exposes the mud and blood. In his ominous panorama, murder for the sake of trifling gain loses its extraordinariness: it is just as inseparable from the day-to-day mechanics of life, propelled by greed and self-seeking, as the Stavisky affair is inseparable from the much higher mechanics of modern finance. Céline shows what is. For this reason he appears as a revolutionist.

But Céline is no revolutionist, and does not aim to be one. He does not occupy himself with the goal of reconstructing society, which is chimerical in his eyes. He only wants to tear away the prestige from everything that frightened and oppresses him. To ease his conscience from terror in the face of life, this physician to the poor had to resort to new modes of imagery. He turned out to be the revolutionist of the novel. Generally speaking, that is the law governing the movement of art: it moves through the reciprocal repulsion of tendencies.

Decay hits not only parties in power, but schools of art as well. The creative methods become hollow and cease to react upon human sensibilities—an infallible sign that the school has become ripe enough for the cemetery of exhausted possibilities —that is to say, for the Academy. Living creativeness cannot march ahead without repulsion away from official tradition, canonized ideas and feelings, images and expressions covered by the lacquer of use and wont. Each new tendency seeks for the most direct and honest contact between words and emotions. The struggle against pretense in art always grows to a lesser or greater measure into the struggle against the injustice of human relations. The connection is self-evident: art which loses the sense of the social lie inevitably defeats itself by affectation, turning into mannerism.

The richer and more solid is national cultural tradition, the more abrupt is the repulsion from it. Céline's power lies in that through supreme effort he divests himself of all canons, transgresses all conventions. He not only undresses life's model, but rips her skin off. Hence flows the indictment of calumny.

But it is precisely in his impetuous radicalism of negating the national tradition that Céline is deeply nationalistic. Just as the French antimilitarists prior to the war were most often desperate patriots, so is Céline a Frenchman to the marrow of his bones, a Frenchman who has torn himself loose from the official masks of the Third Republic. Célinism is moral and artistic anti-Poincaréism. In that is Céline's strength, but, too, his limitation.

When Poincaré compares himself to Silvio Pellico, he is apt

to give one the chills by this combination of smugness and bad taste. But does not the real Pellico, who was incarcerated not in a palace, as head of the government, but in the dungeons of Santa Margherita and Spielberg as a patriot—does he not reveal another and a much higher side of human nature? Instead of this Italian Catholic believer, who was besides a victim rather than a fighter, Céline might have reminded the eminent captive of the Élysée palace of another prisoner who spent four decades of his life in the prisons of France, prior to the time when the sons and grandsons of his jailers named one of the Parisian boulevards after him—namely, Auguste Blanqui. Is that not evidence that there is something lodged in man which is capable of raising him above himself?

Only because there are numerous and well-paid priests serving the altars of false altruism does Céline turn away from greatness of mind and heroism, from great projects and hopes, from everything that leads humanity from out the dark night of the circumscribed I. It seems almost as if the moralist who is so ruthless to himself had been repelled by his own image in the mirror, and smashed the glass, cutting his hands. Such a struggle may enervate, but it does not break out toward the light's glimmer. Hopelessness ever leads to docility. Conciliation opens the doors to the Academy. There has been more than one previous occasion when those who have blasted the literary foundations ended underneath the dome of immortality.

In the music of this book there is a dissonance pregnant with much meaning. By rejecting not only the present but also what must take its place, the artist gives his support to what is. To that extent Céline, willy-nilly, is the ally of Poincaré. But, exposing the lie, he instills the want for a more harmonious future. Though he himself may consider that nothing good can generally come from man, the very intensity of his pessimism bears within it a dose of the antidote.

Céline, as he is, stems from French reality and the French novel. He does not have to be ashamed of his ancestry. The French genius has found its unsurpassed expression in the novel. Beginning with Rabelais, likewise a physician, there has branched, in the course of four centuries, a splendid genealogy of the masters of epic prose: from life-loving belly laughter down to hopelessness and despair, from the brilliant break of day to the depths of the night.

Céline will not write a second book with such an aversion for the lie and such a disbelief in the truth. The dissonance must resolve itself. Either the artist will make his peace with the darkness or he will perceive the dawn.

Stalinism and Bolshevism

(1937)

Reactionary epochs like ours not only disintegrate and weaken the working class and its vanguard, but also lower the general ideological level of the movement and throw political thinking back to stages long since passed through. In these conditions the task of the vanguard is above all not to let itself be carried along by the backward flow: it must swim against the current. If an unfavorable relation of forces prevents it from holding the positions that it has won, it must at least retain its ideological positions, because in them is expressed the dearly-bought experience of the past. Fools will consider this policy "sectarian." Actually it is the only means of preparing for a new tremendous surge forward with the coming historical tide.

THE REACTION AGAINST MARXISM AND BOLSHEVISM

Great political defeats inevitably provoke a reconsideration of values, generally occurring in two directions. On the one hand the true vanguard, enriched by the experience of defeat, defends with tooth and nail the heritage of revolutionary thought and on this basis attempts to educate new cadres for the mass struggle to come. On the other hand the routinists, centrists, and dilettantes, frightened by defeat, do their best to destroy the authority of revolutionary tradition and go backward in their search for a "New Word."

One could indicate a great many examples of ideological reaction, most often taking the form of prostration. All the literature of the Second and Third Internationals, as well as of their satellites of the London Bureau, consists essentially of such examples. Not a suggestion of Marxist analysis. Not a single serious attempt to explain the causes of defeat. About the future, not one fresh word. Nothing but clichés, conformity, lies, and above all solicitude for their own bureaucratic self-preservation. It is enough to smell ten lines from some Hilferding or Otto Bauer to know this rottenness. The theoreticians of the Comintern are not even worth mentioning. The famous Dimitroff is as ignorant and commonplace as a shopkeeper over a mug of beer. The minds of these people are too lazy to renounce Marxism: they prostitute it. But it is not they that interest us now. Let us turn to the "innovators."

The former Austrian communist Willi Schlamm, has devoted a small book to the Moscow trials, under the expressive title *The Dictatorship of the Lie*. Schlamm is a gifted journalist, chiefly interested in current affairs. His criticism of the Moscow frame-up, and his exposure of the psychological mechanism of the "voluntary confessions," are excellent. However, he does not confine himself to this: he wants to create a new theory of socialism which would insure us against defeats and frame-ups in the future. But since Schlamm is by no means a theoretician and is apparently not well acquainted with the history of the development of socialism, he returns entirely to pre-Marxian socialism, and notably to its German—that is, to its most backward, sentimental, and mawkish—variety. Schlamm renounces dialectics and the class struggle, not to mention the dictatorship of the proletariat. The problem of transforming society is reduced for him to the realization of certain "eternal" moral truths with which he would imbue mankind, even under capitalism. Willi Schlamm's attempt to save socialism by the insertion of the moral gland is greeted with both joy and pride in Kerensky's review *Novaya Rossia* (an old provincial Russian review now published in Paris): as the editors justifiably conclude, Schlamm has arrived at the principles of true Russian socialism, which a long time ago opposed the holy precepts of faith, hope and charity to the austerity and harshness of the class struggle. The "novel" doctrine of the Russian "Social Revolutionaries" represents, in its "theoretical" premises, only a return to the socialism of pre-March (1848!) Germany. However, it would be unfair to demand a more intimate knowledge of the history of ideas from Kerensky than from Schlamm. Far more important is the fact that Kerensky, who is in solidarity with Schlamm, was, while head of the government, the instigator of persecutions against the Bolsheviks as agents of the German general staff: organized, that is, the same frame-ups against which Schlamm now mobilizes his moth-eaten metaphysical absolutes.

The psychological mechanism of the ideological reaction of Schlamm and his like is not at all complicated. For a while these people took part in political movement that swore by the class struggle and appealed, in word if not in thought, to dialectical materialism. In both Austria and Germany the affair ended in catastrophe. Schlamm draws a wholesale conclusion: this is the result of dialectics and the class struggle! And since the choice of revelations is limited by historical experience and . . . by personal knowledge, our reformer in his search for the Word falls on a bundle of old rags, which he valiantly opposes not only to Bolshevism but to Marxism as well.

At first glance Schlamm's brand of ideological reaction seems too primitive (from Marx . . . to Kerensky!) to pause over. But actually it is very instructive: precisely in its primitiveness it represents the common denominator of all other forms of reaction, particularly of those expressed by wholesale denunciation of Bolshevism.

"BACK TO MARXISM"?

Marxism found its highest historical expression in Bolshevism. Under the banner of Bolshevism the first victory of the proletariat was achieved, and the first workers' state established. Nothing can erase these facts from history. But since the October revolution has led in the present stage to the triumph of the bureaucracy, with its system of repression, plunder, and falsification—to the "dictatorship of the lie," to use Schlamm's happy expression—many formalistic and superficial minds leap to a summary conclusion: one cannot struggle against Stalinism without renouncing Bolshevism. Schlamm, as we already know, goes farther: Bolshevism, which degenerated into Stalinism, itself grew out of Marxism; consequently one cannot fight Stalinism while remaining on the foundation of Marxism. There are others, less consistent but more numerous, who say on the contrary: "We must return from Bolshevism to Marxism." How? To *what* Marxism? Before Marxism became "bankrupt" in the form of Bolshevism it had already broken down in the form of Social Democracy. Does the slogan "Back to Marxism" then mean a leap over the periods of the Second and Third Internationals . . . to the First International? But it too broke down in its time. Thus in the last analysis it is a question of returning . . . to the complete works of Marx and Engels. One can accomplish this heroic leap without leaving one's study and even without taking off one's slippers. But how are we to go from our classics (Marx died in 1883, Engels in 1895) to the tasks of our own time, omitting several decades of theoretical and political struggles, among them Bolshevism and the October revolution? None of those who propose to renounce Bolshevism as an historically "bankrupt" tendency has indicated any other course. So the question is reduced to the simple advice to study *Capital*. We can hardly object. But the Bolsheviks, too, studied *Capital* and not with their eyes closed.

This did not however, prevent the degeneration of the Soviet state and the staging of the Moscow trials. So what is to be done?

IS BOLSHEVISM RESPONSIBLE FOR STALINISM?

Is it true that Stalinism represents the legitimate product of Bolshevism, as all reactionaries maintain, as Stalin himself avows, as the Mensheviks, the anarchists, and certain Left doctrinaires considering themselves Marxist, believe? "We have always predicted this," they say. "Having started with the prohibition of the other socialist parties, the repression of the anarchists, and the setting up of the Bolshevik dictatorship in the soviets, the October revolution could end only in the dictatorship of the bureaucracy. Stalin is the continuation and also the bankruptcy of Leninism."

The flaw in this reasoning begins in the tacit identification of Bolshevism, October revolution and Soviet Union. The historical process of the struggle of hostile forces is replaced by the evolution of Bolshevism in a vacuum. Bolshevism, however, is only a political tendency, closely fused with the working class but not identical with it. And aside from the working class there exist in the Soviet Union a hundred million peasants, various nationalities, and a heritage of oppression, misery, and ignorance. The state built up by the Bolsheviks reflects not only the thought and will of Bolshevism but also the cultural level of the country, the social composition of the population, the pressure of a barbaric past and of no less barbaric world imperialism. To represent the process of degeneration of the Soviet state as the evolution of pure Bolshevism is to ignore social reality in the name of only one of its elements, isolated by pure logic. One has only to call this elementary mistake by its real name to do away with every trace of it.

Bolshevism, at any rate, never identified itself either with the October revolution or with the Soviet state that issued from it. Bolshevism considered itself as one of the factors of history, the "conscious" factor—a very important but not the decisive one. We never sinned in historical subjectivism. We saw the decisive factor—on the existing basis of productive forces—in the class struggle, not only on a national but on an international scale.

When the Bolsheviks made concessions to the peasant tendency to private ownership, set up strict rules for membership in the party, purged the party of alien elements, prohibited other parties, introduced the NEP, granted enterprises as concessions, or concluded diplomatic agreements with imperialist governments, they were drawing partial conclusions from the basic fact that had been theoretically clear to them from the beginning: that the conquest of power, however important it may be in itself, by no means transforms the party into a sovereign ruler of the historical process. Having taken over the state, the party is able, certainly, to influence the development of society with a power inaccessible to it before; but in return it submits itself to ten times greater influence from all other elements of society. It can, by the direct attack of hostile forces, be thrown out of power. Given a more dragging tempo of development, it can degenerate internally while maintaining itself in power. It is precisely this dialectic of the historical process that is not understood by those sectarian logicians who try to find in the decay of the Stalinist bureaucracy an annihilating argument against Bolshevism.

In essence these gentlemen say: the revolutionary party that contains in itself no guarantee against its own degeneration is bad. By such a criterion Bolshevism is naturally condemned: it has no talisman. But the criterion itself is wrong. Scientific thinking demands a concrete analysis: how and why did the party degenerate? No one but the Bolsheviks themselves has up to the present time given such an analysis. To do this they had no need to break with Bolshevism. On the contrary, they found in its arsenal all they needed for the clarification of its fate. They drew this conclusion: certainly Stalinism "grew out" of Bolshevism, not logically, however, but dialectically; not as a revolutionary affirmation but as a Thermidorian negation. They are by no means the same.

THE FUNDAMENTAL PROGNOSIS OF BOLSHEVISM

The Bolsheviks, however, did not have to wait for the Moscow trials to explain the reasons for the disintegration of the governing party of the USSR. Long ago they foresaw and spoke of the theoretical possibility of this development. Let us remember the prognosis of the Bolsheviks, not only on the eve of the October revolution but years before. The specific alignment of forces in the national and international field can enable the proletariat to seize power first in a backward country such as Russia. But the same alignment of forces proves beforehand that *without a more or less rapid victory of the proletariat in the advanced countries* the workers' government in Russia will not survive. Left to itself, the Soviet regime must either fall or degenerate. More exactly: it will first degenerate and then fall. I myself have written about this more than once, beginning in 1905. In my *History of the Russian Revolution* (cf. the Appendix to the last volume: "Socialism in One Country") are collected all the statements on this question made by the Bolshevik leaders from 1917 until 1923. They all lead to one conclusion: without a revolution in the West, Bolshevism will be liquidated either by internal counter-revolution or by external intervention, or by a combination of both. Lenin stressed again and again that the bureaucratization of the Soviet regime was not a technical or organizational question, but the potential beginning of the degeneration of the workers' state.

At the Eleventh Party Congress in March, 1923, Lenin spoke of the support offered to Soviet Russia at the time of the NEP by certain bourgeois politicians, particularly the liberal professor Ustrialov. "I am for the support of the Soviet power in Russia," said Ustrialov, although he was a *Kadet*, a bourgeois, a supporter of intervention—"because on its present course it is sliding back into an ordinary bourgeois power." Lenin prefers the cynical voice of the enemy to "sugary communistic babble." Soberly and harshly he warns the party of the danger:

> What Ustrialov says is possible; one must say it openly. History knows transformations of all kinds; it is absolutely trivial in politics to put one's faith in conviction, devotion, and other excellent moral qualities. A small number of people have excellent moral qualities. The historical outcome is decided by gigantic masses who, if they are not pleased with this small number of people, will treat them none too politely.

In a word, the party is not the only factor of development and, on a larger historical scale, is not the decisive one.

> One nation conquers another [continued Lenin at the same congress, the last in which he participated]. This is quite simple and understandable to everyone. But what of the culture of these nations? That is not so simple. If the conquering nation has a higher culture than the defeated, it imposes its culture on the latter, but if the contrary is true then the defeated nation imposes its culture on the conqueror. Did not something like this occur in the capital of the RSFSR and was it not in this way that 4,700 communists (almost a whole division and all of them the best) were submitted to an alien culture?

This was said in the beginning of 1923, and not for the first time. History is not made by a few people, even "the best"; and not only that: these "best" can degenerate in the spirit of an alien, that is a bourgeois culture. Not only can the Soviet state abandon the way of socialism, but the Bolshevik party can, under unfavorable historic conditions, lose its Bolshevism.

From the clear understanding of this danger issued the Left Opposition, definitely formed in 1923. Recording day by day the symptoms of degeneration, it tried to oppose to the growing Thermidor the conscious will of the proletarian vanguard. However, this subjective factor proved to be insufficient. The "gigantic masses" which, according to Lenin, decide the outcome of the struggle, became tired of internal privations and of waiting too long for the world revolution. The mood of the masses declined. The bureaucracy won the upper hand. It cowed the revolutionary vanguard, trampled upon Marxism, prostituted the Bolshevik party. Stalinism conquered. In the form of the Left Opposition, Bolshevism broke with the Soviet bureaucracy and its Comintern. This was the real course of development.

To be sure, in a formal sense Stalinism did issue from Bolshevism. Even today the Moscow bureaucracy continues to call itself the Bolshevik party. It is simply using the old label of Bolshevism the better to fool the masses. So much the more pitiful are those theoreticians who take the shell for the kernel and the appearance for the reality. In the identification of Bolshevism and Stalinism they render the best possible service to the Thermidorians and precisely thereby play a clearly reactionary role.

In view of the elimination of all other parties from the political field the antagonistic interests and tendencies of the various strata of the population must, to a greater or lesser degree, find their expression in the governing party. To the extent that the political center of gravity has shifted from the proletarian vanguard to the bureaucracy, the party has changed in its social structure as well as in its ideology. Owing to the impetuous course of its development, it has suffered in the last fifteen years a far more radical degeneration than did the social democracy in half a century. The present purge draws between Bolshevism and Stalinism not simply a bloody line but a whole river of blood. The annihilation of all the old generation of Bolsheviks, an important part of the middle generation which participated in the civil war, and that part of the youth which took seriously the Bolshevik traditions, shows not only a political but a thoroughly physical incompatibility between Bolshevism and Stalinism. How can this be ignored?

STALINISM AND "STATE SOCIALISM"

The anarchists, for their part, try to see in Stalinism the organic product not only of Bolshevism and Marxism, but of "State socialism" in general. They are willing to replace Bakunin's patriarchal "federation of free communes" by the more modern federation of free Soviets. But, as formerly, they are against centralized state power. In fact, one branch of "state" Marxism, social democracy, after coming to power, became an open agent of capitalism; the other gave birth to a new privileged caste. It is obvious that the source of the evil lies in the state. From a wide historical viewpoint, there is a grain of truth in this reasoning. The state as an apparatus of constraint is undoubtedly a source of political and moral infection. This also applies, as experience has shown, to the workers' state. Consequently it can be said that Stalinism is a product of a condition of society in which society was still unable to tear itself out of the straitjacket of the state. But this situation, containing nothing for the evaluation of Bolshevism or Marxism, characterizes only the general cultural level of mankind, and above all—the relation of forces between proletariat and bourgeoisie. Having agreed with the anarchists that the state, even the workers' state, is the offspring of class barbarism and that real human history will begin with the abolition of the state, we have still before us in full force the question: what ways and methods will lead, *ultimately*, to the abolition of the state? Recent experience proves that they are certainly not the methods of anarchism.

The leaders of the CNT, the only important anarchist organization in the world, became, in the critical hour, bourgeois ministers. They explained their open betrayal of the theory of anarchism by the pressure of "exceptional circumstances." But did not the leaders of German social democracy invoke, in their time, the same excuse? Naturally, civil war is not a peaceful and ordinary but an "exceptional" circumstance. Every serious revolutionary organization, however, prepares precisely for "exceptional circumstances." The experience of Spain has shown once again that the state can be "denied" in booklets published in "normal circumstances" by permission of the bourgeois state, but that the conditions of revolution leave no room for "denial" of the state; they demand, on the contrary, the conquest of the state. We have not the slightest intention of blaming the anarchists for not having liquidated the state by a mere stroke of the pen. A revolutionary party, even after having seized power (of which the anarchist leaders were incapable in spite of the heroism of the anarchist workers) is still by no means the sovereign ruler of society. But we do severely blame the anarchist theory, which seemed to be wholly suitable for times of peace, but which had to be dropped rapidly as soon as the "exceptional circumstances" of the . . . revolution had begun. In the old days there were—and probably are now—certain generals who considered that the most harmful thing for an army was war. In the same class are those revolutionaries who claim that their doctrine is destroyed by revolution.

Marxists are wholly in agreement with the anarchists in regard to the final goal: the liquidation of the state. Marxists are "state-ist" only to the extent that one cannot achieve the liquidation of the state simply by ignoring it. The experience of Stalinism does not refute the teaching of Marxism but confirms it by inversion. The revolutionary doctrine, which teaches the proletariat to orient itself correctly in situations, and to profit actively by them, contains of course no automatic guarantee of victory. But victory is possible only through the application of this doctrine. Moreover, the victory must not be thought of as a single event. It must be considered in the perspective of an historic epoch. The first workers' state—on a lower economic basis and surrounded by imperialism—was transformed into the *gendarmerie* of Stalinism. But genuine Bolshevism launched a life and death struggle against that *gendarmerie*. To maintain itself, Stalinism is now forced to conduct a direct *civil war* against Bolshevism, under the name of "Trotskyism," not only in the USSR but also in Spain. The old Bolshevik party is dead but Bolshevism is raising its head everywhere.

To deduce Stalinism from Bolshevism or from Marxism is the same as to deduce, in a larger sense, counterrevolution from revolution. Liberal-conservative and later reformist thinking has always been characterized by this cliché. Due to the class structure of society, revolutions have always produced counterrevolutions. Does this not indicate, asks the logician, that there is some inner flaw in the revolutionary method? However, neither the liberals nor the reformists have succeeded, as yet, in inventing a more "economical" method. But if it is not easy to rationalize the living historical process, it is not at all difficult to give a rational interpretation of the alternation of its waves, and thus by pure logic to deduce Stalinism from "state socialism," fascism from Marxism, reaction from revolution, in a word, the antithesis from the thesis. In this domain as in many others anarchist thought is the prisoner of liberal rationalism. Real revolutionary thinking is not possible without dialectics.

THE POLITICAL "SINS" OF BOLSHEVISM AS THE SOURCE OF STALINISM

The arguments of the rationalists assume at times, at least in their outer form, a more concrete character. They do not deduce Stalinism from Bolshevism as a whole but from its political sins.[1] The Bolshevik—according to Gorter, Pannekoek, certain German "spartakists," and others—replaced the dictatorship of the party; Stalin replaced the dictatorship of the party with the dictatorship of the bureaucracy. The Bolsheviks destroyed all parties but their own; Stalin strangled the Bolshevik party in the interest of a bonapartist clique. The Bolsheviks made compromises with the bourgeoisie; Stalin became its ally and support. The Bolsheviks preached the necessity of participation in the old trade unions and in the bourgeois parliament; Stalin made friends with the trade union bureaucracy and bourgeois democracy. One can make such comparisons at will. For all their apparent effectiveness they are entirely empty.

The proletariat can take power only through its vanguard. In itself the necessity for state power arises from an insufficient cultural level of the masses and their heterogeneity.

---

[1] One of the outstanding representatives of this type of thinking is the French author of the book on Stalin, B. Souvarine. The factual and documentary side of Souvarine's work is the product of long and conscientious research. However, the historical philosophy of the author is striking in its vulgarity. To explain all subsequent historical mishaps he seeks the inner flaws of Bolshevism. The influence of the real conditions of the historical process of Bolshevism are nonexistent for him. Even Taine with his theory of "milieu" is closer to Marx than Souvarine.

In the revolutionary vanguard, organized in a party, is crystallized the aspiration of the masses to obtain their freedom. Without the confidence of the class in the vanguard, without the support of the vanguard by the class, there can be no talk of the conquest of power. In this sense the proletarian revolution and dictatorship are the work of the whole class, but only under the leadership of the vanguard. The Soviets are only the organized form of the tie between the vanguard and the class. A revolutionary content can be given to this form only by the party. This is proved by the positive experience of the October revolution and by the negative experience of other countries (Germany, Austria, finally Spain). No one has either shown in practice or tried to explain articulately on paper how the proletariat can seize power without the political leadership of a party that knows what it wants. The fact that this party subordinates the Soviets politically to its leaders has, in itself, abolished the Soviet system no more than the domination of the conservative majority has abolished the British parliamentary system.

As far as the *prohibition* of the other Soviet parties is concerned, it did not flow from any "theory" of Bolshevism but was a measure of defense of the dictatorship in a backward and devastated country, surrounded by enemies on all sides. For the Bolsheviks it was clear from the beginning that this measure, later completed by the prohibition of factions inside the governing party itself, signalized a tremendous danger. However, the root of the danger lay not in the doctrine or in the tactics but in the material weakness of the dictatorship, in the difficulties of its internal and international situation. If the revolution had triumphed, even if only in Germany, the need of prohibiting the other Soviet parties would immediately have fallen away. It is absolutely indisputable that the domination of a single party served as the juridical point of departure for the Stalinist totalitarian system. But the reason for this development lies neither in Bolshevism nor in the prohibition of other parties as a temporary war measure, but in the number of defeats of the proletariat in Europe and Asia.

The same applies to the struggle with anarchism. In the heroic epoch of the revolution the Bolsheviks went hand in hand with the genuinely revolutionary anarchists. Many of them were drawn into the ranks of the party. The author of these lines discussed with Lenin more than once the possibility of allotting to the anarchists certain territories where, with the consent of the local population, they would carry out their stateless experiment. But civil war, blockade, and hunger left no room for such plans. The Kronstadt insurrection? But the revolutionary government naturally could not "present" to the insurrectionary sailors the fortress which protected the capital only because the reactionary peasant-soldier rebellion was joined by a few doubtful anarchists. A concrete historical analysis of the events leaves not the slightest room for the legends, built up on ignorance and sentimentality, concerning Kronstadt, Makhno and other episodes of the revolution.

There remains only the fact that the Bolsheviks from the beginning applied not only conviction but also compulsion, often to a most brutal degree. It is also indisputable that later the bureaucracy that grew out of the revolution monopolized the system of compulsion for its own use. Every stage of development, even such catastrophic stages as revolution and counterrevolution, flows from the preceding stage, is rooted in it and takes on some of its features. Liberals, including the Webbs, have always maintained that the Bolshevik dictatorship was only a new version of Czarism. They close their eyes to such "details" as the abolition of the monarchy and the nobility, the handing over of the land to the peasants, the expropriation of capital, the introduction of planned economy, atheist education, etc. In the same way liberal-anarchistic thought closes its eyes to the fact that the Bolshevik revolution, with all its repressions, meant an upheaval of social relations in the interest of the masses, whereas the Stalinist Thermidorian upheaval accompanies the transformation of Soviet society in the interest of a privileged minority. It is clear that in the indentification of Stalinism with Bolshevism there is not a trace of socialist criteria.

Their Morals and Ours

(1938)

(In Memory of Leon Sedov)

During an epoch of triumphant reaction, Messrs. Democrats, Social Democrats, Anarchists, and other representatives of the "Left" camp begin to exude double their usual amount of moral effluvia, similar to persons who perspire doubly in fear. Paraphrasing the Ten Commandments or the Sermon on the Mount, these moralists address themselves not so much to triumphant reaction as to those revolutionists suffering under its persecution, who with their "excesses" and "amoral" principles, "provoke" reaction and give it moral justification. Moreover they prescribe a simple but certain means of avoiding reaction: it is necessary only to strive and morally to regenerate oneself. Free samples of moral perfection for those desirous are furnished by all the interested editorial offices.

The class basis of this false and pompous sermon is—the

intellectual petty bourgeoisie. The political basis—their impotence and confusion in the face of approaching reaction. The psychological basis—their effort at overcoming the feeling of their own inferiority through masquerading in the beard of a prophet.

A moralizing philistine's favorite method is the lumping of reaction's conduct with that of revolution. He achieves success in this device through recourse to formal analogies. To him Czarism and Bolshevism are twins. Twins are likewise discovered in fascism and communism. An inventory is compiled of the common features in Catholicism—or more specifically, Jesuitism—and Bolshevism. Hitler and Mussolini, utilizing from their side exactly the same method, disclose that liberalism, democracy, and Bolshevism represent merely different manifestations of one and the same evil. The conception that Stalinism and Trotskyism are "essentially" one and the same now enjoys the joint approval of liberals, democrats, devout Catholics, idealists, pragmatists, and anarchists. If the Stalinists are unable to adhere to this "People's Front," then it is only because they are accidentally occupied with the extermination of Trotskyists.

The fundamental feature of these *rapprochements* and similitudes lies in their completely ignoring the material foundation of the various currents, that is, their class nature and by that token their objective historical role. Instead they evaluate and classify different currents according to some external and secondary manifestation, most often according to their relation to one or another abstract principle which for the given classifier has a special professional value. Thus to the Roman pope, Freemasons and Darwinists, Marxists and anarchists are twins because all of them sacrilegiously deny the Immaculate Conception. To Hitler, liberalism and Marxism are twins because they ignore "blood and honor." To a democrat, fascism and Bolshevism are twins because they do not bow before universal suffrage. And so forth.

Undoubtedly the currents grouped above have certain common features. But the gist of the matter lies in the fact that the evolution of mankind exhausts itself neither by universal suffrage, nor by "blood and honor," nor by the dogma of the

Immaculate Conception. The historical process signifies primarily the class struggle; moreover, different classes in the name of different aims may in certain instances utilize similar means. Essentially it cannot be otherwise. Armies in combat are always more or less symmetrical; were there nothing in common in their methods of struggle they could not inflict blows upon each other.

If an ignorant peasant or shopkeeper, understanding neither the origin nor the sense of the struggle between the proletariat and the bourgeoisie, discovers himself between the two fires, he will consider both belligerent camps with equal hatred. And who are all these democratic moralists? Ideologists of intermediate layers who have fallen, or are in fear of falling, between the two fires. The chief traits of the prophets of this type are alienism to great historical movements, a hardened conservative mentality, smug narrowness, and a most primitive political cowardice. More than anything, moralists wish that history should leave them in peace with their petty books, little magazines, subscribers, common sense, and moral copybooks. But history does not leave them in peace. It cuffs them now from the left, now from the right. Clearly—revolution and reaction, Czarism and Bolshevism, communism and fascism, Stalinism and Trotskyism—are all twins. Whoever doubts this may feel the symmetrical skull bumps upon both the right and left sides of these very moralists.

The most popular and most imposing accusation directed against Bolshevik "amoralism" bases itself on the so-called Jesuitical maxim of Bolshevism: "The end justifies the means." From this it is not difficult to reach the further conclusion: since the Trotskyists, like all Bolsheviks (or Marxists) do not recognize the principles of morality, there is, consequently, no "principled" difference between Trotskyism and Stalinism. Q.E.D.

One completely vulgar and cynical American monthly conducted a questionnaire on the moral philosophy of Bolshevism. The questionnaire, as is customary, was to have simultaneously served the ends of ethics and advertisement. The inimitable H. G. Wells, whose high fancy is surpassed only by his Homeric self-satisfaction, was not slow in solidarizing himself with the reactionary snobs of *Common Sense*. Here everything fell into order. But even those participants who considered it necessary to defend Bolshevism did so, in the majority of cases, not without timid evasions (Eastman): the principles of Marxism are, of course, bad, but among the Bolsheviks there are, nevertheless, worthy people. Truly, such "friends" are more dangerous than enemies.

Should we care to take Messrs. Unmaskers seriously, then first of all we would ask them: what are your own moral principles? Here is a question which will scarcely receive an answer. Let us admit for the moment that neither personal nor social ends can justify the means. Then it is evidently necessary to seek criteria outside of historical society and those ends which arise in its development. But where? If not on earth, then in the heavens. In divine revelation popes long ago discovered faultless moral criteria. Petty secular popes speak about eternal moral truths without naming their original source. However, we are justified in concluding: since these truths are eternal, they should have existed not only before the appearance of half-monkey-half-man upon the earth but before the evolution of the solar system. Whence then did they arise? The theory of eternal morals can in nowise survive without God.

Moralists of the Anglo-Saxon type, in so far as they do not confine themselves to rationalist utilitarianism, the ethics of bourgeois bookkeeping, appear to be conscious or unconscious students of Viscount Shaftesbury, who—at the beginning of the eighteenth century!—deduced moral judgments from a special "moral sense," supposedly once and for all given to man. Supra-class morality inevitably leads to the acknowledgment of a special substance, of a "moral sense," "conscience," some kind of absolute which is nothing more than the philosophic-cowardly pseudonym for God. Independent of "ends," that is, of society, morality, whether we deduce it from eternal truths or from the "nature of man," proves in the end to be a form of "natural theology." Heaven remains the only fortified position for military operations against dialectic materialism.

At the end of the last century in Russia there arose a whole school of "Marxists" (Struve, Berdyaev, Bulgakov, and others) who wished to supplement the teachings of Marx with a self-sufficient, that is, supra-class moral principle. These people began, of course, with Kant and the categorical imperative. But how did they end? Struve is now a retired minister of the Crimean baron Wrangel, and a faithful son of the Church; Bulgakov is an orthodox priest; Berdyaev expounds the Apocalypse in sundry languages. These metamorphoses which seem so unexpected at first glance are not at all explained by the "Slavic soul"—Struve has a German soul—but by the sweep of the social struggle in Russia. The fundamental trend of this metamorphosis is essentially international.

Classical philosophic idealism, insofar as it aimed in its time to secularize morality, that is, to free it from religious sanction, represented a tremendous step forward (Hegel). But having been torn from heaven, moral philosophy had to find earthly roots. To discover these roots was one of the tasks of materialism. After Shaftesbury came Darwin, after Hegel—Marx. To appeal now to "eternal moral truths" signifies an attempt to turn the wheels backward. Philosophic idealism is only a stage: from religion to materialism, or, contrariwise, from materialism to religion.

The Jesuit order, organized in the first half of the sixteenth century for combatting Protestantism, never taught, let it be said, that *any* means, even though it be criminal from the point of view of the Catholic morals, was permissible if only it led to the "end," that is, to the triumph of Catholicism. Such an internally contradictory and psychologically absurd doctrine was maliciously attributed to the Jesuits by their Protestant and partly Catholic opponents who were not shy in choosing the means for achieving their ends. Jesuit theologians who, like the theologians of other schools, were occupied with the question of personal responsibility, actually taught that the means in itself can be a matter of indifference but that the moral justification or judgment of the given means flows from the end. Thus shooting in itself is a matter of indifference; shooting a mad dog that threatens a child—a virtue; shooting with the aim of violation or murder—a crime.

Outside of these commonplaces the theologians of this order made no promulgations.

In so far as their practical moral philosophy is concerned the Jesuits were not at all worse than other monks or Catholic priests—on the contrary, they were superior to them; in any case, more consistent, bold, and perspicacious. The Jesuits represented a militant organization, strictly centralized, aggressive, and dangerous not only to enemies but also to allies. In his psychology and method of action the Jesuit of the "heroic" period distinguished himself from an average priest as the warrior of a church from its shopkeeper. We have no reason to idealize either one or the other. But it is altogether unworthy to look upon a fanatic-warrior with the eyes of an obtuse and slothful shopkeeper.

If we are to remain in the field of purely formal or psychological similitudes, then it can, if you like, be said that the Bolsheviks appear in relation to the democrats and social democrats of all hues as did the Jesuits in relation to the peaceful ecclesiastical hierarchy. Compared to revolutionary Marxists, the social democrats and centrists appear as morons, or a quack beside a physician: they do not think one problem through to the end; they believe in the power of conjuration and cravenly avoid every difficulty, hoping for a miracle. Opportunists are peaceful shopkeepers in socialist ideas, while Bolsheviks are its inveterate warriors. From this comes the hatred and slander against Bolsheviks from those who have an abundance of their historically conditioned faults but not one of their merits.

However, the juxtaposition of Bolshevism and Jesuitism still remains completely one-sided and superficial, of a literary rather than historical kind. In accordance with the character and interests of those classes upon which they based themselves, the Jesuits represented reaction, the Protestants progress. The limitedness of this "progress" in its turn found direct expression in the morality of the Protestants. Thus the teachings of Christ "purified" by them did not at all hinder the city bourgeois, Luther, from calling for the execution of revolting peasants as "mad dogs." Dr. Martin evidently considered that the "end justifies the means" even before that maxim was attributed to the Jesuits. In turn the Jesuits, competing with Protestantism, adapted themselves evermore to the spirit of bourgeois society, and of the three vows of poverty, chastity, and obedience, preserved only the third, and at that in an extremely attenuated form. From the point of view of the Christian ideal, the morality of the Jesuits degenerated the more they ceased to be Jesuits. The warriors of the church became its bureaucrats and, like all bureaucrats, passable swindlers.

This brief discussion is sufficient, perhaps, to show what ignorance and narrowness are necessary to consider seriously the contraposition of the "Jesuit" principle, "the end justifies the means," to another seemingly higher moral, in which each "means" carries its own moral tag like merchandise with fixed prices in a department store. It is remarkable that the common sense of the Anglo-Saxon philistine has managed to wax indignant at the "Jesuit" principle and simultaneously to find inspiration in the utilitarian morality, so characteristic of British philosophy. Moreover, the criterion of Bentham and John Mill, "the greatest possible happiness for the greatest possible number," signifies that those means are moral which lead to the common welfare as the highest end. In its general philosophical formulations Anglo-Saxon utilitarianism thus fully coincides with the "Jesuit" principle, "the end justifies the means." Empiricism, we see, exists in the world only to free us from the necessity of making both ends meet.

Herbert Spencer, into whose empiricism Darwin inculcated the idea of "evolution" as a special vaccine, taught that in the moral sphere evolution proceeds from "sensations" to "ideas." Sensations conform to the criterion of immediate pleasure, while ideas permit one to be guided by the criterion of *future, lasting and higher pleasure*. Thus the moral criterion here, too, is that of "pleasure" and "happiness." But the content of this criterion acquires breadth and depth depending upon the level of "evolution." In this way Herbert Spencer too, through the methods of his own "evolutionary" utilitarianism, showed that the principle, "the end justifies the means," does not embrace anything immoral.

It is naïve, however, to expect from this abstract "principle" an answer to the practical question: what may we, and what may we not, do? Moreover, the principle, "the end justifies the means," naturally raises the question: and what justifies the end? In practical life as in the historical movement the end and the means constantly change places. A machine under construction is an "end" of production only so that upon entering the factory it may become the "means." Democracy in certain periods is the "end" of the class struggle only so that later it may be transformed into its "means." Not embracing anything immoral, the so-called Jesuit principle nonetheless fails to resolve the moral problem.

The "evolutionary" utilitarianism of Spencer likewise abandons us halfway without an answer, since, following Darwin, it tries to dissolve the concrete historical morality in the biological needs or in the "social instincts" characteristic of a gregarious animal, and this at a time when the very understanding of morality arises only in an antagonistic milieu, that is, in a society torn by classes.

Bourgeois evolutionism halts impotently at the threshold of historical society because it does not wish to acknowledge the driving force in the evolution of social forms: *the class struggle*. Morality is one of the ideological functions in this struggle. The ruling class forces *its* ends upon society and habituates it into considering all those means which contradict its ends as immoral. That is the chief function of official morality. It pursues the idea of the "greatest possible happiness" not for the majority but for a small and ever diminishing minority. Such a regime could not have endured for even a week through force alone. It needs the cement of morality. The mixing of this cement constitutes the profession of the petty-bourgeois theoreticians and moralists. They dabble in all colors of the rainbow, but in the final instance remain apostles of slavery and submission.

Whoever does not care to return to Moses, Christ or Mohammed; whoever is not satisfied with eclectic hodge-podges must acknowledge that morality is a product of social development; that there is nothing invariable about it; that it serves social interests; that these interests are contradictory; that morality more than any other form of ideology has a class character.

But do not elementary moral precepts exist, worked out in the development of mankind as an integral element necessary for the life of every collective body? Undoubtedly such precepts exist, but the extent of their action is extremely limited and unstable. Norms "obligatory upon all" become the less forceful the sharper the character assumed by the class struggle. The highest pitch of the class struggle is civil war which explodes into mid-air all moral ties between the hostile classes.

Under "normal" conditions a "normal" man observes the commandment: "Thou shalt not kill!" But if he murders under exceptional conditions for self-defense, the judge condones his action. If he falls victim to a murderer, the court will kill the murderer. The necessity of the court's action, like that of the self-defense, flows from antagonistic interests. So far as the state is concerned, in peaceful times it limits itself to individual cases of legalized murder so that in time of war it may transform the "obligatory" commandment, "Thou shalt not kill!" into its opposite. The most "humane" governments, which in peaceful times "detest" war, proclaim during war that the highest duty of their armies is the extermination of the greatest possible number of people.

The so-called "generally recognized" moral precepts preserve an essentially algebraic, that is, an indeterminate character. They merely express the fact that man, in his individual conduct, is bound by certain common norms that flow from his being a member of society. The highest generalization of these norms is the "categorical imperative" of Kant. But in spite of the fact that it occupies a high position upon the philosophic Olympus, this imperative does not embody anything categorical, because it embodies nothing concrete. It is a shell without content.

This vacuity in the norms obligatory upon all arises from the fact that in all decisive questions people feel their class membership considerably more profoundly and more directly than their membership in "society." The norms of "obligatory" morality are in reality charged with class, that is, antagonistic content. The moral norm becomes the more categorical the less it is "obligatory" upon all. The solidarity of workers, especially of strikers or barricade fighters, is incomparably more "categorical" than human solidarity in general.

The bourgeoisie, which far surpasses the proletariat in the completeness and irreconcilability of its class consciousness, is vitally interested in imposing *its* moral philosophy upon the exploited masses. It is exactly for this purpose that the concrete norms of the bourgeois catechism are concealed under moral abstractions patronized by religion, philosophy, or that hybrid which is called "common sense." The appeal to abstract norms is not a disinterested philosophic mistake but a necessary element in the mechanics of class deception. The exposure of this deceit which retains the tradition of thousands of years is the first duty of a proletarian revolutionist.

In order to guarantee the triumph of their interests in big questions, the ruling classes are constrained to make concessions on secondary questions, naturally only so long as these concessions are reconciled in the bookkeeping. During the epoch of capitalistic upsurge, especially in the last few decades before the World War, these concessions, at least in relation to the top layers of the proletariat, were of a completely genuine nature. Industry at that time expanded almost uninterruptedly. The prosperity of the civilized nations—partially, too, that of the toiling masses—increased. Democracy appeared solid. Workers' organizations grew. At the same time reformist tendencies deepened. The relations between the classes softened, at least outwardly. Thus certain elementary moral precepts in social relations were established along with the norms of democracy and the habits of class collaboration. The impression was created of an evermore free, more just, and more humane society. The rising line of progress seemed infinite to "common sense."

Instead, however, war broke out with a train of convulsions, crises, catastrophes, epidemics, and bestiality. The economic life of mankind landed in an impasse. The class antagonisms became sharp and naked. The safety valves of democracy began to explode one after the other. The elementary moral precepts seemed even more fragile than the democratic institutions and reformist illusions. Mendacity, slander, bribery, venality, coercion, murder, grew to unprecedented dimensions. To a stunned simpleton all these vexations seem a temporary result of war. Actually they are manifestations of imperialist decline. The decay of capitalism denotes the decay of contemporary society with its right and its morals.

The "synthesis" of imperialist turpitude is fascism, directly begotten of bourgeois democracy's bankruptcy in the face of the problems of the imperialist epoch. Remnants of democracy continue still to exist only in the rich capitalist aristocracies: for each "democrat" in England, France, Holland, or Belgium there is a certain number of colonial slaves; "Sixty Families" dominate the democracy of the United States; and so forth. Moreover, shoots of fascism grow rapidly in all democracies. Stalinism in its turn is the product of imperialist pressure upon a backward and isolated workers' state, a symmetrical complement, in its own genre, to fascism.

While idealistic philistines—anarchists of course occupy first place—tirelessly unmask Marxist "amoralism" in their press, the American trusts, according to John L. Lewis (C.I.O.) are spending not less than $80,000,000 a year on the practical struggle against revolutionary "demoralization," that is, or espionage, bribery of workers, frame-ups, and dark-alley murders. The categorical imperative sometimes chooses circuitous ways for its triumph!

Let us note in justice that the most sincere and at the same time the most limited petty-bourgeois moralists still live even today in the idealized memories of yesterday and hope for its return. They do not understand that morality is a function of the class struggle; that democratic morality corresponds to the epoch of liberal and progressive capitalism; that the sharpening of the class struggle, in passing through its latest phase, definitively and irrevocably destroyed this morality; that in its place came the morality of fascism on one side, on the other the morality of proletarian revolution.

Democracy and "generally recognized" morality are not the only victims of imperialism. The third suffering martyr is "universal" common sense. This lowest form of the intellect is not only necessary under all conditions but under certain conditions is also sufficient. Common sense's basic capital consists of the elementary conclusions of universal experience: not to put one's fingers in fire, whenever possible to proceed along a straight line, not to tease vicious dogs . . . and so forth and so on. Under a stable social milieu common sense is sufficient for bargaining, healing, writing articles, leading trade unions, voting in parliament, marrying, and reproducing the race. But when that same common sense attempts to go beyond its valid limits into the arena of more complex generalizations, it is exposed as just a clot of prejudices of a definite class and a definite epoch. No more than a simple capitalist crisis brings common sense to an impasse; and before such catastrophes as revolution, counterrevolution, and war, common sense proves a perfect fool. In order to realize the catastrophic transgressions against the "normal" course of events higher qualities of intellect are necessary, philosophically expressed as yet only by dialectic materialism.

Max Eastman, who successfully attempts to endow "common sense" with a most attractive literary style, has fashioned out of the struggle against dialectics nothing less than a profession for himself. Eastman seriously takes the conservative banalities of common sense wedded to good style as "the science of revolution." Supporting the reactionary snobs of *Common Sense,* he expounds to mankind with inimitable assurance that if Trotsky had been guided not by Marxist doctrine but by common sense then he would not . . . have lost power. That inner dialectic which until now has appeared in the inevitable succession of determined stages in all revolutions does not exist for Eastman. Reaction's displacing revolution, to him, is determined through insufficient respect for common sense. Eastman does not understand that it is Stalin who in an historical sense fell *victim* to common sense, that is, its inadequacy, since that power which he possesses serves ends hostile to Bolshevism. Marxist doctrine, on the other hand, permitted us to tear away in time from the Thermidorian bureaucracy and to continue to serve the ends of international socialism.

Every science, and in that sense the "science of revolution" as well, is controlled by experience. Since Eastman well knows how to maintain revolutionary power under the condition of world counterrevolution, then he also knows, we may hope, how to conquer power. It would be very desirable that he finally disclose his secrets. Best of all that it be done in the form of a *draft program for a revolutionary party* under the title: How to Conquer and Hold Power. We fear, however, that it is precisely common sense which will urge Eastman to refrain from such a risky undertaking. And this time common sense will be right.

Marxist doctrine, which Eastman, alas, never understood, permitted us to foresee the inevitability under certain historic conditions of the Soviet Thermidor with all its coil of crimes. That same doctrine long ago predicted the inevitability of the downfall of bourgeois democracy and its morality. But the doctrinaires of "common sense" were caught unaware by fascism and Stalinism. Common sense operates on invariable magnitudes in a world where only change is invariable. Dialectics, on the contrary, takes all phenomena, institutions, and norms in their rise, development and decay. The dialectical consideration of morals as a subservient and transient product of the class struggle seems to common sense an "amoralism." But there is nothing more flat, stale, self-satisfied and cynical than the moral rules of common sense! . . .

Russia took the greatest leap in history, a leap in which the most progressive forces of the country found their expression. Now in the current reaction, the sweep of which is proportionate to the sweep of the revolution, backwardness is taking its revenge. Stalinism embodies this reaction. The barbarism of old Russian history upon new social bases seems yet more disgusting since it is constrained to conceal itself in hypocrisy unprecedented in history.

The liberals and the social democrats of the West, who were constrained by the Russian Revolution into doubt about their rotted ideas, now experienced a fresh influx of courage. The moral gangrene of the Soviet bureaucracy seemed to them the rehabilitation of liberalism. Stereotyped copybooks are drawn out into the light: "every dictatorship contains the seeds of its own degeneration"; "only democracy guarantees the development of personality"; and so forth. The contrasting of democracy and dictatorship, including in the given case a condemnation of socialism in favor of the bourgeois regime, stuns one from the point of view of theory by its illiterateness and unscrupulousness. The Stalinist pollution, a historical reality, is counterpoised to democracy—a supra-historical abstraction. But democracy also possesses a history in which there is no lack of pollution. In order to characterize Soviet bureaucracy we have borrowed the names of "Thermidor" and "bonapartism" from the history of bourgeois democracy because— let this be known to the retarded liberal doctrinaires—*democracy came into the world not at all through the democratic road*. Only a vulgar mentality can satisfy itself by chewing on the theme that bonapartism was the "natural offspring" of jacobinism, the historical punishment for infringing upon democracy, and so on. Without the Jacobin retribution upon feudalism, bourgeois democracy would have been absolutely unthinkable. Contrasting the concrete historical stages of jacobinism, Thermidor, bonapartism to the idealized abstraction of "democracy" is as vicious as contrasting the pains of childbirth to a living infant.

Stalinism in turn is not an abstraction of "dictatorship," but an immense bureaucratic reaction against the proletarian dictatorship in a backward and isolated country. The October revolution abolished privileges, waged war against social inequality, replaced the bureaucracy with self-government of the toilers, abolished secret diplomacy, strove to render all social relationships completely transparent. Stalinism re-established the most offensive forms of privileges, imbued inequality with a provocative character, strangled mass self-activity under police absolutism, transformed administration into a monopoly of the Kremlin oligarchy and regenerated the fetishism of power in forms that absolute monarchy dared not dream of.

Social reaction in all forms is constrained to mask its real aims. The sharper the transition from revolution to reaction, the more the reaction is dependent upon the traditions of revolution, that is, the greater its fear of the masses—the more is it forced to resort to mendacity and frame-up in the struggle against the representatives of the revolution. Stalinist frame-ups are not a fruit of Bolshevik "amoralism"; no, like all important events in history, they are a product of the concrete social struggle, and the most perfidious and severest of all at that: the struggle of a new aristocracy against the masses that raised it to power.

Verily boundless intellectual and moral obtuseness is required to identify the reactionary police morality of Stalinism with the revolutionary morality of the Bolsheviks. Lenin's party has long ceased to exist—it was shattered between inner difficulties and world imperialism. In its place rose the Stalinist bureaucracy, the transmissive mechanism of imperialism. The bureaucracy substituted class collaboration for the class struggle on the world arena, social patriotism for internationalism. In order to adapt the ruling party to the tasks of reaction, the bureaucracy "renewed" its composition through executing revolutionists and recruiting careerists.

Every reaction regenerates, nourishes and strengthens those elements of the historical past which the revolution struck but which it could not vanquish. The methods of Stalinism bring to the highest tension, to culmination, and at the same time to absurdity all those methods of untruth, brutality, and baseness which constitute the mechanics of control in every class society including also that of democracy. Stalinism is a single clot of all monstrosities of the historical State, its most malicious caricature and disgusting grimace. When the representatives of old society puritanically counterpoise a sterilized democratic abstraction to the gangrene of Stalinism, we can with full justice recommend to them, as to all of old society, that they fall enamored of themselves in the warped mirror of Soviet Thermidor. True, the GPU far surpasses all other regimes in the nakedness of its crimes. But this flows from the immense amplitude of events shaking Russia under the influence of world imperialist demoralization.

Among the liberals and radicals there are not a few individuals who have assimilated the methods of the materialist interpretation of events and who consider themselves Marxists. This does not hinder them, however, from remaining bourgeois journalists, professors or politicians. A Bolshevik is inconceivable, of course, without the materialist method, in the sphere of morality too. But this method serves him not solely for the interpretation of events but rather for the creation of a revolutionary party of the proletariat. It is impossible to accomplish this task without complete independence from the bourgeoisie and their morality. Yet bourgeois public opinion actually now reigns in full sway over the official workers' movement from William Green in the United States, Léon Blum and Maurice Thorez in France, to Garcia Oliver in Spain. In this fact the reactionary character of the present period reaches its sharpest expression.

A revolutionary Marxist cannot begin to approach his historical mission without having broken morally from bourgeois public opinion and its agencies in the proletariat. For this, moral courage of a different caliber is required than that of opening wide one's mouth at meetings and yelling, "Down with Hitler!" "Down with Franco!" It is precisely this resolute, completely-thought-out, inflexible rupture of the Bolsheviks from conservative moral philosophy not only of the big but of the petty bourgeoisie which mortally terrorizes democratic phrasemongers, drawing-room prophets and lobbying heroes. From this are derived their complaints about the "amoralism" of the Bolsheviks.

Their identification of bourgeois morals with morals "in general" can best of all, perhaps, be verified at the extreme left wing of the petty bourgeoisie, precisely in the centrist parties of the so-called London Bureau. Since this organization "recognizes" the program of proletarian revolution, our disagreements with it seem, at first glance, secondary. Actually their "recognition" is valueless because it does not bind them to anything. They "recognize" the proletarian revolution as the Kantians recognized the categorical imperative, that is, as a holy principle, but one not applicable to daily life. In the sphere of practical politics they unite with the worst enemies of the revolution (reformists and Stalinists) for the struggle against us. All their thinking is permeated with duplicity and falsehood. If the centrists, according to a general rule, do not raise themselves to imposing crimes it is only because they forever remain in the byways of politics: they are, so to speak, petty pickpockets of history. For this reason they consider themselves called upon to regenerate the workers' movement with a new morality.

At the extreme left wing of this "left" fraternity stands a small and politically completely insignificant grouping of German emigres who publish the paper *Neuer Weg* (The New Road). Let us bend down lower and listen to these "revolutionary" indicters of Bolshevik amoralism. In a tone of ambiguous pseudo-praise the *Neuer Weg* proclaims that the Bolsheviks are distinguished advantageously from other parties by their absence of hypocrisy—they openly declare what others quietly apply in fact, that is, the principle: "the end justifies the means." But according to the convictions of *Neuer Weg* such a "bourgeois" precept is incompatible with a "healthy socialist movement." "Lying and worse are not permissible means of struggle, as Lenin still considered." The word "still" evidently signifies that Lenin did not succeed in overcoming his delusions only because he failed to live until the discovery of *The New Road*.

In the formula, "lying and worse," "worse" evidently signifies violence, murder, and so on, since under equal conditions violence is worse than lying, and murder the most extreme form of violence. We thus come to the conclusion that lying, violence, murder are incompatible with a "healthy socialist movement." What, however, is our relation to revolution? Civil war is the most severe of all forms of war. It is unthinkable not only without violence against tertiary figures but, under contemporary technique, without murdering old men, old women and children. Must one be reminded of Spain? The only possible answer of the "friends" of republican Spain sounds like this: civil war is better than fascist slavery. But this completely correct answer merely signifies that the *end* (democracy or socialism) justifies, under certain conditions, such *means* as violence and murder. Not to speak about lies! Without lies war would be as unimaginable as a machine without oil. In order to safeguard even the session of the *Cortes* (February 1, 1938) from Fascist bombs the Barcelona government several times deliberately deceived journalists and their own population. Could it have acted in any other way? Whoever accepts the end—victory over Franco—must accept the means—civil war with its wake of horrors and crimes.

Nevertheless, lying and violence "in themselves" warrant condemnation? Of course, even as does the class society which generates them. A society without social contradictions will naturally be a society without lies and violence. However there is no way of building a bridge to that society save by revolutionary, that is, violent, means. The revolution itself is a product of class society and of necessity bears its traits. From the point of view of "eternal truths" revolution is of course "antimoral." But this merely means that idealist morality is counter-revolutionary, that is, in the service of the exploiters.

"Civil war," will perhaps respond the philosopher caught unawares, "is however a sad exception. But in peaceful times a healthy socialist movement should manage without violence and lying." Such an answer however represents nothing less than a pathetic evasion. There is no impervious demarcation between "peaceful" class struggle and revolution. Every strike embodies in an unexpanded form all the elements of civil war. Each side strives to impress the opponent with an exaggerated representation of its resoluteness to struggle and its material resources. Through their press, agents, and spies the capitalists labor to frighten and demoralize the strikers. From their side, the workers' pickets, where persuasion does not avail, are compelled to resort to force. Thus "lying and worse" are an inseparable part of the class struggle even in its most elementary form. It remains to be added that the very conception of *truth* and *lie* was born of social contradictions.

Stalin arrests and shoots the children of his opponents after these opponents have themselves been executed under false accusations. With the help of the institution of family hostages Stalin compels those Soviet diplomats to return from abroad who permitted themselves an expression of doubt upon the infallibility of Yagoda or Yezhov. The moralists of *Neuer Weg* consider it necessary and timely to remind us on this occasion of the fact that Trotsky in 1919 "also" introduced a law upon hostages. But here it becomes necessary to quote literally:

> The detention of innocent relatives by Stalin is disgusting barbarism. But it remains a barbarism as well when it was dictated by Trotsky (1919).

Here is the idealistic moralist in all his beauty! His criteria are as false as the norms of bourgeois democracy—in both cases *parity* is supposed where in actuality there is not even a trace of it.

We will not insist here upon the fact that the Decree of 1919 led scarcely to even one execution of relatives of those commanders whose perfidy not only caused the loss of innumerable human lives but threatened the revolution itself with direct annihilation. The question in the end does not concern that. If the revolution had displayed less superfluous generosity from the very beginning, hundreds of thousands of lives would have been saved. Thus or otherwise I carry full responsibility for the Decree of 1919. It was a necessary measure in the struggle against the oppressors. Only in the historical content of the struggle lies the justification of the decree as in general the justification of the whole civil war which, too, can be called, not without foundation, "disgusting barbarism."

We leave to some Emil Ludwig or his ilk the drawing of Abraham Lincoln's portrait with rosy little wings. Lincoln's significance lies in his not hesitating before the most severe means once they were found to be necessary in achieving a great historic aim posed by the development of a young nation. The question lies not even in which of the warring camps caused or itself suffered the greatest number of victims. History has different yardsticks for the cruelty of the Northerners and the cruelty of the Southerners in the Civil War. A slaveowner who through cunning and violence shackles a slave in chains, and a slave who through cunning or violence breaks the chains—let not the contemptible eunuchs tell us that they are equals before a court of morality!

After the Paris Commune had been drowned in blood and the reactionary knaves of the whole world dragged its banner in the filth of vilification and slander, there were not a few democratic philistines who, adapting themselves to reaction, slandered the Communards for shooting sixty-four hostages headed by the Paris archbishop. Marx did not hesitate a moment in defending this bloody act of the Commune. In a circular issued by the General Council of the First International, in which seethes the fiery eruption of lava, Marx first reminds us of the bourgeoisie adopting the institution of hostages in the struggle against both colonial peoples and their own toiling masses and afterwards refers to the systematic execution of the Commune captives by the frenzied reactionaries, continuing:

> ... the Commune, to protect their [the captives'] lives, was obliged to resort to the Prussian practice of securing hostages. The lives of the hostages had been forfeited over and over again by the continued shooting of prisoners on the part of the Versaillese. How could they be spared any longer after the carnage with which MacMahon's Praetorians celebrated their entry into Paris? Was even the last check upon the unscrupulous ferocity of bourgeois governments—the taking of hostages—to be made a mere sham of?

Thus Marx defended the execution of hostages although behind his back in the General Council sat not a few Fenner Brockways, Norman Thomases, and other Otto Bauers. But so fresh was the indignation of the world proletariat against the ferocity of the Versaillese that the reactionary moralistic bunglers preferred to keep silent in expectation of times more favorable to them which, alas, were not slow in appearing. Only after the definite triumph of reaction did the petty-bourgeois moralists, together with the trade union bureaucrats and the anarchist phrase-mongers, destroy the First International.

When the October revolution was defending itself against the united forces of imperialism on a five thousand mile front, the workers of the whole world followed the course of the struggle with such ardent sympathy that in their forums it was extremely risky to indict the "disgusting barbarism" of the institution of hostages. Complete degeneration of the Soviet state and the triumph of reaction in a number of countries was necessary before the moralists crawled out of their crevices . . . to aid Stalin. If it is true that the repressions safeguarding the privileges of the new aristocracy have the same moral value as the revolutionary measures of the liberating struggle, then Stalin is completely justified, if . . . if the proletarian revolution is not completely condemned.

Seeking examples of immorality in the events of the Russian Civil War, Messrs. Moralists find themselves at the same time constrained to close their eyes to the fact that the Spanish Revolution also produced an institution of hostages, at least during that period when it was a genuine revolution of the masses. If the indicters dare not attack the Spanish workers for their "disgusting barbarism," it is only because the ground of the Pyrennean peninsula is still too hot for them. It is considerably more convenient to return to 1919. This is already history, the old men have forgotten and the young ones have not yet learned. For the same reason Pharisees of various hues return to Kronstadt and Makhno with such obstinacy—here exists a free outlet for moral effluvia!

It is impossible not to agree with the moralists that history chooses grievous pathways. But what type of conclusion for practical activity is to be drawn from this? Leo Tolstoy recommended that we ignore the social conventions and perfect ourselves. Mahatma Gandhi advises that we drink goat's milk. Alas, the "revolutionary" moralists of *Neuer Weg* did not drift far from these recipes. "We should free ourselves," they preach, "from those morals of the Kaffirs to whom only what the enemy does is wrong." Excellent advice! "We should free ourselves. . . ." Tolstoy recommended in addition that we free ourselves from the sins of the flesh. However, statistics fail to confirm the success of his recommendation. Our centrist manikins have succeeded in elevating themselves to supra-class morality in a class society. But almost two thousand years have passed since it was stated: "Love your enemies." "Offer also the other cheek. . . ." However, even the holy Roman father so far has not "freed himself" from hatred against his enemies. Truly, Satan, the enemy of mankind, is powerful!

To apply different criteria to the actions of the exploiters and the exploited signifies, according to these pitiful manikins, standing on the level of the "morals of the Kaffirs." First of all such a contemptuous reference to the Kaffirs is hardly proper from the pen of "socialists." Are the morals of the Kaffirs really so bad? Here is what the *Encyclopædia Britannica* says upon the subject:

> In their social and political relations they display great tact and intelligence; they are remarkably brave, warlike, and hospitable, and were honest and truthful until through contact with the whites they became suspicious, revengeful and thievish, besides acquiring most European vices.

It is impossible not to arrive at the conclusion that white missionaries, preachers of eternal morals, participated in the corruption of the Kaffirs.

If we should tell the toiler-Kaffir how the workers arose in a part of our planet and caught their exploiters unawares, he would be very pleased. On the other hand, he would be chagrined to discover that the oppressors had succeeded in deceiving the oppressed. A Kaffir who has not been demoralized to the marrow of his bones by missionaries will never apply one and the same abstract moral norm to the oppressors and the oppressed. Yet he will easily comprehend an explanation that it is the function of these abstract norms to prevent the oppressed from arising against their oppressors.

What an instructive coincidence: in order to slander the Bolsheviks, the missionaries of *Neuer Weg* were compelled at the same time to slander the Kaffirs; moreover, in both cases, the slander follows the line of the official bourgeois lie: against revolutionists and against the colored races. No, we prefer the Kaffirs to all missionaries, both spiritual and secular!

It is not necessary in any case, however, to overestimate the conscientiousness of the moralists of *Neuer Weg* and other *culs-de-sacs*. The intentions of these people are not so bad. But despite these intentions they serve as levers in the mechanics of reaction. In such a period as the present when the petty bourgeois parties who cling to the liberal bourgeoisie or its shadow (the politics of the "Peoples' Front") paralyze the proletariat and pave the road for Fascism (Spain, France . . .), the Bolsheviks, that is, revolutionary Marxists, become especially odious figures in the eyes of bourgeois public opinion. The fundamental political pressure of our time shifts from right to left. In the final analysis the whole weight of reaction bears down upon the shoulders of a tiny revolutionary minority. This minority is called the Fourth International. *Voilà l'ennemi!* There is the enemy!

In the mechanics of reaction Stalinism occupies many leading positions. All groupings of bourgeois society, including the anarchists, utilize its aid in the struggle against the proletarian revolution. At the same time the petty-bourgeois democrats attempt, at least to the extent of fifty per cent, to cast the repulsiveness of the crimes of its Moscow ally upon the indomitable revolutionary minority. Herein lies the sense of the now stylish dictum: "Trotskyism and Stalinism are one and the same." The adversaries of the Bolsheviks and the Kaffirs thus aid reaction in slandering the party of revolution.

The Russian "Social Revolutionaries" were always the most moral individuals: essentially they were composed of ethics alone. This did not prevent them, however, at the time of revolution from deceiving the Russian peasants. In the Parisian organ of Kerensky, that very ethical socialist who was the forerunner of Stalin in manufacturing spurious accusations against the Bolsheviks, another old "Social Revolutionary," Zenzinov, writes:

> Lenin, as is known, taught that for the sake of gaining the desired ends communists can, and sometimes must, "resort to all sorts of devices, maneuvers and subterfuge" [*New Russia*, February 17, 1938, p. 3].

From this they draw the ritualistic conclusion: Stalinism is the natural offspring of Leninism.

Unfortunately, the ethical indicter is not even capable of quoting honestly. Lenin said:

> It is necessary to be able . . . to resort to all sorts of devices, maneuvers, and illegal methods, to evasion and subterfuge, *in order to penetrate into the trade unions, to remain in them, and to carry on communist work in them at all costs.*

The necessity for evasion and maneuvers, according to Lenin's explanation, is called forth by the fact that the reformist bureaucracy, betraying the workers to capital, baits revolutionists, persecutes them, and even resorts to turning the bourgeois police upon them. "Maneuvers" and "subterfuge" are in this case only methods of valid self-defense against the perfidious reformist bureaucracy.

The party of this very Zenzinov once carried on illegal work against Czarism, and later—against the Bolsheviks. In both cases it resorted to craftiness, evasion, false passports, and other forms of "subterfuge." All these *means* were considered not only "ethical" but also heroic, because they corresponded to political *aims* of the petty bourgeoisie. But the situation changes at once when proletarian revolutionists are forced to resort to conspirative measures against the petty bourgeois democracy. The key to the morality of these gentlemen has, as we see, a class character!

The "amoralist" Lenin openly, in the press, gives advice concerning military craftiness against perfidious leaders. And the moralist Zenzinov maliciously chops both ends from the quotation in order to deceive the reader: the ethical indicter is proved as usual a petty swindler. Not for nothing was Lenin fond of repeating: it is very difficult to meet a conscientious adversary!

A worker who does not conceal the "truth" about the strikers' plans from the capitalists is simply a betrayer deserving contempt and boycott. The soldier who discloses the "truth" to the enemy is punished as a spy. Kerensky tried to lay at the Bolsheviks' door the accusation of having disclosed the "truth" to Ludendorff's staff. It appears that even the "holy truth" is not an end in itself. More imperious criteria which, as analysis demonstrates, carry a class character, rule over it.

The life and death struggle is unthinkable without military craftiness, in other words, without lying and deceit. May the German proletariat then not deceive Hitler's police? Or perhaps Soviet Bolsheviks have an "immoral" attitude when they deceive the GPU? Every pious bourgeois applauds the cleverness of police who succeed through craftiness in seizing a dangerous gangster. Is military craftiness really permissible when the question concerns the overthrow of the gangsters of imperialism?

Norman Thomas speaks about "that strange communist amorality in which nothing matters but the party and its power" (*Socialist Call*, March 12, 1938, p. 5). Moreover, Thomas throws into one heap the present Comintern, that is, the conspiracy of the Kremlin bureaucracy against the working class, with the Bolshevik party, which represented a conspiracy of the advanced workers against the bourgeoisie. This thoroughly dishonest juxtaposition has already been sufficiently exposed above. Stalinism merely screens itself under the cult of the party; actually it destroys the party, and tramples it in filth. It is true, however, that to a Bolshevik the party is everything. The drawing-room socialist, Thomas, is surprised by and rejects a similar relationship between a revolutionist and revolution because he himself is only a bourgeois with a socialist "ideal." In the eyes of Thomas and his kind the party is only a secondary instrument for electoral combinations and other similar uses, no more. His personal life, interests, ties, moral criteria exist outside the party. With hostile astonishment he looks down upon the Bolshevik to whom the party is a weapon for the revolutionary reconstruction of society, including also its morality. To a revolutionary Marxist there can be no contradiction between personal morality and the interests of the party, since the party embodies in his consciousness the very highest tasks and aims of mankind. It is naïve to imagine that Thomas has a higher understanding of morality than the Marxists. He merely has a base conception of the party.

"All that arises is worthy of perishing," says the dialectician, Goethe. The destruction of the Bolshevik party—an episode in world reaction—does not, however, disparage its worldwide historical significance. In the period of its revolutionary ascendance, that is, when it actually represented the proletarian vanguard, it was the most honest party in history. Wherever it could, of course, it deceived the class enemies; on the other hand it told the toilers the truth, the whole truth, and nothing but the truth. Only thanks to this did it succeed in winning their trust to a degree never before achieved by any other party in the world.

The clerks of the ruling classes call the organizers of this party "amoralists." In the eyes of conscious workers this accusation carries a complimentary character. It signifies: Lenin refused to recognize moral norms established by slaveowners for their slaves and never observed by the slaveowners themselves; he called upon the proletariat to extend the class struggle into the moral sphere too. Whoever fawns before precepts established by the enemy will never vanquish that enemy!

The "amoralism" of Lenin, that is, his rejection of supra-class morals, did not hinder him from remaining faithful to one and the same ideal throughout his whole life; from devoting his whole being to the cause of the oppressed; from displaying the highest conscientiousness in the sphere of ideas and the highest fearlessness in the sphere of action, from maintaining an attitude untainted by the least superiority to an "ordinary" worker, to a defenseless woman, to a child. Does it not seem that "amoralism" in the given case is only a pseudonym for higher human morality?

A means can be justified only by its end. But the end in its turn needs to be justified. From the Marxist point of view, which expresses the historical interests of the proletariat, the end is justified if it leads to increasing the power of man over nature and to the abolition of the power of man over man.

"We are to understand then that in achieving this end anything is permissible?" sarcastically demands the philistine, demonstrating that he understood nothing. That is permissible, we answer, which *really* leads to the liberation of mankind. Since this end can be achieved only through revolution, the liberating morality of the proletariat of necessity is endowed with a revolutionary character. It irreconcilably counteracts not only religious dogma but every kind of idealistic fetish, these philosophic gendarmes of the ruling class. It deduces a rule of conduct from the laws of the development of society, thus primarily from the class struggle, this law of all laws.

"Just the same," the moralist continues to insist, "does it mean that in the class struggle against capitalists all means are permissible: lying, frame-up, betrayal, murder, and so on?" Permissible and obligatory are those and only those means, we answer, which unite the revolutionary proletariat, fill their hearts with irreconcilable hostility to oppression, teach them contempt for official morality and its democratic echoers, imbue them with consciousness of their own historic mission, raise their courage and spirit of self-sacrifice in the struggle. Precisely from this it flows that *not* all means are permissible. When we say that the end justifies the means, then for us the conclusion follows that the great revolutionary end spurns those base means and ways which set one part of the working class against other parts, or attempt to make the masses happy without their participation; or lower the faith of the masses in themselves and their organization, replacing it by worship for the "leaders." Primarily and irreconcilably, revolutionary morality rejects servility in relation to the bourgeoisie and haughtiness in relation to the toilers, that is, those characteristics in which petty-bourgeois pedants and moralists are thoroughly steeped.

These criteria do not, of course, give a ready answer to the question as to what is permissible and what is not permissible in each separate case. There can be no such automatic answers. Problems of revolutionary morality are fused with the problems of revolutionary strategy and tactics. The living experience of the movement under the clarification of theory provides the correct answer to these problems.

Dialectic materialism does not know dualism between means and end. The end flows naturally from the historical movement. Organically the means are subordinated to the end. The immediate end becomes the means for a further end. In his play, *Franz von Sickingen,* Ferdinand Lassalle puts the following words into the mouth of one of the heroes:

> ... Show not the *goal*
> But show also the *path*. So closely interwoven
> Are path and goal that each with other
> Ever changes, and other *paths* forthwith
> Another *goal* set up.

Lassalle's lines are not at all perfect. Still worse is the fact that in practical politics Lassalle himself diverged from the above expressed precept—it is sufficient to recall that he went as far as secret agreements with Bismarck! But the dialectic interdependence between means and end is expressed entirely correctly in the above-quoted sentences. Seeds of wheat must be sown in order to yield an ear of wheat.

Is individual terror, for example, permissible or impermissible from the point of view of "pure morals"? In this abstract form the question does not exist at all for us. Conservative Swiss bourgeois even now render official praise to the terrorist William Tell. Our sympathies are fully on the side of Irish, Russian, Polish, or Hindu terrorists in their struggle against national and political oppression. The assassinated Kirov, a rude satrap, does not call forth any sympathy. Our relation to the assassin remains neutral only because we know not what motives guided him. If it became known that Nikolayev acted as a conscious avenger of workers' rights trampled upon by Kirov, our sympathies would be fully on the side of the assassin. However, not the question of subjective motives but that of objective expediencey has for us the decisive significance. Are the given means really capable of leading to the goal? In relation to individual terror, both theory and experience bear witness that such is not the case. To the terrorist we say: it is impossible to replace the masses; only in the mass movement can you find expedient expression for your heroism. However, under conditions of civil war, the assassination of individual oppressors ceases to be an act of individual terror. If, we shall say, a revolutionist bombed General Franco and his staff into the air, it would hardly evoke moral indignation even from the democratic eunuchs. Under the conditions of civil war a similar act would be politically completely expedient. Thus, even in the sharpest question—murder of man by man—moral absolutes prove futile. Moral evaluations, together with political ones, flow from the inner needs of struggle.

The liberation of the workers can come only through the workers themselves. There is, therefore, no greater crime than deceiving the masses, palming off defeats as victories and friends as enemies, bribing workers' leaders, fabricating legends, staging false trials—in a word, doing what the Stalinists do. These means can serve only one end: lengthening the domination of a clique already condemned by history. But they cannot serve to liberate the masses. That is why the Fourth International leads against Stalinism a life and death struggle.

The masses, of course, are not at all impeccable. Idealization of the masses is foreign to us. We have seen them under different conditions, at different stages and, in addition, in the biggest political shocks. We have observed their strong and weak sides. Their strong side—resoluteness, self-sacrifice, heroism—has always found it clearest expression in times of revolutionary upsurge. During this period the Bolsheviks headed the masses. Afterward a different historical chapter loomed when the weak side of the oppressed came to the forefront: heterogeneity, insufficiency of culture, narrowness of world outlook. The masses tired of the tension, became disillusioned, lost faith in themselves—and cleared the road for the new aristocracy. In this epoch the Bolsheviks ("Trotskyists") found themselves isolated from the masses. Practically we went through two such big historic cycles: 1897-1905, years of flood tide; 1907-1913, years of the ebb; 1917-1923, a period of upsurge unprecedented in history; and finally, a new period of reaction which has not ended even today. In these immense events the "Trotskyists" learned the rhythm of history, that is, the dialectics of the class struggle. They also learned, it seems, and to a certain degree successfully, how to subordinate their subjective plans and programs to this objective rhythm. They learned not to fall into despair over the fact that the laws of history do not depend upon their individual tastes and are not subordinated to their own moral criteria. They learned to subordinate their individual desires to the laws of history. They learned not to become frightened by the most powerful enemies, if their power is in contradiction to the needs of historical development. They know how to swim against the stream in the deep conviction that the new historic flood will carry them to the other shore. Not all will reach that shore, many will drown. But to participate in this movement with open eyes and with an intense will —only this can give the highest moral satisfaction to a thinking being!

P.S.—I wrote these lines during those days when my son struggled, unknown to me, with death. I dedicate to his memory this small work which, I hope, would have met with his approval— Leon Sedov was a genuine revolutionist, and despised the Pharisees.

32

Diary in Exile—1935

TRANSLATED BY ELENA ZARUDNAYA

February 7, 1935
The diary is not a literary form I am especially fond of; at the moment I would prefer the daily newspaper. But there is none available. . . . Cut off from political action, I am obliged to resort to such ersatz journalism as a private diary. At the beginning of the war, when I was confined in Switzerland, I kept a diary for a few weeks. Later, after being deported from France to Spain in 1916, I did so again. I think that is all. Now once again I have to resort to a political diary. Will it be for long? Perhaps months; in any case not years. Events must come to a head in one way or another and put an end to the diary—if it is not cut short even sooner by a surreptitious shot directed by an agent of . . . Stalin, Hitler, or their French friend-enemies.

Lassalle wrote once that he would gladly leave unwritten what he *knew* if only he could accomplish at least a part of what he felt able to *do*. Any revolutionary would feel the same way. But one has to take the situation as it is. For the very reason that it fell to my lot to take part in great events, my past now cuts me off from chances for action. I am reduced to interpreting events and trying to foresee their future course. At least this occupation is more satisfying than mere passive reading.

Here my contacts with life are almost entirely limited to the newspapers and partly to letters. It will not be surprising if my diary tends to take the form of a review of newspapers and periodicals. But it is not the world of the newspapermen as such that interests me, but the workings of the deeper social forces as they appear reflected in the crooked mirror of the press. However, I naturally am not committing myself in advance to this form. The advantage of a diary—alas, the only one—lies precisely in the fact that it leaves one free from any literary requirements or prescriptions.

Engels is undoubtedly one of the finest, best integrated and noblest personalities in the gallery of great men. To re-create his image would be a gratifying task. It is also a historical duty. On Prinkipo,[1] I worked on a book about Marx and Engels, but the preliminary materials were burned in a fire. I doubt that I will be able to return to this subject again. It would be good to finish the book on Lenin so as to move on to more timely work, a book on capitalism in the stage of disintegration.

Christianity created the figure of Christ to humanize the elusive Lord of Hosts and bring him nearer to mortal men. Alongside the Olympian Marx, Engels is more "human," more approachable. How well they complement one another! Or rather, how consciously Engels endeavors to complement Marx; all his life he uses himself up in this task. He regards it as his mission and finds in it his gratification. And this without a shadow of self-sacrifice—always himself, always full of life,

[1] [In Turkey, where Trotsky began his exile outside Russia in 1929 after two years in Alma Ata, Siberia. In 1933, Trotsky moved to France where he stayed until 1935, going then to Norway as indicated in these excerpts from his diary, which are published with the kind permission of Harvard University Press.—Ed.]

always superior to his environment and his age, with immense intellectual interests, with a true fire of genius always blazing in the forge of thought. Against the background of their everyday lives, Engels gains tremendously in stature by comparison with Marx—though of course Marx's stature is not in the least diminished by this. I remember that after reading the Marx-Engels correspondence on my military train, I spoke to Lenin of my admiration for the figure of Engels. My point was just this, that when viewed in his relationship with the titan Marx, faithful Fred gains—rather than diminishes—in stature. Lenin expressed his approval of this idea with alacrity, even with delight. He loved Engels very deeply, and particularly for his wholeness of character and all-round humanity. I remember how we examined with some excitement a portrait of Engels as a young man, discovering in it the traits which became so prominent in his later life.

When you have had enough of the prose of the Blums, the Cachins and the Thorezes, when you have swallowed your fill of the microbes of pettiness and insolence, obsequiousness and ignorance, there is no better way of clearing your lungs than by reading the correspondence of Marx and Engels, both to each other and to other people. In their epigrammatic illusions and characterizations, sometimes paradoxical, but always well thought out and to the point, there is so much instruction, so much mental freshness and mountain air! They always lived on the heights.

February 15

Le Temps had published a very sympathetic report from its Moscow correspondent about the new privileges granted to the *kolkhozniks* [collective farmers], especially in regard to their acquiring ownership of horses, cattle, and other livestock. Certain further concessions to the petty-bourgeois tendencies of the peasant seem to be in preparation. At this stage it is hard to predict the point at which they will manage to hold the line against the present retreat. But the retreat itself, brought on as it was by the extremely crude bureaucratic illusions of the preceding period, was not difficult to foresee. Since the fall of

1929 the *Bulletin of the Russian Opposition*[2] has been sounding the alarm against irresponsible methods of collectivization.

In this manipulation of unco-ordinated tempos the foundation is being laid for an inevitable crisis in the immediate future.

The rest is well known: the slaughter of the cattle, the famine of 1933, the untold number of victims, and the series of political crises. At the present time the retreat is proceeding at full speed. For this very reason Stalin is once again forced to cut down everyone and everything that stands to the left of him.

Revolution by its very nature is sometimes compelled to take in more territory than it is capable of holding. Retreats are possible—when there is territory to retreat from. But this general law by no means justifies wholesale collectivization. Its absurdities were not the result of elemental pressure from the masses, but of bureaucratic bungling. Instead of regulating the collectivization according to the productive and technical resources of the country, and instead of extending the radius of collectivization in breadth and depth according to the dictates of experience, the frightened bureaucrats began to drive the frightened *muzhiks* into the collective farms with the knout. Stalin's narrow empiricism and utter lack of vision are nowhere more starkly revealed than in his commentaries on the subject of wholesale collectivization. But now, the retreat is being carried out without commentaries.

February 17

I imagine an old doctor, devoid of neither education nor experience, who day after day has to watch quacks and charlatans doctor to death a person dear to him, knowing that this person could be certainly cured if only the elementary rules of medicine were observed. That would be approximately the way I feel as I watch the criminal work of the "leaders" of the French proletariat. Conceit? No, a deep and indestructible conviction.

[2] [Russian periodical published for several years by Trotsky's followers in Europe.—Ed.]

. . .

Our life here differs very little from imprisonment. We are shut up in our house and yard and meet people no more often than we would at visiting hours in a prison. True, within the last few months we have acquired a radio, but such things probably exist even in certain prisons, at least in America (not in France, of course). We listen almost exclusively to concerts, which now occupy a rather prominent place in our daily routine. For the most part, I listen to music superficially, while working. Sometimes music helps me to write, sometimes it hinders; in general I would say that it helps me to make first drafts of my ideas, but hinders me from working them up. N.,[3] as always, listens with absorption and concentration. Right now we are listening to Rimsky-Korsakov.

The radio reminds one how broad and varied life is and at the same time gives an extremely economical and compact expression to this variety. In short, it is an instrument perfectly suited to a prison.

March 21

It's spring, the sun is hot, the violets have been in bloom for about ten days, the peasants are puttering around in the vineyards. Last night we listened to *Die Walküre* from Bordeaux until midnight. Military service extended to two years. Rearmament of Germany. Preparations for a new *"final"* war. The peasants peacefully prune their vines and fertilize the furrows between them. Everything is in order.

The socialists and the communists write articles against the two-year term, and for the sake of greater impressiveness trot out their largest type. Deep in their hearts the "leaders" hope things will work out somehow. Here also everything is in order.

And yet this order has hopelessly undermined itself. It will collapse with a stench. . . .

March 27

In 1903 in Paris a performance of Gorky's *The Lower Depths* was organized, the proceeds from which were to benefit *Iskra*. There was talk of giving a part to N., very likely on my initia-

[3] [Natalia, Trotsky's wife.—Ed.]

tive. I thought she would play her part well, "sincerely." But nothing came of it, and the part was given to someone else. I was surprised and distressed. Only later I understood that N. cannot "act a part" in any sphere. She always and under all conditions, all her life and in all possible surroundings—and we have changed quite a few of them—has remained true to herself, and has never allowed her surroundings to influence her inner life. . . .

Today on our walk we went up a hill. N. got tired and unexpectedly sat down, all pale, on the dry leaves (the earth is still a bit damp). Even now she still walks beautifully, without fatigue, and her gait is quite youthful, like her whole figure. But for the last few months her heart has been acting up now and then. She works too much—with passion, as in everything she undertakes, and today it showed during the steep ascent up the hill. N. sat down all of a sudden—she obviously just *could not* go any further—and smiled apologetically. What a pang of pity I felt for youth, *her* youth. . . . One night we ran home from the Paris Opera to the *rue* Gassendi, 46, *au pas gymnastique*, holding hands. It was in 1903. Our combined age was 46. . . . N. was probably the more indefatigable one. Once, while a whole crowd of us were walking somewhere in the outskirts of Paris, we came to a bridge. A steep cement pier sloped down from a great height. Two small boys had climbed on to the pier over the parapet of the bridge and were looking down on the passers-by. Suddenly N. started climbing toward them up the steep smooth slope of the pier. I was petrified. I didn't think it was possible to climb up there. But she kept walking up with her graceful stride, on high heels, smiling to the boys. They waited for her with interest. We all stopped anxiously. N. went all the way without looking at us, talked to the children, and came down the same way, without having made, as far as one could see, a single superfluous effort or taken a single uncertain step. . . . It was spring, and the sun was shining as brightly as it did today when N. suddenly sat down in the grass. . . .

"*Dagegen ist nun einmal kein Kraut gewachsen,*"[4] Engels wrote about old age and death. All the events and experiences

[4] ["No herb has grown to remedy this."—Ed.]

of life are arranged along this inexorable arch between birth and the grave. This arch constitutes life itself. Without this arch there would be not only no old age, but also no youth. Old age is "necessary" because it has experience and wisdom. Youth, after all, is so beautiful exactly because there is old age and death.

April 2

Yesterday another period of ill health began for me. Weakness, slightly feverish condition, an extraordinary humming in my ears. Last time, during a similar spell, H. M. was at the local Prefect's. The latter inquired about me, and learning that I was sick, exclaimed in genuine alarm: "This is extremely unpleasant, extremely unpleasant! If he dies here, why, we will not be able to bury him under his assumed name!" Everyone has his worries!

April 4

All the current *"misères"* of our personal lives have receded into the background in the face of our anxiety for Seryozha, A. L., and the children.[5] I said to N. yesterday: "It seems now that our life before we got the last letter from Lyova was almost beautiful and serene. . . ." N. behaves with great fortitude, for my sake, but she feels all this immeasurably more deeply than I do.

The motive of *personal revenge* has always been a considerable factor in the repressive policies of Stalin. Kamenev told me how the three of them—Stalin, Kamenev, and Dzherzinsky—in Zubalovo, in the Summer of 1923 (or 1924) spent the day in a "heart-to-heart" conversation over wine. They were bound together by their campaign against me, which had recently been initiated. After the wine, on the balcony, the talk touched upon a sentimental subject—personal tastes and predilections, something of that sort. Stalin said, "The greatest delight is to

[5] [Stalin persecuted Trotsky's children relentlessly. A son, an engineer uninvolved in politics, disappeared in Russia; a daughter was driven to suicide; another son, a political co-worker of his father, died in suspicious circumstances in a Paris hospital.—Ed.]

mark one's enemy, prepare everything, avenge oneself thoroughly, and then go to sleep."

His craving for revenge on me is completely unsatisfied: there have been, so to speak, physical blows, but morally nothing has been achieved. There is no refusal to work, no "repentence," no isolation; on the contrary, a new historical momentum has been acquired which is already impossible to halt. This is the source of gravest apprehensions for Stalin: that savage fears ideas, since he knows their explosive power and knows his own weakness in the face of them. At the same time he is clever enough to realize that even today I would not change places with him: hence the psychology of a man stung. But if revenge on a higher plane has not succeeded—and clearly it will not succeed—it is still possible to reward oneself with police blows against people close to me. Naturally, Stalin would not hesitate a moment to organize an attempt on my life, but he is afraid of the political consequences: the accusation will undoubtedly fall on him. Blows against my intimates in Russia cannot give him the necessary "satisfaction," and at the same time they cause serious political inconveniences. To announce that Seryozha worked "under the direction of foreign intelligence service"? It's too incongruous; the motive of personal revenge would be revealed too directly; it would be too compromising for Stalin personally.

It is hard right now to work on my book on Lenin; my thoughts simply don't want to concentrate on the year 1893! The weather has changed sharply in the last few days. Although the gardens are in bloom, it has been snowing today since early morning; everything was covered with a white shroud; then it melted; now it is snowing again but melting right away. The sky is gray; from the mountains the fog is creeping down into the valley; in the house it is chilly and damp. N. is fussing over the housework with a heavy weight in her heart. Life is not an easy matter. . . . You cannot live through it without falling into prostration and cynicism unless you have before you a great idea which raises you above personal misery, above weakness, above all kinds of perfidy and baseness.

April 5

The depth and strength of a human character are defined by its moral *reserves*. People reveal themselves completely only when they are thrown out of the customary conditions of their life, for only then do they have to fall back on their reserves. N. and I have been together for almost thirty-three years (a third of a century!), and in tragic hours I am always amazed at the reserves of her character. . . . Whether because our strength is declining, or for some other reason, but I should very much like to fix N.'s image on paper, at least partially.

April 9

The Socialist and the Communist Parties of France are continuing their fatal work: they carry their opposition to a point quite sufficient to embitter the bourgeoisie and to bring about a mobilization of forces of reaction and additional arming of fascist detachments; but it is altogether insufficient for a revolutionary rallying of the proletariat. They provoke the class enemy, as if on purpose, and without giving anything to their own class. This is the shortest and most certain road to destruction.

April 10

Today, during a walk in the hills with N.—it was almost a summer day—I was thinking over my conversation with Lenin about a trial for the Czar. It is possible that besides the time factor (we would "not have time" to bring a big trial to its conclusion, since the decisive events on the front might intervene), Lenin had another consideration with regard to the Czar's family. Under judicial procedures, of course, execution of the family would have been impossible. The Czar's family fell victim to that principle which constitutes the axis of monarchy: dynastic succession.

No news about Seryozha, and perhaps there won't be any for a long time. Long waiting has blunted the anxiety of the first days.

. . .

When I was getting ready to go to the front for the first time, between the fall of Simbirsk and that of Kazan, Lenin was in a gloomy mood. "Russians are too kind," "Russians are lazybones, softies," "It's a bowl of mush we have, not a dictatorship. . . ." I told him: "As the foundation for our military units we should use hard revolutionary nuclei, which will support iron discipline from *within;* create reliable security detachments which will act from *outside* in concert with the inner revolutionary nucleus of the detachment, and will not hesitate to shoot deserters; we should guarantee competent leadership by putting a commissar with a revolver over every 'spets' [Czarist officer serving as technical expert in the Red Army]; we should set up military-revolutionary tribunals and establish decorations for individual bravery in battle." Lenin answered something like this: "That is all true, absolutely true, but there is not enough time; if we act drastically (which is absolutely necessary) our own party will interfere: they will whine, set every telephone ringing, tug at our coattails—in short, interfere. Of course, revolution hardens one, but there is too little time. . . ." When Lenin became convinced by our talks that I believed in our success, he supported my trip wholeheartedly, helped with the arrangements, showed great concern, kept asking about ten times a day over the telephone how the preparations were going, whether we should not take an airplane along on the train, etc. . . .

Kazan fell. Lenin was wounded by the Social Revolutionary Kaplan. We recaptured Kazan. Simbirsk was retaken too. When I made a quick visit to Moscow, Lenin was convalescing in Gorki. Sverdlov told me: "Ilyich would like you to visit him. Shall we go together?" So we went. The manner in which Marya Ilyinishna and Nad. Konst met me made me realize how impatiently and warmly they were expecting me. Lenin was in a fine humor and looked well physically. It seemed to me that he was looking at me with somehow different eyes. He had a way of *falling in love* with people when they showed him a certain side of themselves. There was a touch of this being "in love" in his excited attention. He listened eagerly to my stories about the front, and kept sighing with satisfaction, almost blissfully. "The game is won," he said, changing suddenly to a firm and serious tone. "If we have succeeded in establishing order in the army, it means we will establish it everywhere else. And the revolution—with order—will be unconquerable."

When Sverdlov and I were getting into our automobile Lenin and N. K. stood on the balcony directly above the entrance, and again I felt the same slightly bashful, all-enveloping glance of Ilyich. He looked as if he wanted to say something more but could not find words. At that moment one of his bodyguards brought out some flowers in pots and started putting them into the car. Lenin's face darkened with anxiety. "You won't be uncomfortable?" he asked. I had paid no attention to the flowers and did not understand the reason for his concern. Only as we were approaching Moscow—the hungry, dirty Moscow of the fall months of 1918—did I feel acutely ill at ease; was it appropriate to ride about with flowers at such a time? And just then I understood Lenin's concern: he had anticipated my uneasiness. He did have foresight.

At our next encounter I said to him: "The other day you asked about the flowers; I didn't even grasp, in the excitement of our meeting, what sort of 'discomfort' you had in mind. It suddenly dawned on me only as we were entering the city." "It made you look like a *meshochnik* [illegal trader]?" Ilyich asked quickly, and laughed gently. Again I caught that special friendly glance of his which seemed to reflect his pleasure that I had understood him. How deeply, how distinctly, and how indelibly all the details, large and small, of the Gorki visit are engraved on my memory!

Lenin and I had several sharp clashes because, when I disagreed with him on serious questions, I always fought an all-out battle. Such cases, naturally, were memorable for everyone, and later on much was said and written about them by the epigones. But the instances when Lenin and I understood each other at a glance were a hundred times more numerous, and our solidarity always guaranteed the passage of a question in the Politburo without disputes. This solidarity meant a great deal to Lenin.

· · ·

Last year N. and I were in Lourdes. What crudeness, insolence, nastiness! A shop for miracles, a business office for trafficking in Grace. The Grotto itself makes a miserable impression. That, of course, is a psychological calculation of the clerics: not to frighten the little people away by the grandeur of their commercial enterprise; little people are afraid of shop windows which are too resplendent. At the same time they are the most faithful and profitable customers. But best of all is the papal blessing broadcast to Lourdes by radio. The paltry miracles of the Gospels side by side with the radiotelephone! And what could be more absurd and disgusting than the union of proud technology with the sorcery of the Roman chief druid? Indeed, the thinking of mankind is bogged down in its own excrement.

May 8

Old age is the most unexpected of all the things that happen to a man.

May 16

We are not cheerful these days. N. is unwell: temperature of 38° [C.]—apparently a cold, but there may also be malaria mixed in with it. Every time N. is ill, I feel anew the place that she fills in my life. She bears all suffering, physical as well as moral, silently, quietly, inside herself. Right now she is more upset about my health than her own. "If only you would get well," she said to me today, lying in bed, "that's the only thing I want." She rarely says such things. And she said this so simply, evenly and quietly, and at the same time from such a depth, that my whole soul was stirred. . . .

My condition is not encouraging. The attacks of illness have become more frequent, the symptoms are more acute, my resistance is obviously getting weaker. Of course, the curve may yet take a temporary turn upward. But in general I have a feeling that liquidation is approaching. [A curved line is drawn across these sentences.]

It's been about two weeks since I've written much of anything: it's too difficult. I read newspapers, French novels, Wittels' book about Freud (a bad book by an envious pupil), etc.

Today I wrote a little about the interrelationship between the physiological determinism of brain processes and the "autonomy" of thought, which is subject to the law of logic. My philosophical interests have been growing during the last few years, but alas, my knowledge is too insufficient, and too little time remains for a big and serious work. . . .

I must give N. her tea. . . .

July 13

During the daytime lately I have been lying in the open air, reading and dictating letters to Jan. Newspapers and letters have begun arriving here directly and in ever-increasing numbers.

A few days ago our landlord had guests, also party editors; they came here to make our acquaintance. "Fascism cannot happen in Norway." "We are an old democracy." "We have complete literacy." "Besides we have learned a lot: we have limited our capitalism. . . ." And if Fascism conquers in France? In England? "We shall hold out." Why then did you not hold your currency when it fell in England?

They have learned nothing. Essentially, these people do not suspect that such men as Marx, Engels, and Lenin have lived in this world. The war and the October revolution, the upheavals of fascism have passed them by without a trace. . . . For them, the future holds hot and cold showers.

I have read the biography of Eugene Debs. The biography is bad, lyrically sentimental; but in its way it reflects the lyrical and sentimental figure of Debs, remarkable of its kind, and in any case very attractive.

I am reading Edgar Allan Poe in the original, and am getting on, although not without difficulties. In recent years I have learned to dictate articles in French and German, to dictate to collaborators who are capable of correcting my syntactic errors on the spot. The latter are not infrequent. It has not been given to me to master *completely* any foreign language.

In English (which I know quite badly) I am making progress now with the help of intensive reading. Sometimes I catch myself wondering, isn't it a bit too late? Is it worthwhile to expend this energy not on knowledge, but on language, a tool of knowledge?

In Turkey we lived "openly" under the public eye, but actually under a considerable guard (three comrades and two policemen). In France we lived incognito, first under a guard of our comrades (Barbizon), later alone (Isère). Now we are living openly and without guard. Even the yard gate is wide open day and night. Yesterday two drunken Norwegians dropped in to get acquainted. We chatted with them amiably and parted.

Glossary of Names

Axelrod, Pavel (Paul)—early leader of Russian Social Democratic Party who supported the Menshevik wing.

Bauer, Otto—leader and theoretician of Austrian Social Democratic Party during twenties and thirties.

Bebel, August—early leader of German Social Democratic Party.

Belinsky, Vissarion—distinguished nineteenth-century Russian literary and social critic who pioneered in expounding the social approach to literature.

Black Hundreds—reactionary anti-Semitic group in early twentieth century which conducted physical attacks on Jews and radicals, sometimes with connivance of Czarist regime.

Blanqui, August—nineteenth-century French revolutionary, known as expounder of the *putsch* (an armed seizure of power by small conspiratorial movement).

Blum, Léon—leader of French Socialist Party, premier in Popular Front cabinet beginning June 1936.

Brockway, Fennor—British socialist leader, for a time prominent in Independent Labor Party.

Brüning, Heinrich—leader of Catholic Center Party in Germany; Chancellor between March 1930 and June 1932; tended to rule by decree and to ignore Weimar Constitution.

Bukharin, Nikolai—veteran Bolshevik leader; author of Marxist theoretical works; prominent in Lenin's regime; intellectual spokesman for Right Opposition in Russian Communist Party in 1928; shot after Moscow Trial in 1938.
Cachin, Marcel—a founder of French Communist Party, and for many years a staunch supporter of Stalinism.
Cheidze, N.S.—veteran Menshevik leader of Georgian extraction, prominent in Russian politics during period between February and October 1917 revolutions.
Daladier, Edouard—leader of Radical Socialist Party (neither radical nor socialist, but a lower-middle-class party with secularist tradition); participated in Popular Front under Blum.
Denikin, Antar—Czarist general who later commanded White armies during the Civil War.
Dollfuss, Engelbert—Austrian Chancellor at time of Vienna socialist uprising in 1934, which he put down by force; clerical-reactionary in politics; pro-Mussolini, anti-Nazi; assassinated by Nazis in 1934.
Doumerge, Gaston—conservative French politician, premier between February and November 1934; ruled by decree, which Trotsky described as "bonapartist."
Duma—Russian parliament under reign of Czars, created as concession to 1905 revolution.
Dzherzinsky, Felix—Polish Social Democrat who joined Bolsheviks, became head of Cheka (secret police).
Ercoli—pseudonym, Italian Communist Party leader Palmiro Togliatti.
February Revolution—popular revolution which in early 1917 overthrew the Czar.
Frossard, Louis—a founder of French Communist Party, later Right Wing Socialist leader in thirties.
Father Gapon—Russian orthodox priest who led peaceful workers' demonstration before Kremlin in 1905 requesting constitutional rights and improved labor conditions; police firing on this demonstration sparked 1905 revolution.

Girondists (Girondins)—a party in the French Revolution which favored a moderate development; shattered when Robespierre took power in 1792.

Herriot, Edouard—leader of Radical Socialist Party, who held variety of posts in French cabinets; lukewarm to Popular Front.

Hilferding, Rudolf—leading theoretician, German Social Democracy, distinguished for studies in economics; died in Nazi concentration camp.

Jacobins—the Society of the Friends of the Constitution, political club exercising great influence during French Revolution. Term is generally applied to political tendency led by Robespierre which formed Left Wing of Revolution. In Marxist discussion, it often signifies a belief in a highly disciplined vanguard movement, acting in the name of the people but sometimes imposing its will upon them.

Joffé, Adolf—Soviet diplomat, committed suicide as protest against persecution of Trotskyists.

Kadets—Constitutional Democratic Party of Russia, a bourgeois party committed to a constitutional monarchy and moderate liberalism, which for short time after February 1917 Revolution dominated the provisional government.

Kamenev, Leo—veteran Bolshevik leader, head of anti-Stalin "Leningrad Opposition" together with Zinoviev, which in midtwenties made temporary alliance with Trotskyists. Kamenev and Zinoviev soon capitulated to Stalin but were repeatedly disgraced and then imprisoned. Kamenev was shot after 1926 Moscow Trial.

Kautsky, Karl—leading writer and theoretician of German Social Democracy; in years before World War I defended orthodox Marxism against Eduard Bernstein's "revisionism"; sharp critic of Bolshevik revolution; later, a major spokesman for reformist Social Democracy.

Kerensky, Alexander—a Populist leader who served as premier in short-lived provisional government overthrown by Bolsheviks in October 1917.

Kornilov, Lavr—Czarist general who tried to overthrow the Kerensky regime; was defeated when left parties came to Kerensky's aid.

Kronstadt Rebellion—uprising of sailors against Bolshevik regime in 1921, at Kronstadt naval base near Leningrad; rebellion demanded free elections in Soviets; suppressed by Bolsheviks, but led to concessions of the NEP.

Kulak—Russian term meaning "fist," popularly used to refer to well-to-do peasant who owned land and hired poor peasants to work it.

Left Opposition—formal title of Trotskyist group within Bolshevik Party, formed in 1923.

Leipart, Theodor—leader of German trade unions during the 1920s.

Liebknecht, Karl—German Socialist and anti-militarist, opposed World War I; murdered in 1919 with Rosa Luxemburg.

Luxemburg, Rosa—leader of Polish Social Democracy in World War I period; distinguished Marxist theoretician; active in Germany in immediate postwar period; leader of Left Wing; murdered in 1919.

(Prince) Lvov—belonged to Kadet party, and became first prime minister after February Revolution.

Manuilsky, Dimitri—leader of Communist International, completely faithful to Stalin.

Mensheviks—meaning literally "of the minority," a phrase used to designate group in Russian Social Democratic Party which in 1903 was led by Julius Martov in opposition to Lenin; afterwards, unofficial designation of reformist socialists.

Miliukov, Paul—leader of Kadets and central political figure in interval between February and October 1917 revolutions.

Molotov, Vyacheslav—veteran Bolshevik functionary; rose to prominence as supporter of Stalin faction; for many years foreign minister under Stalin; disgraced by Khrushchev regime.

NEP—New Economic Policy inaugurated in spring 1921 by Lenin regime to relax rigors of War Communism and allow a measure of private trade.

Noske, Gustav—German Social Democratic leader who, together with Philip Scheidemann, put down Communist-led uprisings in 1919-1920; "Noske-Scheidemann" became term of abuse among European leftists.

Old Bolshevik—member of Bolshevik movement who joined before October revolution or, more loosely, veteran of the movement whose history extends to period of underground work in early years of twentieth century.

Papen, Franz von—conservative German politician who succeeded Bruening as Chancellor in 1932 and helped Hitler take power.

Parvus (Alexander Helfand)—prominent in pre-World War I years as Marxist theoretician in eastern Europe; reached conclusions similar to Trotsky's theory of permanent revolution.

Plekhanov, George—usually considered intellectual father of Russian Marxism; a founder of Russian Social Democratic Party; author of numerous theoretical works; a Right Wing Menshevik during World War I and revolution.

Populists—a somewhat loose term referring to those Russian revolutionists and reformers who, rejecting Marxism, looked to the peasants as the class that would overthrow Czarism and reconstruct the nation. One party among the various shadings of Populism was the Trudoviks, a moderate grouping slightly to the left of the Kadets, to which Kerensky belonged.

Pravda—"The Truth," Bolshevik newspaper, first published in 1912.

Radek, Karl—Polish radical, became prominent as major Communist journalist in twenties; for a time collaborator of Trotsky; disappeared after Moscow trials.

Rasputin, Gregory—illiterate Siberian monk who held great influence over Czar and Czarina in World War I years; assassinated December 1916 by members of court.

Renaudel, Pierre—French left-of-center politician, premier for several weeks in early 1936.

Rote Fahne, Die (The Red Flag)—central newspaper of German Communist Party in pre-Hitler years.

Rykov, Alexey—veteran Bolshevik leader, occupied high posts in government under Lenin; Premier of Soviet Union during mid-twenties; leader of Right Opposition in 1928; shot after 1938 Moscow Trial.

Social Revolutionary Party (SRs)—a peasant socialist party descended from Russian populism; at time of October 1917 revolution, a majority of SRs opposed Bolsheviks, while Left SR minority became temporary allies.

Stavisky, Alexander—French financier whose bankruptcy in mid-thirties exposed corruption in many high political places.

Struve, Peter—Russian economist who in early years of twentieth century led group of "legal Marxists" using the Marxist method in form sufficiently abstract and unrevolutionary to allow them to be legally tolerated under Czarism.

Sukhanov, N. N.—Left-Menshevik intellectual whose vivid memoirs form a major source for historians of Russian revolution.

Sverdlov, Jacob—prominent Bolshevik leader, died shortly after revolution.

Tardieu, André—Conservative French politician who in mid-thirties abandoned parliamentary politics for Right Wing street movements.

Thaelmann, Ernst—German Communist leader, imprisoned by Nazis.

Thermidor—on 19th of Thermidor (July 27, 1794) Robespierre and friends overthrown by more conservative wing of Jacobins, which paved way for Directory and liquidation of radical phase of French Revolution. In Trotsky's use of the term, which varied in emphasis from time to time, the general intent is to suggest that the consolidation of Stalinism represented a turn to opportunism and then totalitarian reaction, analogous to that which occurred in France, while nevertheless keeping intact the social gains (property forms) of the revolution.

Tomsky, Michael—Bolshevik trade-union leader, supporter of

Glossary of Names 421

Right Opposition in 1928; committed suicide in 1938 just before Moscow Trial.

War Communism—system of total state control over economy, involving compulsory labor and rationing, introduced in 1919 by Lenin regime to cope with economic collapse and civil war.

Wels, Otto—leader of German Social Democrats during pre-Hitler period.

Count Witte—statesman in Czarist epoch who favored modernization of Russia.

Zemstvo—rural assemblies in Czarist period, late nineteenth and early twentieth centuries, with very limited powers.

Zinoviev, Gregory—close collaborator of Lenin, first chairman of Communist International; shot by Stalin regime after Moscow Trials in 1936.

Zyromski, Jean—French Socialist leader who favored cooperation with Communists.

Index

Adler, Friedrich   294, 295
Adler, Max   109
Alexander III   51
Alfonso XIII   225, 226
Anarchists, Anarchism   364-367, 370
Andreyev, Leonid   70
Anglo-Russian Committee   253
Anti-Semitism   206-215
Axelrod, Pavel (Paul)   125

Babeuf, François   195
Bakunin, Michael   364-365
Bauer, Otto   272, 357, 389
Bebel, August   257
Belinsky, V. M.   317, 318, 321-323
Berdyaev, Nikolai   374
Bernstein, Edouard   72
Biro-Bidjan   214
"Black Hundreds"   48, 211
Blanqui, Auguste   354
"Bloody Sunday"   133
Blum, Léon   385, 402
Bolsheviks, Bolshevik Party   77, 82, 87, 95, 96, 108, 109, 143, 145, 161, 163, 188-205, 192, 193, 197, 249, 250, 255, 286, 356-369, 384, 394
Bolshevism   141, 188, 189, 220, 359, 372
Bonaparte, Napoleon   192, 227
Braun, Otto   251, 256
Brest-Litovsk Treaty   151
British Labor Party   275
Brockway, Fenner   389
Brüning, Heinrich   237-244, 250, 251, 256, 272
Bukharin, Nikolai   164, 167, 180, 192, 211, 212
Bulletin of the Russian Opposition   295, 302, 403

Cachin, Marcel   272, 273, 402
Céline, Louis-Ferdinand   345-355
Cheidze, N. S.   95, 107
Chernyshevsky, N. G.   318
Christianity   155-157, 372-378
Ciliga, Anton   307
Clemenceau, Georges   350

Communist International (Comintern) 189-191, 199, 248, 258-265, 291, 302, 359
Communist Party of Germany 246-266
Constitutional Democratic Party of Russia (Kadets) 47-52, 144, 149
Cossacks 79-83
Cromwell, Oliver 104-108
Czarism 46, 47, 75, 126, 147, 207, 225, 293, 294, 372

Daladier, Edouard 271, 273
Dan, Theodor 250
Darwin, Charles, Darwinism 74, 374, 376, 377
Debs, Eugene 412
de Maupassant, Guy 70
de Rivera, Prima 228-232
Denikin, Antav 119, 145, 147, 150
Dimitroff, George 357
Dollfuss, Engelbert 272
Dostoevsky, Fyodor 318
Doumerge, Gaston 271, 273
Dual Power 101-110, 242
Dzhevzinsky, Felix 70, 406

Eastman, Max 373, 381, 382
Ebert, Fritz 136
Engels, Friedrich 108, 201, 359, 401, 402, 405, 412
Ercoli (Palmira Togliatti) 237

February Revolution 78, 107
Five Year Plans 167, 169, 178-187
Fourth International 301, 306, 308, 392, 398
Franco, Francisco 385, 387, 397
French Revolution 57, 104, 136, 171, 233
Freud, Sigmund 411
Frossard, Louis 269-276

Gandhi, Mahatma 390
Gapon, Father 65, 66
George, Lloyd 150
Gestapo 213, 282
Gide, André 288
Girondists 106
Gogol, Nikolai 317-324
Goncharov, I. A. 318
Göring, Hermann 266
Gorky, Maxim 70
Gorter, Hermann 367
Gotz, A. 250
GPU 193, 210, 213, 280, 283-289, 303, 394
Green, William 385

Hauptmann, Gerhard 70
Hegel, Friedrich 72, 374
Herriot, Edouard 270, 273
Hilferding, Rudolf 109, 251, 357
Hitler, Adolf 207, 241-244, 246, 247, 251, 258, 259, 264, 266, 279, 282, 284, 306, 347, 371, 385, 394, 400

Ibsen, Henrik 70
Iskra 76, 404

Jacobins 171, 172, 192, 195, 197, 383
Jesuits, Jesuitism 371-377
Jews 206-215
Joffé, Adolf 289

Kaledin, A. M. 144
Kamenev, Leo 165, 167, 190, 192, 210-213, 278, 281-285, 406

Index

Kant, Immanuel 72, 374, 378
Kautsky, Karl 109, 143-159
Kerensky, Alexander 95, 107, 143, 236, 249, 250, 254, 255, 358, 392, 393
Kirov, Sergei 211, 279, 280, 295, 397
Kolchak, Alexander 144, 150
Kornilov, Lavr 237, 249, 250, 254, 255
Krasnov, P. N. 119, 121, 144
Kronstadt Rebellion 190, 369, 390
Krupskaya (Lenin's wife) 192
Kulaks 128, 164, 168, 174-185, 200, 202
Kuomintang 255

Labriola, Antonia 72
Lafargue, Paul 158
Lassalle, Ferdinand 59, 396, 397, 400
Left Opposition (Bolshevik-Leninists) 163, 166-168, 178-185, 191, 192, 209, 211, 219, 248, 291, 296, 363, 364
Leipart, Theodor 263-265
Lenin, V. I. 76, 95, 114, 117, 124, 125-141, 160, 162, 180, 189-202, 219, 249, 254, 261, 292, 325-337, 339, 340, 362, 363, 369, 392-395, 402, 408-412
Levellers 104
Lewis, John L. 380
Liebknecht, Karl 109, 255, 295
Ludwig, Emil 347-388
Luxemburg, Rosa 109, 255, 340
Lvov, Prince 107
Lvovna, Alexandra 67, 68, 76

Makhaisky, V. K. 72, 73
Makno, Nestor 369, 390
Manuilsky, Dmitri 238, 244
Marat, Jean Paul 109
Martov, Julius 130, 292
Marx, Karl 60, 68, 73, 108, 132, 225, 359, 374, 389, 401, 402, 412
Marxism 44, 69-74, 123, 124, 130-132, 139, 159, 172, 200, 214, 296-300, 359, 371, 382
Mensheviks, Menshevism 78, 109, 125, 129, 135, 140, 141, 144, 149, 150, 171, 250, 255, 360
Miliukov, Paul 130
Molotov, Vyacheslav 95, 166, 167, 182, 186, 193, 200, 202, 238
Moscow Trials 206, 209, 278-304
Mussolini, Benito 236, 266, 279, 371
Muzhiks 178-183

Nazi-Soviet Pact 305, 306
Nazis, Nazism 234-266
NEP 162, 170, 175, 181, 193, 361, 362
Nicholas II 48
Nietzsche, Friedrich 70
Noske, Gustav 251, 253

October Revolution 108, 132, 145, 207, 219, 360

Pannekoek, Anton 367
Paris Commune 105, 106, 388, 389
Parliamentarism 158-159
Parvus (Alexander Helfand) 133-136

Permanent Revolution, Theory of 123-141, 229
Piatakov, Y. L. 211, 212, 278, 281-285
Plekhanov, George 124-129, 139, 154, 292
Poincaré, Raymond 345-350
Popular Front (People's Front) 267-277, 392
Populists, Populism 69, 71, 124, 130, 132, 139
Pravda 196, 199, 258
Preobrazhensky, E. 211, 212
Pritt, D. N. 279, 280
Pushkin, Alexander 213, 318, 319

Radek, Karl 211, 278, 281-285
Radical Socialist Party of France 269-273
Rakovsky, Christian 193, 194, 195, 211
Red Terror 143, 146, 150, 152, 153
Remmele, H. 244, 250, 251
Renaudel, Pierre 269, 274
Revolution of 1848 54, 108
Robespierre, Maximilian 108
Rykov, Alexey 167, 179, 180, 192

Schlamm, Willi 357-359
Sedov, Leon 287, 370, 399
Shaftesbury, Viscount 373, 374
Shliapnikov, A. G. 95, 96, 98
Social Democrats, German 109, 134, 135, 139, 162, 235-266
Social Democrats, Russian 52, 54, 62, 123, 128, 135

"Social Fascism" 234-265
Social Revolutionary Party of Russia (Social Revolutionists, S.R.'s) 75, 78, 109, 117, 118, 144, 149, 150, 250, 255, 294
"Socialism in One Country" 178, 362
Socialist International (Second International) 240, 279, 357, 359
Sosnovsky, L. 195
Souvarine, Boris 367
Spencer, Herbert 376, 377
Spinoza, Baruch 289
Stalin, Josef 133, 165, 167, 178, 179, 182, 189, 199, 200, 206-213, 238, 244, 280-288, 297, 299-303, 313, 360, 367, 381, 388, 400, 403, 406, 407
Stalinists, Stalinism 131, 141, 356-369, 372, 383-384
Stavisky, Alexander 350-352
Struve, Peter 63, 374
Sukhanov, N. N. 107
Sverdlov, Jacob 114, 409, 410

Tardieu, André 270
Terrorism 290-298
Thälmann, Ernst 244, 249, 250, 259
Thermidor 106, 107, 132, 191, 196-198, 204, 206-215, 300, 308, 363, 383, 384
Thomas, Norman 389, 394
Thorez, Maurice 385, 402
Tolstoy, Leo 74, 318, 390
Tomsky, Michael 167, 180, 192, 289
Trotsky, Leon 210, 281, 282, 285, 297, 299-304, 358
Trotsky, Natalia 404-412

Trotskyism 131, 132, 165, 169, 281-284, 372

Voltaire, François 285
Vyshinski, Andrei 286, 287, 298

Webb, Sidney & Beatrice 169, 369
Wells, H. G. 372
Wels, Otto 251, 256, 263, 264, 272
White Guards 111, 121, 147
White Terror 151-153
Witte, Count 64
Wrangel, Baron 119, 374

Yagoda, G. G. 199, 282, 387
Yezhov, N. I. 282, 387
Yudenich, N. I. 117, 145, 150

Zinoviev, Gregory 165, 167, 190, 192, 210-213, 278, 281-285, 298
Zionism 215
Zyromski, Jean 272